Rethinking
the
Progressive Agenda

Rethinking the Progressive Agenda

The Reform of the American Regulatory State

Susan Rose-Ackerman

THE FREE PRESS
A Division of Macmillan, Inc.
NEW YORK

Maxwell Macmillan Canada
TORONTO

Maxwell Macmillan International
NEW YORK   OXFORD   SINGAPORE   SYDNEY

The Free Press
A Division of Macmillan, Inc.
866 Third Avenue, New York, N. Y. 10022

Maxwell Macmillan Canada, Inc.
1200 Eglinton Avenue East
Suite 200
Don Mills, Ontario M3C 3N1

Macmillan, Inc. is part of the Maxwell Communication
Group of Companies.

First Free Press Paperback Edition 1993

Printed in the United States of America

printing number

1 2 3 4 5 6 7 8 9 10

Library of Congress Cataloging-in-Publication Data

Rose-Ackerman, Susan.
    Rethinking the progressive agenda: the reform of the American
regulatory state / Susan Rose-Ackerman.
        p.   cm.
    Includes bibliographical references and index.
    ISBN 0-02-926845-1
    1. Administrative law—United States.   2. Administrative agencies—
United States.   3. Deregulation—United States.   4. Judicial
review—United States.   5. Courts—United States.   6. Social choice—
United States.   7. United States—Economic policy—1981–
8. Progressivism (United States politics)   9. Policy sciences.
I. Title.
KF5402.R665   1992
342.73´0664—dc20   91-27654
[347.302664]   CIP

For my mother
and in memory of my father

Contents

Preface

This book proposes a new public agenda inspired by recent advances in law and economics. My aim is to reform, rather than dismantle, the regulatory state. Economists began to influence progressive thinking late in the last century when they helped shape the debate over monopoly control of industry. In the 1930s, policy-oriented social scientists began to enter law schools to teach public utilities, trade regulation, and antitrust. These progressive thinkers were later eclipsed by legal and economic scholars centered at the University of Chicago. Particularly during the past twenty years, these scholars, with their emphasis on the benefits of common law courts and unregulated markets, profoundly influenced the legal profession's perception of the links between economics and public law.

In this book I distinguish between the logical structure of economic argument and policy conclusions which derive, not from economic reasoning itself, but from political and ideological commitments.

The progressive approach rests on two intellectual foundations, policy analysis and social choice theory. The outlines of this structure are sketched in Chapter 1; Chapter 2 develops the policy analytic base of the Progressive School and uses it to critique Chicago-style analysis. Part Two introduces the second intellectual foundation, social choice theory, and examines the implications of progressivism for judicial review. Chapter 3 recommends that, unless expressly forbidden by Congress, courts should hold economic regulatory agencies to the standard of net benefit maximization. I argue in Chapter 4 that the courts should make it easier for voters to hold legislators responsible for their actions by requiring that statutes be internally consistent. Chapter 5 proposes to increase political accountability through judicial review of the appropriations process.

Part Three shifts the emphasis from governmental process and the courts to substantive policy. Given the wide range of problems facing the country, I make no attempt to be comprehensive. I concentrate on issues which suggest the range of the approach. The first two chapters provide examples of progressive analyses of the regulation of business and the organization of social welfare programs. Chapter 6 summarizes the federal regulation of occupational safety and health. I contrast existing law with the outcome of an informed policy analysis and argue that judicial review of executive branch actions has been hampered by a failure to understand the nature of the regulatory issues. Chapter 7 demonstrates that a policy analytic approach can be useful, not only in regulatory areas, but also in the reform of government redistributive efforts.

The next two chapters return to the courts. Chapter 8 takes as given a pervasive federal regulatory role in the control of health and safety and isolates the remaining place for tort law in a reformed system. Chapter 9 examines a central question of constitutional law: When must the government compensate owners if public regulatory actions lower the value of their property?

Part Four asks if the Reagan "Revolution" provides any lessons for progressives. My thesis is that the Reagan administration had many sound ideas buried in its overblown rhetoric, but that few of them were actually put into practice. The "revolution" failed to accomplish much of value along any of the three key dimensions of deregulation, decentralization, and privatization, analyzed in Chapter 10, 11, and 12. Its failure stemmed both from a commitment to rhetoric at the expense of analysis and from a failure of political will. Nevertheless, focusing on some of the same issues which preoccupied Reaganites provides a framework for progressive thinking. The book concludes in Chapter 13 with some general thoughts on the nature of modern progressivism.

———————— • ————————

Like all books, this one could not have been written without the help of many people and institutions. Columbia and Yale Universities have both proved to be places where interdisciplinary scholarship is encouraged and rewarded. When I came to Columbia Law School in 1982, I was given the chance to teach what I liked, and I found a segment of the student body eager for a policy-oriented approach to law. As Director of the Law School's Center for Law and Economic Studies, I was able to organize conferences which brought together lawyers, political scientists, and economists interested in the interconnections between their fields. Many of my colleagues at Columbia supported my efforts and taught me a good deal, but I am especially grateful to Peter Strauss, who was unfailingly generous in his efforts to help me master the mysteries of administrative law.

Both institutional and personal support for my efforts has also been strong at Yale Law School with its concentration of both lawyer-economists and others interested in public law and regulatory policy. The Law School's Center for Law, Economics, and Public Policy, which I co-direct, has been a focus of this work for professors and students. In Political Science, where I hold a joint appointment, the opportunity to be part of a new undergraduate major in Ethics, Politics, and Economics has been a stimulating experience. Students in both my undergraduate and graduate seminars will, I hope, see in this book an illustration of the way teaching and research can mutually benefit each other.

Many of my Yale colleagues have contributed to my work. Of special help on particular chapters, or the articles which led to them, were Guido Calabresi, Robert Ellickson, Henry Hansmann, Jerry Mashaw, Roberta Romano, Peter Schuck, Alan Schwartz, and Kate Stith. As always, my husband, Bruce Ackerman, has been an indefatigable critic and a loyal supporter and friend. Even my children, Sybil and John, have gotten so old that they want to talk about public policy.

During the last year of manuscript preparation, two students, Mitu Gulati and Nancy Nieman, provided helpful research assistance. Nancy deserves special thanks for her excellent ability to track down legal and social science sources and her general goodwill in the face of my obsession with footnotes. Gene Coakley of the Yale Law Library was always ready to help solve bibliographic problems. Renée DeMatteo, my secretary, was a constant help, especially in the final weeks of manuscript preparation, and she handled numerous time-consuming tasks in a way which left me free to write.

PART
ONE

INTRODUCTION

For progressives, the modern regulatory-welfare state is at the heart of American Law. The task for law and economics is threefold: first, to define the economic justifications for public action; second, to analyze political and bureaucratic institutions realistically; third, to define useful roles for the courts within this modern policymaking system.

In Chapter 1, I sketch the foundations of the progressive approach. Rethinking fundamentals is especially urgent, given the way economic analysis was discredited by some of the excesses of the Reagan administration. Chapter 2 begins the task of rehabilitation by introducing the fundamental concepts of policy analysis and illustrating the way economic analysis can inform public debate. With this background, I critique the Chicago School. I argue that an overemphasis on the judge-made common law has distorted the focus of law and economics. Like policy analysts, lawyer economists should begin with instances of market failure and consider a wide range of solutions that do not give a privileged position to the common law. The rest of the book begins the more constructive task of using political economic analysis to evaluate specific problems of democratic government and market failure.

1

The New Progressivism

Progressives have taken a beating in the Eighties. At the political level they had to confront a decade of Republican control of the Presidency. The counterweight imposed by the judiciary has steadily eroded as these same presidents have appointed conservative judges. A whole generation of liberal, policy-oriented scholars who came to maturity in the Sixties has seen its hopes for a life of public service undermined by changes in the political landscape.

Life has not been much more comfortable in the law schools. Progressives have been hemmed in by libertarian scholars using the lessons of public choice theory to undercut arguments for public intervention and by Critical Legal Studies scholars who argue that since everything is politics, reasoned argument is pointless. Although their attacks are rooted in vastly different ideologies, these critics converge in viewing a progressive, reformist agenda as naïve wishful thinking. Both the right and the left stereotype economics, which has been at the heart of progressive reform for a hundred years, as a conservative, laissez-faire movement.

While conservatives can oppose government regulatory and spending programs "on principle," a credible progressive movement must incorporate a well-developed respect for the costs as well as the benefits of reform. Economic analysis is essential to this evaluative enterprise. It is, then, both odd and unfortunate that the public has come to associate economics with a set of conservative and, to many, morally dismal ideologies that have no necessary connection with the economic analysis of legal and policy problems.[1]

But progressives and policy-analytic economists should not retreat into self-pity. Some hopeful signs suggest both that policymakers are beginning to recognize the force of progressive arguments and that legal scholarship and education are moving toward a richer interdisciplinary synthesis.

THE PROGRESSIVE TRADITION

What is the progressive tradition? While I shall doubtless get the details wrong, butcher history, and offend some who want to keep the label for themselves, I do have something particular in mind. Progressives acknowledge that irrationality, smallmindedness and greed coexist with rationality, generosity, and frugality, but they are not paternalists. Leaving to one side the education of children, they take people as they find them and deemphasize programs designed either to change values or to prohibit private behavior that imposes no direct cost on others. They favor systems that promote individual choice, such as private markets and democratic political processes. Their preferred policy tools emphasize the creation of incentives, through either taxes or subsidies. Progressives place more emphasis on statutes and government institutions and less on the common law than has been the norm in recent law and economics scholarship. To do this successfully, they need the tools of public policy analysis and social choice theory as well as a heightened knowledge of the operation of government institutions.

In substantive policy, progressives recognize that the existing distribution of property rights is highly contingent and lacks strong normative justification. They approach the question of the just distribution of income without giving much weight to the status quo. They have an egalitarian impulse but recognize the costs of leveling redistributive policies, which reduce the incentives for hard work and the exercise of initiative. Especially disturbing in recent years are increases in the inequality of income and wealth[2] and the persistence of poverty with its growing concentration among single-parent families.[3] Income inequalities by race and gender are a continuing concern in spite of long-term improvements in both measures.[4] While recognizing the importance of a healthy economy and a strong rate of growth in reducing the poverty rate and narrowing income inequalities, progressives stress the need for targeted programs to deal with structural problems. The achievement of distributive justice is not just a question of following sound macroeconomic policies.

Progressives recognize the overarching importance of scarcity and acknowledge the strength of the market in permitting the decentralized choices of individuals to produce a diverse range of goods and services responsive to individual demands. However, they are sensitive to the multiple sources of market failure—ranging from external effects, to monopoly power, to information imperfections, to frictions and lags in the operation of markets.

External effects occur when the action of one individual or firm affects someone else in the absence of a voluntary market transaction. A factory that pollutes the air without paying for the damage is creating an external effect. A bakery that blankets a neighborhood with the smell of fresh bread is also creating an external effect, but one with mostly positive, rather than negative, consequences.

Unregulated monopolists can set prices above the marginal cost of production, can restrict output, and can produce inefficiencies in the allocation of resources. Sluggish responses to changed market conditions can leave workers stranded in regions that offer no jobs and untrained in newly demanded skills. Decentralized choices in capital-intensive industries, such as office building construction, can produce cycles of boom and bust.

Uninformed consumers may purchase products that cause health problems or do not perform as advertised. Uninformed workers may be exposed to hazards that damage their health. While market pressures will induce some producers and employers both to inform consumers and workers and to provide high-quality products and safe workplaces, others will not face strong market incentives. Problems are especially likely to continue if a hazard causes harm only after a delay of some years, if other casual factors are involved, and if the casual connection is statistical.

Each of these market failures creates a presumption in favor of policy intervention, but one that can be overcome by showing that a public program would be excessively costly or ineffective. In promoting the efficient allocation of resources, tradeoffs between the goals of equity and efficiency provide some of the most potent challenges for progressivism. Can public policies be designed that both improve the justice of the distribution of income and enhance the efficiency of the economy? Is the structure of American government capable of responding to a progressive effort at reform?

A TIME FOR REASSESSMENT

Fifty years after the New Deal is a propitious time for a reassessment of the progressive agenda. The postwar period has seen an explosion of new learning in both the economic analysis of policy issues and the political-economic evaluation of government processes. While the optimism of early practitioners of cost-benefit analysis has given way to a sober realism, social scientific thinking continues to influence the way policy problems are framed and evaluated. At the same time, both economists and political scientists have made important contributions to the analysis of social choice issues, studying the properties of voting rules and legislative structures, analyzing the interest group aspects of politics, and modeling the interactions between bureaucracies and legislatures.

While this intellectual ferment was taking place, changes in the substantive law forced both judges and legal scholars to reexamine the roles of Congress, the agencies, and the courts. Laws regulating environmental pollution and safety and health in the workplace, in the home, and on the highway raise issues of public accountability and competence in all branches of government that were not central to earlier regulatory initiatives. These joint developments in the world of ideas and in practical politics suggest the promise of a progressive legal-economic scholarship. The goal is a reformed administrative law that will incorporate a richer range of both empirical and theoretical concerns and will respond more effectively to the needs of public officials, politicians, and private citizens.

Recent problems with the functioning of American government cannot all be traced to the temporary presence in the White House of a president who was out of sympathy with the goals of many of the statutes he was charged with enforcing. More fundamental problems arose from the basic structure of American government. Representative government requires citizens to evaluate the actions of their representatives. Yet for most citizens the legislative process is anything but transparent. In overseeing the work of Congress, however, the courts have frequently permitted the legislature to operate in ways that make it difficult for ordinary people to perceive what is happening in politics. This lack of transparency in the legislative process breeds cynicism in the voting population and can further undermine the representative nature of the state. Using the new learning in social choice and American government, we need to reexamine the role of the courts to take account of recent changes in the operation of Congress. To further democratic ideals, the federal courts may need to act to improve the accountability of the legislature to its constituents and to reexamine the links among agencies, interest groups, and Congress.

Even with a reformed process of judicial review, the courts cannot improve policy by themselves. They can constrain the legislature and the executive, but they lack the training and the legitimacy to take on the substantive policymaking tasks performed by agencies and the Congress. The failures of the Reagan administration were due to failures of analysis as much as to the structural faults of our political system.

REAGANISM AND PROGRESSIVISM

The progressive reform agenda can be understood by contrasting it to the reform efforts of the Republican Right. The simple sorting of people into the Right and the Left is, however, too glib to capture the relationship of the progressive position to Reaganism. Republicans are not the enemy. The progressive reaction to the Reagan record in regulatory affairs is one of disappointment. But you cannot be disappointed with someone in whom you never had any hope. Some of the fundamental positions of the past administration suggested that genuine reform might have occurred. Unfortunately, most have proved to be little more then simplistic slogans, and some have contributed to major disasters, such as the savings and loan collapse and bailout.

At the level of broad substantive principle there was agreement between Reaganites and progressives on the need for regulatory reform. Both believed that government intervention in the economy should be justified by reference to market failures and that, insofar as possible, cost-benefit tests should be used to set regulatory policy. At the implementation stage there was also a convergence between progressive and Reaganite rhetoric in favor of market schemes.

Convergence led to disappointment. Despite its strong language, the Reagan administration did not actually do very much. In a 1989 list of deregulatory accomplishments the Council of Economic Advisers can find little to report after 1984. Many of the earlier initiatives were begun before Reagan took office.[5] Equally surprising, broad-scale incentive-based reforms were not proposed in the regulation of health and safety. Most damning, the administration was often guided more by ideology than by careful thought even when regulatory changes were undertaken.

Paradoxically, the ideology of some of the administration's critics may have inadvertently encouraged and supported the deregulatory efforts of the Reagan administration. Those critics stressed the political uses of expertise and the oppressive possibilities of bureaucracies, thus undermining progressive justifications for the use of public agencies to regulate the economy. The left and the right converged in attacking a common scapegoat—the expert public agency—at a time when the need for informed technical input had become critically important. Furthermore, the seeds of several problems that surfaced in the Reagan administration were sown earlier and were the product, in part, of statutory language and judicial decisions, not Republican ideology.

What kinds of problems do I have in mind? Five typical ones illustrate the range of difficulties.

1. *A retreat from the rules.* This first phenomenon illustrates the convergence of structural and policy failure. General policy can best be made by promulgating general rules that apply prospectively. However, major rules are almost always challenged in court, delaying their implementation and raising the possibility of a remand to the agency to reformulate them. Even an activist agency might seek other techniques. For example, the National Highway Transport Safety Administration soon abandoned rulemaking and emphasized product recalls, which more easily passed muster in court.[6]

In addition, conservative agency heads who wish to minimize the impact of their agency might try to minimize the number of major rules and delay those they cannot avoid considering. They can justify their deliberate pace by pointing to the courts' demand that the agency take a "hard look" before deciding on a policy. The Occupational Health and Safety Administration issued few major rules dealing with health hazards in the past decade, and the Consumer Product Safety Commission all but abandoned rulemaking.[7] In many areas general policy was simply not being made. The result in such areas as automobile and product safety has been to impose a greater implicit regulatory burden on the state and federal courts through the products liability system, a burden the courts are ill-equipped to handle.

2. *A retreat from analysis.* Policy analysis was viewed skeptically by some agency heads in the Reagan administration who feared that it would be used to justify increased agency activity. Although critics saw systematic analysis as a tool used by the administration to reduce the role of government, some inside the government believed the reverse. Both positions are plausible and confirm the notion that systematic analysis of problems is not inherently either conservative or liberal. If you know ahead of time how you want a study to come out, it is risky to employ an independent analyst. Thus at the beginning of the Reagan administration a decision was made to help out the automobile industry.[8] From this position it followed that the passive restraint ("airbag") rule issued by the Carter administration should be rescinded. Policymakers saw no need to analyze the costs and benefits of the alternatives. The Supreme Court, with even the most conservative members on board for the key result, ruled that the agency had to use disciplined analysis to consider the most plausible alternative to repeal.[9]

The most dramatic example of the eviscerating of policy analysis is the Environmental Protection Agency under Anne Gorsuch Burford. The EPA downgraded the importance of analysis and was explicit about its ideological commitment to reducing regulatory burdens.[10] Paradoxically, without analysis, the agency may have increased the burden on business by its inconsistent and indecisive behavior and by implying that business was against a clean environment.

3. *Failure to regulate the deregulated.* The administration did not recognize the basic truth that deregulation along one dimension may imply the need to regulate more stringently along another. Perhaps the most dramatic example here is the savings and loan crisis. At the same time as the thrift industry was permitted to expand the range and risk of its loan portfolios, the number of inspectors monitoring their behavior actually fell.[11] In the presence of an unchanged deposit insurance system, the reduced oversight set the stage for the current crisis. The deregualtion of the airlines produced similar problems. As one of the original architects of airline deregulation has pointed out, deregulation should have been accompanied by vigorous antitrust enforcement to prevent the exercise of monopoly power by airlines.[12]

4. *Misplaced priorities.* If the energy of an agency is taken up with promulgating stringent rules, it will have time to put only a few items on its agenda. Other items will not be regulated at all. This problem was first documented in a study of OSHA health regulation.[13] Even zealous regulators will face this tradeoff between depth and breadth so long as their budgets are limited. In fact, it is essentially a problem for activist regulators. Those who want inactivity face no tradeoff between a few stringent rules and many intermediate controls; such administrators simply want to do as little as possible.

5. *Weak enforcement.* Budget cuts and agency reorganizations resulted in reduced resources for enforcement of many regulatory statutes.[14] Business firms are less likely to comply with regulations if they expect their competitors to be able to get away without meeting their obligations.

INTELLECTUAL ROOTS: POLICY ANALYSIS
AND RATIONAL ACTOR MODELS OF GOVERNMENT

The Progressive School is rooted in the late nineteenth century when economists first organized as a profession.[15] The fledgling American Economic Association helped guide the debate over control of monopoly under the Sherman Antitrust Act and federal regulation of railroads under the Interstate Commerce Act. Legal education felt the influence of progressives in the thirties when policy-oriented economists and political scientists began to enter law schools to teach public utilities, trade regulation, and antitrust.[16] The scholarship of this group is sometimes called the "old" law and economics to contrast it with the "new" law and economics of the common law.[17]

Far from being "old" in the sense of old-fashioned or out of date, a progressive brand of law and economics can be of widespread contemporary significance, as it moves beyond a narrow focus on policy areas such as antitrust and public utilities. Unfortunately, however, the basic intellectual foundations of modern progressivism are not as broadly familiar to lawyers as the microeconomic tools used in the law and economics of torts, contracts, and property. One puzzle for the future intellectual historian is the fairly distinct line between the policy analytic community and the developing field of law and economics in recent decades. Even though legal economists view the common law as playing a regulatory role, they seldom collaborate with scholars studying public programs. Nevertheless, outside of the law and economics community, a number of administrative law scholars are part of the policy analytic establishment.[18] Some of them have moved in and out of positions in the federal government, ending up as judges on occasion.

The other strand of modern progressivism, rational actor models of government, has had only a selective influence on legal thinking. Even here, however, the scholarly literature combining social choice and public law is growing, and the level of sophistication is improving.[19] The association in some minds of social choice theory with the politically conservative position of James Buchanan and the "Virginia School" has kept legal applications limited. For these scholars the existing distribution of wealth and property has a strong normative claim. This belief is combined in Buchanan's work with a deep cynicism about government. He argues that electoral constraints are weak and that unconstrained politicians will seek to maximize the size of the public budget. Taken together, these normative beliefs about private property and positive claims about public officials combine in a proposal for sharp constitutional limits on the scope of public action and the level and type of taxes.[20]

Some liberal scholars familiar only with the Virginia School have rejected all social choice as antagonistic to progressive reform.[21] This rejection is unwarranted. It confuses a method based on rational choice and logical deductive thinking with a philosophical commitment that has no necessary connection to the method. There is nothing inherent in social choice that generates political beliefs favoring the existing distribution of property rights and income or giving priority to market outcomes.[22] In fact, much normative work in social choice is almost radical, based as it is on the proposition that special weight should not be given by the political system to the distribution of property and privilege produced by the market and other nongovernmental institutions. One of the appeals of majority rule as a social decisionmaking rule is its satisfaction of this condition.[23]

The integration of public law with policy analysis and rational actor models of politics has only begun. Moving forward requires a broader collaborative effort by economists, lawyers, and political scientists to understand the politics and economics of the policy process. We need to consider a reform of administrative law on the scale of the changes wrought by the New Deal and codified by the Administrative Procedures Act in 1946.[24] Such an enterprise can provide a strong foundation for the modern administrative state. Sharp differences in politics and philosophy, however, hamper the development of a unified approach. Legal scholars themselves have creative work to do. They cannot simply borrow a ready-made synthesis.

2

Progressivism
and the Chicago School

This chapter begins the work of developing a progressive approach to law and economics[1] by contrasting it with the orthodoxy of what is frequently called the Chicago School. The Chicago School's appropriation of the law and economics label distorts the legal profession's perception of the role of economic analysis in the law. The alternative progressive endeavor promises a political economy of law that does not have the conservative bias of much Chicago work. I concentrate here on the policy analytic portion of progressivism since it presents the clearest contrast to Chicago. To emphasize the most striking differences, I provide rather stark characterizations of each approach, ignoring many subtleties and cross-cutting themes.

I begin with a summary of the development of progressive thinking in the post-war period. This is followed by an overview of the principles of policy analysis. With this background, I place the Chicago School in critical perspective: recognizing its important intellectual contributions while demonstrating its narrow focus and shaky empirical basis.

POLITICS AND POLICY:
A HISTORICAL SKETCH OF MODERN PROGRESSIVISM

In the late Fifties and early Sixties economists developed techniques of project evaluation based on cost-benefit tests and systems analysis. The theoretical underpinnings of these innovations are welfare economics, with its emphasis on externalities and market failures, and the theory of imperfect competition, which focuses on the inefficiency of monopoly power, imperfect information, and monopolistic competition. The political agenda is the correction of market failures by government action.

Cost-benefit techniques began to affect public decisions with the appointment of Robert McNamara as Secretary of Defense in 1961.[2] McNamara peopled the Department with a group of self-styled "whiz kids" committed to systems analysis and economic methods.[3] Several years later, the Johnson administration followed the Defense Department model in establishing offices for Policy, Planning, and Budgeting in agencies with domestic programmatic responsibilities such as Health, Education, and Welfare, and Housing and Urban Development.[4] Eventually, however, the Vietnam War and domestic unrest dampened the optimism of reform-minded students of the federal spending process. The problems of those years were not ones that technocrats could solve on their own. Public policy analysis remained a useful tool for programs with efficiency as their goal, but the claims of its early proponents were recognized as inflated.

As cost-benefit analysts began to accept the limitations of their techniques, public choice scholars started to use economic analysis to undermine the legitimacy of existing regulatory policies. They saw legislation as the outcome of political dealmaking that frequently did no more than preserve or enhance the monopoly power of existing producers.[5] Some concluded that government should be prevented from intervening in the economy since its actions were usually no more than devices to benefit narrow, well-organized interests.

Criticisms of the legislative process complemented demonstrations that existing policies were misguided. In some cases the regulation of price and entry harmed consumers.[6] Even regulatory policies with strong economic justifications, such as environmental protection, were inefficient in practice. Critics urged more reliance on economic incentives to produce compliance.[7] Studies of government spending programs tended to emphasize their weaknesses, showing, for example, that most subsidized housing was built outside of central cities and that many who completed job training programs were unable to find jobs.[8] Although many scholars who criticized existing social welfare and spending programs were deeply committed to the programs' purposes, others used these criticisms to show that government domestic spending and regulatory activity were too intrusive, too costly, and in need of drastic curtailment. These analysts and policymakers used arguments in favor of deregulating airlines or trucking to advocate cutting back environmental protection, and they used critiques of existing welfare policies to argue for drastic reductions in government spending. They interpreted studies showing that social programs had not accomplished all their goals to signify that the goals themselves were not worth pursuing.[9]

Not surprisingly, progressive analysts have not responded sympathetically to this misuse of their work. A counterattack is under way that emphasizes both the real accomplishments of recent regulatory and social programs[10] and the importance of information, ideas, and analysis in determining government policy.[11] Since the private market is riddled with imperfections, one can respond by reforming the state rather than shrinking government. My contribution to this reformation seeks, first, to argue that those concerned with economic efficiency and fairness cannot rely on the common law courts to achieve their aims. The correction of market failures and the improvement of distributive fairness requires statutes. Second, I argue for an active judicial oversight role, and third, I demonstrate that the skeptical political-economic contributions of public choice scholars can complement, not undermine, the progressive approach.

PRINCIPLES OF POLICY ANALYSIS

To understand the differences between the Chicago School of law and economics and the progressive approach, one needs to master the fundamentals of the policy analysis.[12] Public policy analysts are optimistic about politics. They view government as a system that designs policies to promote the goals of efficiency and equity. Policy-oriented economists are central to this effort, producing cost-benefit analyses and other analytic exercises of use to decisionmakers.[13] Professionals working in this tradition recognize both the value of markets in promoting efficiency and the importance of economic incentives in all areas of life, both private and public. They are trying to get the economic incentives right, not eliminate them.

As a central tenet of policy analysis, government should, insofar as possible, select projects that maximize the net benefits flowing to the populace. This calculation should include all costs and benefits, not just those which show up in the government budget. The analyst estimates the opportunity cost of the public program by calculating the value of alternatives forgone. Public policy analysis can evaluate options developed by others, but it is most useful when it aims to specify the options themselves with an eye to their efficiency consequences.

A competent cost-benefit analysis is essentially a step-by-step assessment of the nature of a public program and its impact on the world. It frequently requires scientific, engineering, and sociological skills in addition to economics. Even someone who objects to a full-fledged cost-benefit analysis might nevertheless accept the preliminary stages, in which one is simply sorting out the causal connections and identifying the less obvious implications of a policy.

Sometimes, however, critics object to the disclosure of a program's unintended consequences, as if the analyst were somehow at fault for pointing out unpleasant possibilities. This is a modern version of killing the messenger who brings the bad news. For example, a newspaper column expressed shock when a government analyst suggested that requiring infant seats in airplanes might increase infant deaths.[14] If babies use a seat, they will be charged for it; if they are charged for it, their parents may decide to drive or stay home instead of fly; driving is more dangerous than flying per passenger mile, so if enough families continue to travel, more babies may die. Whatever the truth of this claim, it is not absurd on its face. The argument simply assumes that parents are sensitive to price in making their travel plans. Other examples are easy to find: Requiring more stringent pollution controls on new as compared to old power plants can increase pollution by keeping old plants in operation longer.[15] Controlling rents can hurt the poor by limiting the supply of housing.[16] Stringent quality controls on subsidized day care centers can lead to segregation of children by race and income level.[17]

A cost-benefit analysis, however, does not end with the specification of a causal model. To complete the exercise, one must calculate the net benefit of each option. Since benefits and costs are borne by many people, the analyst needs a common metric to measure and compare gains and losses. Money is the most convenient metric, but sometimes others are superior, such as lives saved or acres of wilderness preserved. The use of money does not imply that only those benefits and costs which are traded in markets should count. Rather, one should identify and measure all the impacts of a program as well as possible.

To illustrate the multiple steps, consider a program to reduce the discharge of wastes into a river. As a first step, one must be able to model the relationship between discharges at particular points and water quality throughout the river. This is an exercise in hydrology and biology, not economics. Next, one must estimate the link between water quality and such physical measures as the number and variety of fish, drinking water quality, or savings in travel time for recreational water users. Third, benefits must be calculated in monetary terms. Fourth, one must estimate the costs of alternative levels of cleanup. In calculating costs the analyst should consider alternatives to in-plant waste treatment such as treating the water in the river rather than in the factory or changing product mix instead of treating waste. If benefits and costs are spread out over several years, they must be expressed in discounted present values, which reflect the fact that benefits obtained today are worth more than benefits with the same dollar value obtained tomorrow. Finally, the option with the greatest net benefits should be identified. Net benefits are maximized, not where total costs equal total benefits, but where *marginal* costs equal *marginal* benefits.[18] Such precision will not always be possible. When most of the benefits are difficult to monetize, the policy analysis may be able to do no more than itemize cost-effective solutions and indicate the dollar cost of such benefits as lives saved or acres of wilderness preserved.

Utilitarian and cost-benefit tests are not identical. Dollar measures permit interpersonal comparisons of benefits, but maximizing the monetary value of a program is not the same thing as maximizing total satisfaction under a utilitarian metric. Utilitarianism requires the direct measurement of satisfaction levels, a task that no one has yet been able to perform convincingly. A utilitarian and a cost-benefit analyst may rank projects differently. A poor person may benefit a great deal from some public policy but might be willing to accept a relatively small sum of money to forgo the benefit. Conversely, a rich person may obtain only a little satisfaction from a project but, because he is rich, be willing to pay a large amount to obtain it.

Cost-benefit analysis is not an appropriate tool when distributive justice issues are paramount. All dollars count equally. The procedure is neutral about who gains and who loses. It is primarily designed to analyze programs that could improve the efficiency of the economy. The neglect of distributive issues in cost-benefit analysis does not imply that economists believe that such issues are unimportant, but only that statutes designed to correct market failures are poor redistributive vehicles. Individual statutes affect only a portion of the population. A policy that concentrates on allocating the benefits and burdens of one statute fairly may well be unfair to those who are excluded from the program's ken. If all public programs concentrated on fairness to the exclusion of efficiency, the result could make most people worse off and would surely produce a crazy quilt of special-purpose benefits that would be difficult to justify. People would be treated differently who differ only in whether or not they happen to come under the jurisdiction of a particular statute. To echo a familiar theme in public finance, redistribution should be accomplished through a general system of taxes and transfers, not piecemeal through the complex of regulatory and spending programs.

Politicians, however, may wish to know the incidence of gains and losses either out of a concern for fairness or to permit them to claim credit for aiding their constituents. The cost-benefit analyst can then provide information about who has been hurt and harmed by a program along with her overall assessment of net benefits. Over and above credit-claiming by political supporters of the program, these data could form the basis for legislative actions to change the agency's mandate or to develop counteracting compensation schemes.

Policy analysts, however, do more than evaluate given projects. They also help design efficient public programs. Subject to overall public goals, the analyst aims to set up programs that economize on the information needs of government and give individuals choices about how to use subsidies or comply with regulations. Thus an economist might recommend an auction to allocate offshore oil leases or a voucher plan to subsidize housing for the poor. The use of effluent charges or pollution rights schemes is a familiar feature of plans to distribute pollution loads efficiently across dischargers. These plans permit each discharger to set its own marginal cost equal to the effluent fee or rights price. The total pollution load would be efficiently distributed across polluters, with high-cost dischargers paying more to the state and discharging more than low-cost dischargers.

Financial incentives have top priority, but if they cannot be implemented, performance-based regulations are preferable to technology-based plans. Efficiency is improved if the government tells regulated entities what they must accomplish, not what they must do. For example, a performance-based pollution control policy would order a plant to discharge no more than x pounds of waste per day, leaving it to the firm to decide whether to treat its waste, change its product mix, or shut down the plant. The government would not specify a required technology. Each discharger would select the cheapest option consistent with the state's pollution goal.

———————— • ————————

With this outline of the progressive approach and an overview of policy analysis and its link to progressivism, I turn now to the Chicago School of law and economics.

THE CHICAGO SCHOOL

To some, the Chicago school is synonymous with law and economics.[19] In fact, it is a rather specialized endeavor based on a particular view of the world and of the justifications for state action. The basic building blocks are clearly defined property relations, competitive markets, and private bargains. While Chicago School scholars have written on topics as diverse as antitrust, family law, taxation, corporations, and racial discrimination,[20] the central core is the economic analysis of the common law. Their analysis is directed toward decisions of Anglo-American courts, focusing on tort, contract, and property law doctrines that have evolved through the judicial system. The Chicago School has contributed a great deal to the integration of law and economics. As a comprehensive view of the relationship of law to economic analysis, it is, however, deeply flawed.[21]

Origins: The "New" Law and Economics

Innovative law and economics scholarship in the Sixties blurred the distinction between public and private law by showing that common law doctrines could have broad effects on the efficiency and justice of society. Early work by Guido Calabresi and Ronald Coase set the agenda for law and economics scholarship in the decades to follow.[22] Borrowing from microeconomic theory and public finance, these scholars urged lawyers to take an ex ante perspective by viewing judicial decisions as affecting future behavior. Tort and contract damages were designed not just to make the wronged one whole. They encouraged efficient caretaking by injurers and victims and efficient dealmaking by buyers and sellers. Legal rules should encourage economic actors to take account of the opportunity cost of their behavior in situations where other forms of price incentives were not available.

In torts, accident law was seen as a response to private market failure. Tort law deters accidents in situations where potential victims would find it very costly either to negotiate with injurers ex ante or to purchase caretaking in a market.[23] Liability should be placed on the individual best able to prevent the harm.[24] If one firm's actions impose costs on many uninformed customers, liability should be placed on the firm, not because the firm is "at fault," but because such a rule will minimize the costs of negotiating a solution to the externality problem.

Similarly, since bargaining is costly, contract law provides a set of fallback provisions that the courts will enforce unless the parties have agreed to alternative contractual language. The expectation measure of damages, designed to make the breached-against party whole, provides an inducement to the breaching party (for example, the seller) to take account of the costs of his action. However, it may encourage the buyer to spend too much in reliance on the contract.[25]

Finally, property law should establish entitlements that facilitate the efficient use of resources. As the Coase "theorem" is famous for demonstrating, if no transactions costs exist, the distribution of property rights is irrelevant. Owners will always negotiate to an efficient solution. The assignment of rights affects the fairness of the distribution of wealth, but not its efficiency. However, as Coase also illustrated, when bargaining costs exist, information is imperfect, or other transactions costs are pervasive, efficiency requires that rights be assigned to minimize these costs. [26]

This research represented a sharp break from the use of economics in specialized legal applications such as the estimation of market concentration ratios in antitrust law or the calculation of rates of return in the regulation of public utilities. Instead, economics could provide fundamental organizing principles for the heart of the standard first-year curriculum: torts, contracts, and property. Nevertheless, this interdisciplinary effort had several conventional features. First of all, it did not challenge the traditional law school curriculum. Reading lists might be revised and casebooks rewritten, but the standard subjects remained, and many of the same "leading" cases would continue to be taught. Second, the economic analysis itself built on familiar concepts of opportunity cost, externalities, marginalism, and static equilibrium. Methodologically, law and economics was not at the cutting edge of economics. Mainstream economists chuckled at the idea that Coase had proved a "theorem."

Compensating for these weaknesses, these early efforts took a broad view of the range of relevant issues that was similar in many ways to the concerns of progressive scholars. While emphasizing the resource allocation role of common law rules, much of this research was also concerned with the distribution of income and wealth and the capacity of legal institutions to resolve disputes fairly and expeditiously. There was no attempt to glamorize the accomplishments of judge-made law. For example, Calabresi's writing has always stressed the importance of direct regulation, subsidies, and taxes as alternatives to the common law. [27]

However, when one looks at this pioneering work as a whole, one is struck by the limited range of substantive issues considered. Even when these lawyer-economists contemplated the field of "public law," they studied problems that were central to the common law, such as automobile accidents, land use regulation, and the Uniform Commercial Code. The progressive agenda, which begins with market failures rather than with the doctrines of the common law, provides a more broad-gauged perspective.

From Interdisciplinary Borrowing to Chicago Ideology

The scholars of the Chicago School built on the ecclectic and nonideological base of this first group of writers. The first wave stressed the need to consider efficiency in evaluating common law doctrines. The Chicago School has gone farther and argued that the observed pattern of common law decisions actually closely approximates the efficient set. It was said that, over time, the common law changed in response to changes in the relative costs and benefits of alternative rules. These scholars claimed that inefficient rules were more likely to be litigated than efficient rules, and a new efficient standard would persist once it was established. Instead of simply analyzing the efficiency properties of common law rules, the Chicagoans defended the common law system as the best public policy system available. In their view, judges had been promoting efficient resource allocation for decades without knowing it.

Any judge who appeared at all self-conscious about what he was doing was canonized. The most prominent example is Learned Hand. He stated in *United States v. Carroll Towing* that in a negligence case, "if the probability be called P; the injury, L; and the burden, B; liability depends upon whether B is less than L multiplied by P, i.e., whether B<PL."[28] In other words, the defendant should be liable if the cost of taking care is less than the probability of an accident times the level of injury if an accident occurs. Richard Posner, the legal scholar most emblematic of the Chicago approach,[29] uses *Carroll Towing* as the epigram for his torts casebook and Judge Hand's portrait as a frontispiece.[30]

As the field developed, it of course generated its own internal disputes. Scholars differed both on the current direction of doctrine and on the efficiency of alternative rules. Posner and Calabresi, for example, debated the relative merits of strict liability versus negligence in torts,[31] and contracts scholars clashed over the issues of liquidated damages and specific performance.[32] These debates were not, however, over fundamental goals, but were instead over the proper behavioral assumptions and the information realistically available to individuals.[33]

Despite these controversies, there is broad consensus among Chicagoans that the central focus of law and economics is the individual transaction, not the market. Building on typical tort, contract, and property cases, Chicago scholars focus on such transactions as automobile accidents, breached contracts, trespassing animals, and hotels that cast shadows on neighboring swimming pools. They praise the market but do not spend much time studying it. Their faith in the market paradoxically implies that it should not be the predominant area for law and economics study. The more efficient the market, the less important is law as a means of promoting efficiency. The closer the world approaches the ideal world of zero transactions costs,[34] the closer law comes to performing a purely distributive function.

The Role of the State

Despite their focus on the common law courts, Chicagoans cannot avoid joining progressives in considering the role of the state. The Chicagoan's political philosophy combines a utilitarian or wealth maximization ethic with a belief in the independent value of individualism and free choice.[35] The political program is based on support of laissez-faire capitalism and a belief that the state should do little more than define and uphold private property rights, enforce private contracts, and preserve external and internal order.

The state's essential function is to establish a system of legally enforceable property rights and to enforce private deals.[36] Since private economic activity is hindered by uncertainty about ownership, the state should behave like a conservative dictator with respect to the definition of property rights. To facilitate private economic decisionmaking, democratic political decisionmaking must be constrained. Free market choice takes precedence over free democratic political choice. Implicit in this work is an authoritarian system for defining property rights that can credibly promise not to redefine rights on which expectations have been based. The dictatorial powers of the state are, however, limited to establishing property rights and perhaps also enforcing laws against monopoly.[37] All other resource allocation choices are made by private individuals acting to maximize their wealth. Democratic choice has little role to play in determining economic policy or in redistributing wealth.

But Chicagoans are concerned not only with the stability of property relationships. They also want a system of rights that reduces the costs of market and negotiated transactions. A stable system of state ownership of the means of production, while not disappointing anyone's expectations, is hardly what they have in mind. Instead, rights should be designed to further efficiency. Thus if one firm creates air pollution that harms many nearby landowners, courts should give these landowners an entitlement to clean air since this solution minimizes transaction costs.[38]

Policy prescriptions of this form, however, move Chicagoans beyond a simple requirement that the state establish *some* set of property rights to a policy analytic argument that it should establish a particular set, supplemented by tort and contract law that takes a particular form. But what if the existing legal doctrines are well-established rules that bear only a very rough relationship to those that would best further efficient private economic behavior? A central tension in the Chicago School is between the progressive notion that changes in property relations can be used to further efficiency goals and the conservative, status quo orientation of much writing with its heavy emphasis on the preservation of existing rights to property.[39] The Chicago School scholars thus risk being caught in a contradiction.[40] In order to encourage investment, the state should be conservative and reluctant to change the rules. However, if the rules encourage inefficient actions, they need to be changed. Even more troubling, how should these scholars enter the policy debate, given their belief that one cannot expect a democratically elected government to view economic efficiency as self-evidently the most basic value? When bureaucracies and legislatures engage the attention of Chicagoans, it is generally to criticize them as bastions of special interest influence and red tape.

One solution is to deny that a contradiction exists in Anglo-American jurisprudence. And Chicagoans have often been tempted in this direction. They argue that very little needs to be done to fine-tune the law by attempting to demonstrate that existing doctrines and property relationships turn out by and large to further efficiency.[41] These doctrines have been promulgated not by democratic legislative bodies but by common law courts whose judges are not directly responsible to the electorate. Legislative meddling would both disrupt private expectations and override efficient legal rules. Doctrines change over time in response to changes in the economic system, but the change is gradual, so that current expectations are not seriously eroded. Thus the property rights "autocrat" turns out to be history, whose rules are interpreted and updated by hundreds of decentralized, professional judges with a powerful respect for precedent.[42]

The claim that common law rules are efficient has been questioned by many progressive scholars and by others both in and out of the law and economics field.[43] Even though scholars do not always agree on what the efficient rule should be, most analysts accept the conclusion that some existing rules are inefficient in some circumstances. The dispute turns on how pervasive and important these lapses are. No empirical work exists which estimates the losses from such rules, but a few doctrinal examples from tort and trespass law should suffice to produce a healthy skepticism.

Consider, first, the case of *LeRoy Fiber Co. v. Chicago, Milwaukee and St. Paul Railway*,[44] a leading case in which railroad sparks set fire to flax stored near the railroad tracks. Justice Holmes's partial concurrence is a model of law and economics reasoning. For him, the owner of the flax would receive compensation so long as it was not "in danger from even a prudently managed engine."[45] The Court majority, however, does not admit the possibility of contributory negligence by the plaintiff so long as the use of the land was a "proper use."[46] The opinion supports the view that landowners can stack flammable products anywhere they wish regardless of the relative costs of caretaking by railroads and landowners. Many other cases adopt this strong entitlements view for landowners. In general, an action may be called a tort simply because it interferes with someone's use and enjoyment of his or her property.[47]

As a second example consider the legal distinction between trespass and nuisance. A trespasser is strictly liable even if no measurable harm has occurred, while an action will be declared a nuisance only if it affects the "use and enjoyment" of land. Thus trespass is a "property rule" that gives the owner the right to keep others out unless they obtain his consent, while nuisance is a "liability rule," which means people can create nuisances so long as they pay off those who are adversely affected.[48] The legal distinction between trespass and nuisance seems to be between physical objects that enter one's land (cattle, a fallen tree, a person) and intangibles that bother a landowner (poisonous gases, noise). This distinction obviously has no economic content. However, some law and economics scholars have tried to argue that the trespass–nuisance distinction maps onto the distinction between two-person and multiperson events.[49] Since transaction costs are lower in the former than in the latter, a property rule is used for the two-person case and a liability rule based on nuisance is used in the multiparty case. While the distinction is fine as an economics exercise, it does not capture the legal categories. A cow that tramples twenty pieces of property is still trespassing, and a drummer still creates a nuisance whether he lives in Manhattan with a hundred neighbors or shares a country road with a single lover of solitude.

More important than the current state of Anglo-American common law is the general observation that even if the case could be proved, such a proof would not resolve the fundamental contradiction in the Chicago School approach. Any finding that the common law is efficient is contingent on the particular historical past and current institutions existing in the United States and Great Britain. Chicago School scholars need to ask policy analytic questions to resolve contradictions between settled expectations and the creation of efficient substantive rules. They also need to join with progressives to consider more fully the role of political institutions other than common law courts.[50]

CONCLUSIONS

Conventional law and economics has begun to incorporate some of the recent innovations in economic theory. Strategic game theoretic insights are appearing in the literature on contracts, and the role of imperfect information is reflected in recent work.[51] Nevertheless, while the importation of recent innovations in the fields of industrial organization and microeconomics promises to enrich the field, standard law and economics analysis has begun to run out of steam. The easy innovations have been made, and some of the current embellishments seem decidedly marginal. The limitations arise, not from a failure of intelligence, but from a narrowness of vision.

The difficulties are most clearly illustrated when law and economics analysis confronts policy problems that test the limits of the courts as regulatory institutions. An especially clear example has arisen in products liability law. Suddenly the common law tort system is attempting to resolve major policy questions concerning the healthfulness and safety of products. Decisions involving design defects in mass tort cases have implications for the organization and competitiveness of markets. Judges and their special masters are aping regulatory agencies. For Chicago School scholars this issue is something of a test of their faith in the efficiency of common law courts versus their belief in leaving businesses and their customer free to contract as they wish. Interestingly, the trend in toxic tort law has led some of the staunchest Chicagoans to question their faith in courts and to propose doctrinal shifts, apparently as a way of avoiding preemptive legislation.[52] Others have even rallied behind federal legislative proposals to preempt the common law. Products liability clearly demonstrates the weakness of a perspective that emphasizes only one aspect of government.

A progressive approach to safety begins, not with the case law, but, in contrast, with the problem of consumer and worker information. There is no a priori commitment to a particular institutional arrangement such as the common law courts. Instead, the effort is directed toward isolating the possible market failures caused by imperfect information and the incentives to reveal or hide it or to produce more knowledge through research. If private market inefficiencies can be isolated, the next step is to consider alternative ways of correcting them with their accompanying costs and benefits. Will a labeling or notice requirement be sufficient, or is more intrusive regulation required? Should firms be charged a tax based on the riskiness of their products or workplaces, or should lawsuits by those who suffered damages be streamlined? How strong is the knowledge linking particular products or substances to accidents and illness? If the causal links are weak, should the government sponsor research of its own or give incentives to firms to discover the relationships? These are difficult questions which illustrate the range of the policy analytic exercise for which the private lawsuit is only one possible tool. I will take up some of these issues in Part Three when I discuss both occupational health and safety and the regulation of consumer products.[53]

PART
TWO

THE COURTS

In the common law fields of torts, contracts, and property everybody recognizes that judges make substantive law. Hard as the courts may try to follow precedent, new situations arise that require creative lawmaking. Economic analyses that argue for the efficiency of particular doctrinal rules are acceptable prescriptive exercises. In contrast, when statutes (or the Constitution) govern behavior and when administrative agencies are active, judicial lawmaking is much criticized. The separation of powers circumscribes the role of the courts. Thus progressive law and economics, when it focuses on judicial review of the other branches of government, cannot rely on the heart of the policy analytic exercise: substantive policy recommendations.

My study of judicial review in this section of the book accepts this constraint but argues that courts should be active in reviewing both administrative agencies and the legislature. In contrast to the common law, this does not mean imposing concrete policies directly. Instead, judges should improve the democratic accountability and technical quality of policymaking in the other branches and enhance the fairness of the political-bureaucratic state. The courts should seek to improve the operation of the political-administrative process staking out an intermediate position between the optimistic "can-do" attitude of public policy analysis and the pessimistic view articulated by some public choice scholars who study government.

Chapter 3 outlines a framework for judicial review of regulatory agency actions under statues concerned with economic efficiency. I apply the lessons of public choice to argue that courts should impose a background norm on agencies operating under vague statutory mandates. Chapters 4 and 5 propose ways for the courts to improve the democratic accountability of the legislative process. Political science research on Congress suggests that elected representatives have an incentive to be less than straightforward with their constituents. Judicial review may be able to improve Congressional performance by examining statutory structure and by monitoring the appropriations process.

3

Policy

Judicial Review
of Agency Action

Many statutes are ostensibly concerned with improving the efficient operation of the economy but leave considerable discretion to the executive branch. Agencies may exploit the freedom given to them by the Congress to favor narrow groups or to further their own agendas. Given this possibility, I argue that courts should impose a background norm on agency deliberations. The norm I propose is one that respects the costs and benefits imposed on all citizens. In the absence of specific language outlawing policy analysis, courts would require agencies to seek the net benefit maximizing solution. Of course, legislation which explicitly rejects this approach should be upheld. Courts should simply give notice to the legislature that without clearcut language, they will impose a policy analytic test in reviewing economic regulation.

I justify my proposal for a judicially imposed background norm both by reference to the normative values of the policy analytic approach and by introducing research examining the problematic links between legislative choice and majority will. This research in political economy suggests that when agencies have been given a broad statutory mandate, no sharp conflict need exist between democratic values and judicial encouragement of policy analysis in agencies. When a statute's purpose is the correction of a market failure, the burden of proof should be on those who argue that net benefit maximization is contrary to democratic principles.

The policy analytic approach was outlined in the preceding chapters. It proceeds by locating instances of market failure and recommending methods to correct them. The aim is to maximize the dollar value of net benefits using private willingness to pay for benefits (or private willingness to be paid to forgo gains) as a criterion. I do not wish to downplay the obvious difficulties with policy analysis as a comprehensive social welfare scheme. For example, only the total gain matters so that dollar costs imposed on one group can be balanced by dollar benefits gained by another. Furthermore, measuring benefits in dollars is not the same thing as measuring them in utility or in votes. Nevertheless, policy analysis does provide a way of isolating market failures and thinking systematically about costs and benefits. If we assume that the efficient operation of markets is a broadly shared goal, cost-benefit tests imposed by the courts might, in the absence of other information, reflect the underlying wishes of the electorate. In the absence of specific legislative directives, it seems to me to provide a better background norm for democratic policymaking than the problematics of common law jurisprudence or a presumption in favor of the status quo.

But why should a background norm be required in the review of statutes? Why won't the legislature both faithfully represent popular sentiment and draft statutes with clearly stated goals? Part of the answer can be gleaned from the social choice literature with its skepticism about any easy association between legislative performance and democratic preferences.

IRRESPONSIBLE DEMOCRACY

Government by technocratic experts is easy to criticize, but compare it with government by elected politicians. The fundamental strength of Congress is that its members must be reelected every few years, while technocrats, who are civil servants or, increasingly, independent contractors, face no such test. If legislators act in an outrageous way, they will face defeat. But if the courts require the administrative process to be open to public input and scrutiny and to act on the basis of competent analyses, is the executive necessarily any less accountable?

I do not wish to downplay the constraints imposed by the electoral process, and I am certainly not advocating authoritarianism. However, recent research in political economy should undermine glib confidence that every action of the legislature is in the interest of a majority of the population. Exaggerated respect by the courts for the "intent" of the Congress is misplaced even for committed democrats. A realistic view of the legislative process provides a justification for focusing on the quality of the administrative process. To establish this point I review political-economic research that casts doubt on strong claims for the quality of legislative output.

Two aspects of this work are relevant. The first, originating with Mancur Olson's *Logic of Collective Action*, studies private incentives for political action.[1] The second, associated with David Mayhew and Morris Fiorina, analyzes how the motivations of individual politicians affect the design of legislation.[2]

The Logic of Collective Action

Political organizations do not spring up full-blown whenever people share a common interest. To an economist political organization of any kind is a puzzle. Why should self-interested people band together to further a common goal when each can take a free ride on the political success of the others? This was the problem with which Olson grappled in the *Logic of Collective Action*.[3] He challenged the prevalent functionalism of political scientists who thought it obvious that shared aims would produce shared political activity. He pointed out that if organization is costly, no one may wish to organize even if all would benefit. He showed that the groups that do organize will represent a selective set of the population and support a nonoptimal level of public service provision.

Sometimes a group may be aided by an individual whose benefits will be so great that he is willing to bear the costs of political action single-handedly. Thus an industry with one dominant firm may let the firm leader do all the lobbying. Even with no dominant firm, however, an industry may organize if it has a small number of similar-size firms that can overcome the costs of collective action.

Private benefits can also induce political action. In the case of a dominant firm, smaller firms might join the effort in an attempt to tilt the political benefits toward their own interests.[4] For example, the largest firm in the steel industry might want import controls on mass-produced steel sheets, while a smaller firm might push for controls on specialty products. Private benefits might also consist of direct inducements, such as discount insurance policies and free credit cards, which encourage individuals to join a group. Organizations that exist for other purposes have a political advantage. Thus industrial labor unions, organized to bargain with employers, can easily turn their energies to politics. Finally, the selective incentives can be moral or social. Organizers can try to make people feel guilty for not doing their part, provide them with pleasant social experiences, and appeal to ethical standards.

Olson, especially as he develops his argument in *The Rise and Decline of Nations,* [5] views most politically active groups as pernicious. While he recognizes that countervailing forces may overwhelm the factors which he emphasizes, Olson is generally pessimistic about interest group politics. The tighter and more established organized groups become, the more redistributive politics occurs, and the worse off society is. Olson places little weight on political organizations that obtain public benefits which improve the efficiency of the economy. He has not carefully integrated his analysis into a theory of representative politics in which information about costs and benefits is politically salient to the general voting public.

Olson's pessimism about political organization is odd, given the intellectual roots of his theory. He has borrowed directly from the economic analysis of public goods. In that theory government action is justified when goods are consumed in common by everyone. National defense is the most familiar example. People may differ widely in their evaluation of the proper level of defense spending, but all consume the same amount. A decentralized private market cannot efficiently provide such goods. State action is necessary to levy taxes and set the level of output. While each citizen would prefer not to pay taxes and take a free ride off others' provisions, tax rates can be set so that everyone would rather live in a state with a coercive tax system than in a world with no public goods. Obviously, in practice, taxes are unlikely to be set in this way, and groups who capture the political system may induce a redistribution of benefits toward themselves. Nevertheless, the lesson of public finance economics is that politics is not just a zero (or negative) sum game in which resources are simply transferred from winners to losers. [6]

While Olson emphasizes the inefficient redistribution that results from the selectiveness of political organization, his work implies that government may be too small in a democracy. Many efficient projects will not be undertaken because no one organizes in their support. Those pushing for inefficient projects may fill the gap, but it is entirely possible that overall public spending will be too low.

Organized groups are not necessarily undesirable; they may sometimes permit the articulation of beneficial public goals. Courts might then try to lower the organizational costs of these groups. One way to do this through the lens of judicial review is to presume a goal of net benefit maximization for economic regulation. Thus broad-based groups would only need to obtain quite general public interest language to accomplish their goals. Groups with a narrower focus could succeed only if the statutory language explicitly singled them out. The aim of the presumption is to make it easier for reform groups to pass laws and attract members since the courts have simplified the political tasks facing such groups. In the face of vagueness in the language of regulatory statutes, the courts would not look to the common law or seek to preserve the status quo, but would require agencies to follow the precepts of policy analysis. Thus my analysis of judicial review builds on Olson's framework but recognizes that groups seeking to correct market failures may have some political success at least in framing the purposes of statutes. A presumption in favor of agency cost-benefit analysis is a modest attempt to reduce the level of political action required of broad-based groups.

I move now to the second part of my social choice argument, which is based, not on the costs of political organization, but on the weak link between legislative actions and majoritarian policy preferences.

Reelection Motives in Congress

Consider members of Congress, not as paragons of public-spirited self-lessness, but as self-interested politicians fundamentally concerned with reelection.[7] Even if they have other aims besides reelection, continued membership in Congress is a necessary condition for the achievement of such goals as a powerful committee chairmanship or passage of a favored bill.

David Mayhew argues that, in seeking reelection, members of Congress engage in three activities, which he calls advertising, credit claiming, and position taking.[8] Advertising is an effort to project a favorable image empty of substantive content. Credit claiming involves maneuvering to be seen as responsible for some specific benefit. The benefit may be a favorable decision by the bureaucracy or a legislative amendment that particularly aids one's constituents.[9] Seldom will one be able to claim credit for a major piece of legislation, and even if one can, the voters may be indifferent. Finally, position taking is a public statement on anything of interest to voters.[10] It may take the form of a roll call vote or a speech or a media interview. Mayhew concludes that reelection pressures, which produce the behavior he outlines, have serious consequences for the quality of legislation. Few members will be much concerned with the detailed coherence of statutory schemes so long as a pet amendment has been included or the symbolism of votes and speeches is clear to voters.

Building on Mayhew's book, Morris Fiorina argues that legislator self-interest will affect the delegation of tasks to the bureaucracy.[11] He argues that legislators satisfy their constituents not so much by position taking on broad legislative initiatives as by doing individual favors for voters. He then argues that Congress will design laws with numerous opportunities for "casework" to aid constituents. After the law is on the books, legislators can earn points with their constituents by intervening in their favor before the agency.

The extent of Congressional delegation to the bureaucracy may depend upon whether benefits and costs are concentrated or diffused. If benefits are diffuse and costs are concentrated, for example, Congress is likely to want to shift the hard choices to an agency. Conversely, when benefits are concentrated and costs are diffuse, members of Congress will be specific about who should benefit from their largess. Even when delegation to the agency seems politically desirable as a way of shifting hard choices to someone else, there are costs for Congress. Agencies are not completely under its control. Studies of the budgetary process show how agencies use control over program information and over the allocation of funds to increase or maintain budgetary appropriations.[12] Public bureaucrats may become powerful advocates for the industries they oversee, pressuring Congress to increase aid. Agencies such as the Department of Agriculture, the Department of Labor, and the Department of Education, whatever else they do, are advocates for their respective sectors.

These conclusions have two implications for judicial review of agency action. First, they suggest that the pronouncements of individual legislators should be given little weight in judging the intent of a statute. These statements will frequently be no more than Mayhew's position taking and are hardly evidence of majority support. The political science scholarship supports the view that courts should concentrate on statutory language, not legislative history. Second, this research implies that statutes may be carelessly or vaguely drafted or constructed to permit subsequent favorseeking. Judicial insistence on net benefit maximization as a default rule can help repair some of the carelessness and can force Congress to be explicit about a statute's narrow focus. It can also constrain an agency from selling out to the groups it oversees. Agency assistance to a narrow group at the expense of greater costs imposed on others would be upheld only if expressly intended by the enabling legislation.

POLICY ANALYSIS AND ADMINISTRATIVE LAW

Background Norms and Judicial Review

The weaknesses of the democratic political process support the use of substantive background norms when courts review agency actions. Policy analysis provides guidance on norm construction, at least for statutes whose stated purpose is the correction of a market failure. Under such statutes, courts should require agencies to use policy analytic methods absent an explicit statutory prohibition. Courts would require agencies to make a plausible case that they have maximized net benefits subject to statutory, budgetary, and informational constraints.[13] A presumption in favor of net benefit maximization will increase the political costs for narrow groups who must obtain explicit statutory language in order to have their interests recognized by court and agency.

Judicial review of agency policy analyses should replace tortured attempts to derive legislative intent from legislative history. Consistent with constitutional limits, however, the courts would enforce clear statutory statements of purpose, even ones that further only narrow privileged interests. Courts would require agencies to follow unambiguous statements of intent in the legislative text and would not engage in judgments about the national interest. The words of the statute would be the courts' fundamental guide, but with the burden of proof on anyone attempting to show legislative intent not to maximize net benefits.[14] No such presumption of legality, however, would apply to legislative history. As the social choice research outlined above suggests, the use of Congressional speeches and committee reports to infer "intent" is problematic. Speeches may represent position taking for the nightly news, and reports may include negotiated deals without enough legislative or popular support to be included in the statute itself.

When, as is usually the case, goals are not precisely specified in the statute, and budgetary appropriations are limited, the imprecision of the statute gives the agency leeway to evaluate both benefits and costs. The judiciary should then insist that agencies make this evaluative effort.[15] Of course, cost-benefit analyses cannot always be carried out with precision. Key pieces of information may be unavailable, and certain harms and benefits maybe unquantifiable. Nevertheless, the agency should be required to make an effort systematically to think through the available options. Such a presumption in favor of net benefit maximization does not imply a lack of concern for distributive justice. Rather, it reflects the principle of institutional competence outlined in Chapter 2. Economic regulatory programs are simply not effective ways to achieve equity goals.

The pursuit of net benefit maximization does not necessarily mean that agencies should do cost-benefit analyses. The technique should be tailored to the nature of the issue. When private individuals and firms possess much of the information needed to develop sound policies, it may be best to give them incentives to reveal this information rather than to centralize analysis and decisionmaking in the agency. Thus while in some cases informal rulemaking guided by cost-benefit principles may make sense, in others a negotiated bargain between the affected interests may be more likely to produce a net-benefit-maximizing result. In still others the agency might create incentives for private individuals and firms to act without specifying a desired result.

Administrative Procedures: Policymaking Versus Implementation

Administrative law is a procedure-oriented field. Since my proposal would require a shift in the direction of substantive judicial review, what would be left of the review of process? To analyze this question I distinguish between policymaking and implementation. These categories overlap with, but are not identical to, the familiar administrative law dichotomy between rulemaking and adjudication.[16] Unlike traditional distinctions, my focus is on the results of the process, not the nature of the procedures. Policymaking concentrates on statutory gap-filling consistent within the basic policy thrust of the law. Implementation includes the followup activities needed to put a policy into effect in concrete cases. One set of procedures is appropriate when a democratically accountable agency makes policy by gathering technocratic information and evaluating data. Another set is required to assure that policy is implemented to impose the costs and benefits of government action in a fair and even-handed manner.

But are policymaking and implementation viable categories? The distinction is out of favor. Policy is not really made until it has been put into practice. The range of practical options depends upon the feasibility of their implementation. Some agencies do little general policymaking. In fact, the trend seems to be away from policy-oriented rulemaking. Adjudicatory procedures can both determine policy and be a step in the implementation process, and other techniques, such as guidelines and product recalls, may be used to circumvent judicial review of general policies.[17] While the courts have limited the use of general guidelines as a substitute for rulemaking, they have permitted agencies wide latitude to decide between rulemaking and adjudication under the Administrative Procedures Act.[18]

To the extent that the courts have thus contributed to the blurring of categories, they should reverse themselves. The policy-implementation distinction is important for the very reason that agencies themselves are important. Agencies are an improvement over laws enforced through case-by-case adjudication in the courts because they permit a systematic overview of a policy problem. Even when agencies can themselves pick which issues to adjudicate, reliance on individualized cases can obscure the broad policy issues involved and overemphasize the details of particular situations. Furthermore, considerable uncertainty is created when regulated firms must infer agency policy from a series of individual adjudications. Adjudications are appropriate when the issue is individualized, as when the decisionmaker must decide if the law has been implemented fairly in a particular case or whether the agency should grant an exception to a general rule. They can be part of a broader implementation strategy, which also includes less legalistic techniques drawn from the methodology of science and social science.

The policymaking process should be compatible with a program's basic goals. Courts should review agencies, not to find out if they have mechanically followed some set of guidelines, but to see if their choices are appropriate given statutory goals and constitutional protections. The courts would not examine policymaking procedures except to determine if the process is sufficiently open to permit political accountability.[19] Agency policy processes should be challenged only on the ground that relevant interests were not kept informed or permitted to provide material to the agency. Over and above substantive concerns, the language of the informal rulemaking provisions of the Administrative Procedures Act would govern.[20] The agency must give public notice of its intent to make policy in a particular area and must give interested individuals, groups, and organizations the opportunity to provide information. The agency's decision must be made public. The imposition of extra procedural constraints by courts would be replaced with direct oversight of the policy choices. The courts should view the use of adjudications to make policy with skepticism since such a practice runs the risk of confusing fairness to individuals with the furtherance of broad policy goals.

In contrast, for implementation, judicial priorities should be quite different. Norms of fairness and equal treatment, not substance, would govern the judicial inquiry. Once the agency has set overall policy, implementation should avoid favoritism and arbitrariness. Judicial analogies are much more appropriate at this stage, although the goal should be, not individualized justice, but fair patterns of agency behavior. The courts should, however, avoid excessively judicializing agency procedures. The goal should not be to recreate the protections of the courtroom for their own sake but to establish fair implementation patterns that do not require judicial intervention on a day-to-day basis. Although everyone cannot be treated absolutely equally, the agency should articulate its principles of enforcement and establish procedures that permit individuals to challenge implementation decisions. Administrative law's traditional concern with protecting individuals from state tyranny would be salient. Constraints of time and money can appropriately limit agency behavior, but budget constraints operate here to limit the fairness of procedures, not—as in the policymaking area—to limit the achievement of efficiency goals. Implementation and policymaking are linked, however, since the more trouble the agency takes over its implementation plan, the fewer resources it will have for policymaking.[21]

In my formulation, then, policymaking and implementation face different sorts of judicial scrutiny. Substantive norms, not procedure, are central to policymaking. In this domain, only procedural requirements that further openness have independent importance. Such procedures do not enhance fairness or improve the quality of policy but, instead, increase the accountability of the government to voters. For implementation, in contrast, procedural fairness is a central goal in individual cases, and the courts would also hear claims that an agency's overall implementation practice is arbitrary and unfair.

CONCLUSIONS

This chapter has demonstrated how progressive law and economics approaches a central problem in administrative law. Policy analysis and social choice complement each other to produce a proposal for judicial review of agency action. The topic is a conventional one, and my analysis respects the basic principle that courts should not substitute their judgments for those of agencies or of Congress. Only the attempt to combine disparate intellectual traditions was novel. The result, though, is at odds with much current legal thinking. It would require a substantial reorientation of judicial roles. Judicial review of policymaking would shift away from the details of procedure and of legislative history and toward the encouragement of improved analytic capabilities. Judges themselves would have to acquire these capabilities, raising a challenge to the notion that the best form of oversight is by generalists with no particular training outside of the law.[22]

The next two chapters develop more unconventional implications of my interdisciplinary approach. They take up judicial review of legislative activity. On the basis of rational actor models of democratic government and normative work in social choice, I argue for judicial oversight to remedy some of the weaknesses of Congress as a representative body responsible to the electorate.

4

Politics

Judicial Review of Congressional Action

When individual people are harmed by government action, the courts require procedural safeguards under the due process and equal protection clauses of the Constitution. When thousands or millions are harmed by statute, the courts are far more deferential.[1] They assert that the political process provides sufficient protection for the populace. This misplaced view has produced an overly passive judiciary. In reviewing legislation the courts seem unable to distinguish between judicial actions that dictate policy and those which enhance the democratic structure of political life.

Modern judges idealize the legislature. They either are naïve about politics or else believe that idealization is a way of avoiding oversight. "[T]he Legislature . . . is presumed to know the needs of the people,"[2] and its statutory products are accepted absent a violation of constitutional prohibitions. This presumption extends from a refusal to evaluate the quality of legislative enactments[3] to an unwillingness to examine the legislative process. In the typical case the courts limit their inquiry to a search for legislative "intent." The judiciary seldom examines the connection between the intent of legislators and majoritarian principles. Even recent Supreme Court cases involving the structure of government stress the separation of powers[4] and the formal stages of the lawmaking process.[5] These opinions involve a mechanical application of the constitutional text to the particular problem at hand without much appreciation of the realistic operation of government.[6]

I argue in this chapter and the next that courts should take a more active role in improving the accountability of Congress to its constituents.[7] Judges should do this, not by trying to determine the popular will, but by requiring Congress to make the legislative process more transparent to voters and to limit the strategic opportunities available to narrow interests. Reconstructions of legislative intent are insufficient. The aim should be to make it easier for voters to understand Congressional actions and hence to hold their representatives responsible at election time.

Much writing on judicial review worries over the "countermajoritarian difficulty." How can an appointed body of nine lawyers justify decisions that contradict the judgments of a representative assembly and an elected president? The conflict is often characterized as one between constitutionally protected individual rights and majority will.[8] I recognize the existence of such conflicts, but they are not my subject. I concentrate on the role of judicial review in improving the democratic and representative character of the political system. True, this may sometimes involve the imposition of constraints on the legislature, but only in the interest of improving its representative character.

LEGISLATIVE CONSISTENCY

I concentrate on one basic problem: the opaqueness of Congressional action to ordinary citizens. Opacity is not inherent in the concept of democracy. It is a pathology of present democratic practice in the United States.

The basic goal of judicial review should be an increase in the accountability of Congress to the voters. Members of Congress seek to claim credit for policies popular with their constituents and avoid blame for unpopular policies. One way to credit-claim is to pass a statute. But in order to obtain majority support a law may need to include provisions that will not be popular with the legislator's constituents. To enact the statute, then, sponsors will emphasize the positive in the preamble or policy statement and bury the negative in details or in legislative history. They may also be less than candid about the subsequent budgetary costs of a new policy. There are, then, strong political forces favoring distorted public presentations of legislative enactments.

I argue that courts should further legislative transparency in two ways. First, judges should demand internal statutory consistency as a way of preventing hidden deals. They should refuse to enforce statutory provisions that are inconsistent with legislative preambles and policy statements. They should focus on the internal structure of individual statutes without judging their ultimate worth or requiring programmatic consistency across statutes. Second, judges should ask if appropriations acts are consistent with statutory purposes. I discuss internal consistency in this chapter and the review of appropriations in Chapter 5.

Although my recommendations may be unconventional, they reflect concerns similar to those raised by such scholars as Gerald Gunther and John Ely. Ely's aim, like mine, is to *reinforce* democratic representation by adding greater realism to judicial interpretation of statutes and review of the legislative process.[9] Gunther argues that "safeguarding the structure of the political process has been acknowledged as a major judicial obligation since the 1930's."[10]

Gunther believes that the Constitution requires statutes to be a rational means to a legitimate end. The requirement should be broadly applied to include "social and economic regulatory legislation."[11] "The yardstick for the acceptability of the means would be the purposes chosen by the legislatures, not 'constitutional' interests drawn from the value perceptions of the Justices."[12] Means scrutiny, he argues,

> can improve the quality of the political process . . . by encouraging
> a fuller airing in the political arena of the grounds for legislative
> action. Examination of means in light of asserted state purposes
> would directly promote public consideration of the benefits assert-
> edly sought by the proposed legislation: indirectly, it would stimulate
> fuller political examination in relation to those benefits, of the costs
> that would be incurred if the proposed means were adapted.[13]

Using social choice theory and political economy, I provide an intellectual foundation for Gunther's claim which complements the prevailing tendency of constitutional law scholarship. For the present, however, I have not tried to build a constitutional foundation for my proposal. Although strong arguments are available,[14] it will suffice to think in terms of a new statute permitting judicial intervention to encourage legislative deliberation and improve voters' capacity to monitor the output of Congressional bargains.

I begin with the empirical claim that voters are poorly informed about the outcome of the legislative process. I also assert that better information would be useful to voters in making political decisions and that representatives' own behavior will be affected by the voters' perceptions. My view of the ideal legislative process can then be articulated in a weak form or in a strong form. The weak form accepts the fact that much legislation is a bargain among self-interested actors. The goal of judicial review is to improve the information available to those affected by the bargain. Within constitutional limits,[15] the courts must accept laws passed by a legislative majority even though they harm both poorly organized groups and those that are well-organized but politically weak. The judicial aim is simply to assure that information about legislative bargains is more widely available to the electorate. Citizens can then decide whether to take political action and, if so, what kind—lobbying, supporting opponents, demanding a compensatory law in another area.[16]

The strong form views the ideal legislative process as essentially deliberative.[17] Here, legislators discuss different points of view and make a good faith effort to formulate policy that reconciles political differences. Participants in policy debates have an obligation to use public interest arguments to justify their positions. Public policy analysis, then, plays a central role. Under this view, partisans are acting illegitimately when they content themselves with asserting that a bill is good for the trucking industry. They must instead articulate reasons why large segments of the public will benefit as well.[18] My proposal does not require a choice between these competing visions. A judicial demand for internal statutory consistency makes sense under either the weak or the strong theory of the legislative process, without requiring that either ideal be fully realized.

Internal consistency would be enforced by judicial insistence that statutes contain statements of purpose, which courts would take as reflecting legislative intent. These statements could express multiple objectives, but to the extent that purposes conflict, the statutory preamble should give some guidance concerning the way tradeoffs are to be made. Anything in the body of the statute inconsistent with the preamble or statement of purpose would be invalidated by the court. Legislators would be forced to articulate aims and to stick with them in drafting specific provisions. Thus the courts would not engage in policy analysis themselves when they review statutes, but they would insist that the legislators both articulate a set of purposes and consider the relationship between means and ends.

To develop my argument further, I first consider the properties of an idealized direct democracy. I show that it would be inconsistent with democratic values for courts to require logical consistency across statutes. Such a strong position would truly be counter-majoritarian. Global consistency cannot be imposed on the legislative process without violating our commitment to democracy.

After articulating principles that courts should *not* apply to legislation, I show how the representative nature of American government creates problems of public accountability that can be addressed by judges. My proposal for review of the internal consistency of individual statutes is one possible response to these difficulties. I then relate my proposal to judicial pronouncements on the rational basis standard, to the current legal status of preambles, and to state constitutional limits on legislative form. Finally, I distinguish my perspective both from the writings of lawyer economists and from those who urge more aggressive conceptions of judicial review.

MAJORITY RULE

While majority rule is fundamental to democratic choice, it has a number of weaknesses as a decisionmaking method—especially its tendency to produce inconsistent results through voting cycles. These weaknesses are inherent in the method. They are not details that can be "corrected" by courts. Furthermore, certain normative principles, such as net benefit maximization or mutual consent, are incompatible with even an idealized majoritarian democracy. Thus, it would be undemocratic for the courts either to insist on consistency across statutes or to require legislation to conform with one or another normative theory. It is only after distinguishing my proposal from these truly antidemocratic suggestions that I will develop the affirmative case for internal-consistency review.

The Case for Majority Rule

A commitment to democracy implies a commitment to a political system that takes individual preferences seriously. A central responsibility of political life is the aggregation of disparate individual desires into a set of public choices. Since people cannot always obtain everything they want from politics, the legitimacy of the method of aggregation is of primary importance. Yet the methods of aggregation are legion. Majority rule is only one among many voting rules ranging from supramajority rules to weighted voting schemes.

Given the large number of alternatives, why does majority rule have such broad appeal? Social choice theory provides one answer by isolating the method's fundamental features and showing that no other voting rule satisfies all these properties.[19] Under pure majority rule a series of votes is taken that pits every option against every other option in a pairwise comparison. For each pair we record the option with the greatest number of votes. The winner is the alternative that beats or ties every other.

To see why pure majority rule might seem appealing, consider the rule as it applies in a simple choice between two, and only two, competing alternatives. In such a case, majority rule always produces a determinate result.[20] This seems preferable to, say, a two-thirds rule, which makes no selection if neither option obtains at least two-thirds support. Second, majority rule gives all voter rankings equal priority. A voter obtains no extra influence because she is rich or beautiful or intelligent or needy. Third, all options are treated equally. In particular, the status quo does not have a favored position. Compare that condition with a rule under which the status quo is maintained unless another option obtains two-thirds support. Finally, majority rule is indifferent between options only if an equal number support each option. It makes choices that are responsive to shifts in the underlying preferences of the voters. There is not a wide range of indifference. No other voting rule based on individual rankings satisfies all these conditions.[21]

The Inconsistency of Majority Rule

In spite of these advantages, majority rule has one crucial drawback. It does not always produce a determinate answer when more than two options are on the table.[22] The basic problem is posed by the possibility of "voting cycles." Suppose, for example, that there are three voters, Alice, Bob, and Cathy, and three candidates, Bush, Nunn, and Gore. Alice prefers Bush to Nunn to Gore. Bob prefers Nunn to Gore to Bush, and Cathy prefers Gore to Bush to Nunn. A majority prefers Bush to Nunn and Nunn to Gore. However, a majority also prefers Gore to Bush. No candidate will beat all the others in a series of pairwise votes.

However, if voters agree that the options lie along a single "left-right" dimension, majority voting does produce consistent choices.[23] For example, suppose that voters judge candidates only on their ideology and that everyone agrees that Bush is the most conservative candidate, Gore is the most liberal, and Nunn is in the middle. Alice and Bob have the same preferences as before, but Cathy is replaced by the liberal Carl, who prefers Gore to Nunn to Bush. When this condition, called "single-peakedness," prevails, voters may differ widely on which option is the best, some preferring right-wing candidates and others wanting leftists. In spite of these differences, they all agree that the alternatives can be lined up along a single-dimensional ideological scale. In my example, Nunn is now preferred to both Gore and Bush and wins the election.

The practical significance of voting cycles has been much debated. Some point out that voting in legislatures does not seem to cycle endlessly. But that observation, while correct, is unconvincing. Legislative rules of procedure may hide cycles. For example, one common rule holds that once an option has been defeated, it cannot be reintroduced. Yet if a cycle exists in the legislators' underlying preferences, the legitimacy of the final result under this rule is called into question. The outcome represents not the will of the majority but the will of the people in control of the order of votes.[24]

One familiar strategic technique suggests that cycles are common: a legislator introduces an amendment in the hope that the amendment will pass, but the amended bill will be defeated. This could happen only if there were a cycle in the underlying preferences.[25] For example, in the spring of 1990 the Senate was considering a bill to amend the Clean Air Act. The bill was believed to have majority support. Senator Robert Byrd of West Virginia introduced a very costly amendment to the bill designed to compensate those who lost their jobs as a result of the new law. Some suggested that Byrd hoped the amendment, which was popular with labor unions, would pass and that, as a consequence, the entire bill would fail. In fact, the Byrd amendment was defeated by one vote, with some who voted against pointing out that passage of the amendment would harm the bill's prospects for passage.[26]

If courts were to seek to reform the legislative process to make it more reflective of public sentiment, the lessons of social choice counsel caution. The search for procedures not subject to strategic manipulation is doomed to fail if one is also committed to democracy. Dictatorships can avoid strategic voting by making voting irrelevant, but all reasonable collective choice mechanisms are open to manipulation. If we are committed to majoritarian principles, the answer is realistically to accept the faults of majority rule, not replace it with another voting system that does not have its advantages and is equally open to strategic manipulation.[27] My proposal is in that spirit. It does not insist on an impossible global consistency that would be inconsistent with majoritarian principles. Instead the courts would seek only to induce the legislature to produce internally consistent individual statutes.

Majority Rule, Net Benefit Maximization, and Unanimity

Majority rule does not take the intensity of voters' feelings into account. Thus the method is inconsistent with utilitarianism or net benefit maximization as overall principles of social welfare. I argued in Chapter 3 that courts should impose cost-benefit tests on agencies that administer open-ended statutes designed to improve economic efficiency. However, democratic principles require that the citizenry be free to reject policy analysis through explicit statutory language. A majority may choose a policy that benefits them while imposing a greater total harm on the minority. It need not even try to maximize net benefits. If it acts in an entirely self-interested manner, it will only try to maximize the net benefits flowing to the members of the majority coalition.[28] Self-interested, majoritarian behavior is not necessarily compatible with the promulgation of policies that pass cost-benefit tests.[29] This conflict between majority rule and net benefit maximization can occur in a direct democracy with no organized interest groups. It does not depend on the power of "big business" or the presence of a privileged elite. Majority rule counts every voter equally and does not weight votes by wealth or intensity of feeling, while cost-benefit analysis takes these factors into account. Although both decisionmaking techniques are grounded in the preferences of individuals, they employ fundamentally different principles of aggregation.[30]

Just as majority rule does not guarantee net benefit maximizing policies, it does not ensure that everyone will be better off as a result of political activity. Only slightly more than half of the voters must agree to a change in policy. So long as only a majority need agree and so long as the existing distribution of wealth is not accorded some special constitutional status,[31] political choices will help some and harm others, and people will seek to be on the winning side. Thus interest group bargains cannot be prevented even in an idealized democracy. They are the cost of voting rules that are not too heavily biased toward the status quo.

When confronting these possibilities, some scholars would have us abandon majority rule. For them, unanimity is the preferred voting rule since, like a free market transaction, it assures that everyone is made better off relative to the status quo. These scholars, represented most prominently by James Buchanan and the "Virginia School,"[32] reluctantly accept lesser voting systems only because of the costs of reaching unanimous agreement in a polity of any size. Since government failure is viewed as more serious than market failure, the constitution should limit the reach of government to only the most necessary tasks such as internal and external security. This leads to proposals to amend the United States Constitution to limit the power to tax and to require balanced budgets. Also consistent with this approach is an activist judiciary aggressively protecting private property against majoritarian incursions.

I disagree with these antimajoritarian sentiments and do not believe they are implied by social choice analysis. Rather, one can use this scholarship to suggest reforms along the lines of my proposal for judicial review. As we have seen, if the existing distribution of income and wealth is not given canonical status, majority rule has claims to legitimacy based on stronger foundations than expediency and practicality. Under the American Constitution, individual rights to life, liberty, and property are preserved, not by the structure of democratic political institutions, but by separate substantive clauses. Courts operating within the American constitutional framework cannot legitimately reject democracy in favor of a competing principle. Therefore, if the courts are to play a constructive role, they must focus on problems with American government that are not inherent in idealized majoritarian governments.

REPRESENTATIVE GOVERNMENT AND JUDICIAL REVIEW

So much for undemocratic visions of judicial review. I proceed now in a more constructive spirit. The United States does not have an idealized direct democracy. The size of the electorate dictates a representative system. Any proposal to improve the accountability of American government must, therefore, focus on Congress.

The previous chapter outlined two problems with representative government: the biases introduced by the differential organizing costs of political actors, and the way the representatives' reelection motives discourage careful legislative drafting and encourage posturing. Call these difficulties the "political organization" problem and the "political image" problem. I now introduce a third—the undemocratic consequences of the organization of the legislature and its rules of procedure. Call this the problem of "legislative structure." Recent work in social choice has shown how the existence of committees, as well as of rules governing the process of voting on amendments, can affect the ultimate outcome of the legislative process.[33]

All three of these difficulties should be on the agenda of political-economic work in law. Confronting these weaknesses of representative government can produce a reformed picture of judicial review.[34] That project is a large one, and I have taken up only a few selected issues here. The previous chapter argued that the problems of political organization and political image justified a presumption in favor of net benefit maximization when courts review the administration of regulatory statutes. In this chapter I argue that reelection motives produce a bias in favor of statutes that promise more than they can deliver and disguise special interest deals in public interest language. The problems of political image and legislative structure combine to distort the statutory drafting process.

To see why Congress might draft statutes that are internally inconsistent, consider the reelection motive. Reelection is a central goal of members of Congress, and citizens, when casting their ballots, have poor information about the actions of legislators. Thus, without constraints, legislators have few incentives to reveal deals that are not obvious to superficial observers. The problem is not interest group bargains per se, but the voters' ignorance of them. Representatives, concerned with their "political image," want to claim credit for politically beneficial actions—emphasizing the positive aspects of the laws they pass and downplaying the negative.[35]

Opponents, both electoral challengers and other members of Congress, may point to flaws in a law, but if the statute appears to be responding to a popular concern (drug abuse, environmental pollution, consumer protection), no one may gain from a curmudgeonly critique of the statutory language or a gloomy prediction about future appropriations. The competitive aspects of politics, while an important check, are insufficient to permit voters to understand the implications of new statutes. Members of Congress can say one thing and do another. They can state grand purposes in a preamble and contradict that language in the body of the statute. They can promise a major program and later fund it inadequately or direct the money to special interests.

The problem of legislative structure is also relevant to the question of legislative accountability. Since members of Congress want to be reelected, they will organize the legislative process to further this goal. Some structural features of the process are, of course, constitutionally mandated, such as the Presidential veto with its accompanying two-thirds override rule, and the need for majority support from each chamber before a bill can be sent to the President.[36] But others, such as the organization and functions of committees, have no constitutional basis, and Congress will take care that its internal procedures aid incumbents, even if the result undermines majoritarian values.

These dual concerns suggest a limited role for the courts in improving the consistency and transparency of statutes. Under my proposal, courts would insist that the substance of statutes be consistent with their preambles or statement of purpose. Inconsistent substantive clauses would be unenforceable. Judges would do less second-guessing of the legislative process than at present, since legislative history would play a far smaller role than is does under current judicial practice. Nevertheless, even though this new role involves no overt review of the structure of Congress, it could change the way Congress does business.[37] Internal procedures would need to be reformed to produce legislation that would survive judicial review.

The internal consistency requirement is meant to deal with two problems. First, some statutes have overly ambitious statements of purpose that cannot possibly be accomplished given the other goals people care about (for example, both protecting the environment and encouraging economic growth, or improving the safety of the workplace while preserving jobs).[38] Internal consistency is designed to inject a note of realism into the preambles of such statutes and, as a consequence, to encourage a more informed, policy analytic debate over tradeoffs. Thus the objective of my proposal is not only to increase the information available to voters but also to encourage Congress to pass laws that represent a coherent response to social problems.

Second, some statutes have well-focused preambles or policy statements (protecting the health of those who need haircuts or eye care) but include provisions with no obvious link to these purposes (grandfather clauses, advertising bans, prohibitions on corporate ownership). Others seem designed to benefit several groups (dairy farmers, dairies, and milk consumers) but are written to favor only some (dairy farmers and dairies).[39] When faced with such special interest statutes, courts would allow legislative judgments to stand only if the preambles clearly stated the acts' purposes (for example, protecting existing barbers, favoring optometrists, or aiding dairy farmers). Laws will pass judicial muster only if they communicate the nature of the political compromises they embody through a visible preamble and a consistent text. Courts would refuse to use committee reports and speeches to determine "real" purposes both because such "legislative history" does not necessarily reflect majority opinions and, more importantly, because much of it may not be part of the public's perception of the statute's aims.[40]

My proposal is meant to give legislators an incentive to produce statutes that are easier for voters to evaluate. The aim is not to override or downplay the reelection motive or to dictate procedures, but rather to give reelection-seeking politicians an incentive to produce statutes that are straightforward efforts to achieve clearly stated goals.

THE "RATIONAL BASIS" STANDARD

At present the federal courts treat the rational coherence and internal consistency of legislation almost as an irrelevancy. For economic regulation, the Justices have chosen "to retain the rhetoric of the rational basis standard, but to apply it so tolerantly that no law [is] ever likely to violate it."[41] Three kinds of dodges are common.

First, the court searches for "rational" statutory purposes irrespective of whether they are plausible as matters of logic or political fact. In both *Williamson v. Lee Optical Co.*[42] and *Railway Express Agency Inc. v. New York*[43] the challenged laws seem designed to restrict competition. The Court, however, was able to invent public interest rationales that might possibly have been served.

Second, the Court posits a legitimate purpose that is so broad as to encompass almost any state action. For example, in *Exxon Corp v. Governor of Maryland*[44] the Supreme Court simply declared that an act's purpose was "controlling the gasoline retail market" without relying on statutory language. Given *this* purpose, it was easy to conclude that a Maryland law forbidding oil companies from owning stations was instrumentally rational. The requirement that some purpose be served was satisfied by simply removing all policy content from the idea of "purpose."

Third, the Court refers to the statute's actual statement of purpose, reads it broadly, and states that no conflict exists between a specific provision and the preamble. Thus in *New Motor Vehicle Bd. v. Orrin W. Fox Co.*,[45] a car dealer challenged a California law giving competitors a right to protest a dealer's entry decision. Without engaging in any analysis, the Supreme Court declared that the public welfare and consumer protection language in the preamble was consistent with that provision.[46]

When individual civil rights are affected, the requirement of a rational connection between means and ends has more salience for lawyers and legal scholars than in the economic sphere.[47] The ends, however, need not be articulated by the legislature.[48] Thus John Ely, in an article that focuses on civil rights, can invoke the "commonly made assumption, that any governmental choice that disadvantages some persons relative to others must . . . be shown to have a rational (at least) connection with some permissible governmental goal."[49] The Court has not, however, required legislators to state their goals explicitly, and sometimes takes a position close to the one in *Williamson v. Lee Optical* in which actual legislative purpose is irrelevant. Thus in *Fleming v. Nestor* Justice Harlan stated that it was "constitutionally irrelevant" whether a legitimate purpose that he had imagined "in fact underlay the legislative decision."[50]

More recently, the Court has expressed a willingness to limit itself to the legislature's "actual purposes." Thus in *U.S. Dept. of Agric. v. Moreno*[51] the Justices struck down as unconstitutional an amendment to the Food Stamp Act that made households of unrelated individuals ineligible for food stamps. They quoted at length from the Act's declaration of policy to show that the purposes were to alleviate hunger and malnutrition among the poor and to strengthen agriculture. Legislative history indicated that the amendment was designed to make "hippies" ineligible, a purpose that was taken by the court to be illegitimate and not part of the original statutory goals. Thus that portion of the act was declared unconstitutional. The opinion did not, however, focus on means/end rationality except to find that the disqualification of unrelated households was not a good way to deal with the legitimate concern regarding fraud.[52]

To summarize, while the Supreme Court retains a rhetorical commitment to means/end rationality in legislation, it has not given this doctrine much bite. Although the legislature's own declarations of purpose are sometimes mentioned, they have not proved determinative if the Court could think up another purpose. The Justices' concern has been more with the imaginative construction of legitimate purposes than with the internal consistency of the statutes themselves. They seek to discover if the questionable law is consistent with the equal protection, due process, or commerce clauses, not to confront the possibly unrepresentative character of the political process.

One should not, however, exaggerate the inconsistency of my proposal with current practice. Although the reform implies an inquiring federal judiciary, capable of understanding and evaluating policy analytic arguments, it does not envisage judges converting their own policy preferences into law. In comparison with the active search for possible legitimate purposes in *Williamson v. Lee Optical, Railway Express,* and *Fleming v. Nestor,* my proposal is deferential to the purposes articulated by Congress. Unless a violation of constitutional rights is charged, the courts would not interfere with the substance of statutes. They would only require a very rudimentary form of internal consistency. Thus Congress could pass a law favoring a small, well-organized group, but this goal would have to be stated in the preamble. The goal is a higher level of legislative accountability to the electorate, not the imposition of substantive judicial norms.

THE LEGAL STATUS OF
LEGISLATIVE PREAMBLES AND POLICY STATEMENTS

My proposal must overcome legal doctrines of statutory construction that support the practice of giving scant judicial weight to statements of purpose and policy. My basic argument is that legal technicalities ought not to govern when the basic responsibility of representative government to its citizens is at stake. Nevertheless, one should, at least, understand the doctrinal objections that might be raised.[53]

The courts at present give preambles little role.[54] If they do come into play at all, it is to resolve ambiguities in the language of other parts of the statute.[55] Thus preambles function much like a superior form of legislative history that has been voted on by the legislature and signed by the President.[56] According to one commentator, a preamble cannot enlarge the scope or effect of a statute.[57] Under that doctrine the legislature could never be penalized for drafting overly ambitious preambles to introduce narrowly focused statutes. Similarly, inconsistencies between preamble and statute do not receive judicial notice so long as the specific clauses in the body of the statute are clear.[58] This doctrine, of course, rules out exactly what I want to encourage.[59]

Indeed, the courts seem to have fostered a vicious cycle. By downgrading preambles and statements of policy they invite the legislature to treat these clauses as legally trivial as well. This legal stance then has produced a self-fulfilling prophecy. While some observers see this as no loss,[60] my claim is that the courts have overlooked a possibility for increasing democratic accountability.

STATE CONSTITUTIONAL LIMITS ON LEGISLATION

While support from federal law is weak, my proposal does build on state constitutional law. Most state constitutions include explicit constraints on the legislative process. Many of these limitations are, like my proposal, designed to accomplish the goals of transparency and accountability to the voters.[61] The most common is a rule that requires that every law encompass a single subject, which is expressed in its title. Also widespread are procedural limitations such as provisions forbidding the legislature from altering a bill to change its original purpose. While the success of these constraints is subject to debate,[62] the impulse behind them is clear enough. Although state courts have given an expansive interpretation to the single-subject requirement, the rule, when it is invoked, is justified in functional terms as a way of improving the democratic responsibility of the legislature.

The Minnesota Supreme Court has been especially clear in interpreting its state Constitution, which states that "[n]o law shall embrace more than one subject, which shall be embraced in its title."[63]

> The function of the title requirement is to provide notice of the interest likely to be affected by the law and "to prevent surprise and fraud upon the people and the legislature by including provisions in a bill whose title gives no intimation of the nature of the proposed legislation." Similarly we have said that the purpose of the requirement that one subject be expressed in the title "is to prevent [the title] from being made a cloak or artifice to distract from the substance of the act itself." [citations omitted][64]

The single-subject rule has an additional goal not embraced by my proposal for consistency review. It is also viewed as a way to prevent logrolling.[65] I would not limit logrolled deals, because such legislative behavior is not necessarily undesirable.[66] While compromise legislation in which one group supports another's program in return for support for its own program can produce bloated government, it may also resolve difficult tradeoffs so that a large proportion of the membership benefits.[67] Furthermore, even if one wished to prevent logrolling, the single-subject clause is a weak tool. While it does increase the cost of logrolling somewhat by requiring that separate bills be proposed for disparate parts of a deal, the constitutional provisions seem poorly targeted.[68]

THE CHICAGO SCHOOL AND JUDICIAL REVIEW

Frank Easterbrook and Richard Posner have applied a political economic framework to the judicial evaluation of legislative purposes. Since they reach a different conclusion from my own, it will clarify my position to contrast it with theirs.

Easterbrook and Posner view most statutes as bargains between conflicting groups.[69] Rather than insist on legislative deliberation, they maintain that courts should uphold legislative bargains. Judges, however, should not go beyond the explicit language of the statute. They ought to read statutes narrowly.

While Posner accepts interest group politics as legitimate, he does recognize that statutes can fulfill a variety of goals. Some laws serve the public interest, others are narrow interest group deals, and still others are a complex mixture of both.[70] All are constitutionally permissible so long as the aims can be inferred from public materials, i.e., statutory language or published reports. On this view, courts impose some check on legislative power politics since to "the extent that legislators use Aesopian language to deceive potential opponents of the interest groups behind legislation, they may fool the courts as well and thereby limit the political power of those interest groups."[71] Beyond this, however, Posner does not go. He treats legislative history as legitimate data *because* "some bills do not reflect the convictions of a majority of legislators voting for it."[72] He does not acknowledge that this judicial practice actually creates additional incentives for low-visibility deals.

Easterbrook follows Posner in arguing that courts should never impute legislative purposes. Courts "cannot reconstruct an original meaning because there is none to find."[73] He would be extremely deferential to Congress, believing with Justice O'Connor that the "task of [the] Court . . . is to interpret the statutory language that Congress enacted into law."[74]

He views statutes as contracts. The judge's job is to enforce that contract "as a faithful agent but without enthusiasm."[75] Easterbrook has analyzed several Supreme Court decisions in this light. His discussion of a case challenging the administration of the Agricultural Marketing Act, regulating dairy product prices, is characteristic.[76] The Court upheld the exclusion of consumers from the Department of Agriculture's administrative process. Easterbrook argues that, in supporting the agency, the Court was implementing the political bargain contained in the statute. He argues that the statute was a deal between Congress and the dairy industry that excluded consumers. Yet in summarizing the statute, he does not mention that the actual nature of the bargain had been blurred in the statutory preamble by bows in the direction of consumer interests. Although the detailed statutory provisions do not mention consumers, the preamble implies that they were intended as beneficiaries. Even on his own terms Easterbrook has not proved his claim.

In equating laws with "contracts," Posner and Easterbrook ignore some of the most important lessons of research in social choice. In contrast to private bargains, all affected parties need not agree to the terms of a legislative deal. Only a legislative majority is needed, and even Congressional supporters may represent many people who are opposed to the new law. While third parties may also be affected by private contracts, legislation can be far more redistributive than typical contracts. There is a special need for public sector institutions to ensure that all affected individuals have the chance, at the very least, to find out what is happening with only a little inconvenience. In developing their contractual view of the statutory law, Posner and Easterbrook fail to emphasize the importance of publicity and responsibility to the electorate in their assessment of the judicial function. Theirs is not a true social choice analysis, but draws instead on a glib analogy to private contract doctrine.

Another author in the political economic tradition is Jonathan Macey, who raises concerns about the public-regarding character of legislation that are similar to mine.[77] Moving beyond Posner and Easterbrook, he distinguishes two kinds of private-regarding laws called "open-explicit" and "hidden-implicit" statutes. Macey shares my view that accurately described special interest legislation (open-explicit statutes) should be upheld by the courts so long as it does not violate other constitutional guarantees. The citizens' ability to discipline their representatives through the ballot box must remain the principal check.

Macey then goes on to argue for a narrow, literal reading of statutes that embody "hidden-implicit" deals. He argues for a conventional approach to statutory interpretation that looks to "plain meaning" in both statutes and legislative history and does not try to reconstruct backroom bargains. Judicial interpretation will then discourage "hidden-implicit" deals since they will not be upheld by the courts. While I have no quarrel with Macey as far as he goes, I do not believe he goes nearly far enough. Instead of his Pollyannaish belief in a return to old-fashioned techniques of statutory interpretation, I argue for a stronger judicial posture that not only refuses to enforce hidden-implicit deals but also tests statutes themselves for internal inconsistency. Inconsistency is simply not recognized by Macey as a problem that requires judicial notice. He also ignores the possibility that courts may give a public interest gloss to special interest legislation that has been packaged in attractive rhetoric. Both possibilities require more than a "plain meaning" approach: the former, because there is no plain meaning; the latter, because the "plain" meaning is misleading.

Finally, his characterization of "open-explicit" legislation is, to mind, overly broad since it includes laws where the special interest deals can be found in committee reports. Committee reports are public only in a formalistic sense. They may not make much operational difference to the citizenry, which only hears politicians claiming credit for public interest legislation. Even using Macey's categories, I would shift some laws from "open-explicit" to "hidden-implicit" and require courts to look to what Congress enacted, not to what it claims to have done via the legislative "history."

REVIEW FOR PUBLIC-REGARDING PURPOSES

In an important article, Hans Linde challenges the validity of means/end rationality both as a workable criterion for courts and as a valid theory under the Constitution.[78] Linde characterizes idealized, rational law-making as a system where decisionmakers learn about a problem, consider what goals to pursue in responding to it, and decide what actions will further these goals.[79] Courts, however, have never held legislatures to procedures designed to produce this kind of behavior, and Linde states that this judicial posture is correct as a matter of constitutional law.[80] His supposedly clinching argument does not, however, succeed. He claims that the constitutional acceptability of popular initiatives shows that no due process can be required of political decisions. This example, however, misses the point. The *representative* character of the legislature creates problems of democratic legitimacy not present in referenda.[81]

In the end, however, Linde's position seems quite close to mine since he saves his most scathing criticism for those who want the courts to impose limits on the acceptable ends of legislation. He claims that

> [o]ur institutions and procedures are designed to curb power to make law capriciously, on merely personal or inarticulate impulse, without preventing the enactment of measures that can win deliberated assent, even though they cater to a selfish minority, even if they are doubtful means toward divergent goals.[82]

Our most important point of difference is Linde's skepticism about the value of requiring Congress to articulate statutory goals.[83] His concern that Congress will hypocritically mouth public interest language is less of a problem under my suggested reform. In my proposal the courts would ratify most any goal, no matter how narrow, so long as it was clearly stated. Only goals directly contradicting constitutional provisions, such as the first amendment, would be impermissible.

At the other extreme from Linde are scholars who would hold the legislature to substantive standards—with the courts acting as expositors of values within government. These authors would not actually have the courts invalidate large numbers of laws, however. Instead, creative statutory interpretation would usually suffice to limit congressional purposes. Robert Bennett, Jerry Mashaw, and Cass Sunstein are perhaps the most prominent proponents of such review.[84]

Bennett takes as his subject laws that raise due process and equal protection problems. He discusses the issue of "legitimate" purposes in a way that highlights the fact that legislative "purpose" is "a figure of speech." Individual legislators have purposes, but not the collective body as a whole.[85] Bennett argues that courts should find laws unconstitutional if their purposes can be shown to do nothing more than favor one interest group or individual rather than another. He gives an example of a law with a preamble announcing that its purpose is to favor a Ms. A by giving her company tax credits. According to Bennett: "Few will doubt that the legislation would fail the rationality requirement: the purpose would be found illegitimate,"[86] because "unalloyed personal favor is beyond the legislative pale."[87] Bennett would have courts look for "real" purposes in spite of the admitted difficulty of this inquiry.[88]

Mashaw has also argued for increased attention by courts to the public-regarding character of regulatory legislation in the economic sphere. He claims that "the appropriate constitutional demand is not for 'rational' or 'efficient' legislation, but for legislation that is public-regarding—that can make a coherent and plausible claim to serve some public, rather than a merely private, interest."[89] This is a requirement "grounded in no particular text, but in the Constitution as a whole."[90] Interestingly, Mashaw looks to the constitutional preamble for support.[91] At bottom, he is reaching for the same distinction between public-regarding and private-regarding legislation as Posner and Easterbrook. They would have courts interpret the former broadly and the latter narrowly. Mashaw would find the latter unconstitutional. In the more usual mixed cases, courts should weigh the gains and losses and uphold "the legislative choice unless its cost-benefit calculation is patently unreasonable,"[92] and unless important interests appear to be underrepresented. Mashaw is concerned with inconsistency since he would have courts ask, for example, if a stated legislative purpose of aiding consumers is, in fact, accomplished by the statute. He is not clear, however, about whether courts should only consider purposes stated in the statute or look elsewhere as well. Also, he is, of course, not solely concerned with consistency but with locating public purposes. He would have courts invalidate laws that *consistently* advance private interests and uphold laws that serve public ends different from those explicitly stated in the statute.

Sunstein contends that there is a

> fundamental constitutional norm against naked interest-group transfers. That norm proscribes legislative efforts to transfer resources from one group to another simply because of political power.[93]

He admits that the courts seldom seem to apply this norm, "almost always finding a public-regarding justification for legislation."[94] For him this is not evidence against the norm's validity since courts can enforce it less obtrusively through statutory construction. However, if a deal is "unambiguously reflected in the law," it should be respected.[95] But this seems a rather strange position. If the norm against "naked interest group transfers" is fundamental, why shouldn't courts make this clear in an effort to influence the lawmaking process? Sunstein refers to the "institutional position of the judiciary."[96] But his argument for the norm's constitutional status would seem an argument for a change in the courts' role. Little improvement in the legislative process can be expected from judicial dissembling.

CONCLUSIONS

Believing—with Linde, Easterbrook, Posner, and most judges—that Courts should not generally review the substantive aims of legislation, I would reject the proposals of Bennett, Mashaw, and Sunstein. Some concerns, such as the preservation of individual rights and the prevention of discrimination, are important enough to override the presumption of constitutionality. But substantive review is outside the appropriate role of the courts in most regulatory and policy areas.

Courts are better able to structure legislative deliberations to produce greater accountability than they are to review laws for "goodness." The aim of accountability review is not the technical one of improving the logic of legislative enactments. Its goal instead is to increase public accountability through a legislative process that produces statutes which can be more easily understood by voters. If voters are concerned about special interest laws, they will, at least, be able to know that such laws have been passed. The courts would set the stage for lawmaking that is more responsible to popular concerns without having the judges actually articulate these concerns themselves.

In this same spirit, I turn in the next chapter to the role of courts in policing another fundamental legislative arena: the appropriations process. Despite its importance, appropriations have been given even less scrutiny by courts and commentators. Yet repeated budget crises suggest that Congressional behavior is in need of a new look.

5

Judicial Review
and the Power of the Purse

The passage of a law is only the first step. Policymaking statutes are meaningless without money to bring them to life. Democratic accountability depends as much on the appropriations process as it does on statutory drafting. How can the courts encourage Congress to develop straightforward and realistic connections between budget appropriations and substantive statutory policy? I make two proposals. Each responds to a different problem arising from the representative character of American politics. First, the legislature may undermine the stated purposes of an act with appropriations and special interest amendments hidden in portmanteau spending bills and their accompanying committee reports.[1] The courts should invalidate spending provisions in appropriations acts that clearly benefit a narrower range of interests than those contemplated in the original substantive act. I would also have the courts limit the ability of Congress to use appropriations acts for substantive lawmaking. My objection is not to omnibus bills per se but only to their use to further interests that could not obtain independent majority support.[2]

Second, members of Congress may claim credit for broad, public-interested statutory mandates while failing to support the use of public funds to accomplish these goals. The judiciary should flag instances of obvious underfunding, give Congress time to respond, and, if it does not, give de jure status to Congress's de facto repeal of the underfunded provisions. This second proposal gives priority to appropriations statutes by using low spending levels as evidence of presumptive repeal of the underfunded statute. Congress can refute this presumption by subsequent action, but if it fails to act, the judgment of repeal would stand. Congress would then have to endure the negative publicity associated with a show-ing that it promised more than it could deliver. The object of such judicial actions is to prevent inflated promises in the first place.

Notice that the first proposal gives priority to the underlying statute, while the second implies that appropriations trump authorizing statutes. The paradox dissolves, however, once one recognizes that both proposals aim to improve the accountability of Congress to the voters. The first does this by limiting Congress's ability to make low-visibility deals through the appropriations process. The second deters Congress from passing ambitious-sounding laws that it has no intention of funding adequately.

My proposals do not require Courts to order Congress either to appro-priate money or to pass laws to further particular policies.[3] I call on courts to give Congress incentives to improve the consistency between appro-priations acts and prior enabling legislation.

AMENDING STATUTES
THROUGH THE APPROPRIATIONS PROCESS

Congressional Rules and Legislative Practice

Both houses of Congress have rules that forbid the amendment of statutes through appropriations acts.[4] While the Supreme Court takes these rules seriously,[5] Congress does not. They are routinely violated or waived.[6]

During the Eighties the consolidated budget process encouraged such activities. The Budget Committees, established under the 1974 budget reform act, imposed spending limits which were meant to constrain the operation of the appropriations subcommittees.[7] These constraints may have fostered delay as committee members wrestled with hard choices. Although Congress retained the presumption that it would pass thirteen separate appropriations acts,[8] this failed to happen in several years, with Congress appropriating funds at the end of the fiscal year under massive continuing resolutions.[9] Oddly, normal House rules do not apply to continuing resolutions.[10] Thus when continuing resolutions replaced appropriations bills, even the formal constraint imposed by the House rulebook was missing.

Ironically, the combination of Budget Committee constraints and the inexorable passage of time may have improved the prospects for special interest manipulation. Each member could calculate how far Congress could be pushed before a special benefit added to an appropriations bill was sufficient to threaten passage of the bill. The more comprehensive the bill and the closer the fiscal year deadline, the greater the cost of delaying passage, and the more room there was for private interest amendments.[11] The problem was exacerbated if, as occurred in the Eighties, the approach of the deadline actually increased the omnibus character of appropriations measures.

In 1990 the budget process was modified. Through fiscal 1995 the appropriations committees face annual spending constraints. The constraints can only be violated if the new programs are self-financing. Thus it appears that the 1990 act has made unauthorized spending more difficult. The modifications, however, impose no constraints on the inclusion of substantive provisions with no direct budgetary impact.[12] In fact, since specialized spending provisions are now more difficult to include, we might expect an increase in substantive clauses in appropriations acts.

Congressional rules allow members to raise a point of order when an appropriation is unauthorized[13] or when a substantive provision appears in an appropriations bill. However, the House Rules Committee generally waives the rule, especially for legislation that might actually provoke a response.[14] While points of order are more often raised in the Senate,[15] objections are, in fact, uncommon despite widespread violations. The result, I shall argue, is an abuse of democratic principles of accountability.

A Conceptual Framework

There are good policy reasons to consolidate the appropriations process. The annual budgetary cycle should require both Congress and the executive to consider the overall level of spending and the size of the deficit. Of course, the accounting conventions used in the federal budget are not designed to facilitate an informed judgment on these matters, but these imperfections should not obscure the basic point: A comprehensive annual look at the government's impact on the economy is a crucial aspect of modern democratic practice. A broad-based view of the budget also permits the Office of Management and Budget (OMB) and the Congress to set priorities by making financial tradeoffs between competing programs. The scarcity of resources forces decisionmakers to make ongoing judgments about the relative value of programs. I do not mean to challenge, then, the basic premises of the Congressional Budget and Impoundment Control Act of 1974, which consolidated the budget process.[16]

Nevertheless, we must recognize that consolidation creates strategic opportunities for experienced politicians. The Constitution and the Antideficiency Act require that appropriations precede spending.[17] Several times during the Eighties, the difficulty of satisfying the newly consolidated budget process produced a year-end crunch. Massive continuing resolutions, called Omnibus Budget Reconciliation Acts, passed late in one fiscal year or early in the next, included a high proportion of appropriated funds.[18] In such crisis situations the high cost of failing to pass a spending bill before the end of the fiscal year gives leverage to members of Congress who threaten to delay passage to gain an advantage for special constituency interests.[19]

A simplified scenario will illustrate the basic argument. Holding taxes constant, suppose that every member of Congress prefers early passage of a fiscally responsible budget (FRB) over recommitment to the appropriations committee and a delay of several months. Every member also wants to add special provisions for his or her constituents or contributors. Except for a given member, everyone else prefers the FRB to the FRB amended to include the special interest provisions. Suppose, however, that a senior legislator can get his specialized provisions included by the appropriations committee and that the amending process on the floor is restricted. If the bill comes to a vote near the deadline, most members may refuse to close down government merely to force the enactment of a pure FRB.[20]

The basic argument is similar to the familiar story of Gordon Tullock's in which majority rule produces an inefficiently large government budget.[21] The driving force of his argument is a public spending program, say repair of roads by individual farms, that has no public goods characteristics. Every farmer supports inefficiently high levels of spending on the road by his house because a dollar of public outlay only costs him $1/n$ dollars, assuming a head tax levied on n taxpayers. A majority can band together to tax 100 percent of the citizenry and overmaintain their own roads. The budget is further bloated by the instability of any majority coalition. After one coalition forms and obtains good roads through high taxes, the minority may bid away enough voters to transform itself into the majority and vote taxes to repair *its* roads. The key here is the voters' support for publicly provided private benefits under conditions where they do not bear the full cost of marginal budgetary increases.

My Congressional scenario differs from Tullock's, however, because specialized benefits may be provided without the organization of *any* majority coalition. Instead, the cost of missing the fiscal year deadline and Congressional procedures limiting floor action combine to give insiders on the appropriations committees the ability to obtain special benefits. These benefits may, for example, be spending provisions earmarked for the member's district. The extent of such behavior is constrained, however, by a voting public that penalizes incumbents who go along with massive budgets. Even if an incumbent's constituents benefit from specialized provisions, at some point the overall size of the deficit has a countervailing influence.[22]

This constraint does not seem sufficient, however, especially under current budget processes. Not only do these practices permit earmarked spending not authorized by substantive statutes; they also allow substantive provisions in spending bills. This second pathology is especially troublesome given the spending limits legislated in 1990. The public's opposition to taxes and large budget deficits will be ineffective against provisions with no direct budgetary impact. Such provisions will thus be particularly tempting to Congress at times of budget deficits.[23]

Once again a simple illustration will suffice. Assume a one-house legislature where each member can make one proposal to the appropriations committee. The proposal can be for a special budgetary appropriation, e.g., funds for construction of a hometown stadium, or it can be a substantive legal change, e.g., a provision, added to the appropriations for the Forest Service, permitting logging on federal land in the member's district. Suppose that the committee seeks to report a bill that will pass the legislature under a rule restricting amendments. The committee wants to obtain a rule for floor consideration under which the only proposal in order is one to return the bill to the committee for revision. Such a rule, however, must be broadly acceptable to the legislators, or they will refuse to accept it.[24]

Individual legislators seek to maximize their chance of reelection by trading off overall spending levels against benefits to their home districts. At low appropriations levels one might suppose that constituents prefer higher budget levels to lower ones. Suppose, however, that, given nondiscretionary spending commitments, appropriations are so large that everyone prefers less overall spending to more, holding district benefits constant. As the fiscal year deadline approaches, members also prefer spending bills to pass sooner rather than later to avoid shutting down the government. Suppose that these two concerns unite in the notion of a threshold budget: For any given level of district benefits, there is a maximum tolerable overall spending level that a legislator will accept with no remand to the committee. The committee, facing numerous nondiscretionary calls on the budget, has a minimum FRB required for the operation of government. If the committee adds no amendments, the appropriations required under this budget will pass in the first round. However, if the committee accepts no specialized amendments, members of Congress will vote down proposals for restrictive rules and will insist on the right to propose amendments from the floor. This process will delay passage and runs the risk of making it impossible to pass any appropriations act.[25] Thus the committee has an incentive to accept enough district-specific proposals to assure acceptance of a restrictive rule.

In evaluating the special interest proposals of legislators, the committee will accept amendments with the highest marginal benefits in producing votes for the comprehensive budget. These must be proposals from districts where one dollar of district benefits will produce a tolerance for an overall budget increase of more than a dollar. Suppose, for example, that in a five-member legislature the baseline budget of 100 would obtain three votes when put against a proposal to recommit the bill to the committee. However, with an open amendment rule all five voters will submit special interest proposals and no equilibrium may result. The cost of inducing the three "cheapest" representatives to refrain from challenging a restrictive rule is 4, 5, and 6 respectively, for a total budget increase of 15. These "payoffs" will succeed only if the new total budget of 115 is acceptable to these voters. The committee must consider not just the level of specialized benefits but the tolerance of the legislators for higher overall totals. A key question for the appropriations committee is whether such an equilibrium exists. There may be no way to keep the appropriations total within a majority's acceptable range while providing enough district-specific benefits to sustain a restrictive rule.

Obviously, an equilibrium is more likely if special interest benefits do not show up as dollar-for-dollar increases in the overall budget and if benefiting one legislator also advantages others who can be made part of the majority. (In the process, of course, costs could be imposed on other districts, but so long as these costs are targeted and fall on those who are already opposed to the committee proposal, they are politically irrelevant.) For both these reasons, substantive statutory changes will be more appealing to the committee than special purpose appropriations.

It is the likelihood of these abuses that frames my proposal: courts should prohibit Congress from waiving its own rules governing appropriations. On the one hand, Congress should be barred from including substantive provisions in spending bills. On the other hand, it should also be prevented from including narrowly focused spending provisions not expressly authorized by substantive statutes. Such a change in legal doctrine might be more effective than the Gramm–Rudman law, which enshrined a particular and controversial view of correct macroeconomic policy and proved open to gimmickry.[26] Representatives would have less reason to oppose restrictive rules on floor amendments when an FRB is proposed if the class of amendments most likely to be accepted by the committee is ruled out of order. The aim is not only to limit "rent-seeking" in the budgetary process but also to encourage a more visible and realistic debate over statutory goals at the time substantive, programmatic statutes are enacted. Ex post political compromises would be made more difficult.

I want to be clear about one thing my proposal does *not* do. It does not prohibit Congress from passing substantive statutes that benefit narrow groups or limited geographical areas. Its aim is to limit the range of strategic maneuvering, not to forbid special interest legislation. If the citizenry will accept a program of building dams on a few favored rivers, the courts should not intervene. I do not believe Tullock's problem can be "solved" within the framework of a democratic commitment to majority rule. My concern is narrower: to cut off strategic possibilities for rent-seeking created by emerging budgetary practices.

Judicial Ambiguities

So much for my proposal. How does it fit into existing judicial doctrine? The courts have an uncomfortably ambiguous attitude toward the rules of Congress.

On the one hand, the Supreme Court has given normative force to Congressional rules forbidding substantive legislation in appropriation statutes.[27] Writing for a unanimous court in *Andrus v. Sierra Club*, Justice Brennan supports "the traditional distinction which Congress has drawn between 'legislation' and 'appropriations,' "[28] and asserts that Congress has maintained a "careful distinction" between appropriations and legislation. "[A]ppropriations requests do not 'propose' federal actions at all; they instead fund actions already proposed."[29] Ignoring the frequency with which Congress violates or waives its own rules, Brennan follows *TVA v. Hill* by going on to cite the rules of both houses and concludes (erroneously) that appropriations "have the limited and specific purpose of providing funds for authorized programs."[30]

These strong pronouncements coexist, on the other hand, with a second line of doctrine. Here the courts have given force to substantive provisions inconsistent with prior law even though they are found in appropriations statutes. Judges do not view violation or waiver of the internal rules of the House and Senate as undermining the legality of a statute. Hence clear substantive language in appropriations acts takes priority over authorizing laws.[31] The Supreme Court has, however, directly confronted this question only in cases involving personnel disputes, such as the pay of judges and soldiers, not general policy issues.[32] A possible exception involves the Hyde Amendment, a rider to an appropriations act that prohibits the use of federal funds for abortions.[33] While the Court did uphold the amendment, it did not claim to be giving priority to the appropriations act over prior substantive legislation. Instead, it argued that the rider was consistent with the original statute.[34]

My suggested reforms, then, are not obviously inconsistent with recent Supreme Court rulings on the use of appropriations acts to change policy. They build on the view of the appropriations process expressed in cases like *Andrus* and *Hill*. As I have argued, the new budgetary procedures make preservation of the line between appropriations and substance even more important to maintain in the face of pressures for special deals as deadlines approach. The federal courts should require Congress to keep substantive policy changes and unauthorized, targeted benefits out of appropriations.

GOALS VERSUS APPROPRIATIONS

In the preceding chapter I proposed judicial review of statutes for consistency between stated aims and detailed statutory provisions. Now I propose review for consistency between substantive statutes and subsequent appropriations. The aim of this second recommendation is the same as the first: greater honesty and clarity of purpose in the drafting of substantive, policymaking laws. If Congress passes a policymaking law and then later funds it at markedly inadequate levels, the courts should infer a Congressional intention to repeal the underfunded provisions.[35]

Courts would not order an increase in spending. They would use lack of funding as evidence that Congress does not view the statute as a serious policy initiative.[36] This would be a rebuttable presumption. First, not all statutes would come under this doctrine. It would cover only those with a clear policy thrust which require funding to become operational. Second, the burden would be on the persons challenging the adequacy of appropriations. Third, even if funding is found inadequate, Congress would be given two or three years either to amend the statute in accordance with funding priorities or to appropriate funds sufficient for a good faith implementation effort. The goal is not to make dead letters of a multitude of statutes but to encourage legislators to consider the spending consequences of high-flown statutory promises.

The problem I have isolated is a real one. Conflicts between grand stated goals and niggardly appropriations are widespread in federal social welfare and regulatory programs. The most straightforward examples involve subsidized housing. The Housing Act of 1949 stated that "as soon as feasible" its goal was "to provide a decent home and suitable living environment for every American family."[37] This formula was repeated in the 1968 Act without any qualifying language about feasibility.[38] As of 1975 only about one in seven families in the targeted income class actually received benefits.[39] Even when production was high, assistance payments have generally been under 1 percent of the federal budget.[40] Lack of funds played an important role in restricting the success of housing programs.[41]

The Community Development Block Grant program of 1974 had a similar gap between rhetoric and funding. The objective of the act was nothing less than

> The elimination of slums and blight, . . . The elimination of conditions detrimental to health, safety, and public welfare, . . . The conservation of the Nation's housing stock in order to provide a decent home and suitable living environment for all persons. . . . The expansion and improvement of the quantity and quality of community services.[42]

This program never accounted for more than 1 percent of the federal budget.[43] The housing portion of the Act, which was 35–40 percent of the total, produced an average of four to five rehabilitated units per month in the cities surveyed by one researcher.[44]

In the regulatory area, conflicts between budgetary stringency and statutory goals are a familiar feature of many current programs. Among those reaching the courts are cases involving the numerous deadlines included in environmental statutes. Deadlines appear to be a politically attractive way to signal that one is serious about the environment. Congress gives voters the impression that it is taking a tough stand without having to do the difficult work of really understanding the problem addressed in the statute. These deadlines are widely ignored. One study found that the Environmental Protection Agency had met only 14 percent of its deadlines.[45] While critics in Congress and the environmental movement blame lack of commitment at the EPA, at least part of the explanation seems to be the low level of appropriations, which makes speedy compliance impossible.[46]

A Conceptual Framework

To begin the analysis, consider the way substantive statutes are proposed and enacted. Committees in both houses play a salient role in developing legislation and deciding which bills should be reported to the floor. The leadership then determines which bills will come before the full chamber and sets the rules for debate and amendment. Committees thus perform a gatekeeping function and, if bills are considered under rules restricting amendments, can affect the substantive provisions of statutes as well. Some contend that this system biases the legislative process toward the preferences of committee members and away from the median of the floor.[47] If this were so, a procedure like mine, which seeks consistency between substantive language and subsequent appropriations, might seem to have little to recommend it. Why not permit the de facto amendment of statutes to pass unnoticed if the appropriations process has greater claims to legitimacy than the process of enacting substantive statutes?

There are two responses to this criticism. First, the party leadership appoints committee members. If the leadership represents the median of its party, it will not create committees that diverge too far from the wishes of the chamber as a whole. If outliers are appointed, they will be balanced by more moderate members. There is considerable evidence that, in spite of claims to the contrary, committees have preferences close to the chamber median.[48] Furthermore, the rules under which bills are considered on the floor may reflect the leadership's assessment of the bill's acceptability. A bill that is just barely preferable to the status quo may not be placed on the legislative calendar or may be considered under a relatively open rule permitting many amendments. Thus there appear to be strong forces preventing the passage of very unrepresentative bills.

Second, the appropriations process cannot easily be distinguished from the process by which ordinary statutes are passed. Specialized subcommittees organized by subject matter consider each appropriations bill, and these bills are often voted up or down on the floor under very restrictive rules, especially in the House. As pointed out in the previous section, the opportunity for successful special pleading seems as likely for bills that govern spending as for substantive bills. While both processes may be in need of reform, one is not obviously more representative than the other. For both these reasons, it seems plausible to accept the working hypothesis that substantive statutes are legitimate reflections of the sentiments of a majority of the representatives. My focus is then on whether representatives have misrepresented to voters the policy commitments implied by these statutes.

Two pure and opposite types of legislation would never run afoul of the inconsistency between purpose and funding that is at the center of my concern. The first type is "rights and duties" laws, which impose responsibilities or create rights in ways that do not require the expenditure of substantial public funds. By their mere existence, such statutes change the fundamental character of the social contract and reorient the status quo from which people deal with each other. Individuals may, of course, violate such laws, but they should not be allowed to plead as a defense that the law is void because of the low level of public funds devoted to its enforcement. The most obvious examples here are statutes dealing with tort, contract, and property law. A person who injures another in a blasting accident cannot defend against the tort claim on the ground that the government ought to have monitored dynamite users more closely. Similarly, a right to own private property is not void because the government has not subsidized mortgages so that more people can afford to own homes.

The second type of law is an "expenditure-driven" statute. Such laws mean nothing unless accompanied by funding allocations. Examples include federal revenue sharing programs for states and localities, and laws permitting an agency to build public works projects. The statute merely sets up a program with no statement of goals beyond the disbursement of money.[49] Such acts can never be inconsistent with subsequent appropriations.

A third, essentially trivial, type of legislation also creates no problems. This is the purely hortatory proclamation often used to establish a particular date as national "worthy cause" day.[50] Such proclamations are expressions of public concern that require no budgetary appropriations or programmatic development.[51]

My concern, instead, is with a fourth kind of statute characteristic of the modern regulatory state. These "policymaking laws" create special difficulties. Such statutes contain statements of purpose that express fine sentiments and may invoke the language of rights and duties. However, the statutory purposes have little meaning in the absence of the expenditure of government funds. The acts are not cast as open-ended entitlements or, if they impose duties, as orders to the executive to spend all that is necessary to achieve compliance. Instead, the intentions of Congress may be inferred by the generosity or stinginess of its funding choices under subsequent appropriations measures. In spite of the legislative rhetoric a transformation in public attitudes is unlikely on the strength of the act's exhortations alone.[52]

Drastically underfunded "policymaking laws" have been essentially repealed by implication through Congressional inaction. I propose that the courts simply publicize, and give legal status to, the consequences of Congress's inaction. The judiciary would not threaten inconsistent substantive statutes with immediate invalidation. Instead, it should give the Congress some fixed amount of time to respond[53] by amending the underlying statute or by appropriating more money. Courts would not express any views on the merits of the substantive law. They would not rule on whether a public value would be served by fully funding some program. Their actions would be fully consistent with my refusal to give them a direct policymaking role.

The task of the courts would be the narrower technical one of judging if there is a minimal sense of proportion between the stated aim of a statute and subsequent appropriations. The standard should be deferential, placing the burden of proof on those arguing for inconsistency. The aim is to locate clear examples of overinflated rhetoric, not to involve the court in a policy analytic exercise. The proposal accommodates the well-understood presumption that no law can be 100 percent effective. The basic standard would be whether the average voter (analogous to the "reasonable person") would have been misled by the programmatic statute into expecting a level of budgetary commitment substantially above what was forthcoming.

Operational Questions

To make my proposal operational, I must address several specific issues: the definition of "adequate funding," the timing of suits, the bundling of appropriations, and standing.

Funding Adequacy: Absent some basic knowledge about the nature of the problem and its possible solutions, the "average voter" and, by extension, the reviewing judge cannot evaluate the adequacy of the budgetary commitment. In order to determine if there is a "rational" connection between means and ends, the courts will need to learn something about the substance of the policy issues raised by underfunding cases. Such knowledge is notoriously difficult to obtain for many social programs. Insofar as the problem is the lack of bureaucratic incentives to generate such data, my proposal should increase the pressure on agencies to come up with the relevant data. Insofar as the problem is inherent in the nature of the program, deeper problems exist. Hard cases will be those which challenge the courts to distinguish between goals that cannot, in principle, be evaluated quantitatively, and others that have been stated obscurely to frustrate review.

Furthermore, even if data are available, analysts may differ on how to measure success. Social and economic well-being can be expressed in absolute terms (the number of poor families); in relative terms (the proportion of substandard housing units); or as a rate of change (the percentage decline in pollution discharged into the air). For difficult social problems, even a well-designed program funded at a high level may not quickly reduce the magnitude of the problem. The rate of improvement can be high, while the level of harm or suffering also remains high. In such cases, if the ultimate statutory goal has been stated in absolute terms, courts should not declare the program underfunded. The achievement of high rates of improvement seems consistent with the basic intent of such programs.

The courts need not carry out complex policy analytic exercises that seek to link policies to results. Instead, they must only determine if the goals of the act are somehow being achieved. For example, if housing quality improves because of increases in income and falls in mortgage rates, an act to improve housing quality would be upheld even if appropriations were very small. Conversely, a very effective but small-scale program to reduce drug addiction in one urban neighborhood would be inconsistent with an act whose goal was the elimination of drug addiction in the nation.

Timing: The timing of lawsuits must reflect the fact that quick fixes are not possible in many policy areas. Legal challenges should be delayed until Congress has been given some time after passage of an act to appropriate sufficient funds. Suits should be heard only after the law has been on the books for several years.

Bundling: The current Congressional practice of combining several programs into a single line item in an appropriations bill would create further interpretive problems.[54] Congress could claim that it has appropriated sufficient funds, but that bureaucratic priority setting has gutted the program. Such arguments should not be acceptable defenses. Otherwise Congress will have an incentive to provide fewer details than at present. Rather, the burden should be on Congress to approve sufficient funds to meet the test of "minimum effectiveness."[55]

Standing: Who should have standing to sue under this doctrine, and who would actually have a incentive to bring suits? To analyze the first question, recall the distinction between rights-and-duties statutes and expenditure-driven statutes. When an act is close to the rights-and-duties end of the spectrum, the principle that a person should not profit from his own wrong should govern. If the act can plausibly be viewed as changing the expectations of private individuals concerning acceptable behavior, then violators should not be able to claim exemptions on the ground of inadequate government funding. Potential murderers should not be allowed standing to argue that the criminal statutes have been implicitly repealed by underfunding. Conversely, robbery victims might be given standing to sue to require the current town government either to acknowledge that it did not consider robbery to be a crime or to appropriate more funds for the police.

As one moves toward the expenditure-driven end of the spectrum, the notion that an act creates private claims independent of funding levels loses its force. Now those who would benefit from repeal and would be harmed by increased funding can be admitted as plaintiffs. Consider, for example, a housing act whose goal is "a decent home and suitable living environment for every American." Both individuals unable to find affordable decent housing and opponents of subsidized housing should be given standing to challenge the existing combination of organic statute and appropriations.

Let us move to the second aspect of the standing question. Even if standing were generously granted, who, if anybody, would have an incentive to go to court? The ability of the courts to discipline Congress depends on the willingness of individuals to challenge inconsistent legislative behavior. Thus my proposal will be most effective when a group named in a statute's statement of purpose expects to benefit by reconsideration in the legislature. [56]

Pennsylvania v. Lynn suggests another route by which Congressional funding decisions might be tested when neither beneficiaries nor cost-bearers have an incentive to sue. [57] In that case a federal court approved the Secretary of HUD's decision to suspend several housing programs on the ground that they could not effectively accomplish their goals. By analogy with that case, an agency's top administrator could determine that appropriations were too low to accomplish the purposes of an act and refuse to carry out the law. This challenge to Congressional spending authority could be adjudicated by the courts. A finding in favor of the administrator would imply implicit repeal of the statute unless Congress decides to appropriate additional funds. [58]

Judicial Precedents

My proposal does not sit easily with current precedents. Although a generous reading of some recent cases is consistent with my approach, its adoption would require a shift in direction by the courts.

In at least one case federal judges have inferred that a statute "implicitly carries with it all means necessary and proper to carry out effectively the purposes of the law." [59] The case involved the unwillingness of a *state* government to provide aid to illiterate voters under the Voting Rights Act of 1965 and did not implicate a federal agency. Nevertheless, the opinion, based as it is on the language of the statute rather than the Constitution, seems a direct challenge to the Anti-Deficiency Act. Since adequate funding is clearly one "means" of carrying out a statute, the breadth of this statement seems to encompass calls on the Treasury. [60]

Subsequent lower court opinions have expanded the scope of this case to include a requirement that Hispanic voters be provided with election materials in Spanish. Compliance with such orders obviously involves the expenditure of public funds.[61]

But these cases are really quite exceptional. Except when a contractual "obligation"[62] or a constitutional requirement exists,[63] federal courts generally do not require Congress to appropriate or authorize funds.[64] Congress is free to set appropriations at zero without explicitly repealing the law.[65] The result is to encourage members of Congress to include language in substantive statutes that appears to promise benefits that legislators have no intention of funding adequately.

Perhaps the clearest example is provided by the Supreme Court's opinion in *Pennhurst State School v. Halderman*.[66] The Court left standing language in the Developmentally Disabled Act even though it could not be implemented with the extremely low level of funding granted by Congress. The "overall purpose" of the act was to assist the states to aid people with developmental disabilities.[67] The Act includes the following "Bill of Rights for the Developmentally Disabled."

Congress makes the following findings respecting the rights of persons with developmental disabilities:

(1) Persons with developmental disabilities have a right to appropriate treatment, services, and habilitation for such disabilities.

(2) The treatment, services, and habilitation for a person with developmental disabilities should be designed to maximize the developmental potential of the person and should be provided in the setting that is least restrictive of the person's personal liberty.

(3) The Federal Government and the States both have an obligation to assure that public funds are not provided to any institution . . . that—(A) does not provide treatment, services, and habilitation which is appropriate to the needs of such persons; or (B) does not meet the following minimum standards . . .[68]

Justice Rehnquist, writing for the majority, found that this section did not create substantive rights. The act provided federal money to the states but at a level far below that which would be needed to provide the listed benefits.[69] Rehnquist argues that Congress can properly enact vague and hortatory statutes. The opinion quotes with approval *Rosado v. Wyman*:[70]

Congress sometimes legislates by innuendo, making declarations of policy and indicating a preference while requiring measures that, though falling short of legislating its goal, serve as a nudge in the preferred direction.

While the *Pennhurst* decision seems to be a correct interpretation of Congressional purposes, it encourages Congress to pass similar statutes in the future. The difficulties raised by this opinion help illustrate the point that legislative intent should not be the only grounds for review. Either the Court is unconcerned with the proliferation of hortatory statutory language, or it has not considered how its opinion could affect the future behavior of Congress. In contrast, a judicial finding of inconsistency would have forced Congress to reconsider the scope of the Bill of Rights for the Developmentally Disabled in a way that would highlight the tension between broad goals and limited resources. The ultimate result would have been more careful Congressional consideration of policy tradeoffs whenever a new statute was passed. Faced with the need to reconsider the issue in the future if appropriations prove inadequate, Congress might well have chosen to make some difficult choices today.

Pennhurst v. Halderman should be overruled insofar as it refuses to take seriously the inconsistency between statutory language and financial commitments. The Court should hold, in some future case, that the relevant portion of a statute has been repealed by implication, subject to a grace period of two to three years to give Congress time to remedy the inconsistency.[71]

CONCLUSIONS: A MODEST PROPOSAL

Some judges may view my modest proposals as if they were similar to Jonathan Swift's famous solution to the Irish famine.[72] Nevertheless, I urge them to think again. Courts *do* have a responsibility to recognize the serious structural difficulties involved in maintaining a responsive representative democracy. Rather than idealizing Congress, they must try to help keep democratic institutions minimally accountable to the electorate.

This theme has organized the last three chapters. I began by arguing that judges should interpret regulatory statutes against a background norm of net benefit maximization. While Congress should be free to make explicit exceptions to this norm, I argued that courts would serve democratic values by requiring a rule of clear statement for all exceptions. Similarly, chapters four and five have sought to define more creative roles for judges in assuring the transparency of the legislative process to voters. The aim is to enable citizens more easily to hold incumbents responsible for their actions. For the appropriations process, my goal is much the same. Judges should strive to improve the deliberative process at the time a statute is passed and to limit backdoor policymaking through the budget. The proposals are modest in that they do not interfere directly with the committee structure of Congress or with any of its other procedural rules and practices. Courts would make no direct effort to limit interest group influence or to circumscribe legislative purposes. The ultimate responsibility for public policy rests with the voting population.

Judicial review of statutes and appropriations for consistency is, of course, only one response to the weaknesses of the legislative process as a majoritarian institution. Other problems also bear consideration. Is there anything courts can do to facilitate the political organization of diffuse groups? Should courts examine the rules of procedure of the House and Senate to determine if they introduce any systematic biases into the legislative process? These questions are beyond the scope of this book, but they are suggested by my general approach—an approach that locates antidemocratic features of the political process and asks if courts can effectively improve democratic accountability.

THREE

FROM
PROCESS TO POLICY

Most lawyers are not judges. They are legislators, bureaucrats, lobbyists, and advocates. As a consequence, many will either perform policy analyses themselves or evaluate and act on the studies of others. Lawyers cannot afford to view substance with suspicion. Policy analysis is not simply something other people do. While administrative law's concentration on the courts provides a way to distinguish law schools from policy schools, this focus leaves lawyers unprepared for many of the roles they perform in the American political system.

The application of economic analysis to antitrust and public utility law is familiar. While economists may criticize the reasoning of judges and legal commentators, the market failure arguments are well known to those with legal training. Not so widely accepted in the legal profession are policy analytic approaches to social regulation and to public spending programs. In the next two chapters I introduce these themes in the context of occupational health and safety regulation and the provision of social services to needy people. Chapter 6 considers the regulation of risk and the efficacy of the market in allocating the costs of exposure to hazards. Chapter 7 argues that even when the public goal is redistributive, market incentives may be useful. The particular proposal I consider is "proxy shopping," a plan to use the choices of paying customers to ensure high-quality services for needy beneficiaries.

While judicial review of administrative and legislative actions tries to avoid substance, judges themselves cannot always sit above the policy fray. When statutory regulation overlaps with the traditional concerns of the common law, the courts must consider the proper role of each. When constitutional doctrines influence the government's ability to administer public programs, judges cannot avoid considering the substantive policy impact of their decisions.

To make the point that judges must be policy analysts, I consider situations that force courts to confront policy issues directly. In Chapter 8 I link the law and economic analysis of torts with the statutory regulation of consumer products such as drugs, toys, and automobiles. My analysis explains how the legal system might be reformed to encourage the complementary development of tort and regulatory law. Finally, I show in Chapter 9 that even constitutional jurists cannot entirely avoid economics. The constitutional doctrine of takings, long a bastion of ad hoc legal reasoning, can be reformulated in social scientific terms.

Regulation

Occupational Safety and Health

Public policy analyses of regulatory issues are commonplace. Yet lawyers often dismiss such exercises without seriously confronting their strengths and weaknesses. To introduce policy analytic thinking to the skeptical, I work through an example: the safety and healthfulness of the workplace. This example is instructive both because it has been well studied and because the courts have become directly involved in evaluating the government's policy analytic efforts. Judicial review of the Occupational Safety and Health Administration is an object lesson in the costs of relying on a judiciary unable to evaluate analysis competently. Justice Rehnquist's position in these cases also permits a further evaluation of the proposals for review of legislative consistency outlined in Chapter 4.

A POLICY ANALYTIC FRAMEWORK

Efficient Risk Regulation

The regulation of occupational health and safety is essentially a problem in the control of risk.[1] Hence my analysis begins with three familiar points: (1) Everyone voluntarily takes many risks in their daily lives because of the accompanying benefits. They drive cars, fly in airplanes, cross streets, go to the movies during the winter flu season, eat shellfish. No one lives as if his or her main goal in life were maximizing the number of breaths taken.[2] But (2) people tend to be poorly informed about the actual levels of risk. Many studies have documented these misperceptions and the general tendency to overestimate the probability of events that are beyond one's control while underestimating other risky possibilities.[3] Worse yet, (3) it is often difficult to present risk assessments in ways that can be easily used by ordinary people in their daily lives.

These observations lead directly to an analysis of health and safety risks in the workplace. The simple economic story told by Chicagoans posits a labor market with many competing employers. If workers are informed about risks, they will demand higher wages for high-risk jobs. They will also sort themselves across jobs depending upon their preferences toward risk.[4]

Even in this simple competitive world, one complication must be immediately introduced. Knowing that they must compensate workers to take risks, employers would like to keep job hazards secret. The market will then work efficiently only if potential new employees can observe the riskiness of jobs. (Does one have to climb on girders high above the ground? Is liontaming in the job description?) One way such information might be provided is through a feedback process. The first round of employees are uninformed of the risks, but after they are injured, other members of the labor force observe their injuries and illnesses and infer that the company should pay a wage premium or reduce workplace hazards.

There are several reasons why this feedback process will work poorly. First, many hazards take a long time to produce injuries. Second, even if they happen quickly, potential employees will not observe many of the injured in a large labor market. The only exception here would be a fast-acting agent that is harmful but not disabling. Then a look around the shop floor would be sufficient. If everyone has green skin, or if half the workers are missing fingers, demand a wage supplement. Third, the level of hazard depends on workers as well as workplaces. Some workers are more susceptible to hazards because of their genetic characteristics or their life-style, for example, whether or not they are smokers. Thus it may be difficult to infer one's own risk by observing the harm suffered by others. Fourth, workplace conditions change with technology and chemical processes, so the past may be a poor guide to the future. For all these reasons, regulations that require employers to inform employees of hazards are easy to justify. The information must, however, be provided in a form that employees can understand and use to compare job market options.[5]

But the mere provision of information may not be sufficient for several different reasons. The first turns on the limited information-processing capacities of people, especially when it comes to probabilistic information. Rather than engage in a massive educational campaign, it may be more efficient to regulate employers directly through administrative orders or incentive schemes. This justification will be especially strong when the employer's action affects all employees, the plant employs a large number of people, and most people, if informed, would assert that the benefits of added safety outweigh the costs. The second has to do with monopsony power. Some employers operate in labor markets where employees have very poor options. Then the employers can make take-it-or-leave-it offers to workers, which include worker acceptance of unhealthy and unsafe working conditions. One supposes, however, that this strategy requires poorly informed workers. Well-informed workers who saw a hazard they wanted corrected would accept a pay cut in return for the increase in safety. The monopsony power of the employer should be irrelevant. One would not expect health and safety regulation, by itself, to help workers in weak bargaining positions. It might even hurt them by reducing their options. The basic problem for these workers is their weak bargaining position, not the fact that they are willing to accept risks in return for higher pay.

A third justification concerns the production function for health and safety. Many actions an employer can take are "local public goods" so far as workers are concerned. If dust collectors are installed, they will benefit all employees on a shop floor. If a harmless chemical is substituted for a toxic, everyone who comes in contact with the material will benefit. However, if the employees are not organized into a union, individual workers may be unwilling to modify their wage demands enough to make the health and safety investment worthwhile. If employers do not know how much value workers place on safety, they may be unwilling to experiment with costly changes that may not pay off in lower wage increases or improved productivity. Established employers are especially unlikely to act if there are irreversibilities in the labor market so that money wages cannot be reduced in the face of an acknowledged improvement in working conditions.

Finally, there is a second-best argument for regulating workplace health and safety. Given the widespread existence of health insurance, welfare, and publicly subsidized health care for the poor and old, individuals do not bear all of the costs of their illnesses and injuries. Furthermore, individuals may not properly weigh the pain and suffering of their relatives and friends. If we take as given a public commitment to redistributive policies, especially in health care, then individuals may fail to take into account all the social costs of their risky employment decisions. Individuals, but not society as a whole, are insulated from some of the costs of workplace accidents and illness. This insulation provides a final public policy justification for public regulation of these risks.[6]

The False Promise of Distributive Justice

The efficiency arguments for risk regulation are powerful and suggest the need for federal regulation that emphasizes the establishment of baselines and the provision of information. These arguments need to be taken seriously by political actors because the more familiar distributive justice claims are, I believe, deeply flawed. They are based on a distorted view of the way labor markets respond to health and safety regulations.

Let us begin by assuming that workers have a right to a safe workplace, and then consider the next step: Should workers be entitled to trade this safety right for higher pay, or should this right be made inalienable? Inalienability is supported by those who take a paternalistic interest in workers' health but not in their overall level of well-being. It is also supported by those who do not wish to acknowledge that base wages are so low that people are willing to sacrifice health for income. Imposing costs on workers because of the squeamishness of others, however, hardly seems like good public policy, especially for a program ostensibly designed to benefit workers.[7] The more consistent response would be a program of redistributive taxation and subsidy that leads most people to choose improvements in health over marginal improvements in income.

If, however, relative money income matters to workers, then they may themselves prefer to be prevented from trading safety for wages. Caught in a "prisoners' dilemma," workers may agree to higher pay in return for accepting greater risks. If everyone does this, no one ultimately benefits. Relative positions remain unchanged. Most workers might then wish to bind themselves not to make such deals.[8] While this argument for inalienability is provocative, it requires more empirical testing. Why do workers care only about relative money income? Might not workplace conditions also affect relative status? Do highly paid construction workers have higher status than more poorly paid white collar workers?

However the inalienability issue is resolved, one must consider whether the right itself, in whatever form it takes, is worth fighting for in the absence of a right to one's job or to a particular wage. As it stands, the right has the following form. *If* a person holds a job with a particular employer, *then* he or she must not face certain hazards. Wages, however, can be adjusted to take account of these hazards, and the size of the workforce can be reduced.[9] In a prosperous industry unionized workers may obtain real short-term gains if firms spend more on health and safety and cannot adjust wages under the contract.[10] Over the long term, however, government regulation of workplace health and safety is unlikely to have much of a redistributive aspect. In order for workers to obtain *all* the benefits, regulation must impose on the firm a fixed cost that is not large enough to cause it to shut down. Thus the firm must be earning some monopoly profits before the regulation is imposed, and marginal costs must be unaffected.

Unfortunately, while such conditions may sometimes hold in the short run, they are unlikely to hold in the long run. Regulation is likely to reduce employment levels and the real value of take-home pay and to raise product prices even if workers who retain their jobs are better off. Regulation may still be desirable, because the workers benefit from better health and fewer accidents, but it should not be lightly presumed that most benefits will be received by workers, with the costs imposed on the owners of capital and on consumers.

POLICY PROPOSALS

The government policy suggested by this analysis occupies a middle ground—between the Chicagoans' faith in free markets and the present regulatory system under the Occupational Safety and Health Act. Its main features are: First, employers should be required to inform workers and job applicants of the hazards they face in the workplace. This information should be provided both in a clear and nontechnical form and in the technical form necessary for independent research.[11] Second, the government should sponsor research designed to discover the level of risk posed by various substances, tools, capital equipment, and generic work practices. It should also sponsor research on the treatment of work-related health problems.[12] Third, a subset of hazards should be restricted by regulation to avoid serious risks that most people would not plausibly pay to accept. The emphasis should be on covering a large number of hazards with standards set at levels that are clearly cost effective. The standards should be expressed in terms of benefits to be achieved, not particular techniques or ambient levels. Fourth, the agency should set a second tier of more stringent benchmark standards for some health and safety hazards. These would have a different legal status from the mandated minimal standards. The minimal standards should be firm, well-enforced requirements. The secondary standards should be designed to give workers leverage in their bargaining with employers either individually or through their unions. Employers should be required to comply with these secondary standards unless the workers agree to permit their relaxation in return for other job-related benefits.[13] Fifth, new chemical substances would be prescreened to eliminate or control severe hazards. The pre-screening procedures would be expedited with the burden on the government to show a major risk of harm to workers. Care would be taken to be sure that new substances are not disadvantaged relative to existing substances.[14] Finally, the workers' compensation system should be reformed to make it operate as an insurance system that gives more incentives to employers to reduce accidents.[15]

FEDERAL POLICY

The conclusions suggested by policy analysis diverge significantly from the requirements of the Occupational Safety and Health Act.[16] The points of difference involve the language of the statute, agency priorities and standards, and the courts' interpretation of the statutory language.

The Act

The OSHAct is specific about procedures and vague about policy. Congress has given almost no guidance on the substance of health and safety regulation, while setting up a novel administrative structure involving the Department of Labor, the Department of Health and Human Services, a National Advisory Committee, and an independent enforcement agency. Insofar as Congress has expressed policy goals, moreover, they seem premised on erroneous distributive presumptions.

The Act supposes that federal regulation will be beneficial to workers unless a plant is actually forced to close. The assumption seems to be that employers will be unable to shift the initial costs to workers. Despite this master premise, the statute contains some ambiguous language that expresses concern with the possible burden on workers, as well as the costs imposed on employers and their customers. Thus the declaration of purpose mentions "possibility" and "practicality."[17] Occupational health and safety standards must be "reasonably necessary or appropriate to provide safe or healthful employment and places of employment."[18] If the hazard is a toxic material or a harmful physical agent, standards must be "feasible" and must take account of "the latest available scientific evidence."[19] Congress, however, has neither articulated a view of how the labor market works when threats to health and safety exist nor clarified how tradeoffs between the interests of workers, employers, and customers should be made.

Beyond the vague, hortatory language, the only explicit statutory guidance is the insistence that, within two years, the Secretary [of Labor] shall "by rule promulgate . . . any national consensus standard, and any established Federal standard, unless he determines that the promulgation of such a standard would not result in improved safety or health for specially designated employees."[20] These standards are only the first step. The Secretary can modify them in accordance with procedures set out in the Act[21] but is given no general guidance about how to set standards beyond that provided in the definitional section.[22] A special paragraph does deal with "toxic materials or harmful physical agents." As the numerous lawsuits it has engendered indicate, this subsection is a model of ambiguity in which qualifying phrases follow other qualifying phrases.[23]

But the OSHAct is not so vague as to be entirely meaningless. While it does not follow the suggested policy outlined above, it does incorporate some progressive ideas. In particular, it requires disclosure of workplace hazards,[24] mandates standard setting for serious hazards,[25] permits performance standards,[26] and supports research on hazards and the collection of statistics.[27] However, the Act does not have any provision for two tiers of standards, does not give guidance on setting priorities, and has no prescreening requirement.[28] In short, the Act is not only vague but both too stringent and too lax.

As a substitute for clear policy guidance, the Act creates a complex administrative structure. While primary authority is given to the Secretary of Labor, it creates a gaggle of quasi-independent bodies. The National Institute of Occupational Safety and Health is established in the Department of Health and Human Services to do research and recommend standards to the Department of Labor.[29] A National Advisory Committee on Occupational Safety and Health advises the Secretary, who may also convene other, broadly representative, committees to advise on specific hazards.[30] Finally, an Occupational Safety and Health Review Commission, which looks very much like an independent agency, hears appeals from citations issued by the Secretary and issues orders to employers.[31] The legislative drafters have substituted a grab bag of institutions for a serious attempt to confront the vexing tradeoffs inherent in the regulation of occupational health and safety.

The Agency

Given the Act's broad delegation, a great deal depends on the central policymaking agency—the Occupational Safety and Health Administration (OSHA). While certain activities, such as prescreening, are clearly beyond the statutory mandate, OSHA has considerable discretion both in setting priorities and in determining standards. Unfortunately, OSHA has failed to make intelligent use of its policymaking freedom. In a pair of cogently argued books, John Mendeloff develops this thesis in detail.[32]

Consider safety regulation first. While Mendeloff's empirical work indicates that safety regulation does seem to have had some effect on accident rates,[33] the overall impact has been small, and the wholesale adoption of national "consensus" standards has led to overconcentration on trivial infractions. There is some evidence, however, that OSHA safety standards have improved the bargaining power of workers by permitting them to file a complaint with the agency. Given infrequent OSHA inspections, workers can use the threat of a complaint as a bargaining chip.[34] OSHA standards, therefore, may act somewhat like the second tier of standards proposed in my policy discussion. If, however, enhancement of workers' bargaining power is really the main benefit of OSHA, it should be explicitly acknowledged in the language of the statute, and not permitted to occur by default.

In the regulation of toxic substances, Mendeloff argues that OSHA regulates too few hazards but overregulates the few it focuses upon.[35] The result is both under- and overregulation—a few substances are severely controlled while many others are ignored. By setting very stringent rules for some substances, OSHA practically guarantees court challenges that will drag on for many years.[36] OSHA needs quickly to put into effect and then stringently enforce baseline regulations for a wide range of hazards that represent well-thought-out revisions of existing consensus standards.[37] Once this first step is taken, OSHA can go back and consider raising the standards for selected hazards. In the meantime, however, the baseline would be in place.

The difficulty Mendeloff has isolated in toxic substance regulation derives from the method OSHA has used to set individual standards. There are two aspects to the problem: first, the stringency of the standards, and second, the form that the regulations take. In the early years, OSHA had little policy expertise and did not make effective use of the available information. Over time, however, executive orders requiring cost-benefit analyses have induced OSHA to expand its policy analytic capabilities.[38] The agency did begin to perform the required studies in spite of the obvious difficulty of measuring the value of health benefits and reductions in the risk of death.[39] Unfortunately, the improvement in OSHA's capacities has been accompanied by a political climate hostile to regulation, so that few major rulemakings have been undertaken. Overall rulemaking priorities appear to be guided more by political criteria than by cost-effectiveness.

Even when OSHA has engaged in cost-effectiveness analyses, it has typically framed its regulations in primitive command and control language. In drafting regulations it has either required particular control techniques or, at best, focused on ambient air quality rather than workers' exposure levels. Engineering controls are favored over personal protective devices. More outcome-oriented approaches do seem to be possible under the statute and have been proposed by OSHA for some hazards.[40] These recent innovations should be expanded.

The Courts

Policy Analysis

Could this distinctly mediocre performance by Congress and the agency have been improved by artful judicial intervention? Maybe so, but the Supreme Court has not tried to find out. Instead, the Justices have rejected the use of cost-benefit techniques by OSHA in the regulation of toxic substances and have uncritically adopted the questionable distributive rhetoric of some of OSHA's supporters.

In its benzene and cotton dust decisions[41] the Supreme Court went beyond the strict requirements of the statute to impose an excessive amount of irrationality on OSHA. The Justices provided a highly formal and artificial interpretation of the statutory language, even quoting the dictionary at one point to bolster their argument.[42] In setting forth their interpretation of the statute in the benzene case, they rejected the more systematic policy analytic view of the lower court, which drew useful analogies with other statutes regulating risks and with tort law.[43]

Consider how OSHA must set standards for toxic substances under the Court's rulings.[44] It must first determine which hazards create a substantial risk to health. In making this determination it may use cost-benefit criteria, but once the hazard has been placed on the agenda, a cost-benefit test is taboo. Second, OSHA must calculate the costs of progressively more stringent standards. Third, it must choose the one that is as stringent as possible subject to the constraint that the industry remains "viable." The OSHA standard may thus be set at a point where the marginal gain in health is small and the marginal cost is very large. The emphasis on industry viability means that very dangerous occupations in marginally profitable industries may be unregulated while other jobs may be made so safe at such a high cost that employment levels and money wages will shrink. Thus "feasibility" analysis, as envisaged by the court, can exacerbate the tendency to over- and underregulation that is the object of Mendeloff's criticism. Such a standard-setting technique completely ignores one of the basic lessons of policy analysis, which advises a focus on *marginal* costs and benefits at all stages of the analysis.

The juxtaposition of the cotton dust opinion with the Reagan administration's commitment to reducing the level of regulatory activity has meant that OSHA did little more than stall on toxic regulation during the Eighties.[45] Since agenda setting is not judicially reviewable, OSHA appears to have sought to avoid putting items on the agenda, because once they get there, the severe reasoning upheld in the cotton dust case must be applied.

Workplace health regulation could be stronger and more effective today if a more policy analytic interpretation of the statute had been fostered by the Supreme Court majority. An opening had been provided to the Justices by the lower court opinion. In the benzene case the Fifth Circuit applied a cost-benefit test, developing an analogy to the regulation of consumer product safety and the cost-benefit test proposed by Learned Hand in tort law.[46]

In the Supreme Court, however, only Justice Powell followed the lower court's lead. For Powell, a finding that the costs were commensurate with the benefits would have been necessary to demonstrate that a significant risk existed.[47] Thus he implicitly recognizes that a regulation that saved very few lives but did so very cheaply would be worth pursuing. He would have permitted OSHA to issue regulations even though the underlying data were weak, so long as OSHA made good use of what was available.[48] He concluded, with the fifth circuit, that

> the statute . . . requires the agency to determine that the economic effects of its standard bear a reasonable relationship to the expected benefits. An occupational health standard is . . . [not] "reasonably necessary" . . . if it calls for expenditures wholly disproportionate to the expected health and safety benefits.[49]

Why did no other Justices join in Powell's concurrence? The answer lies deeper than the Court's formalistic approach to statutory construction. Instead, there is evidence that some of the Justices adopted unreflectively the flawed distributive arguments that have been central to the political debate over OSHA.[50] Lacking the tools of economic theory, they took Congressional pronouncements at face value. Higher standards were simply assumed to benefit workers. But as we have seen, workers' welfare does not necessarily improve with greater stringency. A court that recognized the complexity of the distributional issues could have provided a more reasoned critique of the agency's actions. At the very least, judges should ask if the arguments presented hold together logically.

While this requirement is far short of a cost-benefit test, it does suppose that judges can understand policy analytic arguments.[51]

The Nondelegation Doctrine: Toward Legislative Consistency

In the context of the multiple failures of Congress, agency, and courts, we can now step back and consider the relevance of the more general framework statute I sketched in Chapter 4. Building on the public choice literature, my analysis explained why laws may be drafted with vague and overbroad statements of purpose. The OSHAct is just such a statute.[52]

Justice Rehnquist recognizes this difficulty, but his remedy is the revival of the nondelegation doctrine, a little-used judicial principle limiting the extent to which Congress can delegate policymaking authority to the executive. He argues that the entire OSHAct is unconstitutionally vague. Such a holding would, he believes, force Congress "to reshoulder the burden of ensuring that Congress itself make[s] the critical policy decisions."[53] While Rehnquist's approach is oversimplified and heavy-handed, he has pointed to some serious problems with the OSHAct that might be better dealt with by the framework statute I have proposed.

Rehnquist's solution is too draconian. Statutes that delegate hard choices to agencies should not be held unconstitutional, and detailed statutes are not, per se, desirable. Many regulatory issues, including occupational health and safety, are technically complex and involve difficult valuation problems. In the case of OSHA the arguments for delegation involve both scientific complexity and the inherently difficult issue of valuing injuries, illness, and death. Thus a better approach is suggested by the consistency analysis elaborated in Chapter 4. Like Rehnquist's, my approach would use courts to improve the accountability of the legislative branch to the citizens. But it would achieve this goal neither by flat invalidation nor by judicial scrutiny of the substance of statutes, but by scrutiny of the clarity and logical consistency of legislative ends and means. This exercise in judicial oversight, whether supported by statutory or by constitutional provisions, does not ask courts to engage in policy analysis directly, but it does require them to understand and evaluate policy analytic arguments. Judges should ask a series of questions of the legislative product. Does the act clearly state its purposes, and are the statutory details consistent with these purposes? Are the costs of a policy recognized, and is the executive branch provided with guidance about how to make the major policy tradeoffs? Are subsequent appropriations sufficient to carry out the statutory mandate? Has the act actually helped those whom Congress identified as the intended beneficiaries?

This perspective permits delegation when technical expertise or detailed case-by-case judgments are necessary, while at the same time insisting that Congress make critical policy choices concerning how much of society's resources (public and private) should be used to further a program's basic goals.[54] Thus a statute might be judged both impermissibly vague because basic policy goals are not stated concretely and overly specific because the agency faces constraints that are inconsistent with effective performance.

CONCLUSIONS

This chapter has contrasted policy analytic thinking on occupational health and safety with the language of the OSHAct and the behavior of the agency and the courts. It has, I hope, illustrated the power of that approach even to those who disagree with my particular conclusions.

The discussion suggests that, at a minimum, the Supreme Court should reexamine the principles articulated in the cotton dust and benzene cases. At the same time, responsible policy analysts should propose to the Congress legislative alternatives that focus on the costs and the distributive consequences of health and safety regulation as well as on the benefits. Absent any of these fundamental reforms, the agency should, at least, follow up its somewhat tentative efforts at comprehensive health regulation.

7

Social Services
Proxy Shopping

Organizations that provide subsidized services to needy people are frequently discouraged from competing with one another. Many policymakers view the duplication of the competitive market place as wasteful and stress coordination, not competition.[1] They claim that quality can be controlled by direct regulation and by the participation of needy clients in suppliers' decisions. Many of these attempts to improve quality have, however, been failures. Direct regulation has proved expensive and has often been ineffective.[2] Attempts to raise the quality of services through client participation on boards of directors and advisory groups have often foundered on the indifference and inaction of client representatives.[3]

In response to these difficulties some commentators have looked to economic analysis for help in obtaining high-quality social services. Isolating providers from the market, these commentators claim, will not eliminate unnecessary duplication, but will instead lead to low-quality, wasteful operations.[4] Various plans have therefore been offered for exposing social service providers to market pressures.

Under the most familiar proposal, needy clients are supplied with vouchers that can be used to purchase the services of any qualified supplier. Vouchers, however, will ensure efficiently provided, high-quality services only if beneficiaries or their guardians are able to make informed decisions about quality. Yet even when vouchers are not feasible, alternative techniques may preserve some of the benefits of market discipline. This chapter considers one such method, called "proxy shopping," which makes use of the market choices of unsubsidized clients to ensure high quality for the needy. Under the system, funding agencies reimburse suppliers directly for services delivered to the needy. The rate of reimbursement is equal to the amount paid by unsubsidized customers for the same services.[5] This method is particularly well suited to situations in which vouchers are ineffective because program beneficiaries are poorly informed or immobile, or because choices made by their legal guardians are thought to be unreliable.

I present a model of a social services market that can be used both to identify the strengths and weaknesses of proxy shopping and to examine the desirability of using proxy shopping to finance several particular social services. I hope to demonstrate that proxy shopping should receive serious consideration as a quality-control device by government agencies and by private charitable organizations that provide subsidy funds to a range of nonprofit, for-profit, and governmental suppliers of social services.

I discuss the possibility of using paying customers to monitor quality in three contexts: care of the "deinstitutionalized" mentally retarded, health maintenance organizations and nursing homes, and integrated schooling. I conclude that proxy shopping can be helpful in monitoring community-based care for the retarded and can provide limited but valuable assistance in health care. In education, however, where integration by race and class is an important goal, the mobility of the wealthy can make it harder, rather than easier, for the poor to obtain high-quality services.

PROVIDING HIGH-QUALITY SOCIAL SERVICES: THE LIMITS OF VOUCHERS

Voucher plans are the most widely discussed method for introducing market pressures into the provision of social services. The beneficiaries of a voucher plan receive "tickets," which can be used only to purchase specified goods or services, such as food, housing, or education, but can be used at any qualified supplier chosen by the beneficiaries. Suppliers then redeem the vouchers for cash from the funding agency.

Under a voucher plan, at least in principle, suppliers face the same market pressures in serving subsidized customers as they do in serving unsubsidized ones. A subsidized customer who is dissatisfied with the price–quality combinations offered by a supplier is free to search for another who can provide higher-quality goods or lower prices. This creates competition among suppliers and should result in a market where the various quality levels that customers demand are sold for the lowest price that will cover suppliers' marginal costs.

The assumptions that underlie a pure voucher program—that is, one with no supplementary regulation—are based on a curious mixture of free choice and paternalism. On the one hand, vouchers can be spent only on particular goods or services that reflect the wishes of those who fund the program. Thus, the funding agency does not leave beneficiaries entirely free to make choices according to their own preferences. On the other hand, since beneficiaries are allowed to choose their own suppliers, the funding agency must assume that beneficiaries are capable of making rational tradeoffs between quality and quantity, that they are effective judges of quality, and that they have access to adequate sources of supply. Absent the subsidy, they would consume less of the service, but this consumption pattern would not arise from a lack of information or of viable alternatives but simply from a lack of resources.

Vouchers are currently used in programs that subsidize food, housing, and medical care, and many commentators advocate extending the use of vouchers to other social services, such as education. Most of the current and proposed programs, however, impose supplementary quality-control regulations, thus diluting the effect of market decisions by the beneficiary on the quality of the service.[6] Of the few pure voucher programs that exist, only one, food stamps,[7] exclusively aids the needy. The Department of Agriculture, which administers the food stamp program, does not impose special quality-control regulations on suppliers who accept food stamps[8] and does not try to control the diets of beneficiaries. Unlike the food stamp program, the other pure voucher programs are not designed exclusively to aid the poor. They are administered through the federal income tax system, and thus provide no benefits to people too poor to pay taxes. Indeed, these programs generally are not even characterized as voucher plans. Nevertheless, deductions and tax credits for such services as child care, medical treatment, legal fees, and housing are essentially voucher plans, which lower the costs of certain services and impose few restrictions on consumers' choices of suppliers.[9]

The reluctance of policymakers to endorse a pure, unregulated voucher plan reflects a pervasive difficulty. The premise underlying a pure voucher is that informed market decisions by recipients of services will ensure optimal quality. Yet in many contexts such informed choice is unlikely or impossible. This disadvantage is particularly acute when the beneficiaries are very young, very old, sick, or handicapped.[10] The efficacy of vouchers designed to aid such needy people would depend on the choices of those who care for them. If many beneficiaries have no guardians, vouchers can be of no use at all. Even if most dependent people do have parents or family members who can be charged with spending the voucher, the funding agency may believe that these people will not adequately represent the beneficiaries' interests. For example, a pure voucher plan cannot ensure high-quality nursing home care for senile old people if their relatives are not sufficiently concerned about the welfare of their elderly family members to investigate thoroughly the quality of various nursing homes.

Supplementing a voucher plan with direct regulation of suppliers might remedy the unwillingness or inability of guardians to make informed choices, but the advantages of a voucher plan are obviously attenuated if vouchers must be accompanied by direct controls on quality. Direct regulation of quality is, moreover, often cumbersome and ineffective. It would be preferable to develop a plan that used market pressures for quality control but did not have the disadvantages of vouchers. I shall show that proxy shopping can be used in some conditions to ensure high quality without the need for direct regulation of quality. This system would be especially useful for situations where vouchers are ineffective because beneficiaries, for one reason or another, are incapable of making choices among various suppliers.

PROXY SHOPPING:
USING PAYING CUSTOMERS TO MONITOR QUALITY

Consider now a stylized social service "market" designed so that proxy shopping is a more effective quality-control mechanism than either vouchers or direct regulation of quality. In this market, there are many suppliers of a similar service, but needy beneficiaries are each limited to a single supplier. Age, sickness, disability, or poverty restricts their mobility. [11] The funding agency wishes to make sure that the needy receive reasonably high-quality services under a plan that pays suppliers the market price. Vouchers, however, are useless as a quality-control method, since the needy are entirely immobile. Moreover, I assume that direct regulation is not feasible because the funding agency has difficulty both discovering suppliers' cost of production and monitoring service quality. [12] The same service is also demanded by unsubsidized customers, however, who are mobile, well informed, and not economically disadvantaged.

The basic proxy shopping plan is simple. In contrast to a voucher program, the funding agency reimburses the supplier directly for services rendered to subsidized customers. In order to receive reimbursement a supplier must have a certain number of unsubsidized paying customers. The funding agency pays any supplier who meets this requirement an amount equal to the price paid by unsubsidized customers multiplied by the number of subsidized customers served by the supplier.

Although the basic mechanism of a proxy shopping plan is simple, the desirability of such a plan depends on the presence of a detailed set of conditions. I first present a social services market in which these conditions are met so that a proxy shopping plan without any supplementary regulations ensures that subsidized customers receive the same level of quality as paying customers. I then go on to consider situations in which a pure proxy shopping plan encounters difficulties that can be corrected through modification in the scheme. Even when proxy shopping must be supplemented with various regulations, it will often still be more effective than a voucher system or a plan that controls quality entirely through direct regulation.

Conditions for Proxy Shopping

Using Paying Customers' Choices

Before implementing a proxy shopping plan, a funding agency must determine that the needy should receive the same quality levels as the unsubsidized. The agency must therefore ask (1) whether paying customers themselves receive reasonably high quality levels, and (2) whether the needy and the unsubsidized have comparable tastes, so that the choices of paying customers are acceptable surrogates for the choices the needy would make if they were capable of shopping for themselves.

To demonstrate the potential of proxy shopping I begin by assuming that quality can be measured with a single index. This condition implies that both needy and paying customers assign the same weights to various aspects of service quality. Moreover, although needy and paying customers have different willingnesses-to-pay for quality, they both value increments in the quality index, and there is no point at which either group ceases to derive benefits from increases in quality. [13] To simplify further, suppose that people purchase at most one unit of the service. This condition permits me to concentrate exclusively on the quality-control issue.

In addition, suppose that market participants are rational maximizers. Paying customers seek to maximize their level of satisfaction given their incomes, while suppliers choose the price–quality level that most benefits them: for-profit firms maximize profits; nonprofit firms—both charities and government instrumentalities—maximize revenues subject to a break-even constraint. Hence, producers have an incentive to provide the price–quality combinations demanded by paying consumers.

To ensure reasonably high quality for paying customers, the market for the service must be relatively competitive. In other words, there must be many suppliers of the service, each of which competes for the business of customers by trying to produce high quality for low prices. Therefore, scale economies must be small relative to the size of the market so that paying customers have a choice of providers. Although a wide range of circumstances can produce diseconomies of scale, the diseconomies in this market are assumed to result from the presence of congestion, a circumstance that is particularly characteristic of social services and of other goods that are consumed communally. Communal goods are those, such as day care centers and movies, that can be consumed by several people simultaneously, as opposed to private goods, such as ice cream, that can be consumed by only a single individual. I can watch the same movie as you without interfering with your enjoyment, but if I am eating an ice cream cone, you cannot eat it also. Congestion occurs because, after serving a certain number of customers, a communally used facility becomes crowded, and quality can be maintained only be incurring additional cost. Therefore, it generally will be efficient for several suppliers to exist even if they all provide the same quality of service.

The Feasibility of Using Paying Customers' Choices

If the funding agency concludes that the needy should obtain the same quality as that chosen by paying customers, it must then consider whether proxy shopping is an effective substitute for direct regulation of quality. The agency must therefore ask (1) whether it is reasonable to expect paying and subsidized customers to use the same suppliers, and (2) whether suppliers are likely to provide subsidized customers assigned to them with the same level of quality they provide to paying customers.

Three conditions must be met to ensure that there are no obstacles to the use of the same suppliers by both needy and paying customers. First, a substantial proportion of paying customers must not care who else consumes the service along with them and so not be reluctant to use suppliers that serve subsidized customers. Second, suppliers must be indifferent to the mix of customers so long as the subsidy rate equals the market price. The needy are assumed to be no more or less expensive to care for, on the average, than are those who pay their own way. Third, suppliers to which paying customers have access must include providers who realistically could be used to provide services to the needy. This condition, which I call the mixing-and-sorting condition, itself has two preconditions. One of them is that, since people of similar incomes tend to live near each other, transportation and search costs must be low enough and homogeneous income clusters small enough to permit paying customers to shop outside their immediate neighborhood. [14]

The other precondition is that scale economies, although small enough to ensure a competitive market structure, must also be large enough to make it efficient for firms to provide services to a substantial number of customers. For example, suppose that babysitters provided the most economical form of full-time child care. Individual sitters would not generally be able to care for the children of more than one household, and proxy shopping could not be used.

Proxy shopping will succeed only if the quality of service a person obtains from a particular supplier is independent of whether he or she is a paying customer. I refer to this as the nondiscrimination condition. This condition is met if suppliers have either one of two characteristics. First, the service may be organized so that everyone consumes the service in common. Suppliers can exclude unsubsidized customers who are unwilling to pay the entry fee, but once people are "inside the door"— whether through subsidies or by their own resources—everyone is treated alike. Second, if the service is consumed individually rather than communally, it must be provided by staff members who do not distinguish between paying and subsidized customers. This could occur for any of three reasons: Admissions may be separated from service provision so that the staff is unable to identify paying customers; the staff may be trained in a profession that teaches that equal care should be given to all clients; or the staff may be reimbursed in a way that removes any incentive to discriminate between clients.

Proxy Shopping in a Simple Market

To see how proxy shopping would operate, I first consider a simple market with no subsidized customers, and second, introduce a subsidy program. Suppose that all paying customers have equal incomes and tastes and that all firms have identical production functions. In market equilibrium all paying customers must be equally well off. If one supplier provides higher-quality services than another, this is exactly balanced by a higher price. Thus, all consumers are indifferent between suppliers. Since the market is competitive, all producers set price equal to marginal cost. Any producer who tries to charge a higher price loses all its customers. Let us assume further that the firms' cost functions have a special form: the cost of producing increments in quality is such that given identical consumers there is only one equilibrium price–quality combination that maximizes profits or revenues.

Now suppose that each supplier serves a fixed number of needy clients. Suppose, moreover, that each supplier has a single source of subsidy payments—e.g., the United Fund, a government agency, or a single wealthy donor—which has the power to withhold funds from managers. An effective subsidy strategy for the funding agency has two parts: the conditions under which the agency provides funds, and the subsidy level it provides to eligible firms. A proxy shopping plan would require each provider to serve at least one paying customer. If this condition is met, the funding agency would then provide a fixed per client subsidy multiplied by the number of needy clients cared for by that firm, where the fixed subsidy equals the price charged to paying customers. Proxy shopping is a fully effective quality-control device under these conditions, and no direct regulation is necessary. The funding agency has succeeded in assuring that both the subsidized and unsubsidized receive the same quality level.[15]

The payment specified above is the only subsidy level that efficiently fulfills the funding agency's quality-control goal. A lower rate would not permit suppliers to break even in competition with suppliers who serve fewer subsidized customers. A higher rate also has little to recommend it as a subsidy strategy. A higher subsidy rate would permit the firms to raise quality levels, lower prices, and attract more paying customers. If the subsidy were proportional to the number of needy clients, then providers with larger numbers of subsidized customers would attract a larger number of paying customers. A funding agency that wished to support the needy would pay the congestion costs of increased numbers of customers, and paying customers would end up obtaining part of the benefit of the subsidy. Instead of using paying customers to ensure high-quality care for the needy, the proxy shopping plan would subsidize high-quality care for the wealthy.[16]

A proxy shopping plan in this simple market raises only one question of fairness, and it can be dismissed quickly. Whatever quality level beneficiaries receive, they may still complain that they "need" higher levels of quality. Since needy beneficiaries, like paying customers, have utility functions without satiation in quality, they will want as high a quality level as possible when its price is zero. The failure to satisfy these demands, however, can hardly be seen as a weakness of proxy shopping. The needy receive the same level of quality as the unsubsidized, and no principle of equity would seem to demand that society bear the cost of providing the needy with still higher-quality services.

Variations in Price–Quality Combinations

In the preceding discussion I assumed that paying customers all had the same income and preference functions and that producers all had the same production functions. I assumed further that the form of the production function implied that only one price–quality combination was produced. If, in contrast, paying customers have a range of incomes and tastes, then producers will offer a range of price–quality combinations, and a proxy shopping scheme may suffer from two defects. First, it may fail to assure that the needy receive adequate levels of quality—the quality of service obtained by the lowest-income paying customers might be unacceptably low. Second, it may be horizontally inequitable—not all needy people would be treated alike.

Suppose, first, that paying customers have a wide range of incomes. Lower-income people, in general, choose lower-quality and lower-priced services than do richer people, and the funding agency must ask if the lowest quality produced by the market is acceptable for the needy. If the lowest quality is unacceptable, this could be remedied by expanding the scope of the program: the near-poor could receive vouchers that subsidize a percentage of price.

The remaining variance in quality levels may, however, continue to create horizontal equity problems among the subsidized. Instead of treating the needy equally, the plan would give them benefits that would depend upon the particular suppliers to which they had access. The same problem might arise if paying customers had different preference functions, or if firms produced a range of price and quality combinations even when paying customers had identical incomes and preference functions. The wider the range of price–quality combinations provided to paying customers, the more unequally the needy are treated. Under these conditions, a proxy shopping plan is most attractive for those policymakers who wish to avoid subsidizing very low quality levels but are not especially concerned with variations above some acceptable minimum.[17]

Several methods could be used to correct this problem of horizontal inequity. One approach would restrict the choices of paying customers: taxes or regulations might limit the range of quality levels available. If the funding agency were a government with taxing power, it might be able to levy a sales tax on the service tied to the paying customer's income. This would discourage the purchase of luxury services. Obviously, such an equalizing strategy is feasible only if the good is not transferable between customers. A regulation restricting the permissible range of quality would provide an even more drastic solution to the horizontal equity problem.

There are, however, two ways to minimize horizontal inequity without increasing the scope of the program or imposing uniform quality levels on everyone. On the one hand, poor people assigned to luxury suppliers could be required to pay something for the higher benefits they obtain. So long as higher prices are, as I have assumed, associated with higher quality, charging subsidized clients fees based both on their income and on the price of services would further horizontal equity.[18] On the other hand, the needy could receive cash benefits based inversely on their incomes and on the quality of services they obtain. This, of course, would raise the costs of the program.

Regulation of Commercial Firms

In the basic model, the funding agency need not require all firms to service subsidized customers. The assumption that individual subsidized customers are no more costly to serve than paying customers generally ensures that they are just as attractive to suppliers. In addition, the model's nondiscrimination condition implies that providers give comparable services to all customers.

In reality, neither of these conditions may hold in the absence of government intervention. Thus, in many situations suppliers may be in a position to discriminate against their immobile, subsidized clients by charging them the same price as unsubsidized customers while providing them with lower-quality services. This discrimination may be preventable only by requiring that firms adopt costly organizational reforms in order to receive a subsidy. Because of the cost of such reforms, commercial firms[19] that refused to serve subsidized customers would be able to supply high-quality services to paying customers less expensively than would firms with a mixture of subsidized and unsubsidized customers. Proxy shopping would thus become unworkable.

To be effective in the face of these difficulties, proxy shopping must be combined with controls on commercial firms, and a means must be found to assure that these controls do not cause firms to refuse to serve the subsidized. One solution is to permit firms to operate only if they adopt an organizational form that prevents discrimination. If this organizational form can be adopted more cheaply by firms with no subsidized clients, the commercial firms must further be required to accept a share of the needy. Of course, regulations of this kind, like direct regulation of quality, are not costless. Thus, such restrictions would not be efficient if the state could rely on the unregulated market to control quality. These regulations are a second-best response to the problem of quality control.

The Requisite Number of Paying Customers:
Ineffective Shoppers, Corruption, and Integration

The assumptions made so far ensure that if a supplier serves a single unsubsidized customer, needy customers assigned to that supplier receive adequate levels of quality. Under realistic conditions, however, eligible suppliers should be required to serve more than one unsubsidized customer. Even if paying customers are better shoppers than the needy, some of them may not have the time or information to make fully adequate judgments about quality. Requiring suppliers to serve more than one paying customer reduces the likelihood that an especially ineffective paying customer is the only control on the quality provided by a particular supplier. A related problem is the possibility of corruption through collusion between paying customers and managers. This problem will be discussed more fully below in connection with medical care. In brief, it may be necessary to require the supplier to serve a significant percentage of paying customers in order to reduce the risk that all of a supplier's paying customers will be corruptible.

Finally, consider a situation, such as education, in which the needy benefit from integration with paying customers: The ratio of paying to nonpaying customers is itself a measure of service quality for the needy. If this is the case, proxy shopping cannot by itself guarantee high quality, and the share of paying customers in the total may need to be regulated directly.

CONTROLLING COST:
A COMPARISON OF PROXY SHOPPING AND VOUCHERS

Proxy shopping can be superior to a voucher plan when the needy are less effective shoppers than are unsubsidized customers. Proxy shopping, unlike vouchers, compensates for the inability of the needy to shop for quality. Suppose, however, that the funding agency believes that the needy are as well-informed and mobile as the rich, but that they ought to consume a higher quality level than they would choose if supplied with a pure income grant. The agency, for example, might believe that the poor should consume more nutritious food or better-quality housing. The agency, however, not only wishes to encourage the beneficiaries to consume higher quality levels of the good but also would like to achieve this goal in the most cost-effective way.

Voucher programs can take several forms, but I consider the two most commonly proposed varieties: a voucher that pays a fixed sum and one that finances a specified percentage of the price. Consider, first, a fixed-sum voucher plan, where beneficiaries receive vouchers worth a set amount, which can be used only to purchase a particular good. Thus, the funding agency pays the entire cost up to a fixed ceiling, and beneficiaries pay all costs above that level. Such a plan has little to recommend it as a means of encouraging increased consumption of quality while controlling costs. If the ceiling is exceeded, beneficiaries will consume the same level of quality as they would if they received a cash grant.[20] By hypothesis, though, the funding agency wants them to consume a level of quality higher than this. If, alternatively, the ceiling is not exceeded, the needy exhaust the full value of the voucher on the highest-quality service available, even if increments in quality are worth very little to them. Thus, a fixed-sum voucher plan either will fail to encourage the consumption of quality beyond that chosen with an income grant, or will be unnecessarily costly.

Second, suppose that the voucher is designed to reimburse the supplier for a specified percentage of the price charged to the beneficiary. Beneficiaries now have an incentive to be cost conscious: if they choose a more expensive good, their own contribution will rise. Although perhaps preferable to fixed-sum vouchers, percentage-of-the-price vouchers are not clearly superior to proxy shopping, even when the needy are effective shoppers. In order to make beneficiaries as well off as they would be under the comprehensive subsidy given by a proxy shopping plan, the funding agency may have to subsidize a very high percentage of the price. This could happen if the needy have a very weak demand for quality. With proxy shopping, they receive a fixed quality at no cost. With percentage-of-the-price vouchers they must pay something for each increment in quality. Thus, the quality selected by the needy could require a higher per capita subsidy with percentage-of-the-price vouchers than with proxy shopping.

The escalation in medical care costs and in spending for Medicare and Medicaid—programs similar to open-ended percent-of-the-price vouchers—appears to reflect exactly the problem described above.[21] Proposals to halt this escalation would continue to permit beneficiaries to choose the quality levels they consume but would reduce the share of costs reimbursed by the government. The needy, though, may be better off under a variant of the proxy shopping plan, which subsidizes all or a high percentage of cost, but requires the needy to consume the same quality levels as paying customers. As I show below, however, proxy shopping is not a panacea. Some of the quality-control problems in medical care are too deepseated to be solved by an increase in competitive pressures.

APPLICATIONS OF THE PROXY SHOPPING PROPOSAL

If a market provides adequate quality levels to paying customers, and if the needy and the unsubsidized have comparable tastes, the funding agency may well decide that its quality-control goals will be fulfilled if the needy obtain the same quality as paying customers. Proxy shopping can be used to attain this goal if four conditions are met: (1) a large proportion of paying customers are indifferent to consuming the service alongside the subsidized; (2) suppliers are willing to accept subsidized customers on the same financial terms as unsubsidized clients; (3) the market allows the mixing of customers with different income levels (the mixing-and-sorting condition); and (4) suppliers serve subsidized customers in a nondiscriminatory manner (the nondiscrimination condition). If, in addition, paying customers are mobile and subsidized customers are not, proxy shopping will assure high quality while vouchers will not.

With these conditions in mind, I illustrate the strengths and weaknesses of proxy shopping when compared with both vouchers and more direct methods of regulation. I consider its application to three important problems: the care of the deinstitutionalized mentally retarded, the provision of subsidized health care, and the integration of classroom instruction by race and class. None of these services satisfies all the assumptions of my model, but deinstitutionalization comes the closest. In addition, my proposed system can play a limited but useful role in controlling the quality of health care. It will, however, be entirely unworkable in education if paying customers are prejudiced and dislike integrated instruction.

Care of the Deinstitutionalized Mentally Retarded

In recent years, a major change in the treatment of the mentally retarded has occurred.[22] Thousands of retarded children and adults have been released from large state residential institutions and now live at home or in smaller regional centers, group homes, and skilled nursing facilities.[23] During the daytime, sheltered workshops, specialized day care centers, and regular public schools provide programs. This deinstitutionalization movement has attracted many committed supporters among professionals who care for the retarded,[24] and has spread quickly, if unevenly, across the country.[25] The program obtained political support as a result of highly publicized scandals involving the low quality of care provided by some large institutions.[26] Predictably, however, quality-control problems are also arising in the newly decentralized systems. State funding agencies are not adequately equipped to monitor suppliers, and investigative journalists have uncovered poor conditions in group homes, special schools, and sheltered workshops.[27] Clearly, direct monitoring and inspection by the state are more costly and difficult when one hundred small suppliers, instead of two or three large ones, supply a highly differentiated service. It seems worthwhile, then, to ask whether market mechanisms might be used to help assure quality.

Since the retarded cannot be expected to judge quality by themselves, any marketlike scheme must rely on the parents and close relatives of the retarded. Many retarded children and adults, however, have no families willing to take this responsibility. A voucher plan obviously would be ineffective for that group. Nevertheless, it may be possible to use proxy shopping to provide market pressures for high-quality care since the basic preconditions appear to be approximately satisfied. It is especially important, however, to be sure that the nondiscrimination condition is fulfilled. Favored treatment of unsubsidized clients is less of a problem when all clients consume services in common. For example, discrimination is less likely in a sheltered workshop, which gives retarded people experience in working with others, in sharing equipment, and in being part of a cooperative activity. The nondiscrimination problem becomes more serious when services are provided to retarded clients individually. Then, the suppliers must be organized so that the staff either does not know which clients receive subsidies or has no incentive to treat clients differently. If it is impossible to organize the agency in this way, the establishment of professional training programs that emphasize equal treatment of clients regardless of wealth might accomplish the same end.[28] As argued earlier, these methods of providing individualized care must be coupled with a policy that carefully regulates entry to prevent firms that accept no subsidized clients from attracting all the paying customers.[29]

Of course, many poor retarded people do have relatives to make choices for them, and vouchers could be given to this group. Even in that case, however, funding agencies may believe that the choices of paying customers will more adequately protect the interests of the retarded than the choices of relatives. There are two reasons for this belief. First, policymakers may believe that poor parents are likely to have relatively little leisure time or money available to investigate quality. The opportunity cost of shopping for quality may be lower for paying customers than for needy clients.[30] Second, the funding agency may fear that some parents will sign up for the voucher scheme even though they care very little about their retarded offspring. They might then try to monetize the vouchers by turning them over to low-quality suppliers in return for cash. In contrast, the parents of unsubsidized children, who by definition are willing to pay some of their own income for care, must have at least some minimal concern for their children's welfare. This is not to say that poor people in general are less caring than wealthy people, but rather that, with vouchers, it is impossible to sort out uncaring people ex ante.

If some of the retarded have relatives who are effective monitors while others do not, then it may be possible to set up a fixed-sum voucher system constrained by the requirement that a facility also serve a substantial number of paying customers. Retarded clients without families would simply be assigned to a supplier.

Health Care: HMOs and Nursing Homes

In the current debate over health policy, several commentators have suggested using Health Maintenance Organizations (HMOs) to provide subsidized care to needy people.[31] Recognizing that quality control could be a problem in HMOs, Clark Havighurst has proposed mixing subsidized and unsubsidized patients together as a way of improving quality for the poor. He recommends using the fees charged to unsubsidized patients as a guide to help determine the government's subsidy rate and points out that this kind of reimbursement scheme "makes each potential private subscriber a sort of proxy who would 'shop' for health services not only for himself but also for . . . [needy] clients."[32] Some of his ideas are reflected in the Health Maintenance Organization Act of 1973, which attempts to promote the growth of HMOs.[33] Regulations originally promulgated under the act limited Medicaid and Medicare beneficiaries to no more than fifty percent of the total enrollment in a particular HMO.[34] However, reimbursement rates appear to have been set so that paying customers subsidize Medicaid and Medicare patients.[35] Proxy shopping cannot work to assure high quality under such conditions.

The chief problem with Havighurst's proposal, however, is not that it has been misapplied but that he did not carefully consider the conditions necessary for its success. He therefore has overstated the potential benefits of proxy shopping in this context. While the scheme has merit in controlling some aspects of health care quality, its value should not be exaggerated.

Havighurst's analysis has three weaknesses. First, although he recognized that an HMO should not be permitted to establish a ghetto branch and a suburban branch,[36] Havighurst appears to believe that each individual HMO office will, without any direct regulation, provide the same quality of service to all patients. He fails to recognize that satisfaction of the nondiscrimination condition is essential to the success of proxy shopping and that, absent regulation, discrimination between subsidized and paying customers is likely. Since most health care is inevitably individualized, the nondiscrimination condition will not automatically be satisfied. There is no analog to the classroom or the sheltered workshop. Therefore, organizational reform must accompany any move to proxy shopping. HMO regulations must make sure that the staff either does not know which patients are subsidized or has no incentive to discriminate. To ensure a mix of paying and nonpaying customers, the plan must regulate or outlaw for-profit and commercial nonprofit HMOs that serve only paying customers. This could be done, for example, by requiring all HMOs to take a share of the subsidized population.[37]

Second, Havighurst does not explicitly discuss the possibility of corruption. Through collusion between suppliers and paying customers, the latter might be nominally overcharged. Since the amount the funding agency pays for each subsidized customer depends on the amount charged paying customers, the supplier would illicitly profit from the nominal overcharge. He would then kick back a portion of this amount to the paying customers who collude in this scheme. Managers could also use kickbacks to compensate for lower-quality service, or secretly redesign the service to provide specialized benefits to those who pay fees.[38] In fact, "paying customers" might not even turn up for services. The manager could invent paying customers by constructing fake patient records or pay kickbacks larger than the fee to induce people to register who receive no services. To make these strategies costly for managers, the state could require that a significant fraction of clients be paying customers. Havighurst does, in fact, recommend that at least one-half of each HMO's patients be unsubsidized.[39] He does not explain why 50 percent is better than 1 percent, but perhaps he implicitly recognizes the possibility of corruption and favored treatment.

Third, although Havighurst realizes that HMOs may have an incentive to provide too little care in a condition of patient ignorance,[40] he seems remarkably sanguine about the ability of patients—either paying or subsidized—to judge quality. He defends his proposal by saying that it "would control costs to the government not by introducing a cumbersome system of quality and cost audits but by relying on the private consumer, who is still the most sensitive indicator of relative values yet discovered."[41] Yet it is a commonplace in medical economics to observe that neither paying customers nor their relatives are likely to be good judges of many dimensions of quality.[42] The demand for health care is determined in significant part by doctors rather than patients, and widespread insurance coverage blunts the price consciousness of consumers. Thus, relying on the market decisions of paying customers as the central means of assuring high quality for the subsidized seems unrealistic in the context of medical services.

Nevertheless, patients can evaluate some aspects of health care quality, such as the length of the wait in the HMO office, the length of the appointment, the pleasantness of the doctors' personalities, the availability of equipment, and the appearance of the offices and waiting rooms. Unfortunately, none of these services is priced separately. Therefore, HMOs might reduce the quality of other services in order to compete on the basis of easily observable characteristics. However, even if patients cannot diagnose their own ailments, an HMO's general reputation is likely to be fairly well-known. Thus large-scale misrepresentations of this kind may be relatively difficult to sustain. Furthermore, since paying customers are unlikely to patronize HMOs that score very badly on these characteristics, all HMOs catering to this group must supply these services at fairly high levels of quality. Only HMOs that face no market pressures can seriously skimp. Of course, this list of observable characteristics does not by itself add up to high-quality medical care, but it is one small but important part of the package of services. So far as proxy shopping is concerned, however, only the last two items on the list—equipment and appearance of facilities—are consumed jointly by patients. Thus, the first three services could be provided in a discriminatory way to the locked-in, subsidized patients. The length of a paying customer's appointment may, for example, be a poor measure of the appointments of subsidized patients.

Two scholars have developed a similar proxy shopping proposal for Medicaid reimbursement of nursing home care.[43] Ralph Andreano and John Nyman propose a sliding scale under which payments increase with the proportion of paying customers a nursing home can attract. They believe that their variant on the proxy shopping plan will help assure the high-quality, efficient operation of nursing homes, but they recognize that the government may need to provide information on homes to private customers and that it will have to regulate directly those characteristics which are difficult for ordinary customers to observe or evaluate.[44] However, the authors ignore the possibility that nursing homes may systematically discriminate against subsidized customers in some aspects of care. As with Havighurst's model, direct regulation may be needed to assure that the nondiscrimination condition is met. For example, devising payment mechanisms that would keep management and staff ignorant of which customers are subsidized would help to accomplish this end.

In spite of these caveats, proxy shopping seems a potentially more effective quality control device for nursing homes than for HMOs, because nursing home care is subject to less professional control and requires less esoteric scientific training. Most nursing home employees are not medical doctors, and most of the services they provide are fairly easy for lay people to evaluate. Thus, market decisions by paying customers can be used to help assure high quality for the needy.

In contrast, only trained professionals can fully ascertain the quality of medical care offered by HMOs. Despite this drawback, the use of proxy shopping in HMOs merits continued consideration, especially in light of the inadequacy of existing quality-control mechanisms. Exposés of fraud and poor care in some HMOs catering only to the poor[45] show the need for very basic quality checks. Although proxy shopping cannot, for example, assure regulators that doctors perform only operations that are medically justified, it can at least uncover the existence of understaffed, underequipped offices located in out-of-the-way places and open only at inconvenient times. Proxy shopping could then be combined with the current system in which beneficiaries can choose which HMO, doctor, or hospital to use. In situations where fraud and incompetence are a problem, requiring HMOs to serve some paying customers might be an effective way to remedy the worst abuses, even if—for the reasons described above—it fails to equalize treatment for rich and poor. In sum, although difficulties arising from the individualized nature of health care and the ignorance of consumers limit the usefulness of "proxy shopping" for HMOs, it may still be of significant value as a complement to other quality-control methods.

Integrated Schooling

In elementary and secondary education, voucher plans that give students a choice of school have been a controversial reform proposal since Milton Friedman espoused them in *Capitalism and Freedom* in 1962.[46] A number of respected scholars, not associated with the far right, have recently begun to recommend market-oriented reforms. They call for plans that would give parents more choice, stressing the gains of reduced bureaucratization, better school organization, and closer family–school relationships.[47]

For vouchers, the mobility of consumers is an essential prerequisite to ensuring the distribution of high-quality social services. Absent mobility, the consumer can make no meaningful, quality-based choices, and the system does not effectively regulate quality. In contrast, under proxy shopping the poor can be entirely immobile. Provided that the unsubsidized are mobile, nonpaying consumers will be assured high-quality service.

For education, however, a pure proxy shopping plan is infeasible since the state subsidizes the education of all children. Thus mobile, high-income parents do not face the entire opportunity cost of their choices. Even if well-off parents are permitted to use their own funds to supplement the public subsidy, their choices may not be a reliable guide to quality. Neither vouchers nor proxy shopping can be viable mechanisms for regulating quality without substantial continuing public regulation.

But the problem with market-based plans for education runs deeper than this. The mobility of some students may make it more, rather than less, difficult to provide high quality to the rest. Suppose that the needy benefit from integration. Poor children might learn more if put in classrooms with middle-class children. Suppose, however, that high-income parents are prejudiced against the poor. In that case, unregulated proxy shopping and voucher plans will be completely ineffective, since schools that serve low-income students will be unable to attract mobile, high-income students. With proxy shopping, suppose that parents pay for the education of their children if their income is above a certain level. Many different schools are available to these parents. The education of poor children is subsidized by the state, and these children are assigned to particular schools. The school board relies on the choices of the wealthy to ensure high quality for the needy. A school is subsidized only if some unsubsidized parents send their children to that school. If, however, the wealthy prefer their children not to interact with the poor, new schools will be founded that cater only to wealthy children. The system will break down with the unsubsidized and subsidized clustering in different schools.

A voucher plan that subsidized the education of all students would not be any more effective. Clustering by income level would still occur unless all schools are required to enroll a share of the needy, or unless the wealthy are compensated to accept integration.[48] Recognizing this problem, voucher proponents would resolve concerns about inequality by having the state guarantee equal or greater resources to the disadvantaged. Regulations would ensure racial balance in the face of parents who would seek white-only schools in a completely free market.[49] Thus, somewhat ironically, voucher plans in education may increase the regulation of private schools.[50] In fact, the very distinction between public and private schools would evaporate under proposals that both forbid parents from spending their own money to supplement voucher amounts and create a set of uniform regulations governing all elementary and secondary schools.[51]

Unregulated choice plans, whether vouchers or proxy shopping, could provide a cover for an even greater segregation of children by class, race, religion, and ethnic group than exists at present. The concern is not simply that predominantly white schools may be of better educational quality, but that the survival of democracy in a polyglot republic is itself threatened by plans that encourage children to cluster together with people like themselves. While residential patterns and private school alternatives already promote segregated schooling, vouchers or proxy shopping might exacerbate this situation.

CONCLUSION

An antimarket ideology that seeks to purge social services of any link to the price system has frequently hampered the design of mechanisms to ensure high-quality social services. Richard Titmuss was probably the leading advocate of this antimarket view. In his famous study of human blood, he concluded that a market in blood would produce lower-quality supplies than a system based on gift-giving.[52] While his observations may be relevant when charities are concerned with the quality of donated inputs, the main issue of quality control for most public welfare activities is not the supplier's monitoring of donors, but the monitoring of the supplier by private donors and public-funding agencies. Even if all inputs are donated, an organization must combine them to produce services. Private donors and public agencies may then have difficulty knowing whether the provider produces high-quality services. Given this difficulty, isolating social-service providers from market pressures can lead to low-quality, wasteful operation. My analysis of the merits of proxy shopping thus contrasts sharply with Titmuss's broad indictment of the use of market incentives to support altruistic public welfare goals.

Any endorsement of proxy shopping must, however, be tempered by a note of caution. In assessing the value of paying customers as monitors of quality, policymakers must analyze each service on its own merits, contrasting proxy shopping with a system of vouchers, with direct regulation, and with various mixed policies. Several questions must be answered. Are the needy poorly informed or limited to a few suppliers? If so, then vouchers are not feasible and proxy shopping should be considered. Is it desirable to use the choices of paying customers as proxies for the choices of the needy? Are paying customers good judges of quality? Do they rank quality levels in the same way as do the needy? Can the industry efficiently support enough suppliers to ensure that paying customers have adequate options? If these questions are answered affirmatively, it may be desirable to use paying customers to ensure high-quality services for all.

Before proxy shopping can be advocated, however, four further questions must be resolved. First, is a substantial fraction of paying customers indifferent to the mix of rich and poor? Second, can the services be organized so that the suppliers' staffs either have no incentive to, or cannot, distinguish between paying customers and the needy? Third, will new firms that serve only paying customers be permitted to enter the sector? If they do enter, must they be regulated? Entry is desirable if providers need not be organized to prevent special treatment of paying customers. Otherwise, such firms must either be outlawed or regulated to prevent "cream-skimming." Fourth, how will donors or government funding agencies reward suppliers? If a supplier obtains funds from several sources, all of them must act together.

The choice of proxy shopping as the most effective regulatory scheme ultimately turns on these empirical issues as well as on judgments about the effectiveness of vouchers and direct regulation. Although pure examples in which proxy shopping is the only workable scheme are hard to locate, it is an idea worth taking seriously given the difficulty of finding effective methods of quality control. The widespread dissatisfaction with direct regulation and the quality-control potential of market pressures, therefore, suggest that a creative combination of vouchers, proxy shopping and direct regulation may, in a range of real-world cases, be the best regulatory alternative.

8

Tort Law
in the Regulatory State

I now return to the courts, but from a different perspective. Previously, I asked how judges might contribute to effective legislation and administration. I now consider them as "front-line" policymakers using the common law of torts, contracts, and property to influence private behavior. Whenever the accumulation of past decisions does not resolve a current case, judges should self-consciously face the policy consequences of their opinions.

Tort law can regulate behavior through injunctive relief and the award of damages.[1] Legal-economic scholarship provides guidance on the efficient allocation of responsibility and the calculation of damages. Much of this work, however, views tort law as a closed system existing independently of other legal constraints on behavior.[2] In the modern world, however, the multiplication of regulatory statutes has gone far beyond that contemplated by nineteenth-century common lawyers and has brought tort law increasingly in contact with the public regulatory system. Legal-economic scholarship must confront the existing mixed system of statutes and tort doctrine. Can anything be done to make these alternative regulatory structures complementary rather than antagonistic?

The courts' task has been complicated, on the one hand, by the growth of statutes concerning issues that are the province of tort law and, on the other, by the challenge of mass tort suits brought against the manufacturers of dangerous products and the providers of risky services. The overlap between tort cases and regulatory initiatives and the strains introduced by mass tort cases suggest the importance of examining the complementarities and conflicts between tort and statutory law. The line between common law tort actions and regulatory interventions has blurred in recent years as courts look for design defects, agencies propose incentive schemes, and statutes permit private rights of action.

The increase in the regulatory role of courts in products liability and medical malpractice occurred as the federal government began to regulate risks in areas formerly left to the tort system. In the mid-1960s Congress passed a law to improve automobile safety just as courts held auto manufacturers liable for design defects that contributed to the seriousness of an accident.[3] The Consumer Product Safety Commission was established in 1972 as product liability suits grew in importance.[4] Occupational health and safety regulation, which responded to the perceived inadequacy of workers' compensation, was passed as workers began to sue the manufacturers of workplace hazards.[5]

I argue in this chapter that statutes should generally dominate so long as agencies can use rulemaking to shape policy. The trend to replace these more systematic regulatory techniques with case-by-case adjudication and product recalls should be resisted.[6] Common law torts should be limited to activities not covered by statutes and to situations in which courts can complement the statutory scheme with a supplementary enforcement and compensation mechanism. The adjudication of mass tort claims has encouraged judges to behave like regulators, a role for which they are ill-suited. Legislatures should address the public policy issues raised by these claims.

If, as I believe, we should rely more on statutes, then these laws should be designed with a more explicit concern for the compensation of victims. Tort law provides compensation for at least some victims, and this aspect of the private law is one of its strengths. Nevertheless, the pattern of compensation produced by the tort system has haphazard qualities. Only those who sue or threaten to sue obtain relief. If the standard is negligence, only those injured by a careless defendant are "made whole." Those injured as a by-product of careful behavior must bear their own losses. If the implementation of a statutory scheme requires that private tort actions be preempted, this creates an opportunity to design alternative and fairer methods of compensating victims, such as social insurance. If, instead, policymakers wish to preserve private rights of action for damages, these could be based on violation of the statutory standard. Even in a world with expanded social insurance for victims, private suits might be maintained as a supplemental enforcement device.

In an era of deregulation, a proposal to increase the scope and generality of regulatory statutes may appear quixotic. But I propose regulatory reform, not increased regulation. Of course, some risk situations may best be regulated through private contracts, and some instances of social regulation arguably fit into that category. As we have seen in the discussion of occupational health and safety, there are numerous situations in which private contracts fail to incorporate all costs and in which tort suits are therefore the only feasible common law alternative to statutory regulation.

I first outline the distinctions between the common law of torts and the traditional scheme of statutory regulation. Next I explain how the tort system could complement a system of standard-setting under statutes. I then consider what role tort law should play if statutory schemes were reformed to permit greater reliance on performance-based structures and on incentives. The final section discusses non-tort compensation schemes.

TORTS VERSUS STATUTES

The fundamental differences between tort law and regulation center, not on substantive standards or on the distribution of benefits and harms, but on procedures. In contrast to tort law, statutory regulation uses agency officials to decide individual cases instead of judges and juries; resolves some generic issues in rulemakings not linked to individual cases; uses nonjudicialized procedures to evaluate technocratic information; affects behavior ex ante without waiting for harm to occur; and minimizes the inconsistent and unequal coverage arising from individual adjudication. In short, the differences involve who decides, at what time, with what information, under what procedures, and with what scope.

Steven Shavell has developed a useful four-category schema to organize a discussion of alternatives.[7] He distinguishes between ex post (backward-looking) and ex ante (forward-looking) options, and between privately initiated and state-initiated systems. This framework produces four alternatives: tort liability (ex post, privately initiated), court injunctions (ex ante, privately initiated), command-and-control regulation or corrective taxes (ex ante, state initiated), and fines for harm done (ex post, state initiated). For our purposes the most important comparisons are between tort liability and ex ante state-initiated approaches.

Five factors, according to Shavell, should influence the choice between these two approaches. First, state action is desirable when the harm is so diffuse that individuals have little incentive to sue on their own and cannot cheaply organize to sue as a group. Second, if injurers are too poor to pay for the harm they cause, a system based on ex post payments will not effectively deter them. If criminal sanctions are ruled out, then either injunctions or direct regulation must be used.

Third, regulations or taxes applied ex ante can shape behavior without a showing of causal links between particular parties. Thus when harm can be demonstrated on a statistical but not an individual basis, tort suits may either be impossible or require judicial innovation to determine causation. The twists and turns of the market share test in the DES cases[8] and the courts' discomfort with probabilistic evidence[9] suggest that such innovation does not come easily.

Fourth, an ex ante regulatory system will be preferable when the same information about costs and benefits is relevant to many instances of harm. Then an agency can impose ex ante rules uniformly on similarly situated injurers; there may be little additional information to be gained by considering individual cases. But if each injury situation has unique benefit and cost features and if the potential injurer and victim are in the best position to balance these factors, then general administrative rules may be less effective than tort (and in some situations, contract) law.

The option of state-levied fines for harm done may make sense even when each case of injury has unique cost-benefit features. This option could be superior if the state has carried out research that gives it better information than victims or if those harmed are too numerous and diffuse to organize for litigation. Similarly, injunctions in individual lawsuits are preferable when cost-benefit information is specific to individual cases but injurers cannot be deterred through ex post liability. For injunctions to be effective, however, the parties must have access to that information and be able to present it clearly to the courts.

Fifth, administrative costs are an important consideration. If the probability of harm is low, ex post systems need only come into play when damage occurs. Under this criterion, the choice among policy instruments should depend upon the cost of ex ante controls relative to the administrative cost of adjudicating each injury multiplied by the number of expected injuries.

Shavell's underlying assumption is that tort law is a regulatory system that should be evaluated in terms of its consequences for the efficient control of accidents. This implies that rather than seek to turn the tort system into a regulatory agency manqué, we should preempt tort law with statutes wherever torts are a costly and ineffective method of control.

Which areas of tort law are ripe for statutory preemption? Ironically, tort law may be most ineffective in precisely those areas where judicial doctrine has been most innovative—toxic torts, products liability, and medical malpractice. These are all areas where ex ante regulation enjoys distinct advantages. Some critics, such as Peter Huber,[10] point to the courts' incompetence concerning technical issues of health and safety—incompetence arising from lack of expertise, inadequate staff, and procedures ill-suited to the discovery of scientific truth.

Others lament the vague, inconsistent signals sent by a decentralized tort system. For example, Justice Powell worries that "juries of lay persons, selected essentially at random" will impose "unfocused penalties solely for the purpose of punishment and some undefined deterrence."[11] Scholars cannot even agree whether tort law in these areas is overdeterring or underdeterring injurers. Some point to large jury awards in particular cases, while others emphasize the infrequency with which victims sue and the small average awards.[12]

Unpredictable, inconsistent adjudications introduce additional risk into corporate decisionmaking that serves no productive purpose but creates costly, essentially random, noise. Inconsistent decisions can also affect firms' competitive positions in the same or related industries in ways that distort economic relationships. Statutes, of course, can also be enforced haphazardly and arbitrarily, but there, at least, enforcement is subject to judicial and political review.

This critique of tort law is not widely accepted even in the toxic torts and products liability areas. The right of individuals to present their claims to a judge and a lay jury is a well-entrenched social value. Many view the tort system as a way to counter the biases of state action despite the fact that some statutes, such as workers' compensation, the Wagner Act, and veterans legislation, were adopted to benefit ordinary people by substituting neutral administrative determinations for biased courts and costly lawyers.[13] Support for the tort system persists even when the logic of efficient risk control demands ex ante regulation. Given this reality, our next task is to consider how tort law might be used to further, not distort, the deterrence goal and to isolate those situations where preemption would be desirable.

TORTS AS A COMPLEMENT TO STATUTORY REGULATION

Let us consider, then, a situation favoring statutory regulation over torts—for example, the safety of automobiles, drugs, or medical devices, where many people are at risk and information about product design is often relevant to harm. To highlight the differences between statutes and torts, assume that regulatory standards are set through rulemaking under a command-and-control scheme. The next section considers the special problem of integrating tort and regulatory law when incentive systems are part of the statutory scheme.

Ideally, tort law and regulatory standards work together to further deterrence and compensation goals. I consider situations in which torts and regulations can be complementary: (1) when tort doctrines are stopgaps which apply absent more stringent statutes; (2) when regulatory standards are intended as minimums that more stringent tort doctrines can supplement, and (3) when a regulatory standard is set at the socially optimal level and tort doctrine imposes either strict liability or a standard of care less than or equal to that required by the agency. However, when the regulatory standard is set optimally while the tort standard of negligence is interpreted to require an even higher level of care, conflicts can arise under a system of compensatory damages. Such conflicts are even more likely when punitive damages are available.

Tort Law as a Stopgap

Legislatures have other aims besides constructing rational regulatory systems, and they often fail to establish regulatory programs in all of the areas in which regulation would in theory be superior to tort law. In such cases courts should not idealize the pattern of common law regulation created by their past adjudications, but should see tort law as a stopgap pending future statutory regulation.[14] If a regulatory statute is then passed, courts should resolve conflicts between tort doctrines and regulatory principles by according priority to the statutes. When Congress enacted a statute regulating automobile safety, for example, federal courts rejected common law actions based on the manufacturers' failure to install air bags, citing Congress's newly manifest desire for uniform standards in this area.[15]

But viewing tort law as a stopgap may reflect circular reasoning. No statute is a fully specified document. When issues of interpretation arise, courts often construe statutes in light of the common law principles existing at the time the statute was passed, unless those principles contradict the statute.[16] This mode of statutory interpretation loses much of its justification if the courts view their prior decisions not as setting a background standard but as simply performing a holding action. Since the common law lacks canonical status, the courts should avoid circularity by looking not to the common law but to the statute's basic purposes. Since the judicial habit of using the common law to interpret statutes dies hard, legislatures should make clear their intention to bar such interpretations.

Regulatory Standards as Minimums

Regulatory standards are sometimes designed to establish only a baseline. While violation of such standards usually amounts to negligence per se in a tort suit, compliance is merely evidence for the jury to consider in determining reasonable conduct. Note the asymmetry here. Because the standard sets a minimum, the plaintiff can argue that a higher standard should be imposed in a particular case, but the defendant cannot invoke special circumstances to justify its violation of the basic standard. The courts have viewed regulations as minimums in many cases involving the safety of products and workplaces.[17] Similarly, tort suits involving automobile design are not preempted by regulatory statutes,[18] and criminal prosecutions for occupational health and safety conditions have been permitted by some state courts in spite of a federal regulatory presence.[19]

While treating statutory standards as minimums is sometimes appropriate, it destroys whatever uniformity the standard imposes and substitutes the judgments of judges and juries for the policy decisions of agencies. Only great skepticism about agency actions and great faith in courts might justify such a system. This justification, however, seems unpersuasive whether one views agency officials as technocrats or as politicians. If they are technocrats, it undermines their expertise by supposing that agencies can set lower, but not upper, limits on care levels. If they are politicians, their political compromises would be set aside by the supposedly apolitical courts, an outcome that violates the familiar administrative law norm that courts should not prefer their own policy judgments to those of agencies.

Careful statutory drafting can help prevent these conflicts. If the courts view regulatory standards as minimums, there is no conflict if the agency itself has set a low standard in the belief that case-by-case adjudication is the best way to respond to the regulatory problem.[20] Although this may sometimes be a plausible strategy, the plaintiff should bear the burden of demonstrating that the legislature intended it. Absent such a showing, a regulatory statute should be taken to imply a legislative judgment that a comprehensive, state-centered, ex ante approach is the best way to deter harm. The difficulties of judicial standard-setting should lead judges to accept the stopgap role and to reject the notion that regulations are merely minimums unless the legislature or agency has explained the regulations in these terms. If the regulations are indeed too lax, statutory or administrative reform is appropriate, not ad hoc judicial actions that respond to individual needs while producing systemwide inequities and inefficiencies.

Tort Law as an Enforcement and Compensation Mechanism

Under either negligence or strict liability, courts can complement a system of statutory regulation, producing both a more consistent tort law and a more effective regulatory system. To accomplish this, however, judges must be prepared to surrender some of their independence in setting standards of care and assessing damages.

Consider a negligence rule that seeks to mimic the regulatory standard. In addition to holding violators of the statute negligent per se, the courts would also recognize a per se *defense* for injurers who meet the regulatory standard.[21] Regulatory law would then resemble the criminal law. The state would establish standards of good behavior, prosecute wrongdoers, and set the stage for private civil damage actions against violators. The wrongdoer could thus be punished twice: by whatever sanctions the state imposes through the criminal or regulatory process, and by paying damages to private litigants. While this may seem unfair to the wrongdoer, it is not inefficient even if the sum of the penalties exceeds the social costs of violating the standards. Convicted wrongdoers would pay "too much," but anyone can avoid this overcharge by simply conforming to the regulatory requirements. Any penalty that equals or exceeds social costs provides the correct deterrent by encouraging potential wrongdoers to conform to the standards. This optimistic view is true, however, only if agencies set clear standards, and courts accept these standards in determining liability and apply them competently to individual cases.[22]

Suppose now that the tort standard is not negligence but true strict liability, which holds a manufacturer liable for all harm caused by its product and requires the court only to determine causation, not to assess the risks and benefits of product design. True strict liability differs substantially from the "strict liability" of products law, which essentially requires the jury to make a negligence-like risk/utility calculation.[23] True strict liability would convert manufacturers of such risky products as drugs and household chemicals into insurers even where the consumers can bear the risk more cheaply and would prefer to do so in return for a lower price.

Under true strict liability, torts and regulation need not conflict if damages are set equal to the harm caused by the tortfeasor. The possibility of a tort judgment will simply give the regulated entity an additional incentive to comply with the statute. The conditions assuring complementarity, however, do not now exist. To achieve them would require substantial tort reform, yet attempts to reshape tort doctrine according to its behavioral effects would be difficult. True strict liability under the common law applies to abnormally dangerous activities such as blasting or keeping wild animals where both determining causation and assessing damages are relatively straightforward exercises.[24] Harm caused by latent cancer risks and air pollution, however, fits awkwardly within these categories. Problems in assessing causation and in setting and apportioning damages will complicate judicial efforts to coordinate with regulatory policies.

Conflicts with an Efficient Standard

Tort law can work at cross purposes to statutes when the regulatory standard is set at the socially optimal level of care, but the courts impose a more stringent negligence standard. While lawyer-economists argue that negligence should be equated with socially inefficient choices, tort law does not perfectly reflect the learning of economics.[25] Two cases need to be considered: compensatory damages and punitive damages.

Judges sometimes sharply distinguish the two, finding punitive damages "regulatory" and compensatory damages not. Dissenting in *Silkwood v. Kerr-McGee*, Justice Powell stated: "There is no element of regulation when compensatory damages are awarded."[26] Under this view, the goal of compensatory damages is merely to make the victim whole, not to induce behavioral changes in potential injurers; thus compensatory damages cannot conflict with a regulatory purpose. If tort actions only provided compensation and if the agency's own enforcement mechanisms effectively assured compliance with its standards, this view might be correct. But these assumptions are always false where no statute exists (the stopgap case) and are often false even when one does.

To see Powell's error, suppose that a regulatory agency such as the Consumer Product Safety Commission or the Food and Drug Administration has set a standard at the optimal level, but courts nonetheless find that complying firms have been negligent or have defectively designed their product. Those firms which just comply with the regulations must pay damages to anyone who has been harmed. If they meet the court's standard, however, they pay no damages. A firm will then compare the extra costs of meeting the court's standard with the damages it must pay victims if it merely complies with the lower regulatory agency standard. If it can increase profits by complying with the court's negligence standard, the firm will do so. At this care level, however, it will surpass the optimal agency standard, and marginal costs will exceed marginal benefits. Even with purely compensatory damages, then, tort doctrine can have regulatory effects.

This conclusion does not depend upon the correctness of the agency's standard. If, for example, the negligence standard were optimal while the agency's standard was too low, the same result would still occur. The issue is not whether tort law has a regulatory effect, but which mechanism—statutory standards or tort adjudication—is the most effective way to regulate behavior.

Judges who distinguish between compensatory and punitive damages, however, are not completely misguided. Suppose that punitive damages are a multiple of actual damages, with the multiple increasing the lower the defendant's level of care. Such a damage schedule provides a greater marginal incentive for caretaking and safe product design than compensatory damages. If the courts impose a higher standard of care than is required by a socially optimal statute, economic distortions will occur. For example, suppose that courts award punitive damages in automobile design defect cases so that marginal damage awards exceed actual marginal damages, with the excess increasing the farther the automotive firm falls below the tort standard. If the firm will be sued for all violations of the tort standard, it will never select the agency's optimal standard of automotive design. At the agency's optimal point, marginal punitive damages levied by the courts exceed the marginal cost of greater care. The firm can improve its profitability by increasing safety. It will choose one of two options (depending upon which is profit-maximizing): compliance with the tort standard where no damages are levied, or a level of safe design (somewhere between the socially optimal level and the tort standard) at which its marginal costs equal marginal punitive damages.[27]

———————————— • ————————————

Thus we have seen how tort law can complement a statutory scheme, but we have also demonstrated that the two systems may work at cross purposes. The tort system can be a way of responding to specialized situations not explicitly addressed in a statute designed for the typical case. Unfortunately, the common law can also undermine regulatory efforts. The most consistent way of merging the two systems is to use true strict liability or to apply statutory standards to define negligence, invoking common law principles only where statutes or administrative rules do not govern. When a regulatory statute exists, punitive damages would be levied only if agency enforcement were weak and the courts expect that only a proportion of the injured will sue.

REGULATORY REFORM

Viewing regulation as nothing more than standard setting could have serious consequences in an era of regulatory reform. Commentators have long urged legislators and regulatory agencies to charge fees set to reflect the risks created by regulated firms. Incentive-based reforms allocate regulatory costs to those who can bear them most efficiently, encourage firms to search for innovative ways to reduce harms, and force producers' prices to reflect the risks they impose on society. Well-designed reforms can improve the market's competitiveness and efficiency.

Incentive schemes require a fundamental rethinking of the relationship between tort law and statutory law. Following the conventional wisdom of economists and policy analysts, regulators have begun to use incentives and subsidies to affect behavior in lieu of command-and-control standards. The EPA has experimented with "bubbles," "offsets," and "banking."[28] The 1990 Amendments to the Clean Air Act seek to control acid rain through a system of tradable pollution rights.[29] Similar proposals exist to pay workers to use protective devices under OSHA and to establish marketable rights for water pollution.

Such reforms, however, could be undermined by an insensitive judiciary. If courts equate regulation with standard setting, they may treat only command-and-control regulation as behaviorally significant. In a recent case, for example, the Superfund law was described as "not a regulatory standard-setting statute" because polluters pay for the cost of abating hazardous wastes "through tax and reimbursement liability."[30] This view is misconceived. Taxes, subsidies, and government-mandated liability regulate behavior as surely as direct orders.

How should courts handle claims by defendants that incentive-based regulatory statutes preempt tort actions? Judges who view regulation as confined to standard setting might allow tort actions on the ground that these statutes are not "regulatory" because they do not establish uniform standards but "only" create incentives. Yet the argument for preemption of tort law is even stronger in the case of incentive-based regulations than in the case of command-and-control regulation. With standard setting based on either technology or performance, tort actions can complement regulatory agency activity if agency enforcement is not comprehensive or if the fines levied bear little relationship to damages. In contrast, if fee schedules have been set to reflect the social costs of the regulated firm's activities, then tort actions would be redundant at best and counterproductive at worst. A well-designed incentive system signals to a firm the social costs of its activities. A fee system resembles a tort liability system:

No fixed standards are set, but firms respond to the cost of damages. The regulated entity must purchase the right to impose social costs in the same way that a tort judgment requires payment for harms. The main difference is the comprehensiveness of a fee schedule, which the state sets so that all firms are covered. A firm's liability does not depend on the contingency of private litigation and jury damage awards.

Tort judgments would undermine such a regulatory scheme, especially if courts applied a strict liability standard, the type of standard that some judges have found least "regulatory."[31] Thus incentive-based statutes should include a provision clearly preempting tort actions. For example, if the Environmental Protection Agency charges effluent fees, those damaged by the discharges that occur should not be able to sue since this would create inefficient caretaking incentives on the margin.[32]

The only remaining role for private individuals would be suits against delinquent regulated firms.[33] Such suits might permit private recovery of damages for harm caused by lax enforcement. For example, the Consumer Product Safety Act permits suits for damages against firms that violate agency rules.[34] In situations where the damages are too diffuse to motivate private litigation, the recovery could be some multiple of fees that the agency could have exacted and could be paid to the Treasury with the public interest litigant recovering legal fees. Thus although ordinary tort actions would be preempted, certain specialized private remedies might supplement agency enforcement just as do tort actions that use regulatory standards as the standard of negligence.

COMPENSATION

Tort law provides more than a set of regulatory incentives; behavior modification is not its only legitimate function. It is also a compensation system triggered by victims' complaints. If a regulatory statute bars private tort actions, those who were previously able to sue for damages will be disadvantaged, a result courts seem reluctant to permit. In finding that Karen Silkwood could sue in state court for punitive damages from exposure to radiation in spite of a federal statute that preempted state regulation of the nuclear industry, the Supreme Court noted that the statute did not provide for compensation. It stated, "It is difficult to believe that Congress would, without comment, remove all means of judicial recourse for those injured by illegal conduct."[35] If compensation of victims is not addressed by a purely regulatory statute yet remains a policy goal, conflict may arise between the statute and tort law. Compensation-oriented courts may apply conventional tort doctrines that are at cross purposes with regulatory policies.

In one class of cases, however, regulatory policy can reduce the conflict by using the doctrine of assumption of risk to identify those victims who should not receive compensation because they have made an informed choice, analogous to a contract, to engage in a dangerous activity or use a risky product. Examples are the warnings on cigarette packages and advertisements and the cautionary material supplied with prescription drugs and consumer products at the behest of regulatory agencies. The effectiveness of the warning is ordinarily treated as a regulatory issue to be resolved by the agency. However, even in this case, reform of tort doctrine may be necessary since courts sometimes treat an agency's prior approval of warnings as legally irrelevant to the firm's tort liability.[36]

When a strategy of providing effective information is not possible, uninformed consumers may be injured. Then we need to focus on situations where regulatory policies conflict with a compensation-oriented tort law. Where innocent victims exist, denying compensation to those who formerly could bring damage actions is unjust and unwise. Yet retaining conventional tort actions in the face of regulatory statutes can undermine the behavioral impact of statutes. Other solutions must be found to the problem of providing compensation.

If the victims are numerous and their losses fall into broad, easily identified categories, such as lost limbs or particular types of cancers, then the compensation goal could be served by direct subsidy programs like workers' compensation and the black lung program.[37] In contrast, if the victims are few in number and their problems are idiosyncratic, the law should either permit private rights of action for damages,[38] or allow tort actions under strict liability principles solely as a means of achieving compensation.

CONCLUSIONS

The tort system has shown itself inadequate to deal effectively with problems, like latent cancer risks and attenuated chains of causation, that do not fit easily into traditional tort categories. The innovations that the judiciary has developed to manage class actions and consolidate cases are transforming the courts into quasi-regulatory agencies. Real agencies are likely to perform better than awkward judicial hybrids, which have many of the disadvantages of both forms.

If Congress reforms the regulatory system to rely more heavily on incentives and on performance-based standards, the judicial role should become even more modest. Under incentive schemes requiring firms to pay for the damage they cause, statutes should preempt tort actions in order to avoid overdeterrence. For programs affecting many people, compensation should be effected through a separate system of social insurance. Private lawsuits would be permitted under the statute only to compel regulated entities to comply with existing regulatory standards.

But in policy areas that have not yet been reformed, a limited role remains for tort law or, at least, for private causes of action embedded in statutory schemes. Negligence law can be complementary to command-and-control regulation if it adopts the agency's standard, not just as a minimum, but as the measure of due care. Conversely, a true strict liability regime would obviate the need for a judicial risk–benefit calculation; courts would need only to determine causation. The choice between negligence and strict liability should then depend on how society evaluates the importance of giving victims an incentive to take care versus the distributive effects of initially shifting all losses to injurers. In the absence of any statutory standards, the common law would be a stopgap with no independent legal status once a statute has been passed.

In short, the widespread presumption favoring a vigorous tort system should be replaced with a more comprehensive view of the alternative ways to achieve both deterrence and compensation. Privately initiated lawsuits, brought either under tort principles or under regulatory statutes, should be quite limited and targeted on augmenting regulatory enforcement and responding to unusual situations that would be poorly resolved by broad-based regulations.

9

Constitutional Law
Regulatory Takings

While the economic consequences of the common law are a familiar law and economics topic, constitutional law is a relatively neglected area. Although the basic structure of American government has been of tremendous importance in permitting the development of a capitalist market economy, most constitutional provisions do not lend themselves to straightforward economic interpretation. One exception is the Fifth Amendment to the United States Constitution, which provides that no private property shall be taken for public use without just compensation.[1] To the policy analyst this phrase seems compatible with the view that government should balance benefits against costs. The central policy analytic issues are the efficiency consequences of takings doctrine for private investors and public officials, and the fairness of alternative rules.

The Supreme Court has not adopted a policy analytic approach in resolving takings questions. Instead, it has required compensation when tangible things are appropriated by the government and has refused compensation when the citizen "merely" suffers a diminution in value of his property.[2] Easy cases requiring compensation occur when the government physically invades your property by building a highway through your cornfield or condemning your housesite for use as a public swimming pool. Hard cases, which do not usually generate compensation, arise when a superhighway keeps your gas station intact but provides no exit ramp nearby, or when a sports stadium is built next to your apartment house.[3]

In recent years, as the regulatory impact of the government has grown, a festering issue of takings law has achieved new importance. If a public regulation limits the value of your property, can you sue for compensation? The Supreme Court appears to be reexamining this issue. Thus it seems appropriate to bring a policy analytic perspective to bear since an affirmative answer to this question would have a major effect on the implementation of regulatory statutes.

The Supreme Court's own position is aggressively ad hoc. The Court seems to be inordinately proud of the unprincipled nature of its takings opinions and has reiterated its support for case-by-case balancing in the recent crop of regulatory takings opinions.[4] Thus, Justice Stevens in a 1987 case[5] cites with approval the statement in an earlier case that

> this court has generally "been unable to develop any 'set formula' for determining when 'justice and fairness' require that economic injuries caused by public action be compensated by the government, rather than remain disproportionately concentrated on a few persons." Rather, it has examined the "taking" question by engaging in essentially ad hoc, factual inquiries that have identified several factors—such as the economic impact of the regulation, its interference with reasonable investment backed expectations, and the character of the government action—that have particular significance.[6]

Justice Rehnquist, dissenting in the same case, found nothing to disagree with here: "Admittedly, questions arising under the Just Compensation Clause rest on ad hoc factual inquiries, and must be decided on the facts and circumstances in each case."[7] The only exception to the general support for balancing occurs in a partial dissent by Justices Scalia and O'Connor in another case.[8]

THE PERILS OF CASE-BY-CASE ANALYSIS

The Court's glorification of ad hoc balancing is impossible to reconcile with a policy analytic approach to the takings issue. A fundamental aspect of such an enterprise is a belief in the importance of preserving "investment-backed expectations." Takings law should be predictable, on this view, so that private individuals can confidently commit resources to capital projects.[9] Nevertheless, as many economically oriented writers have argued, no taking can legitimately be claimed if the property owner correctly anticipated that an uncompensated state action was possible and if this belief affected the price paid for the asset.[10] According to Justice Holmes, writing in 1922, some property values "are enjoyed under an implied limitation and must yield to the police power."[11]

If, however, takings jurisprudence is both ad hoc and ex post, investors may have a very difficult time knowing whether a particular predictable state action will or will not be judged to be a taking. Therefore, even if the menu of possible state actions is known and probabilities can be assigned to each policy, investors will not be able to make informed choices because the Court has not given them clear standards to determine when compensation will be paid. [12] The shifting doctrines of takings law introduce an element of uncertainty into investors' choices that has nothing to do with the underlying economics of the situation. This uncertainty creates two problems. First, investors do not know whether or not damages will be paid. Second, in the event damages are not paid, investors will be left bearing the costs of an uninsurable risk. Thus, the Justices need to recognize that the "investment-backed" expectations they discuss are themselves affected by the nature of takings law. To the extent that investors are risk-averse, the very incoherence of the doctrine produces inefficient choices. When legal rules affect behavior, clarity is a value in itself, independent of the actual content of the rule.

The problem of judicially created uncertainty is exacerbated by the ex post nature of court decisions. Judges are reluctant to decide cases until someone has "actually" been harmed. Not only are they reluctant to articulate general principles of takings law, but judges are also unwilling to make general rulings on the status of state actions under individual statutes. Thus, in one recent case Justice Stevens, in discussing an earlier opinion by Justice Holmes, dismisses Holmes's analysis of the general validity of a statute regulating coal mining as an uncharacteristic "advisory opinion."[13] Stevens then goes on to argue that no taking has occurred under the similar Pennsylvania law at issue in the case before the court, because at the time of the lawsuit no coal company could actually demonstrate that it had been harmed. The companies were asking the Court to pass on the general legitimacy of the statute, and this the majority declined to do.[14] Similarly, in another recent case an association of landlords was given standing to challenge a portion of San Jose's rent control ordinance, but their claim that a taking had occurred was dismissed as "premature" because no landlord had actually suffered harm from the disputed provision.[15] Thus, in the field of regulatory takings, where the future direction of the law is unclear, economic actors cannot obtain a prospective ruling from the court on whether a particular law will effect a taking. They must wait until a concrete harm has occurred before the statute can be tested. In the face of this uncertainty investors may forgo otherwise profitable activities, and thus the current state of the law may produce an inefficiently low level of investment.

Investors are not the only ones adversely affected by the incoherence and unpredictability of takings law. Government officials may be affected as well since the vagueness of the doctrine may act as a force for conservatism among public officials. Risk-averse officials facing the possibility of damage suits against their jurisdictions may restrict their activities simply because they dislike uncertainty. As Justice Stevens notes in dissent: "It is no answer to say that '[a]fter all, if a policeman must know the Constitution, then why not a planner?' To begin with, the Court has repeatedly recognized that it, itself cannot establish any objective rules to assess when a regulation becomes a taking. How then can it demand that land planners do any better?"[16]

As the Court moves to reconsider the regulatory takings area, it appears to be developing a jurisprudence that is working against the fundamental goal of the takings clause. The clause is basically an attempt to reconcile an unpredictable, democratically responsible policy with the existence of a capitalist economy based on private property and individual initiative.[17] The ad hoc nature of the law could introduce an element of uncertainty into private investment decisions that could make the coexistence of democracy and private property more, rather than less, difficult.

TOWARD A TAKINGS JURISPRUDENCE

Let us move now from criticism to prescription. If the courts did try to make sense of the takings issue as a general matter, what should they say? The answer has both an efficiency and an equity component. I first outline an efficiency analysis of the takings issue that stresses its impact on both private and public investment and on the distribution of risk in society. The next section considers the role of takings law in enhancing political legitimacy and contributing to the fairness of the distribution of wealth.

As economists have long argued, the distinction between physical and regulatory takings is not meaningful in efficiency terms, and it also has little to recommend it under most ethical theories. Although this distinction retains a hold on the legal mind,[18] the takings jurisprudence outlined below does not begin with that dichotomy as a first principle. The analysis instead provides a general overview of the takings issue.

Efficiency

To begin, one must distinguish between efficient and inefficient compensated takings. The efficiency question has three prongs: (1) the possibility of over- or underinvestment by private individuals (the "private investment" issue); (2) the problem of government-created uncertainty (the "insurance" issue); and (3) the impact of takings doctrine on the decisions of public officials (the "public investment" issue).

The private-investment issue concentrates upon the use the government intends to make of the property. The fundamental distinction is between improvements to property that the government will use and improvements that it will destroy. On this first efficiency ground only the former should be completely compensated. Full compensation in other cases generally will be inefficient, because it will produce overinvestment. If you expect to be fully compensated for a public policy that destroys your property, you will invest too much in the property.[19] Thus, a homeowner should be compensated both when the state takes his home to turn it into a tourist attraction and when the state passes a regulation requiring the homeowner to permit public access to his garden one month a year. On this first rationale, however, he should not be fully compensated for the value of a house that is destroyed to make way for a highway. Under such a compensation system, when the state destroys existing investments, homeowners will behave efficiently when compensation is set between zero and the level of investment that would be efficient in the absence of any compensation for the taking. Leaving aside the insurance issues discussed below, a level of compensation above zero would be required on efficiency grounds only if courts wished to force governments to take into account the opportunity costs of their actions.[20] In such cases the Court would need to judge the efficient level of homeowner investment ex ante given the possibility of future governmental use.

Notice that in this case the compensation decision would depend only on the government's use of the property. This compensation policy is designed solely to produce optimal investment decisions by private owners and government bodies. Both the economic status of the owner and the magnitude of the loss would be irrelevant. Therefore, owners should be compensated for any land use regulation, such as a historical preservation ordinance, when public benefits flow from past investment spending by individuals. Unfortunately, in practice, the probability of compensation is highest in just those areas where overreliance is most likely. If the state destroys your "thing," it usually will be required to pay you for it.[21] In contrast, if it merely uses your assets without taking title to them by, for example, requiring you to comply with historical preservation standards, the state generally will not be required to compensate you.[22] This gives owners of buildings that might in the future be declared landmarks an incentive to tear them down quickly so that the issue will not arise.[23] Economic analysis suggests a rule that is directly opposed to the idea that government should pay only for things that it physically appropriates.

A compensation rule designed to limit overreliance would have the hypothesized behavioral consequences, however, only if government actions are reasonably predictable so that investors can base their decisions on informed predictions about what the government will do in the future. Thus, the compensation rule proposed above should, in principle, be supplemented with a public policy of announcing public actions in advance and by stating at the same time that compensation will be paid only to those in possession of the property at the time of the announcement. Subsequent sales contracts would be required to include clauses explaining the future government action.

A requirement that governments announce their actions in advance, while fine in principle, misconceives the nature of most political processes.[24] At any point in time, a wide range of public policies is possible. Some may be enacted this year, some next year, and others never. Thus, few policies will be wholly unexpected, and none will be completely certain. Nevertheless, takings law should require property owners to make informed guesses and should encourage governments to be as specific as possible about their plans. A rule tying compensation to the date a project is announced would further this goal.

Given the uncertainty that is, I believe, an inherent feature of representative democratic government, the insurance branch of the efficiency analysis becomes of critical importance. The problem of risk spreading, unlike the issue of overinvestment, is tied to the situation of the private owner, independent of the government's use of the property. Because of its contrasting focus, this second efficiency concern produces results that will sometimes conflict with the first. Conflicts can be resolved by deciding whether government is best viewed as a well-organized process with known probabilities attached to possible future actions or as an essentially random and unpredictable enterprise, at least in its impact on particular persons. When the latter view is closest to being correct, compensation may be justified because it acts as a form of insurance. Even if the state is certain to carry out a particular policy, such as building a highway, no one may be able to predict who will be affected adversely, that is, what route will be chosen. If the ex ante probability of being harmed is distributed broadly across the population and if *no* compensation is paid, two different results are possible. On the one hand, if people are risk-neutral, they all rationally cut back their investment just enough to compensate for the risk of expropriation.[25] On the other hand, if people are risk-averse, the uncertainty created by the threat of harm may lead them to underinvest and to hold their assets in a form that is unlikely to be affected by the public program.

Underinvestment would not occur if insurance were available, but the risks discussed here are generally uninsurable in the private market both because of the arbitrary incidence of harm and the problems of moral hazard and adverse selection. Moral hazard occurs when the existence of insurance leads the insured person to take actions that increase the probability or the magnitude of the loss. In this context, it occurs if property owners secretly lobby to have their property taken or at least do not actively oppose a policy that will produce that result. While such lobbying is possible when the government pays compensation itself, the obvious budgetary consequences of such behavior will help to check abuses. Adverse selection occurs if insurance companies cannot adequately sort property owners into risk classes. Then high-risk and low-risk owners are charged the same rate, so that very low-risk owners may decide to self-insure. The remaining pool of insured owners is now riskier, and premiums must rise. Now the remaining low-risk owners may opt out of the pool. If the insurance companies have less information about risks than property owners, profitable insurance contracts may be impossible to write.[26]

Therefore, when government creates risks for which private insurance is unavailable, efficient risk distribution provides an economically oriented reason for basing the compensation decision on the magnitude of the harm suffered. In considering the degree of harm, courts must decide what standard of comparison to use. For example, should they define the plaintiff's property as the coal that cannot be mined because of a regulatory statute so that 100 percent of it has been taken, or as the firm's entire mining operation, so that only a small share has been lost?[27] A generally accepted rule of thumb is that individuals behave in a risk-averse way when a major portion of their total wealth is threatened. Since owner-occupied housing represents a large proportion of most owners' personal wealth, government should compensate homeowners when it takes their houses either through physical confiscation or through a regulation that makes them uninhabitable.[28] Conversely, if it confiscates their toasters or passes an ordinance making them unusable, no compensation would need to be paid on risk-spreading grounds. In short, the standard of comparison should be the individual's total wealth, not just the property "affected" by the taking. In contrast, broadly held corporations should be viewed as risk-neutral, even toward large losses, because shareholders and other investors can insure by holding a diversified portfolio of investments. Compensation might, however, be provided to employees and owners of specialized assets if either group will suffer large declines in permanent income or wealth relative to their expectations in the absence of the public program. The courts should develop some simple rules of thumb that, while not perfectly adapted to all the individual situations that arise, will nevertheless provide insurance protection to most of those who would demand it.

The final element in an efficiency analysis concerns the impact of takings law on the calculations of public officials. The compensation requirement can be understood as a way to force public policymakers to consider the opportunity costs of their proposed actions. Policies that "take" private property would then have concrete budgetary impacts that would be immediately reflected in tax bills or borrowing capacity. The efficiency consequences of a comprehensive compensation requirement depend upon one's view of the way government policy is made. If cost-benefit tests are used, actual compensation is not required since the analyst can be expected to take into account all costs and benefits, not just those that show up in the budget. Efficient takings rules can depend entirely upon the impact of compensation on the behavior of private individuals. Conversely, if decisionmakers are imperfect agents of the public, compensation requirements may have little impact on their choices, because the required payments come from taxpayers, not from the decisionmakers' own pockets. Once again, but for very different reasons, takings rules can be structured to focus on affecting the investments of private individuals. In contrast, if public choices are the result of the competition of various groups for political benefits, powerful groups will not need a constitutionally mandated takings doctrine in order to preserve their interests. They will be able to insist that the overall legislative package be beneficial to them. Left out of this account, however, are politically ineffective individuals severely harmed by some public policy. Efficiency requires that their costs be taken into account; yet the operation of the political process may not incorporate these costs. Under this view of the political system, compensation should be paid for these losses to force politicians to recognize their existence.[29]

Therefore, since government policymaking can, at least sometimes, be characterized as a struggle between organized groups,[30] takings law should consider whether the affected individuals suffer special difficulties in having their interests taken seriously by the political process. The takings clause, however, is unlikely to be an effective means of equalizing the power of various population groups. It can be most effective as a way to protect the property interests of unorganized individuals with nothing in common except that they would otherwise bear the costs of some public policy.

Thus, an efficient takings doctrine should not be primarily concerned with the impact of the doctrine on the calculations of public officials. Instead, except for special claims advanced by the politically weak, the emphasis should be on encouraging efficient actions by private property owners. This perspective produces the following rough guide to deciding cases. Always compensate for property that will be used by government in the form in which it is provided by the owner. In other cases, compensate when the asset represents a major proportion of the owner's wealth so that a hypothesis of risk-aversion is plausible. Employ a presumption in favor of risk-aversion for individuals and risk-neutrality for publicly held corporations. In addition, compensate even risk-neutral individuals whose loss represents a large proportion of their wealth if these individuals are politically ineffective.

To counteract the moral hazard created by compensation, courts should develop a notion close to the requirement to mitigate damages in contract law.[31] When government appropriation becomes likely, owners should be reimbursed only for new investments that either can be used by the government or would be rational if no compensation were to be paid. To minimize the private burden of this last provision, employ a presumption in favor of the private property owner with burden of proof on the government to show both that it has given notice and that the investment was excessive.

Political Legitimacy and Fairness

Efficiency is not the whole story in analyzing the takings doctrine. When public policies are uncertain and have unpredictable impacts on small groups in the population, the legitimacy of the state may depend upon the payment of compensation to mitigate the arbitrary distributive consequences of many public policies.[32] Citizens whose assets have been taken are unlikely to be satisfied with the argument that the system is fair ex ante. Compensation is then a substitute for imposing severe restrictions on the substance of public policies or the degree of consent required. Thus, the Court has interpreted the Fifth Amendment as designed to prevent

> the public from loading upon one individual more than his just
> share of the burdens of government, and says that when he surren-
> ders to the public something more and different from that which is
> exacted from other members of the public, a full and just equivalent
> shall be returned to him.[33]

Similarly, Justice Scalia, in finding that a taking had occurred in a case involving California beachfront owners, argues that even if the California government's policy is sound, it does not follow that coastal residents "can be compelled to contribute to its realization . . . if [the California Coastal Commission] wants an easement across [their] property, it must pay for it."[34]

However, the United States Constitution, in permitting policies to be adopted by majority votes in representative assemblies and approved by the President, did not contemplate that all statutes would meet with unanimous approval. Some people would suffer losses while others benefited. The status quo is not given the deeply privileged position that it would have under an unanimity rule. "[G]overnment could not exist if a citizen had the unfettered right to use property."[35] Therefore, since some losses can be imposed constitutionally, the problem for takings jurisprudence is to decide when an individual has borne more than his or her "just share of the burdens of government."[36] This is a question that should be taken up in a self-conscious way by the Court.[37] While a comprehensive theory of the takings clause cannot be developed here, I can nevertheless isolate three situations in which compensation should *not* be paid.

The first issue is the specification of the property entitlement itself.[38] Compensation should not be paid when the complainant cannot legitimately claim to be entitled to the benefits that are lost when the government acts.[39] For example, courts have found that individuals do not have the right to create a nuisance. Thus, if the state imposes regulations or confiscates a nuisance, the owner has no right to claim compensation. Nothing has been taken that the individual had a right to claim as his own. The classic statement is in *Mugler v. Kansas*: "All property in this country is held under the implied obligation that the owner's use of it shall not be injurious to the community."[40] Citing *Mugler* with approval, a recent opinion states that the Court hesitates "to find a taking when the state merely restrains uses of property that are tantamount to public nuisances."[41]

The difficulty with this doctrine is twofold. First, Ronald Coase has shown that in a two-sided controversy it is not straightforward to decide who "caused" the harm.[42] Second, this doctrine may tie the regulatory state too closely to doctrines of the common law that may be obsolete in particular regulatory situations. This compensation rule makes some types of regulatory programs much more expensive than others. In practice, however, courts seem not to have limited themselves to common law nuisances. The *Mugler* case itself dealt with brewery property made valueless by a Kansas constitutional amendment prohibiting the manufacture and sale of intoxicating liquors, and the opinion's language is quite broad:

> The power which the States have of prohibiting such use by individuals of their property as will be prejudicial to the health, the morals, or the safety of the public is not—and, consistently with the existence and safety of organized society cannot be—burdened with the condition that the State must compensate such individual owners for pecuniary losses they may sustain, by reason of their not being permitted, by a noxious use of their property, to inflict injury upon the community.[43]

Justice Stevens quotes this statement twice in recent cases, once in a majority opinion[44] and the second time in dissent.[45] Justice Rehnquist, however, would read the nuisance exception quite narrowly to accord more closely with common law doctrine. He argues that "the nuisance exception to the taking guarantee is not coterminous with the police power itself."[46] It is instead a "narrow exception allowing the government to prevent 'a misuse or illegal use.' "[47] A similar contrast in views is evident in *Nollan v. California Coastal Comm.* Justice Scalia argues that the state has taken an "essential stick in the bundle of rights," while Justice Brennan finds that the owners have no legitimate claim.[48] These different views of the content of legitimate property entitlements imply that prior to any resolution of the takings issue the Court must resolve fundamental questions concerning the nature of property.[49] These questions should be resolved without giving a canonical status to common law jurisprudence.

Second, the state should be authorized to appropriate excess profits. This principle, implicit in antitrust law,[50] provides a justification for the Supreme Court's refusal to find a taking when the State of Pennsylvania regulated underground coal mines. The Court found that all mines would continue to operate and that the losses would not be severe.[51] This finding, if correct, implies that the companies were earning excess profits that could be used to pay for the regulation without causing anyone to go out of business. This standard also supports Brennan's dissent in *Nollan.* He argues that the property owners "can make no tenable claim that either their enjoyment of their property or its value is diminished by the public's ability merely to pass and re-pass a few feet closer to the seawall beyond which appellants' house is located."[52] Thus, the appellants' claim could be viewed as an attempt to extract rents from their exclusive control of a piece of beach needed for convenient access between two public beaches. Under this view, they do not deserve compensation, because they had no right to these economic rents. Finally, in a challenge to rent control in San Jose, the Court reiterates previous decisions finding that the monopoly power of private business provides a justification for public action that lowers these returns.[53]

Third, compensation should not be paid if the government action is analogous to a private action that is seen as one of the risks of economic life. For example, if the government competes with a private business, this should not produce a takings claim, because competitive losses do not give rise to damage claims in the private sector. These losses, labeled pecuniary externalities by economists, do not have the adverse efficiency consequences of externalities that arise when individuals use scarce resources for which they do not pay. The distributive consequences produced by market pressures are a cost of maintaining the incentives needed to make markets work efficiently. Thus, if the government sells surplus military supplies, it should not compensate private firms selling competing products. Similarly, the Tennessee Valley Authority should not have to compensate competing power companies for lost business. Finally, a regulation that is cheaper for one firm to comply with than another should not give rise to a compensation claim from the disadvantaged firm.

CONCLUSIONS

While this chapter provides no full-fledged answer to the takings question, my main message is that such an effort is sorely needed. While the Court can try for a principled resolution, this is one legal area in which almost any consistent, publicly articulated approach is better than none. Clear statement, even if not backed by clear thinking, will do much to preserve the investment-backed expectations the Court talks so much about. Clear thinking would be even better, and here I have provided only a rough guide. My outline, however, illustrates how the federal courts might employ the tools of policy analysis and social choice to enlighten a thorny constitutional issue. The suggestions based on efficiency, equity and political legitimacy must, however, be supplemented with an understanding of just what it is that people can be said to own. In attempting to answer that question, historically generated expectations may need to be preserved for the sake of fairness, but they should not straitjacket our thinking about the future.

BUILDING
ON THE EIGHTIES
*A Progressive
Response to Reaganism*

The Reagan administration shared some common aims with progressive reformers. Economists from all parts of the political spectrum have long urged greater reliance on market tests in regulation, have recommended the dismantling of some regulatory systems to enhance competition, have sought to tap the energies of private enterprise in the provision of public services, and have urged an efficient division of tasks between levels of government. Policy analysts interested in structural change and in maximizing the net benefits of public programs entered the Reagan administration with considerable hope that progress was possible. After all, the President had committed himself to regulatory reform and to a rethinking of the relationship between the federal government and both lower-level governments and private firms.

In spite of the initial promise, conscientious and thoughtful reform was sacrificed to rhetoric and to a singleminded preoccupation with reducing the size of the federal government's domestic programs. More nuanced analytic perspectives were seldom successful. Exceptions to the concentration on budget reduction were usually attempts to gain political advantage.

Reagan's advisers did, however, undoubtedly locate key problems with modern government when they emphasized deregulation, decentralization, and privatization as the triad of issues central to modern efforts to restructure government. My aim in this section of the book is to take these categories seriously, outline the failures of the past administration, and propose a principled framework within which to analyze reform proposals.

10

Deregulation

Deregulation was an article of faith for many policymakers in the Reagan administration. They saw their political mandate as a crusade to get the government "off the backs" of the people so that the benefits of free enterprise could flourish.[1] The Ford and Carter administrations and the Congress provided the momentum with legislation that moved toward the deregulation of air travel, intercity trucking, railroads, and banking and financial services.[2] The Reagan rhetoric was, however, more sweeping and less nuanced than that of its predecessors. Earlier officials had sought regulatory *reform*—revising regulations and statutes to improve their effectiveness and removing those which lacked a strong policy justification.[3] Reagan policymakers, in contrast, favored regulatory *relief*—reducing the "burden" of both economic and "social" regulation[4] on consumers and businesses.[5] Without a careful assessment of the causes of ineffective regulation, they began with a presumption that government was lumbering, cumbersome, and even corrupt so that the burden of proof on anyone making a proposal for government intervention was very high.[6]

In spite of such rhetoric, the last administration did not succeed in dismembering the regulatory state. No major regulatory legislation was repealed,[7] and in the latter portion of Reagan's tenure an important regulatory statute was strengthened, and others were reauthorized.[8] In 1983 the White House formally terminated its regulatory relief program.[9] Although the administration claimed to be shifting its emphasis from reducing the burden of administrative regulations to the overall reform of the principal regulatory statutes, its efforts were concentrated on economic regulation, and largely ignored social regulation.[10]

The administration's approach to social regulation was more subtle and may ultimately turn out to have been more destructive than a straightforward attempt at statutory reform. Its strategy was to encourage inaction by regulatory agencies that imposed costs on business and to encourage quick and politically salient actions by agencies that had favors to bestow. This was done by appointing people committed to supporting Reagan's ideology even if they were not well informed about the programs of the agencies in which they served,[11] and if such people were unavailable, by failing to appoint people to fill key regulatory positions.[12] It was also furthered by simply not initiating many major rulemaking proceedings except those required by the courts,[13] and by downgrading enforcement activities.[14] These actions fueled the claims of those wishing to discredit the regulatory policies of the administration and made efforts at constructive reform suspect as well. "Regulatory reform" was taken by critics to be a code word for selling out to business.[15]

The polarization between Reagan loyalists seeking to dismantle the regulatory state and critics wishing to discredit the administration is unfortunate. Given the deep flaws in most regulatory statutes, even those which seek to correct obvious and important market failures, informed debate is required, not name-calling. It is no answer to the imperfections of the Clean Air Act[16] simply to repeal the act. Amendment of existing statutes and changes in the practices of regulatory agencies can, in principle, bring regulatory policy closer to the ideal of an economically efficient program.[17] Some of the policies of the Reagan administration could, in fact, be part of such a progressive reform of administrative law. Regrettably, critics have lumped them with other initiatives directed in a simplistic way toward reducing the influence of government on the economy.[18] The Reagan administration invited such criticism by administering its purported regulatory reforms in a way that left the White House open to the charge of selling out to special interests.[19]

Four different types of action and inaction pushed regulatory policy in a retrograde direction in the last decade. First, the White House attempted to impose rationality and coordination on executive branch regulatory agencies in a way that invited criticisms of undue political influence. Second, by assuming that deregulation was per se desirable, policymakers neglected to observe that deregulation of one set of industry practices might increase the need to regulate other aspects of behavior. Third, in areas of social regulation, such as environmental policy and occupational health and safety regulation, where the underlying statutory purposes are popular, the administration shied away from genuine incentive-based reforms. Finally, even in its own terms of reducing regulatory burdens, the administration failed to the extent that agencies were poorly run with unqualified appointees, vacant posts, and key decisions not made.

WHITE HOUSE OVERSIGHT

The first difficulty arose in the context of White House oversight attempts. Early in the Reagan administration the President issued an Executive Order that required Cabinet-level departments to prepare cost-benefit analyses justifying major rules. These analyses would be scrutinized by the newly established Office of Information and Regulatory Affairs within the Office of Management and Budget (OMB) in the White House and approved or returned to the agency for revision.[20] In 1985 the White House issued a second Executive Order requiring these same agencies to submit a regulatory plan detailing the agency's priorities for the next fiscal year and reporting regulatory actions taken.[21] This assertion of White House involvement in agency rulemaking was not an entirely new initiative. Similar programs were carried out in the Ford and Carter administrations.[22] The Reagan plan, however, was more secret, more centralized in the White House, and did not provide for public input or for public reports from OMB.[23] From the beginning the goals of the first executive order were confused: was it designed to produce better, more well-thought-out regulations and improve interagency coordination, or was it set up to give the White House more political control over regulatory programs?[24] Accusations of undue political influence were countered by technocratic arguments about the merits and demerits of particular rules, by data showing that few rules were delayed, and by revisions in OMB practices to provide for a more open, accountable process.[25] Even if the claims of political influence were overdrawn,[26] one can, nevertheless, be concerned that the appearance of politicization can be used to discredit all attempts to introduce more rationality and consistency into the regulatory process.[27]

In spite of doubts about the effectiveness of the oversight process even on its own terms, the OMB staff appears to have frequently pointed out serious deficiencies in individual regulations, and the quality of staff work seems to have been quite high.[28] The earnestness and professional commitment of the staff is well reflected in the memo prepared by a staff member, entitled "Regulatory Impact Analysis Guidance," which was designed to help agency bureaucrats responsibly comply with the order.[29]

To those in the policy analysis community committed to the proposition that regulators should consider all of the effects of their policies, the aims of the Order appear laudable. [30] Agencies, focusing only on the benefits expected to flow from the statutes they administer, may avoid the hard work of assessing costs. While definitive cost-benefit analyses will frequently be impossible, and, while concerns with distributive consequences and fair process are also often important, I have already argued that a well-focused attempt to assess social costs as well as benefits should be part of regulatory policymaking. [31] Such efforts do not represent a sellout to business. Many of the costs nominally imposed on business end up being reflected in prices and wages. Reductions in profits affect long-term investment decisions and the overall mix of goods and services in the economy. An assessment of these costs should be as much a part of a regulatory analysis as the benefits. Recognition of these costs does not, however, imply an unwillingness to tolerate them. If an industry has been imposing environmental costs on society for free, it should pay for them. Costs can be taken into account without giving them undue weight.

In an adversarial atmosphere with a Democratic Congress and a Republican President, however, the long-run result of the Executive Orders may be harmful. Convinced that the White House was not attempting a responsible analysis but was simply trying to cater to business and to delay all regulations, [32] Congress may counterattack by writing laws with strict deadlines. While deadlines are routinely violated by all regulatory agencies in all administrations, [33] the courts do take such deadlines seriously. [34] In dicta a Federal District Court judge declared that OMB

> has no authority to use its regulatory review . . . to delay promulgation of EPA regulations arising from the 1984 Amendments of the RCRA [Resource Conservation and Recovery Act] beyond the date of a statutory deadline. Thus, if a deadline already has expired, OMB has no authority to delay regulations subject to the deadline in order to review them under the executive order. If the deadline is about to expire, OMB may review the regulations only until the time at which OMB review will result in the deadline being missed. [35]

If this judicial assertion is followed, Congress has a convenient way to emasculate OMB review. It simply writes a statute with very tight deadlines and relies on the agency to meet the statutory schedule with no time left for OMB review. Such deadlines are already common. The RCRA amendments at issue in the preceding case contain forty-four deadlines, twenty-nine to be satisfied within twenty months of the 1986 case. [36] The result can be hurried and poorly researched standards—a worse result than a statute with more permissive deadlines and OMB review. The final irony of Congressional attempts to hurry up rulemaking and prevent

OMB oversight may be successful court challenges on the ground that the rules are arbitrary and capricious.[37]

THE REGULATION OF DEREGULATED MARKETS

The major deregulatory successes of the Eighties occurred in industries that do not share the natural monopoly characteristics of traditional public utilities. The phasing out of price, entry, and quality regulation in industries ranging from airlines to stock brokerage to telecommunications has markedly increased competition in the deregulated sectors.[38] While most of these deregulatory efforts began before Reagan took office and involved Congressional action, Reagan officials did actively support these efforts and made marginal contributions to their implementation.[39]

Unfortunately, however, the deregulation of these "structurally competitive industries,"[40] was accompanied by a failure of vision. The problems are not the ones emphasized by the popular press. The mere fact that some airlines and banks have gone out of business and some cities are served by fewer air carriers and financial institutions than before deregulation does not imply policy failure.[41] One must distinguish the inevitable costs of life in a competitive market, where firms are permitted to fail in the interest of maintaining efficiency,[42] from genuine market imperfections that may become more important when firms are given more freedom of action. The response to such issues should not be a return to the regulatory patterns of the past, but a careful attempt to isolate the remaining sources of market failure and regulate them effectively.

Deregulation of one area of the economy may itself produce the need for more regulation somewhere else. In moving toward a more competitive situation in one dimension, bottlenecks and market imperfections in other dimensions may become newly relevant. The Reagan administration poorly incorporated this lesson into its deregulatory efforts.

Consider airline deregulation, for example. An increase in flights and congestion generated by competition on some routes has placed additional strains on the systems regulating airline safety and allocating space in airports.[43] In both safety and airport management there are strong economic arguments for a public sector role, and these arguments are stronger the *more* deregulation of routes and fares increases air travel.[44] The Federal Aviation Administration requires more resources for inspectors and air traffic controllers, and the construction of airport capacity is a public works issue of central importance, not just to the citizens of the city involved, but also to those affected by flights in and out.[45] Similarly, deregulation may require more diligent government efforts to enforce the antitrust laws and to protect consumers from misrepresentation and "violations of implicit contracts."[46] Both types of government intervention may be required to deal with examples of monopoly pricing on thin routes and complaints of "lost baggage, misleading scheduling, last minute cancellations of flights with few bookings, involuntary bumping of passengers on overbooked flights, and severe delays."[47] Unfortunately, the Reagan administration essentially ignored these problems and focused instead on simply defending airline deregulation against its critics.[48]

As a second example, consider the deregulation of financial institutions, which has permitted much diversification by banks and other financial service companies.[49] In the banking and savings and loans industries no changes in the deposit insurance system accompanied the loosening of constraints on loan portfolios. With more and riskier investment possibilities available after deregulation, the need for public monitoring increased.[50] However, at least in the savings and loan industry, the opposite appears to have occurred. In keeping with the deregulatory spirit of the times, budgets and personnel did not keep pace with the growth in industry assets.[51] As two policy analysts at the Federal Home Loan Bank have written:

> A private insurer implements immediate changes when faced with an important structural event. First, it collects data to determine if the actuarial basis for its pricing system needs to be changed; then if it remains profitable, it offers insurance. Second, it examines the behavior of those insured to determine if insurance should be limited or denied. Third, the insured are segmented by risk characteristics, with the deductible and premium established for each segment.
>
> The federal deposit insurers took none of these actions when faced with the deregulation of the institutions whose deposits they insured. In fact, in some important ways, the federal insurers took actions directly opposite to those that would have been taken by a private insurer. By not instituting practices more similar to those of private insurers, the guarantee aspect of federal deposit insurance became more important.[52]

By the end of the Reagan administration even the economists on the President's Council of Economic Advisers recognized the importance of this problem. The advisers' last report called for reform of banking regulation and oversight in response to previous deregulation efforts. They supported reform of the deposit insurance system and a redefinition of "the appropriate sphere of competition for depository institutions."[53] Unfortunately, nothing could be done at that point to prevent the costly accounting for past mistakes.

In short, deregulation in one area often requires new regulation and oversight somewhere else. Failure to see this point expresses a rigid ideology in which capitalist symbolism is elevated above the substance of ensuring a more efficiently operating economy.

INCENTIVE-BASED SYSTEMS

The Reagan administration also failed to reform the system of social regulation. The administration introduced no systematic reforms in the areas of environmental law or health and safety regulation.

Too often liberals view incentive schemes, which use prices or subsidies as part of a regulatory plan, as deregulatory and therefore suspect.[54] Thus one might have hoped in 1981 that an administration inoculated against liberal skepticism about such rhetoric might have sought to introduce incentive-based elements into the regulation of environmental and product quality.[55] Yet this did not happen. Some limited attempts at reform were made at the Environmental Protection Agency[56] and the Federal Communications Commission,[57] but the mood was deregulatory, not reformist. One explanation may be that incentive systems require regulated firms to pay for the damage they do. Therefore, the very firms that praise the virtues of the market in other contexts may oppose these reform proposals.

Nevertheless, such marketlike schemes are essential for the cost-effective achievement of statutory goals. In such areas as pollution of the air and the water, market tests and efficiency imply regulation, not deregulation. The use of financial incentives may mean that higher levels of cleanup are possible than with command-and-control regulation. Such schemes could produce genuine reform, not a sellout to the regulated firms. Efficient regulation implies a concern for both costs and benefits; it does not imply less regulation.[58]

With its support of the pollution rights scheme included in the 1990 amendments to the Clean Air Act, the Bush administration appears to be moving in a progressive direction. However, the new pollution rights provisions that apply to sulfur dioxide emissions are marred by their grant of free discharge rights to existing discharges.[59] While this distribution should, in principle, have no impact on the ultimate pattern of pollution loads—high-cost polluters will buy rights from low-cost pollutors—it provides a windfall to existing dischargers that cannot be justified on the grounds of distributive justice. Since such an allocation plan has the obvious advantage of dampening the opposition of dischargers, it presents a clear conflict between equity and political expediency.

Other proposals have been made to pay workers to accept personal protective devices, to charge firms an "injury tax," to sell rights to the microwave spectrum, to tax gasoline on the basis of its pollution content, to auction landing slots at congested airports, and to permit auctions for the right to such natural monopolies as cable television franchises.[60] Economists have developed schemes to determine the level of public goods through demand-revealing mechanisms and have applied them in some limited contexts such as the choice of television programs for public television stations.[61] Some of these ideas are not operational at present, while others have been used in limited contexts. Nevertheless, political support for incentive schemes seems to be higher than ever before, and proposals that were made by economists twenty or even thirty years ago are suddenly being viewed as dramatic new developments.[62] While we should avoid jumping uncritically on the bandwagon, I believe that a sober evaluation of these proposals would show that many of them are promising and can be made operational. In a world of tight budgets and opposition to general tax increases, fee schemes have undoubted appeal.[63] The Reagan administration has, at least, performed the function of placing these ideas on the agenda.

DEREGULATION AND THE BUSINESS COMMUNITY

A final failure of the Reagan administration is filled with irony. The administration often failed even in its perception of what was best for the business community. Accepting the inevitability of regulation and wanting some clarity and certainty in their environment, business leaders sometimes pressed recalcitrant agencies to promulgate regulations.

A federal government that has hobbled itself by cutbacks in regulatory budgets and personnel[64] is unable to respond expeditiously to business calls for clarity and uniformity. It seems simply a mistake to suppose that business wants regulatory agencies to run poorly. They might wish the laws off the books, or at least amended, but given their reality, I would suppose that firms, in general, favor competent administration.[65]

Business may, of course, benefit from efforts by regulatory agencies to repeal or revise existing rules. However, if an agency acts in a rushed and careless manner, its efforts may not be upheld by the courts. The most important example of this was the Reagan administration's effort to repeal the passive restraint standard for automobiles without a careful analysis of alternatives. The Supreme Court turned back this initiative, with even the most conservative members of the Court supporting the basic requirement that obviously relevant options be considered.[66] Countering this decision were two other Supreme Court cases giving agencies discretion to overrule a previous administration's interpretation of a statute and upholding an agency's power to determine its own enforcement agenda.[67] Nevertheless, the lesson of these cases, taken together, seems to be that regulatory reform within agencies can succeed only if officials articulate a principled justification based on an understanding of the facts.[68] Simple inattention can reduce the pages in the *Federal Register*,[69] but genuine reform requires expertise and commitment.

While the business community as a whole may prefer competence and clarity, an individual firm or industry may in a particular instance benefit from the inattention and incompetence of a regulatory agency. Cases are beginning to reach the courts in which firms use the understaffing or inattention of an agency as an argument for delaying compliance with some public rule or order. The courts have been unsympathetic to such excuses, giving firms yet another reason not to support ineffective agencies. For example, in a case involving OSHA Judge Posner refused to allow the absence of a quorum on the Occupational Safety and Health Review Commission to generate a remand to that body now that an appointment had been made. The Commission had only one member out of three at the time of the original appeal. Posner was unwilling to allow the administration's slowness in appointing commissioners to permit a firm to reap a benefit.[70]

CONCLUSIONS

What lessons for regulatory reform can we learn from the Reagan experience? Each failure should be seen in the context of the political-economic justifications for reform. First, efforts to review agency rulemaking and priority setting and to coordinate overlapping statutes can improve the performance of government. Yet the Reagan experience teaches that no matter how competent and objective the technocrats charged with these tasks are, if they are not isolated from political pressures the entire effort will lack credibility. If, in addition, the reviewing office has inadequate resources and personnel, it will be open to criticism for superficiality as well.

Second, even when deregulatory policies have a strong efficiency justification, simply repealing existing statutes is unlikely to be sufficient. Genuine market failures that were hidden or controlled by a comprehensive regulatory statute may now surface. The government may need to engage in such activities as increased antitrust surveillance, as in airlines, or monitoring, as in bank lending. It may need to spend more on complementary public services such as traffic control, safety, and airports in the case of airline deregulation.

Third, reforms that promote economic efficiency are not the same thing as reforms that favor business. Requiring firms to pay for pollution cannot be expected to garner much business support. Yet incentive-based schemes promise considerable social cost savings. They need to be developed and justified as effective policy tools, not as sellouts to corporate America. Finally, the incompetence and bias of some Reagan regulatory appointees demonstrated the value of competence even to those who would have preferred repeal of the basic law. Many regulatory problems, especially in the area of social regulation, are genuinely complex. Expertise cannot be avoided. Ideology is not a substitute for knowledge and energy.

11

Decentralization

I n his first inaugural address President Reagan declared:

It is my intention to curb the size and influence of the federal establishment and to demand recognition of the distinction between the
powers granted to the federal government, [and] those reserved to
the states or to the people.[1]

During the President's second term he issued an Executive Order reiter-
ating a commitment to federalism. The White House stated:

The nature of our constitutional system encourages a healthy diversity in the public policies adopted by the people of the several States
according to their own needs and desires. In the search for enlight-
ened public policy, individual States and communities are free to
experiment with a variety of approaches to public issues. . . . Un-
certainties regarding the legitimate authority of the national government should be resolved against regulation at the national level.[2]

The administration's rhetoric, however, was not accompanied by sustained efforts to repeal laws that preempt or supplement state initiatives.[3]
The first year of Reagan's presidency saw the successful consolidation of
numerous spending programs into a series of block grants. In subsequent
years, however, the administration implemented the "new" federalism,
not through the legislative route, but by cutting funds and freezing budgets in health, housing, and other social welfare areas;[4] by failing to issue
regulations; and by increasing the pace of formal delegation and relaxing
federal oversight of state implementation of environmental and health
and safety laws.[5] Cuts in federal grant assistance to state regulators ac-

companied the increased emphasis on state-level implementation.[6] In contrast, other policies worked against decentralization by preempting state government regulations and mandating lower-level governments to act in particular ways.

The Reagan administration is not the place to look for a thoughtful analysis of federalism and intergovernmental relations. Its inability to defend its own initiatives in a principled way has bred suspicion of policies to "rationalize" the intergovernmental system. Yet a principled analysis is required to understand and critically evaluate the division of authority across levels of government and the foundations of cooperative federalism. Both politics and economics are central to this task. Assessments of the relative political power of groups at the local, state, and national levels must complement economic work on the efficient division of authority and the role of intergovernmental grants. The most important puzzle involves the benefits and costs of interstate diversity and competition. After discussing the relatively straightforward problems of interjurisdictional externalities, administrative costs, and citizen participation, I shall concentrate on sorting out the vexing cross-currents arising from intergovernmental competition for residents and business investments.

REAGANISM AND FEDERALISM

The Reagan administration had a simple philosophy, which guided its efforts to decentralize government. Like deregulation, decentralization was justified as a way to limit the influence of government. With the exception of national defense, government was too large and too intrusive. Not only was spending too high, but regulations were too bothersome and constraining. The worst offender was the federal government, but less spending and regulating at the state and local level was also desirable. Thus the Administration's goal was not so much devolution per se as it was an overall reduction in public spending and regulatory activity achieved through the mechanism of devolution.[7]

First, consider spending. Federal grants-in-aid to state and local governments as a percentage of the federal budget reached a peak in 1978, two years before Reagan took office. In fiscal year 1978 grants to state and local governments totaled almost $78 billion dollars, which amounted to 17 percent of total federal outlays, 26.5 percent of state and local outlays, and 3.6 percent of GNP.[8] By 1988 the level had fallen to 10.8 percent of federal outlays, 18.2 percent of state and local outlays, and 2.4 percent of GNP, a shift that represented a return to 1970 levels.[9] The largest spending reductions were in community and economic development, education, social services, and employment and training.[10] While a decline could have been expected no matter who occupied the presidency, and while some observers feel that the magnitude of the cuts has been exaggerated,[11] the extent and nature of the cuts does seem related to the presence of Reagan in the White House.

In spite of the spending cuts, few intergovernmental programs were actually terminated, although seventy-seven were consolidated in 1981 into nine block grants.[12] After 1981, no bold strokes were taken. In 1982 the administration proposed an intergovernmental swap in which the federal government would take over Medicaid while the states accepted responsibility for welfare, food stamps, and numerous other smaller programs. This proposal, lacking a principled justification, died amid criticism that it was designed principally as a way to reduce federal spending.[13]

Subsequent to the abandonment of the "swap" plan, nothing much happened on the fiscal federalism front. A working group of the Domestic Policy Council did issue a report in 1986 calling for limits "on the national government's ability to invade the sovereign authority of the States,"[14] and an Executive Order required agencies to consider the federalism implications of their actions,[15] but neither of these actions appears to have had much concrete impact. The administration continued to seek to hold the line on spending, but no attempt was made to rationalize the system of intergovernmental grants.[16] The pattern was similar to the deregulation effort—an early burst of effort followed by inaction designed to limit spending.

Second, the Reagan administration's push to deregulate applied to intergovernmental programs as much as it did to regulation at the national level. The federal government aimed to reduce both its oversight of lower-level governments themselves and its monitoring of the federal regulatory programs administered by state agencies. In both cases, however, the administration ran up against countervailing pressures, which pushed it toward increased control of state and local governments and the preemption of state initiatives.

Consider, first, federal regulation of state programs. The move to block grants implied a reduction in federal oversight of the details of state spending. For example, under the education block grant 667 pages of regulations were replaced with twenty pages.[17] The Office of Management and Budget estimated that the 1981 block grants saved state and local governments 5.9 million hours of work.[18] Yet the administration was inconsistent. The program with the least oversight, General Revenue Sharing, was disliked by the Reagan administration and was eventually canceled at the President's urging. The Revenue Sharing program died in

1986, the same year in which the deductibility of several state and local taxes was also eliminated.[19]

The presidency's inconsistency went even farther. One might have supposed that the most objectionable federal regulations for Reaganites would be those that simply mandated lower-level governments to do something without providing the funds. For states and localities mandates are easily the most disliked form of federal intervention. Yet in times of budgetary stringency such programs are obviously tempting even to those otherwise committed to encouraging decentralization. Congress and the president can claim to be solving a national problem without spending money on it and without creating a new federal bureaucracy. In spite of the administration's commitment to decentralization, it did give in to this temptation in a number of cases. According to a General Accounting Office study, "state and local governments became subject to hundreds of new program standards and administrative requirements" during the Eighties.[20]

As for federal regulatory programs administered by state governments, these activities experienced reductions in federal financial support. One way in which such cuts can be made tolerable is, of course, to fail to monitor state enforcement of the law. The federal government can still claim credit for supporting a strict law and then blame the lower-level governments for laxity. Something like this may have occurred in the environmental and health and safety areas, although the data are sketchy.[21] The very sketchiness of the data is, however, suggestive since if you do not want the outside world to review your behavior, one way to accomplish this goal is to fail to give your critics information. One of the "accomplishments" of the Gorsuch period at the EPA was the virtual elimination of the backlog of State Implementation Plans awaiting approval under the Clean Air Act.[22] The very speed with which the state plans were approved suggests, not that bureaucrats had suddenly become extremely efficient, but that they had been instructed to be extremely deferential. Perhaps this was the way to promote good policy, but one cannot infer that simply from the rapid reduction of the backlog.

When concerned citizens can observe lax enforcement and sue under statutory citizen suit provisions, they can cause political difficulties for state governments.[23] These difficulties were exacerbated by the reduction in federal regulatory personnel and budgets. With no change in the substantive law, state governments bore a greater regulatory burden.

The administration did not always favor the devolution of regulatory authority to the states. When the wish to decentralize government conflicted with the wish to benefit industry, industry frequently won support for centralized regulation. The Reaganite belief that a decentralized government would also have a smaller impact on society was based on faulty logic. Organized groups, unable to prevail at the national level, turned to the states.[24] The idea that states in competition with each other for business investment would cut back on regulations often proved false. Instead, if the central government is inactive, state and local governments may step in to fill the gaps. This can produce a multitude of different rules, which are costly for national firms selling and producing in many markets. Such regulations may be explicitly designed to favor locally based firms over others. Furthermore, political actors who have lost power at the national level may be able to reassert it at the state level and in ways that might be more harmful for the Republicans' allies than a compromise national law. For example, in the area of food labeling many state governments have been active.[25] Similarly, product safety has become an increasing concern of state courts applying the common law of torts.[26]

The Reagan administration's response to the growth of state regulatory activity was to propose preemptive regulations in such areas as nuclear power, trucking, state workfare, drug labeling, products liability, coastal zone management, taxicab licensing, affirmative action, the minimum drinking age, and the transport of hazardous waste.[27] According to one study, ninety-one explicit federal preemption statutes were enacted during the two Reagan administrations. These statutes represented 25 percent of all federal preemption laws enacted since the founding of the republic.[28] This seems an odd outcome to emerge from an administration supposedly committed to the "new federalism" of increased state authority. Yet it is one more indication of Reagan's reactive stance and his advisers' failure to think through the principles of federalism in a systematic way.

PRINCIPLES OF FEDERALISM

The Reaganite commitment to lower levels of public spending, decentralized government, and aid to industry clashed in the administration's approach to intergovernmental relations. The conflicts were handled on an ad hoc basis that had White House officials urging greater devolution of spending and regulatory authority at the same time as they supported mandates and preemptive statutes and worked to kill Revenue Sharing.

A political economy of federalism can provide a more consistent and principled framework for the development of policy than was evident in the Reagan program. Considerable research by public finance economists has laid the groundwork for a reform of intergovernmental relations that avoids slogans and provides arguments to counter the pleas of the self-interested.

Although Republican rhetoric linked devolution of authority to the states with regulatory and tax relief, these issues are distinct. The important normative question for the study of federalism is the proper location of decisionmaking and spending authority, given a particular public end. The key variables are: (1) the effects of externalities, (2) economies and diseconomies of scale in administration, (3) citizen participation, (4) the benefits of diversity versus uniformity, and (5) the possible existence of "prisoner's dilemmas."[29] The first three isolate a set of problems where the controversies are mainly empirical. The last two combine economic and political concerns and must be considered together since they overlap and intersect in complex ways.

Externalities

Economic theory provides a straightforward answer to the problem of drawing "optimal" jurisdictional boundaries. Individual states have little incentive to consider benefits and costs that accrue to out-of-state residents. Hence, jurisdictional boundaries should internalize these external effects.[30] For example, a single authority should regulate upstream and downstream water users. Dischargers and breathers in a single air basin should be included in the same jurisdiction. As a practical matter, however, this principle may lead to an unmanageable number of overlapping governmental entities. Thus federal matching-grant programs might be designed as a substitute. Without creating new government authorities or redrawing boundaries, grants could give states and localities an incentive to take responsibility for the externalities imposed on others.[31] Managing interstate externalities thus provides the first normative argument for incentive-based cooperative federalism.

Implementing matching-grant programs under this principle would itself be a complex enterprise. The federal government cannot simply set a single matching rate and leave it at that. Most interstate externalities are not imposed symmetrically. Instead, asymmetry is common, where one group of states (e.g., upstream polluters or energy-producing states) tries to impose costs on other states (e.g., downstream water users or energy-using states). The disadvantaged states have no corresponding costs they can impose on their upstream neighbors. The states' interests in federal versus local control are clearly opposed in the asymmetric situation. Economic efficiency requires federal legislation to correct the externality, but, without some form of logrolling (e.g., federal grants), only the disadvantaged states will favor a federal law.[32]

Existing matching-grant programs, however, often have proved an ineffective way to compensate the producers of interjurisdictional externalities. They lower the price of certain inputs (e.g., the capital cost of sewage treatment) but do not directly regulate output. In principle, it would be better to tie the federal subsidy to reductions in interstate externalities (e.g., the interstate transport of water pollution). Conversely, instead of subsidizing pollution control, states could be taxed on their interstate emissions. Either carrots or sticks are, in principle, possible. One implication of such a policy would be vastly different tax or matching rates across state lines depending upon the degree of interstate externality. The result would be not only different tax and subsidy rates, but different state choices concerning pollution levels. Individual states could select different goals constrained only by federal incentives designed to reflect interstate effects. A politically difficult reform of the system of intergovernmental grants would thus be required to fulfill the externality reduction goal efficiently. Upstream states, for example, would either find their water pollution programs more heavily subsidized than downstream dischargers or face stiffer taxes on their discharges.

The necessary diversity in regulatory standards does not, however, require a federal–state program. A preemptive federal statute regulating automobile pollution or airport noise, for example, could be designed to take account of geographical differences.[33] Nevertheless, diversity within wholly federal regulatory programs has proved politically difficult to achieve in practice. Regulatory diversity may be easier to achieve by carrying out a federal program in conjunction with state governments.

Economies and Diseconomies of Scale in Administration

Much regulatory activity requires the production and transmission of information. Some information relevant to the entire country can be most efficiently created by the federal government. National institutes can study public health problems, develop models of ambient air and water quality, and test the safety of products for the benefit of all. In areas such as these, which no state would finance on its own, economies of scale demand national action.

Other information, however, may be specific to a particular time, place, and circumstance and may be virtually useless outside a local area. Furthermore, if information must be transmitted up a long bureaucratic chain to federal decisionmaking officials, the data may be lost or misinterpreted. Where such diseconomies are important, state administration of federal statutes may be preferable to a decentralized federal administrative structure. The argument for devolution on grounds of administrative efficiency is further strengthened if state governments already have agencies charged with similar tasks. In this case, overlap and duplication are reduced through cooperation.

Nevertheless, "cooperative" and incentive-based schemes are worthwhile only in areas where the law serves some federal purpose. Otherwise both spending and regulatory authority might better devolve to the states under a states' rights system.

Political Responsiveness and Citizen Participation

Some defenders of decentralized government emphasize the advantages of smallness rather than the advantages of multiplicity and variety.[34] Smaller governmental units may be "closer to the people" and more responsive to the political activity of individuals. Yet much citizen participation in state and local activities results from requirements in federal statutes and regulations.[35] These requirements indicate that national politicians believe the ideal of citizen participation to be undervalued by state and local officials. The opportunity for participation is apparently not a "natural" result of decentralization. If this is true, an increase in the authority of state governments to set policy may produce laws that are less, rather than more, responsive to citizen preferences.

Consider also James Madison's argument in *Federalist Paper* No. 10 that a large republic will be less likely to succumb to the will of narrow, self-interested factions. In a modern context, the advantage of centralized lawmaking may extend beyond the organizational problems of factions in large polities. In addition, democratic control may be facilitated by the national publicity that accompanies attempts to pass or amend federal statutes. Only a few states have populations large enough and diverse enough to support a full range of single-issue-oriented interest groups or an effective stable of statehouse reporters. Devolution to state government may produce, not democratic responsiveness, but capture by special interests. As we shall see in the next section, this observation is also relevant to the evaluation of interjurisdictional diversity and competitiveness.

Choice, Variety, and the "Prisoners' Dilemma"

In a perfectly competitive market the free choices of buyers and sellers produce an efficient outcome. Noncooperative, self-interested behavior produces socially optimal results. Prices equal marginal costs and mar ginal rates of substitution are equalized for producers and consumers. In equilibrium no one can be made better off without making someone worse off. There are no alternatives unanimously preferred to the market outcome. A wide variety of goods and services is produced, reflecting the diverse tastes of the populace. For a given pattern of demand, the selection of goods available depends upon the relative costs of producing many types of goods versus the cost of supplying larger quantities of fewer sorts. [36] This sanguine view of competition suggests that a multigovernment system ought to imitate the structure of the market in order to reap the same benefits.

In contrast to defenses of the competitive market, other writing emphasizes the pathologies of noncooperative, self-interested behavior. The most well-known game-theoretic example is the "prisoners' dilemma." Two prisoners who have been accomplices in a crime are placed in separate rooms unable to communicate with each other. If one confesses and the other does not, the confessor is set free and rewarded, and the one who fails to confess will be more severely punished than if both confess. If neither confesses, both are set free with no rewards. Each prisoner has an incentive to confess under these conditions. No matter what the accomplice does, the prisoner is better off confessing. However, the problem is constructed so that the joint maximum is for neither to confess. Decentralized, noncooperative behavior makes both individuals worse off and results in a suboptimal outcome from the point of view of the prisoners. In the intergovernmental context the question is whether states and localities should be analogized to firms selling in a competitive market or to prisoners.

Neither analogy fits perfectly, or rather, sometimes one and sometimes the other holds. This complexity makes simple commitments either to decentralization or to federal government control unwise. We need to consider the strengths and weaknesses of intergovernmental competition and then apply the analogies sensitively to particular cases.

The market-based case for a multiple government system has three aspects. First, intergovernmental competition for both residents and business investments may induce governments to satisfy the demands of constituents and firms at least cost. Governments cannot waste resources on excess civil service employment and "edifice complexes" if they want to survive as viable entities. Under this view multiplicity would be desirable even if everyone had identical tastes. Second, a multiple government system is well suited to a population with diverse tastes for public services. Communities can specialize in particular mixes of services, and each one will attract those people and businesses which value its choices over others. The emphasis is not so much on productive efficiency as on the benefits of diversity. Third, a multiple government system may promote the search for new ideas that might be adopted by other states and localities or even by the federal government. Many governments might have the same goal—for example, educating children—so that the benefit of multiple governments is not the promotion of either efficiency or variety, but is, instead, the encouragement of diverse efforts to solve a common problem. Intergovernmental migration need not be an important force so long as the results of experiments can be observed by outside observers.

On the other side of the ledger is the obverse of these potential benefits. State and local governments may operate, not in a marketlike setting, but in a prisoners' dilemma game. Firms and individuals do not always have congruent interests, nor do national corporations and local businesses. As in all government activity, state and local governments are engaged both in providing services that benefit all and in distributing tax costs and service benefits across groups. For example, even if everyone prefers an efficient government to an inefficient one under a given tax structure, some may prefer an inefficient government if it offers them a break on their taxes.

These possibilities produce three arguments against decentralization in a multiple government system. First, interjurisdictional competition favors groups that are relatively mobile over those which are not. Thus business firms that can invest in any state gain relative to immobile citizens. Firms with little fixed capital or ones that can credibly threaten to go out of business have a political advantage. Wealthy center city residents who can move to more homogeneous suburbs may be favored by urban governments. Second, the variety in service mixes and regulatory stringency across jurisdictions may reflect, not a sensitive response to taste differences, but the differing mixes of political influence. This variety, if applied to the regulation of consumer products, may increase costs for firms selling in many states. Third, programs with an experimental cast may merely represent gambles for electoral support by politicians in trouble. Such "bold new initiatives" are unlikely to be structured to permit intelligent evaluation by outsiders. [37]

An attempt to sort out these conflicting tendencies begins with a world of purely private goods where people with a variety of tastes can live side by side without difficulty. Each person simply purchases a different bundle of goods and consumes it privately. In contrast, when some goods are congestible public goods, consumed and financed in common, people may be better off if they can cluster together in communities with others who have similar tastes. This insight was developed by Charles Tiebout in a now-classic article[38] that has spawned a large literature in economics.[39] So long as this clustering does not create interjurisdictional externalities or undermine distributive goals, diversity in tastes argues for a states' rights system with a minimal central government. Tiebout's result, however, depends on a number of special assumptions: citizens are well informed and free to move between a large number of available communities; the level of public goods provision and taxes is the only determinant of location; and public services become congested so that there is an efficient population size for each level of service. Equally important is the presumption that individuals are the only mobile group and that they pay head taxes, which reflect the average cost of public service provision. Political struggles between rich and poor, or businesses and voters, are assumed away.

In reality, because of the link between job location and residence and the importance of existing housing, most people have only a few viable options. Therefore, especially at the state level, the use of competitive pressures as a substitute for politics is unlikely to produce optimal results. The frictions and imperfections of the system are too large.[40] Nevertheless, the possibility that citizens will leave a jurisdiction is a check on the behavior of state and local politicians. The multiplicity of state and local governments permits variety that can respond to the tastes of residents even if the costs of migration ensure that few governments will consist of people with homogeneous tastes.

Economists have long recognized that the Tiebout theory is inapplicable to redistributive policies, which inevitably have different impacts on different people. State and local redistributive efforts are vulnerable to erosion in political systems with many competing governments. A prisoner's dilemma operates: individual governments are unable to carry out large-scale redistributions of income because they fear that their high-income residents and businesses will relocate to lower-tax jurisdictions. Furthermore, the pattern of redistribution that does emerge is likely to have little to recommend it on social justice grounds,[41] with wealthier states generally providing higher levels of benefits for "their" poor.[42] Thus, economic analyses of federalism commonly recommend that income redistribution, whether achieved directly through taxation or indirectly through regulation, be made a federal responsibility.[43] Interjurisdictional competition over redistributive policy has none of the optimality properties of competitive markets.

A variant of the Tiebout story focuses on competition among the states for business investment. Under this version, states seek to produce efficient public services and helpful regulations in order to attract job creating firms. Frank Easterbrook and Ralph Winter have argued that this interstate competition for business will produce a "race to the top" that will encourage a search for innovative and efficient public sector programs.[44] The state with the best set of laws will win the competitive struggle.

The conditions for the Easterbrook–Winter result to hold are, however, just as restrictive as Tiebout's. There must be no interstate externalities and no prisoners' dilemmas. The laws used to attract firms must not have an impact on anyone else in the state; managers must be good agents for stockholders, and state politicians must be good agents for voters. If any of these conditions is absent, the argument that interstate competition produces efficient regulation is unpersuasive. For example, Winter himself argues against permitting states to determine rules governing mergers and takeovers, because he fears that managers may not be good agents for shareholder interests. Moreover, state-level regulations may fail to reflect the interests of those harmed by the external costs of productive activity. States try to attract business to their jurisdictions through tax breaks and regulatory laxness. In this competitive environment, each state tries to outdo the others in offering low levels of taxation and regulation. Even when regulation cannot be entirely avoided, it may be administered to favor business interests. For example, before the passage of the federal water and air pollution control acts in 1970 and 1972, many states included representatives of the polluting industries on boards charged with overseeing environmental control.[45]

Of course, anyone who defines low levels of regulation as synonymous with the public interest will view the leverage of business as a benefit, not a cost. But clearly no general conclusion of this sort is warranted depending as it does on a particular view of the relative political power of ordinary citizens, local industry, and national firms under alternative government systems.

Even the factual claim has been proved wrong by events in the Eighties. As we have seen, the states did not respond to federal inaction with a race to lower regulatory restrictions. In some areas regulatory activity actually increased, creating the possibility, not of low uniform rules, but of diverse, stringent, and possibly inconsistent regulations. Apparently labor, environmental, and consumer interests can sometimes overcome even businesses' threats to withdraw from high-regulation states. In fact, in a striking reversal of position some consumer advocates are lobbying against federal statutes in an effort to preserve state-level gains. Furthermore, locally based industries may successfully obtain regulations that disadvantage out-of-state competitors. They too will oppose national preemptive laws.

The Federal Response to Interjurisdictional Competition

The federal policy response requires a three-pronged inquiry. A federal role will be justified, even when interjurisdictional competition seems vigorous, (1) if a prisoners' dilemma exists, (2) if a narrow group's political power is high at the state and local level because it has captured the machinery of government or because of a credible exit threat, or (3) if the costs imposed on national firms and other organizations are not balanced by the benefits of interstate diversity.

First, when states and localities compete under prisoners' dilemma conditions, individually rational actions produce a result that is worse than a cooperative solution. While a state can gain in the struggle to attract business if it establishes a low-tax and low-regulation environment when other states do not, if all the other states follow suit, only the businesses come out ahead.[46] Thus state officials may support federal laws (or interstate compacts) limiting their ability to compete with each other. Because states will also have an incentive to undercut each other at the implementation stage, state officials may also support federal enforcement efforts.[47]

For example, in the regulatory area, state politicians have supported federal requirements. A subcommittee of the National Governors' Association welcomed devolution of regulatory authority from the EPA, but argued that "successful delegation of programs can only be accomplished with strong technical and financial assistance from EPA, a national presence of EPA in standards' setting and resolving interstate pollution problems, and strong federal research."[48] The subcommittee thus recognized that, left to themselves, state politicians might try to use their authority both to impose costs on the citizens of other states and to benefit at their expense.

Second, citizens may favor federal intervention to counter the political bargaining power of narrowly focused groups that are more powerful at the state and local level than they are nationally. Under the first problem, the citizenry favors policies to attract business, given what other governments are doing, but it recognizes that federal preemption would improve matters. In the second case, the citizenry supports a federal presence to shift the political balance of power in their direction. Federal preemption can protect voters from state legislation favoring local firms over local consumers and from laws that benefit those who can credibly threaten to move to another state or locality, but not to another country.

Local firms may seek state product regulation as a way of improving their competitive position vis-à-vis other firms in the same industry.[49] If a local firm has a product mix somewhat different from that of its national competitors, it may seek regulation that will increase its market share at the same time that it raises prices or lowers the product variety available. Such a firm will be more likely to achieve the desired regulation if it is locally owned, if its use of inputs is important to the local economy, and if it can move out inexpensively. These firms will also oppose any federal attempts to reduce their monopoly power at the state level.[50] The interstate diversity produced by this pattern of political action can hardly be justified as furthering economic efficiency. It represents a series of deals designed to maintain local monopoly power.

Third, even if lower-level governments and their constituents express no dissatisfaction with the competitive situation, federal action may be justified if the costs of the resulting diversity in rules outweigh the benefits. Uniform national regulation may produce economies of scale for private firms in interstate commerce. Federal preemption reduces search costs, maintains economies of national scale in production and distribution arrangements, and tends to produce a more stable and predictable jurisprudence.

For example, in the chemical industry even large national firms appear to have a relatively weak bargaining position at the state level: moving costs are high once capital is in place, and the industry is very capital-intensive. Thus, large chemical companies have actively supported uniformity in a number of regulatory areas. The chemical industry joined with OSHA in support of uniform national labeling standards.[51] Under the Resource Conservation and Recovery Act, the Chemical Manufacturers Association (CMA) favored uniform federal standards both to avoid the costs of complying with a multiplicity of requirements and to maintain "competitive balance" among firms in the industry. The CMA worried that "variations in state priorities could result in cost disadvantages for existing facilities due to geographic location."[52]

Therefore, in areas without absolute federal preemption, efficiency may sometimes require an active federal agency that establishes uniform rules.[53] Corporations are often on the side of federal uniformity rather than interstate diversity and competition. One business critic claimed that the new federalism resulted in a "state regulatory nightmare, a 50-headed hydra."[54] Another, using equally colorful language said, "I would rather deal with one federal gorilla than 50 state monkeys."[55] Firms that sell in national markets (e.g., railroads, trucking, and telecommunications) and compete with local firms in some markets (e.g., supermarket chains and producers of beer, mineral water, dairy products, or prefabricated houses) will often prefer national regulation.[56] Even if a firm's bargaining power is high in most states, the benefits of uniform national laws may outweigh the costs resulting from a higher average level of regulation.[57] If state and local laws seem designed to protect local businesses rather than reflect genuine differences in tastes across jurisdictions, the federal government should take a hard look to determine the possible interference with interstate commerce.

CONCLUSIONS

The Reagan administration put little effort into finding a balance between centralization and decentralization. It was given to rhetorical pronouncements on the value of strong state governments, which failed to account for the subtleties of twentieth-century intergovernmental relations.[58] While it did succeed in devolving some of its authority through spending cuts and both formal and informal reductions in federal oversight, in other areas it sought federal preemption. The end result fits into no principled defense of the intergovernmental system. States and localities were given more responsibilities for many redistributive programs where the argument for federal funding and oversight is high. Conversely, increases in federal constraints occurred in areas where some of the administration's own arguments for decentralization seem especially powerful.

An ideological commitment to states' rights in the design of public policies is misguided. Devolution may have unfortunate consequences, not only for efficiency, but also for the perceived legitimacy of democratic governance. "Closeness to the people" must be carefully weighed against the increased possibility of "capture." Sensible regulatory relief might as easily demand a stronger federal presence as delegation of power to the states.

We are left, then, with a rather weak argument in favor of interstate diversity in regulations. Externalities, prisoners' dilemmas, and redistributive goals argue in favor of a strong federal presence. National uniformity produces economies of scale in administration and compliance and prohibits protectionist state laws. In contrast, decentralization may promote freedom of choice, responsiveness, and desirable forms of interjurisdictional competition. Interstate competition and diversity may undermine the political power of groups that can reach a critical mass only at the federal level and opens up the possibility that new and useful ideas may emerge when states design their own programs.[59] Given this tradeoff in political influence and policy, it is desirable to have a mixed system of regulation and public spending that imposes some level of national uniformity but allows state experimentation in those areas that are most uncertain and least open to opportunistic manipulation. No general claim in favor of devolution will survive analysis.

12

Privatization

C alls for privatization during the last administration suffered from the same rhetorical overkill as calls for deregulation and decentraliza-tion.[1] Much of value was submerged in overblown claims for the benefits of private economic activity. Particularly in Reagan's second term the rhetoric of privatization came to the fore as policies to deregulate and decentralize faltered.[2] Yet when powerful political forces opposed priva-tization plans, the administration demonstrated that free market ideology was to be used only for rhetorical effect, not to override political expe-diency.[3]

Privatization covers a collection of concepts of central importance to progressive reformers. We should not let ideological antagonisms swamp thought. Sensible analysis is hampered, however, by ambiguity about what the term means. At its strongest "privatization" means eliminating a government presence, as either spender or regulator, and leaving the activity entirely to private actors.[4] For programs with no specialized cap-ital this would involve simply canceling the program. When the govern-ment owns capital, it would be sold either piecemeal or as a going concern. Thus a privatizer might recommend the sale of the Tennessee Valley Authority[5] or, more controversially, the national forests and parks and the United States Postal Service.[6] The sale of Conrail was a prime example of such a privatization strategy[7] as was the sale of national corporations in Great Britain under the Thatcher government.[8] On this interpretation the debate is not about the form of the public program but about proper governmental functions. Important as these questions are, they cannot be usefully addressed by starting with the presumption in favor of the private sector implied by those who use "privatization" as a watchword. Since much of the rest of this book concerns justifications for government action, I put these issues to one side here to focus, instead, on the role of private firms and market incentives in the provision of services under existing programs. I concentrate on privatization either as a plan for using private firms to provide public services directly through contracts and franchises or as a way of importing market incentives into the public sector by giving beneficiaries a choice of service provider.[9]

The use of outside contractors has been pervasive at all levels of governments for many years.[10] The Reagan administration sought, however, to increase their role further. In 1983 the White House issued a circular intended to require contracting-out in cases where it would save money.[11] While some criticized the circular for its poor design and limited impact,[12] it does seem to have had an effect.[13] For example, at the Environmental Protection Agency, the budget for contractors increased by 300 percent in the Eighties.[14] In the National Aeronautics and Space Agency, contract employees account for more than half of NASA's workers.[15] The Department of Housing and Urban Development has given wide discretion to private lenders.[16]

The use of market incentives in the provision of public benefits is much less widespread. The federal government has ongoing voucherlike programs in food stamps and health care. In addition, a few local governments have experimented with vouchers for such services as elderly programs, paratransit, day care, and health care.[17] The Reagan administration proposed an expanded plan for existing housing that would be combined with overall funding cuts.[18] The association of budget cuts with vouchers tarnished the proposal,[19] however, and only a small program has been funded.[20] The debate has become most visible to the general public in educational policy, where some state and local experiments have begun, with Washington providing supportive rhetoric.[21]

THE ROLE FOR PRIVATIZATION

The first type of privatization, contracting-out, cuts government monitoring of program administration by reducing direct government control over the production process.[22] Corruption and scandal can be the result.[23] For contracting to be desirable, these costs must be balanced by the benefits of increased efficiency or higher quality.[24]

Under the second sort of privatization, based on market incentives, vouchers are provided to beneficiaries who can "shop around" for the best provider among for-profit firms, and possibly nonprofits and public agencies as well. Such plans imply less direct government control, but the emphasis is on market incentives, not organizational form. The presumption is either that for-profits will respond most effectively to market incentives or that competitive pressures will wipe out the operative differences between types of providers.

To evaluate one or another privatization plan, we must clarify the way in which benefits arise. Putting the privatization label on a program does not guarantee that the benefits of market competition will magically appear. Of the putative advantages of privatization, five seem most important.

1. The use of private firms can be a way to avoid government restrictions that hamper effective program administration (e.g., civil-service requirements, purchasing restrictions) and to lessen political pressures on administrators.

2. Competitive pressures for productive efficiency and high-quality performance can substitute for direct regulation of service delivery. In situations such as mineral exploitation on public lands, where the government is already committed to the use of private producers, auctions or other types of pricing systems can allocate the benefit to the most efficient producers.

3. Program beneficiaries may be given a greater degree of choice.

4. Private providers may offer a greater variety of services and represent greater ideological diversity than public providers, and they may be more likely to innovate.

5. Public funds may stimulate private spending if they take the form of matching grants to private organizations. Nonprofit charities with access to private donations can use the matching grants to encourage private gifts. For-profit firms may be willing to invest in projects with public benefits if a portion of their costs is subsidized by the state.[25]

COST SAVINGS AND COMPETITIVE PRESSURES

The benefit of avoiding government restrictions, while probably quite important in practice, is simply an expedient end run around legal constraints.[26] If that is all there is to privatization, the more straightforward response would be reform of the laws governing public bureaucracies.[27] For example, some governments have created state-owned enterprises largely to avoid the constraints on public bureaucracies while retaining state ownership.[28]

Furthermore, the use of nongovernmental organizations to insulate a program from politics is likely to be unsuccessful as the organizations themselves band together to maintain the public programs that benefit them.[29] One need only look at the political activity of defense contractors to see that this is a realistic concern.[30]

The second possibility raises the question of whether one should equate privatization with the benefits of competitive markets. Clearly, there is no easy analogy. Private investment funds may not be available unless the government can credibly promise not to nationalize the firm, levy confiscatory taxes, or impose severe regulatory burdens. If the government wants the service provided but cannot make credible commitments, it may have no choice but to produce the service itself.[31] This outcome is distinctly second-best but may be the only outcome possible absent a major governmental reform.

When private production is feasible, the government will obtain none of the benefits of competition if only a single provider is available.[32] Thus some studies of the performance of public and private electric utilities suggest that public firms are more efficient. The private firms are monopolies that must be regulated to prevent the accumulation of monopoly profits. The appropriate contrast is thus not between public production and perfect competition but between public production and regulated private production.[33]

Even when only a single provider can efficiently serve the public, however, the government can let potential suppliers compete for the right to provide the best combination of price and service quality. Thus auctions might be held to allocate rights to cable television franchises or to supply electricity or water.[34] In some states private firms have bid to provide prison services.[35] In practice, however, when the service is, like prisons, one that is already being provided by the state, it may be politically difficult to structure an auction that focuses only on the criterion of economic efficiency. For example, some contracts with private firms have included job security for existing civil servants. Such contract clauses obviously limit the ability of private firms to take advantage of the cost savings from replacing unproductive workers or eliminating unneeded positions.[36] Conditions of this sort have sometimes made private firms unwilling to participate in privatization plans.[37]

Furthermore, a competition for the right to supply a service cannot be the end of direct public involvement. The agency must monitor the winning organization to be sure it lives up to its commitments.[38] If the opportunities for cheating or renegotiation ex post are substantial, the benefits of competition between private firms may be very limited compared with direct public provision.[39] Thus some students of government contracting have argued that sealed bidding procedures facilitate collusion and have few countervailing benefits since government agencies routinely approve claims for cost overruns. They argue that efficiency would be improved by underemphasizing competitive bidding.[40]

In contrast, when many firms can simultaneously provide the service, ongoing competitive pressures can help assure high quality and low cost. Studies of a wide range of public services, particularly those provided by local governments, have demonstrated that in many situations private provision can often be more cost-efficient without a decline in quality.[41] There is, however, no necessary connection between private firm production and cost saving for government. Both genuine competition and careful monitoring are required. In many instances the difficulty of writing enforceable contracts will counsel against a wholesale turnover of service provision to private firms. A city can contract out towing services but not the arrest of criminal suspects. It can contract for food service in prisons, but should be more cautious about contracting for the operation of entire prisons.

The costs of contracting-out have surfaced at the federal level. The use of private contractors at the National Aeronautics and Space Administration has led to claims, not of cost savings and efficiency, but of cost overruns and false certification of parts.[42] Part of the problem may be a corresponding fall in the agency's technical and monitoring capabilities, a failing that may undermine the agency's performance. Some observers of the Department of Housing and Urban Development claim that private lenders vastly overvalued property that was being mortgaged, leading to losses for the government.[43] Similar problems have arisen in other federal loan programs.[44] The Environmental Protection Agency's policy of contracting out inspection tasks to private firms led to lawsuits under the Clean Air Act in which federal appeals courts have split on the legality under the statute of using nongovernment employees for monitoring.[45]

Reagan officials seem to have jumbled together the goal of deregulating the private sector and privatizing the provision of government goods and services. Just because it is efficient to deregulate the airlines and the trucking industry, it does not follow that the state should relax the monitoring of its own contractors or use private firms whenever it is technically possible to do so.

It is surely not a sign of high-quality private sector management to hire a contractor to carry out a customized project and then to let it simply submit bills with little oversight. Private firms "get on the back" of contractors if they have no confidence in arms-length relationships. In fact, firms are likely to engage in vertical integration or joint ventures in many areas where government agencies sign contracts. A more "businesslike" government does not necessarily mean one that uses more outside contractors and monitors them less.

Suppose, finally, that a policy decision has been made to permit private exploitation of a publicly owned resource. Policymakers need only decide who should be permitted to use the resource. Then the government can auction off the right to use the resource to the highest bidder.

While broad concerns with social justice ought to predominate when the public resources represent most of a country's productive capacity, as in Eastern Europe and the Soviet Union, these issues should be put to one side in the United States, where the publicly owned resources are a specialized lot. Not much can be done to correct inequities in the distribution of income and wealth by giving away oil leases or rights to cut timber. The tradeoff between equity and efficiency can be better resolved by auctioning off the rights to the high bidder and using the proceeds for redistributive purposes. While the federal government does employ user fees and auctions for some resources, a good deal more could be done. Some user fees have been introduced or increased in recent years. For example, fees have been instituted for some water projects, but only for those outside of Republican strongholds in the West.[46] Federal oil leases are auctioned off for both land-based and offshore sites.[47] Proposals have been made to auction off satellite spots in equatorial orbit.[48] In contrast, timber continues to be sold in marginal forests at bargain prices,[49] and grazing fees on public lands have fallen.[50]

CHOICE AND VARIETY

When competition is possible, the third benefit of greater choice for clients may also be realized. Here is where vouchers, or the "proxy shopping" plans discussed previously, can be useful. Vouchers appear to be a promising innovation for subsidy programs, such as housing and day care, where individual beneficiaries can be expected to have some competence in selecting suppliers. Nevertheless, even for such goods and services, supplementary regulations are likely to be necessary. Not only do beneficiaries lack complete information on service quality, but even if they were fully informed, market efficiency under voucher plans is less than in a free, competitive market. Since beneficiaries are not paying the full cost of the services they consume, their incentives to make informed choices are reduced. Proxy shopping does not suffer from that particular difficulty since the choices of unsubsidized paying customers govern. Nevertheless, as I have outlined above, the conditions under which the unsubsidized are good proxies for the needy are fairly restrictive. Thus while vouchers and their close cousins should be one of the options considered in the design of social service programs, they should be supported only if the conditions for efficient market operation are met and if cost-effective service delivery is indeed a goal.

The fourth privatization benefit of innovation and diversity can result from a voucher plan or from contracting-out for services. Here the emphasis is on the way multiple suppliers can enlarge the range of choice and further the development of new ideas. One must be careful, however, not to oversell this benefit. Private for-profit firms are not per se innovative and diverse. All we know for sure is that they seek to make money. Thus they must be rewarded for innovation and diversity in order to produce them. Similarly, while nonprofits do provide a way for people with ideas to put them into practice, diversity is not inherently desirable if it is not responsive to the demands of beneficiaries.

For an example of the way privatization might be expected to encourage innovation, consider one aspect of the national space policy announced in February 1988. The plan called for the issuance of "space transportation vouchers" that would permit the research missions queued up for the space shuttle to purchase alternative, commercial U.S. launch services. The hope was that such a program would stimulate the entry of private providers of space transportation who would experiment with new methods.[51] Similarly, those who support education voucher plans which include both private and public schools expect them to stimulate the development of innovative educational methods.[52]

Contracting-out with private nonprofit and for-profit providers of social services is justified as a way to promote innovation and flexibility.[53] If experimentation and diversity are important goals, however, then especially in the fields of social welfare and the arts, the state might favor nonprofits over either public agencies or for-profits. Nonprofits can produce diversity, at least along ideological dimensions, since they are more likely than other types of firms to be controlled by people who want to reify their ideas. The example of day care illustrates this possibility; here for-profit firms are fairly uniform in approach, while nonprofits represent a variety of ideological positions and theories of child development.[54]

In some situations, however, the very presence of public funds may reduce the diversity of services supplied. Here we once again face the tension between the benefits and costs of decentralized provision. If the government has some general goals for service quality, it may try to impose them along with the grant of funds. Its conditions may need to be applied to the services provided to all clients whether or not they are publicly subsidized. For example, capital requirements, staffing ratios, and equal treatment requirements must apply to the institution as a whole. Thus the diversity of service provision will be reduced. This may not be viewed as a loss if it means the end to segregated schools or substandard facilities, but it can undermine the original justification for favoring private nonprofits in the first place.[55]

LEVERAGE

As a final benefit, privatization might be a backhanded way of limiting the substitution of public for private spending. Government grants and subsidies can be used to encourage both private charity and private investment by profitseeking corporations.

Consider private giving first. Generally, if the government spends more on a service, we would expect that private charitable donations for this purpose would fall.[56] However, if public funds flow to private organizations that also accept private gifts, then it may be possible to stimulate giving instead. The most obvious way to do this is to provide matching grants to charities in the hope that the effective fall in the price of giving will generate additional gifts.[57] The leveraging of public funds with private gifts is viewed by state and local social service agencies as one of the prime benefits of purchase-of-service contracts with private organizations.[58] Yet the government cannot presume that gifts will increase even with matching grants. While some of the strings attached to public funds may be welcomed by donors as a way to improve the accountability of managers, others may impose costs on donors if the rules force a change in mission.[59]

In spite of the Reagan administration's commitment to increased private sector financing of social welfare,[60] however, it instituted a contrary policy with the help of Congress. By reducing marginal tax rates and cutting back on matching grants to nonprofits, the federal government reduced the incentive to donate. A study of the nonprofit sector showed that nonprofits generally responded to these changed conditions by raising fees since increases in gifts did not match the fall in public support. The income effect of reduced taxes and the substitution effect of reduced government spending were not strong enough to overcome the price effect of lower marginal tax rates.[61]

Second, consider how public funds can leverage private profitseeking resources. Leaving to one side the obvious cases of interest rate subsidies and loan guarantees, governments at all levels have experimented with a range of alternatives that blur the conventional distinction between the public and the private sectors. For many of these situations it is difficult to tell if the public sector is using private funds or if private interests are receiving public subsidies. Is the government stimulating private spending or is the level of private spending stimulating the government to appropriate more funds? For example, some state and local governments have become equity partners in such projects as shopping malls, office buildings, stadiums, and central business district development.[62] In other cases, private firms have financed public infrastructure, sometimes as a way of obtaining development rights, while in yet others private firms provide the capital for facilities that are then leased to the government.[63]

Though the federal government has not been aggressively pursuing opportunities for joint ventures,[64] some hybrid corporations have been financed by both public and private funds and are operated under varying degrees of direct public control.[65] Examples include the Corporation for Public Broadcasting (CPB), the Communications Satellite Corporation (COMSAT), and the National Corporation for Housing Partnerships (NCHP).[66] The goal of tapping private funds for public purposes was powerful in each of these cases. At least for COMSAT, the government anticipates the possibility of earning profits. However, the cautions expressed by William Colman, an observer of the varied experiences of state and local governments, seem to be applicable to the federal government as well. He points to the likelihood that the government will be saddled with most of the costs if the project fails. He also emphasizes the problem of conflict of interest if the private partners are also regulated by the state in other contexts.[67]

CONCLUSIONS

What then are the basic outlines of the privatization issue? One must look at both the demand and the supply side and analyze the interaction between government-supported output and private demand. Is the service one that private individuals do not purchase, such as a space shuttle, a prison, or an army tank? Then, at most, privatization ought to mean competition among firms for the right to provide the service accompanied by heavy government oversight. Attempts by the last administration to reduce oversight in such situations have predictably led to revelations of shoddy work and even fraud. At the other extreme (food stamps), publicly subsidized clients consume the service (food) alongside paying customers in a market characterized by a large number of providers (supermarkets and corner groceries). Market pressures regulate price and quality, and the government can limit itself to certifying eligibility and determining the form of the voucher so that beneficiaries have some incentive to patronize efficient, high-quality providers. In between are a multitude of intermediate possibilities that require sensitive, innovative mixtures of public control and private initiative.

The Reagan administration did not engage in a fine-grained analysis of institutional and market alternatives. It let sloganeering dominate analysis and rhetoric substitute for genuine reform. The goal of shrinking government by whatever means (unless political expediency dictates otherwise) hardly provides a solid grounding for a sophisticated assessment of alternative organizational forms and competitive structures in producing low-cost and high-quality goods and services. The administration's focus on the dynamism of private firms did, at least, put privatization on the policy agenda. Clearly, program designers need to examine the role of private for-profit and nonprofit firms in serving public goals and consider the use of price incentives to improve the quality of subsidized services. Reform proposals, however, must incorporate a realistic view of the weaknesses as well as the strengths of the market.

FIVE

CONCLUSION

13

Progressive Reform and the Regulatory State

Self-interested behavior is a fact of life. People who recognize this are neither liberal nor conservative. They are realists. The dream of forging a public policy consensus is just that. People have different goals, tastes, talents, and resources. Procedures for managing conflict are central to the design of social institutions.

The market is one such institution. Its great strength in a diverse world is its impersonality. I do not have to like you in order to trade with you. But the market cannot bear the entire burden of managing conflict. Political institutions and decisionmaking procedures are required for decisions that can only be made collectively. An individualistic perspective on politics concentrates on the translation of personal preferences into collective decisions, recognizing that compromise is inevitable. Social choice analysis has conclusively demonstrated that no simple solution to the problem of aggregating diverse preferences exists. This should not be surprising in a world of scarce resources where the legitimacy of the existing distribution of wealth is one item on the political agenda.

The difficulty of the problem is not, however, an argument for not attempting to resolve it. Progressivism must accept the fundamental tension at the core of democratic government. The aim must be to remove problems that are not inherent in democracy, problems that arise from the representative nature of politics and the difficulties of political organization. For this reason I have focused on the need for improving the accountability of political agents and on improving the design of public programs.

But is it realistic to expect reform? Don't the very theories of social choice that I have used to identify pathologies in representative government themselves counsel against expecting reform efforts to succeed? The structural reform of government and the rationalization of regulatory policy can never provide television pictures as compelling as a bombing raid, a plane crash, or poignant images of the victims of urban crime and poverty. How then can structural reform become politically salient? Criticism of Congress and the bureaucracy is commonplace but has a fatalistic air in much popular discussion. Dramatic, easy to understand events drown out subtler and more complex issues. Does democracy then imply that the only items on the policy agenda will be colorful problems with simple, photogenic solutions? While the need to attract people's attention will always be a concern, I am not so pessimistic. Expertise can coexist with democracy if the potential for public accountability exists. Difficult but unglamorous problems can engage a minority of concerned individuals until the issues reappear on the policy agenda. The very diversity of the American intellectual establishment can help keep the study of unfashionable problems alive and provide alternative reform proposals.

Committed progressives must be willing to concentrate on fundamental problems without being diverted by surface agitations and without falling into rhetorical traps comparable to those of the Republican right. Tools from the fields of policy analysis and social choice facilitate that enterprise, but they demand care and time to employ. The temptation to forgo analysis and rely on slogans exists for people of all political persuasions eager to engage the public's attention. This temptation should be resisted, not only in the interest of producing effective policy responses, but also in the name of democratic accountability itself.

My approach has combined a belief in the value of expert analysis with a commitment to democracy. The use of experts is viewed by some as inherently undemocratic. This need not be so if basic policymaking authority resides in Congress and the President and if elected officials are ultimately responsible to the electorate. While some systematic policy biases are inherent in the structure of representative government, others are an artifact of particular practices and can be the target of reform. Thus the two aspects of progressivism that have engaged my attention are complementary. On the one hand, we need to improve the quality of expert analysis designed to translate individual costs and benefits into public policies. In the same spirit, program designers should concentrate on ways to harness the powerful forces of self-interest to further progressive policies. On the other hand, a commitment to technocratic solutions, even ones like cost-benefit analysis, which are tied to individual preferences, can be supported by democrats only if the government system is genuinely responsible to the citizenry. Political accountability is necessary not only because policy analysis aggregates individual desires differently from most collective choice rules, but also because experts may be captured by narrow interests or seek to further their own personal agendas.

CONGRESSIONAL PROCEDURE AND JUDICIAL REVIEW

Criticism of Congress falls into two broad, but very different, categories. Some claim that Congress has been captured by special interest groups and passes laws supporting these groups that harm the general public. Others argue that a representative body filled with reelection-seeking politicians supports shortsighted policies favored by their constituents, which will ultimately undermine the prosperity of the economy. The former think the problem is too little democracy; the latter, too much.

The latter problem is inherent in the notion of a representative democracy. It cannot be solved by structural reforms without undermining the commitment to democratic processes. Citizens should not be protected by a paternalistic government from their own political mistakes. Insofar as solutions exist, they involve subsidizing the provision of information, facilitating competitive elections, and encouraging public debate between candidates and among citizens.

My own emphasis has been on the first problem. I have tried to articulate a role for the courts that improves the transparency of the political process without granting judges free-floating authority to invalidate statutes they find substantively distasteful. My proposal has three parts. First, courts should review statutes for internal consistency. They would require a statutory statement of purpose and require the body of the statute to be consistent with these explicit pronouncements. Thus an act to protect the public health by regulating druggists could not legally include clauses exempting existing druggists or forbidding advertising. Only if the legislature were willing to state explicitly that the act was intended to assure the economic health of existing druggists could these clauses stand. The legislature retains the right to pass special interest legislation so long as it publicizes what it is doing.

Other lawsuits might challenge a statute for setting unrealistic goals in the preamble that cannot plausibly be achieved by the detailed statutory scheme. Such judicial activism aims not to make laws inoperative but to encourage legislatures to draft statutes that articulate reasonable goals consistent with statutory details. In the end, judges would make it easier for voters to evaluate the work of their representatives. They would be working on behalf of democracy, not against it.

Second, courts should determine if appropriations made under a statute are adequate to carry out statutory purposes. If not, courts would hold that the underfunded provisions had been repealed. The goal is to prevent Congress from passing laws it has no intention of seriously implementing. Since resources are always scarce, the judicial standard should be a deferential one, but the doctrine should aim to prevent pure puffery and misinformation.

Third, courts should give legal status to congressional rules preventing the inclusion of substantive provisions in appropriations acts and forbidding the appropriation of money for unauthorized purposes. Such provisions permit statutes to be amended in quite invisible ways. Even when the portmanteau character of a spending bill is public knowledge, publicity may be insufficient to prevent its passage if, for example, it includes appropriations to keep the government operating for the next fiscal year.

While these proposals would require courts to take on unfamiliar tasks, they represent limited and principled reform efforts. The courts would not be mandating any particular procedures within the legislature. They would focus, as they do in other cases of statutory interpretation, on the language of the statute itself. They would not express any opinion on the merits of the laws being reviewed. The legal materials are familiar ones. Only the use made of them would be new.

PUBLIC POLICY AND THE ADMINISTRATIVE PROCESS

Progressive reform of government programs challenges the simplistic economic analysis used by right-wing critics of the regulatory-welfare state. While progressives value individual choice and recognize the efficacy of incentives in affecting behavior, they do not make a fetish of private firms or unconstrained free market choice. This perspective produces recommendations for regulatory reform, for a reorientation of intergovernmental relations, and for the limited use of private firms and vouchers in implementing public programs. These proposals are not, however, based on a deep distrust of government institutions, but envisage an active role for the state in setting policy and in monitoring redesigned programs. The goal is not to dismantle the state but to reform it.

In the economic regulation of prices, entry, and service, the "easy" victories have been won and further progress requires an understanding of how too little and too much regulation can coexist in the same industry. Deregulation along one dimension can produce the need for a heightened government presence along another. Thus permitting free competition of airlines for routes has increased the need for safety regulation, improved air traffic control, and the efficient allocation of landing slots.

My hunch is that, at the federal level, most real progress can be made in the reform of social, as opposed to economic, regulation. In the area of social regulation, statutes should emphasize agency rulemaking rather than adjudication as the preferred method of setting general policy. The administrative process should be streamlined so that agencies institute broad-gauged policies of wide coverage rather than concentrating on a few squeaky wheels. Statutory reforms should make more use of economic incentives to reduce costs and add flexibility. Such proposals have been prominent features of policy analysis for decades, and several applications have been tried. The most ambitious is the pollution rights scheme for the control of acid rain established by the 1990 Amendments to the Clean Air Act. The challenge is to extend these innovative ideas beyond the regulatory sphere to unlikely-seeming programs like social welfare, where proxy shopping and vouchers have promise.

In developing my proposals for regulatory reform and an increased use of policy analysis, I have avoided one common comprehensive recommendation. I have not espoused a "regulatory budget" or any of its variants.[1] These plans seek to impose budgetlike constraints on those agencies that make few demands on the Treasury but that nevertheless may impose large costs on the private sector. I oppose these proposals because they suffer from a failure to incorporate benefits and focus undue attention on the costs of regulation. Although some regulatory statutes, agency rules, and judicial decisions have certainly gone too far in overemphasizing benefits and ignoring costs,[2] that is no excuse for going in the opposite direction. Both the costs and the benefits of regulations are largely outside of the federal budget and are therefore unconstrained by the check-writing ability of the Treasury. A regulatory budget would simply invite creative accounting with very few means or incentives for the Treasury to monitor such behavior. Far better, it seems to me, is a system that encourages agency-specific attempts at cost-benefit analysis—attempts that can be frank about information imperfections and unquantifiable benefits and costs.

Absent statutory reform, the courts should examine the efficiency properties of rulemakings. Courts would enforce a rebuttable presumption in favor of policy analysis. The presumption could be rebutted when economic efficiency would not further statutory goals or where Congress has included an explicit statutory prohibition of cost-benefit or cost-effectiveness analysis.

In addition to improving the policy analytic activities of federal agencies, reformers need to consider the role of lower-level governments and private organizations. Decentralized administration and the transfer of authority to the states are not per se desirable—especially for regulatory programs like air pollution, which have important interstate effects. The states themselves recognize the potential for destructive interstate competition and do not want the federal government to abdicate responsibility. Instead, policymakers should take account of the geographic extent of problems without making a blanket commitment either to devolution or to national uniformity. Thus water pollution must be regulated at the river basin level, and air pollution control must take account of the long-distance transport of pollutants. Of course, when problems are truly local—such as the provision of urban open spaces or the regulation of local aesthetics—individual communities should have primary authority. The presumption in favor of local control could, however, be overcome by showing that aesthetics or open space zoning are covers for efforts to exclude low-income people.

The role of private contractors, both for-profits and nonprofits, needs to be much more clearly defined. Proponents of privatization should have the burden of establishing that competitive pressures will exist and that these pressures will work to the benefit of the government. After all, private firms can compete to pay the highest bribe to the federal procurement officer just as well as they can compete to provide the best product at the lowest price.

RETHINKING PROGRESSIVISM

The issues that have occupied me in this book are no more than a first step toward a reconstituted progressivism. They suggest how economic analysis can, as in the past, serve the cause of law reform. A fully developed progressive agenda must go farther to include foreign affairs, defense policy, economic growth, and macroeconomic stability, as well as problems of discrimination, poverty, and the distribution of income and wealth. Such issues are central to the policy debates between liberals and conservatives, but they did not seem to me the best place to begin.

To narrow the range of disagreement, I chose substantive topics whose economic content is unproblematic, and widely recognized procedural issues such as the public accountability of government officials. Even here, however, I have shown that a commitment to economic analysis does not imply an unquestioned faith in the unregulated free market and the common law. In defending the value of the competitive market, economics provides a strong justification for public intervention when markets fail. In recognizing that issues of distributive justice cannot be solved scientifically, it clears the way for political and philosophical discussions of the fairness of the distribution of resources.

Progressive law and economics requires a commitment to individualism. But, to me, this seems a small concession for a democrat. Democratic government makes little sense unless individuals have interests, goals, and aspirations that exist apart from the political institutions of the state. While citizen attitudes may be shaped by the system of government, Americans are not simply resultants of social forces without wills of their own. Beginning with this individualistic base, I have tried to develop a realistic understanding of collective action—one that not only encourages the development of thoughtful policy proposals but also fosters political accountability in a necessarily complex representative democracy.

Notes

CHAPTER 1

The New Progressivism

1. Many of the earliest practitioners of law and economics were liberal reformers. See Hovenkamp, 1990, Kalman, 1986.

   For an example of polemical writing that encourages the popular association of law and economics with the political right, see McConnell, 1987, pp. 23–24. Although McConnell admits that law and economics "has no overt ideological element" (id. at 23), he nevertheless claims that "law and economics scholars will—with only rare exceptions—take positions compatible with libertarian conservatives." (id. at 24)

2. Minarik, 1988; and "Rich Got Richer in 80's; Others Held Even," *New York Times*, January 10, 1991, reporting on a Census Bureau survey.

3. Sawhill, 1988.

4. Blau and Ferber, 1990; Gold in, 1990; Jaynes and Williams, 1989.

5. U.S. President's Council of Economic Advisers, 1989, pp. 198–214.

6. Mashaw and Harfst, 1990.

7. OSHA issued one major rule in each of the years 1986, 1987, 1988. On the CPSC see Scanlon and Rogowsky, 1984.

8. Crandall, Gruenspecht, Keeler, and Lave, 1986; Leone, 1984.

9. *Motor Vehicle Mfrs. Assn v. State Farm Mutual Automobile Ins. Co.*, 463 U.S. 29 (1983).

10. See Harris and Milkis, 1989; Crandall and Portney, 1984; Kraft and Vig, 1984.

11. Barth and Bradley, 1988, pp. 46–47.

12. Kahn, 1988, pp. xviii–xxiii.

13. Mendeloff, 1987. The idea was picked up by Cass Sunstein and applied in a more general context in Sunstein, 1990b, pp. 413–16.

14. Crandall and Portney, 1984, p. 69; Kraft and Vig, 1984, pp. 428–29.

15. Ross, 1991, pp. 108–122. Richard T. Ely, one of the founders of the American Economic Association in 1885, stated in a prospectus sent to recruit members:

> While we recognize the necessity of individual initiative in industrial life, we hold that the doctrine of laissez faire is unsafe in politics and unsound in morals; and that it suggests an inadequate explanation of the relations between the state and the citizens. [Ely, 1938, p. 136]

16. Walton Hamilton, a Brookings Institution economist appointed to the Yale faculty in 1927, taught public utilities, trade regulation, constitutional law, and torts. (Kalman, 1986, p. 110) Hamilton, however, was the last person without a law degree to be appointed to the Yale Law School faculty for eighteen years. (id. at 111) Both Aaron Director at the Chicago Law School and Ward Bowman at Yale taught antitrust in the postwar period.

    If Richard Ely, the progressive economist, had had his way, law and economics might have developed forty years earlier at the University of Wisconsin. He believed that

    > it was logical to connect the work of the law and economics departments, because these two subjects constitute different approaches to the same territory. They both deal with value and exchange, with property and contract. Perhaps it can be said that economics is the spirit of the law and that law applies economics to practical life. When you read the great original decisions of the Supreme Court, you find in them sound economics. . . . Since the law faculty [at the University of Wisconsin] did not at all sympathize with my plan. . . . all that remains of my first efforts to bring law and economics together may be found in the catalogue of the law school where my name appeared. [Ely, 1938, pp. 188–89]

17. Rowley, 1988; Veljanovski, 1985.
18. For representative samples of this work, see Ackerman and Hassler, 1981; Breyer, 1982; Diver, 1981; Edley, 1990; Mashaw, 1981; Rabin, 1977; Stewart, 1975; and Sunstein, 1990a.
19. Public choice material is used in Cass, 1986; Farber and Frickey, 1988, 1990; Macey, 1986; Spitzer, 1980; Levine and Plott, 1977; DeBow and Lee, 1988; and Sunstein, 1986.
20. See Brennan and Buchanan, 1980. For a critical review, see Rose-Ackerman, 1982a. For an application of "Virginia School" thinking in the legal literature, see Mayton, 1986. He claims that the legislative system effectively requires supramajorities for any change and hence gives special weight to the status quo produced by private ordering. (id. at 958)
21. For an example drawn from an otherwise quite thoughtful article see Starr, 1988. Starr simply defines "public choice" as "both a branch of microeconomics and an ideologically-laden view of democratic politics." p. 23
22. See especially Sen, 1970, 1972.
23. See, for example, May, 1952, pp. 680–84. May imposes a condition called neutrality, which guarantees that no alternative has a preferred status under the procedures used.
24. U.S.C. title 5, §551 et seq.

CHAPTER 2
Progressivism and the Chicago School

1. Minda, 1988, p. 3, n. 3, identifies a "New Haven" school that "has attracted liberal practitioners who adopt the common methodology of the Chicago school but believe that there is a larger need for state intervention in order to cure problems of market

failure." My Progressive School, while incorporating portions of the work of some of my colleagues, is not pervasive enough at Yale Law School to warrant using my home town as a label.

2. McKean, 1958; Dorfman, 1965; Maas, Hufschmidt, Dorfman, Heinz, Marglin, and Fair, 1962.

3. Hitch and McKean, 1960.

4. For a selection of papers from Congressional hearings on the PPB process held in 1968 and 1969, see Haveman and Margolis, 1970.

5. Posner, 1974b; Stigler, 1971; Peltzman, 1976.

6. See, for example, MacAvoy, 1970; Moore, 1978; Wilson, 1971, p. 39.

7. Ackerman, Rose-Ackerman, Sawyer, and Henderson, 1974; Kneese and Schultze, 1974; and Schultze, 1977.

8. See e.g. Aaron, 1972; Nelson, 1977; and Steiner, 1971.

9. For examples see Anderson, 1964; Murray, 1984; and Savas, 1982. These arguments were accepted by some officials within the Reagan administration. For an explication and critical review of the goals and philosophy of the Reagan policymakers in a variety of areas, see Palmer and Sawhill, 1984.

10. See, for example, Schwarz, 1988; Sawhill, 1988; and Marmor and Mashaw, 1990.

11. Kelman, 1987; Levine, 1981; Robyn, 1987.

12. Those who wish a more thorough treatment should consult any of the numerous texts designed for students at policy schools. Three recent examples are Friedman, 1984; Stokey and Zeckhauser, 1978; and Weimer and Vining, 1989.

13. Standard works are Musgrave and Musgrave, 1973; Okun, 1975; and Jaskow and Noll, 1981. See also the texts cited in note 12.

14. John Cushman, "Washington Talk: A Cost-Benefit Blend That's Hard to Swallow," *New York Times*, June 21, 1990.

15. Ackerman and Hassler, 1981; Huber, 1983.

16. Downs, 1988; Friedman, 1984, pp. 440–61. See also Irene Peterson, "Wielding New Studies, Landlords Ask Albany to Undo Rent Laws," *New York Times*, February 16, 1991, p. 29.

17. Rose-Ackerman, 1983c.

18. For a critical review of a policy analytic effort of this kind see Ackerman, Rose-Ackerman, Sawyer, and Henderson, 1974.

19. The most comprehensive presentation of this approach is in Posner, 1986, Part II. The seminal article was by Coase, 1960. Also important was Calabresi's work on torts, which began with Calabresi, 1961. Calabresi's work, however, has never had the laissez-faire orientation of the Chicago School and should not be grouped together with that work except insofar as it has emphasized the common law field of torts.

20. See Posner, 1986, for an overview.

21. Of course, not all legal-economic scholarship shares the weaknesses of my stark characterization of the Chicago approach. Models of self-enforcing contracts and of legal systems with asymmetric information in contract law represent especially promising lines of work. See e.g. Schwartz and Wilde, 1979, 1983; Goetz and Scott, 1983; Kornhauser, 1976; Schwartz, 1977.

22. Calabresi, 1961; Coase, 1960.

23. For an overview of work in this area by two leading representatives of the Chicago School see Landes and Posner, 1987.

24. Calabresi and the Chicago School scholars agree on this principle, although they disagree on the best legal rule. See Calabresi, 1970.

25. Shavell, 1980a, 1984.
26. Coase, 1960; Furubotn and Pejovich, 1974.
27. Calabresi, 1970.
28. 159 F. 2d 169, 173 (2d Cir. 1947). This standard, as every student of cost-benefit analysis knows, is not the correct efficiency test. Instead, the level of care should be set where marginal costs equal marginal benefits. In *Carroll Towing*, however, the defendant appears to have faced the dichotomous choice of whether or not to leave a barge unattended in a busy harbor. Thus the Hand formula would produce the correct result. In general, this would not be true. In subsequent writing on this issue, Posner recognizes the weaknesses of Hand's formula but maintains that with a "'little relabeling'" it can be rewritten in marginal terms. (Landes and Posner, 1987, p. 88)
29. At least until recently. See Posner, 1990, pp. 353–92.
30. Posner, 1982a, pp. xxxviii and 1. His casebook is designed "to provide a unifying perspective to tort law through repeated use of the Hand formula and of the economic concepts that it encapsulates." (id. at 9)
31. Calabresi and Hirschoff, 1972; Posner, 1973; see also Shavell, 1980b.
32. See, for example, Kronman, 1978; Schwartz, 1979; Rubin, 1981; and Goetz and Scott, 1977.
33. Occasionally, as in the controversy over the efficiency of comparative negligence rules, the problem is essentially definitional. Participants in the debate simply defined the key term differently. Haddock and Curran, 1985, have sorted out the confusion. In other cases confusion arose when a standard legal term, such as negligence, was given a specialized economic meaning. Thus in law and economics a person is judged negligent if the marginal cost of greater care is less than the marginal benefit. (Brown, 1973) This definition is then imported into the law, even when the fit is awkward.
34. Coase, 1960.
35. See Rowley, 1988, for a discussion of the tensions in Richard Posner's work between these not always consistent principles.
36. DeAlessi and Staaf, 1988.
37. Posner, 1986, Part III, for example, discusses antitrust policy and the regulation of public utilities.
38. Calabresi and Melamed, 1972.
39. DeAlessi and Staaf, 1988.
40. Calabresi's work does not fall into this contradiction, because it is less concerned with the preservation of the status quo and less respectful of private arrangements than the work of Chicago School scholars. His work and much of the work of such scholars as A. M. Polinsky and Steve Shavell belong to what one might call the Reformist–Common Law tradition. See, for example, Calabresi, 1970; Polinsky, 1989; Shavell, 1987.
41. See Landes and Posner, 1987; Posner, 1986.
42. The evolutionary-institutional approach to economics might seem to provide a foundation for the Chicagoans' belief in the efficient evolution of the common law. This approach holds that property rights systems evolve over time in response to changes in technology and society. (DeAlessi and Staaf, 1988; Schmid, 1988) Property rights evolve in a way that is consistent with efficient resource allocation. Policy activism may them prove unnecessary. Some evolutionary scholars argue that changes in legal regimes, whether imposed by courts or by legislatures, will track changes in the underlying economic situation. (Demsetz, 1964, 1967)
   Much evolutionary work, however, focuses on private arrangements rather than law and cannot be neatly cabined within the Chicago tradition. See especially the

work of Oliver Williamson collected in Williamson, 1985. Private individuals and firms develop functional ways of dealing with economic problems in spite of the formal nature of the law.

43. See Rowley, 1988, pp. 123–29; Cooter and Kornhauser, 1982; Rose-Ackerman, 1989; Rubin, 1983; Priest, 1980; Priest and Klein, 1984; Shavell, 1982; Rose-Ackerman and Geistfeld, 1987.

44. 232 U.S. 340 (1914).

45. Id., p. 353.

46. Id., p. 349.

47. For more examples, see Rose-Ackerman, 1989, pp. 35–38.

48. The distinction between property rules and liability rules is due to Calabresi and Melamed, 1972.

49. Landes and Posner, 1987, p. 34.

50. Chapter 4 will discuss such work as exists by Chicago School scholars on the legislative process.

51. Ayres, 1990; Ayres and Gertner, 1989; Katz, 1989; Landa and Grofman, 1981; Wiley, 1987.

52. Landes and Posner, 1987, pp. 263–69.

53. See Chapter 6 for a fuller discussion of the policy analytic approach to occupational health and safety and Chapter 8 for an attempt to contrast tort law and regulation in the products liability field.

CHAPTER 3

Judicial Review of Agency Action

1. Olson, 1971.

2. Fiorina, 1977; Mayhew, 1974.

3. Olson, 1971.

4. Stigler, 1974.

5. Olson, 1982, pp. 36–74.

6. See Mueller, 1989, pp. 103–11, for a thoughtful discussion.

7. Mayhew, 1974; Fiorina, 1977; Ferejohn, 1974; Shepsle, 1978.

8. Mayhew, 1974.

9. A good example here are so-called transition rules in tax laws. These are provisions that exempt or subsidize particular projects in members' districts. For journalistic examples see Lawrence Haas, "Rostenkowski's Way," National Journal, July 22, 1989, p. 1860, and Carol Matlack, "Zap! You're Taxed," National Journal, February 3, 1990, p. 268.

10. On the importance of positiontaking, see Robyn's, 1987, study of the passage of the Motor Carrier Act of 1980. She writes: "Appearances are all-important in Congress. In part because the link between actions and results is difficult to demonstrate in the policy area, legislators are often judged by the positions they take rather than the effects of those positions." (p. 250)

11. Fiorina, 1977; Fiorina and Noll, 1978.

12. Fiorina, 1985; Niskanen, 1971; Arnold, 1979; Wilson, 1980.

13. For a related suggestion see Sunstein, 1990b. One of his twenty-eight "interpretative principles for the Regulatory State" is what he called "proportionality." Under this principle: "Statutes should be construed so that the aggregate social benefits are proportionate to the aggregate social costs." (p. 181) He contends that the principle

is most appropriate for economic regulation, but in other situations metrics other than private willingness to pay might be used. He does not, however, provide any guidance on how to use other metrics when other values are at stake (p. 182). For an overview of recent efforts by courts to evaluate costs and benefits of agency actions see Heimann et al. 1990, pp. 606–621.

14. Compare this position with that of Justice Scalia in *Hirschey v. FERC*, 777 F. 2d 1, 7–8 (D.C. Cir. 1985). Scalia would also focus on the statutory language and avoid relying on legislative history, but he apparently would not support a presumption in favor of net benefit maximization.

15. Shapiro, 1988, p. 186, n.20, also argues that courts should give agencies leeway to set priorities in the light of the "'fudge language" in many regulatory statutes. He stops short, however, of recommending the imposition of policy analytic tests by courts "Because most costs of government regulatory programs are shifted to the private sector and therefore are not subject to trimming and prioritizing by the appropriations process, the agencies themselves must do the trimming and prioritizing."

16. Administrative Procedures Act, 5 U.S.C. §§551–59, 1982.

17. On the use of recalls in the regulation of auto safety, see Mashaw and Harfst, 1990.

18. See *NLRB v. Bell Aerospace Co.*, 416 U.S. 267 (1974).

19. For a similar proposal, see Edley, 1990, p. 210.

20. Administrative Procedures Act, 5 U.S.C. §553.

21. The courts have occasionally recognized this fact. See Justice Black's dissent in *Goldberg v. Kelly*, 397 U.S. 254, 271–79 (1970).

22. Edley 1990, pp. 57, 239, also recommends social science training for judges.

CHAPTER 4
Judicial Review of Congress

1. The Supreme Court denied a hearing to Denver landowners affected by a citywide reassessment on the ground that their rights were protected "by their power, immediate or remote, over those who make the rule." (*Bi-Metallic Inv. Co. v. State Bd. of Equalization*, 239 U.S. 441, 445 [1915]) Justice Holmes in this opinion does not consider whether the affected group actually did have access to the legislative process but instead states that the court "*must assume* that the proper machinery has been used." (id., emphasis supplied) Holmes distinguished the taxpayer-plaintiffs in *Bi-Metallic* from those in *Londoner v. Denver*, 210 U.S. 373 (1908), who were granted a hearing on the ground that they were protesting an individualized governmental choice.

2. *Townsend v. Yeomans*, 301 U.S. 441, 451 (1937). See also *Southern Railway v. Virginia*, 290 U.S. 190, 197 (1933): "*In theory, at least*, the legislature acts upon adequate knowledge after full consideration and through members who represent the entire public." (emphasis added)

3. See, for example, Justice Frankfurter's concurrence in *A.F. of L. v. American Sash Co.* 335 U.S. 538, 557 (1948): "Because the Court is without power to shape measures for dealing with the problems of society but has merely the power of negation over measures shaped by others, the indispensable judicial requisite is intellectual humility, and such humility presupposes complete disinterestedness." He also states (id. at 557): "Matters of policy . . . are by definition matters which demand the resolution of conflicts of value . . . Assessment of their competing worth involves difference of feeling; it is also an exercise in prophecy. Obviously, the proper forum for mediating a clash of feelings and rendering a prophetic judgment is the body chosen for those purposes by the people. Its functions can be assumed by this Court only in disregard of the historic limits of the Constitution."

4. *Bowsher v. Synar*, 478 U.S. 714 (1986); *Mistretta v. U.S.*, 488 U.S. 361 (1989); *Morrison v. Olson*, 487 U.S. 654 (1988).

5. *INS v. Chada*, 462 U.S. 919 (1983).

6. Even when the Justices have understood the nature of the political struggle, they have not intervened. Thus Justice Black describes the "no-holds-barred" fight that is "commonplace" in legislatures. (*Eastern R.R. Presidents Conference v. Noerr Motor Freight, Inc.*, 365 U.S. 127, 144 [1961]) The interindustry contest for influence described in that case "appears to have been conducted along lines normally accepted in our political system, except the extent that each group has deliberately deceived the public and public officials." (Id. at 145) Black, while deploring this deception, found that it did not violate the Sherman Act, the only grounds of the appeal.

7. While my argument is not primarily a constitutional argument, there is general support in the Constitution and in commentaries on it for the proposition that American political institutions should be responsive to popular sentiment. *Federalist* 57 states that the "electors [of the federal government] are to be the great body of the people of the United States." (*The Federalist* no. 57 [Rossiter, ed., 1961, p. 351]) Ely claims that "constitutional development over the past century has . . . substantially strengthened the original commitment to control by a majority of . . . the governed . . . [Furthermore,] whatever the explanation, and granting the qualifications, rule in accord with the consent of a majority of those governed is the core of the American governmental system." (Ely, 1980, p. 7)

8. See, for example, Frug, 1978; Sidak, 1989.

9. Ely, 1980. He argues that a representation-reinforcing approach to judicial review is supportive of the underlying premises of American democracy and focuses on tasks for which judges are particularly well suited. (id. pp. 88, 101–4) The Supreme Court should help improve the visibility of the legislative process because "popular choice will mean relatively little if we don't know what our representatives are up to." (id. at 125) Ely, however, is concerned with issues different from those I am addressing, and he takes an explicitly constitutional perspective. He studies political speech, voting rights, and unconstitutional classifications. He is not concerned with the possibility that legislators will mislead voters and says that requiring clear statements of purpose would be a costly reform. (id. at 129) He is more skeptical than I am about the potential of courts to help produce candor and argues that competition for political office should be the primary check. (id., pp. 129–31)

10. Gunther, 1972, p. 44. See *Harper v. Va. Bd. of Elections*, 383 U.S. 663 (1966), on voting.

11. Gunther, 1972, p. 23.

12. Id. at 21. See also Bennett, 1979, p. 1058, who argues for this position and goes on to claim that the Court is less willing to supply purposes than in the past. (p. 1060) Gunther's position differs from that of scholars like John Ely and Paul Brest, who would have the Court scrutinize legislative motives not articulated in the language of the statute. However, even these writers would use stated purposes, if they exist, as evidence of intent and would require means to be rationally related to these purposes. See Brest, 1971; Ely, 1980.

13. Gunther, 1972, p. 44.

14. A constitutional argument can, I believe, be made on the basis of the due process and equal protection clauses as well as on a general understanding of the purposes served by the governmental structure created by the Constitution. See note 7 supra. Ely, 1980, urges constitutionally based review of statutes based on the process followed in their enactment. (p. 74) He looks to the due process and equal protection clauses to support his position (pp. 14–41) and argues that the Constitution as a whole is fundamentally concerned with government structure and process. (p. 90)

15. For a discussion of these limits, see Ackerman, 1985.

16. But cf. Olson, 1971, who discusses the difficulties of organizing for collective action. See Chapter 3 for a discussion of Olson.

17. Cf. Mashaw, 1980; Sunstein, 1990a.

18. See Kalt and Zupan, 1984; Levine, 1981.

19. The classic article here is May, 1952.

20. The result might, of course, be a tie, but only if exactly equal numbers support each alternative.

21. The formal proof of the result stated informally in the text is in id. For a justification of the use of majority rule for issues not involving the fundamental distribution of wealth, see Ackerman, 1980, pp. 273–301.

22. In other words, unless the range of individual preferences is restricted, majority rule does not necessarily generate a "social welfare function" when more than two alternatives exist. This is a special case of Arrow's Impossibility Theorem. (Arrow, 1951) Arrow hoped to find a way of aggregating individual preferences that would produce a social welfare function that had the same rationality properties of transitivity, reflexiveness, and completeness that he was willing to attribute to individuals.

   Arrow was looking for an aggregation procedure that would (1) accommodate all possible individual preference orderings. No one is to be excluded from the state because of his or her "odd" preferences. (2) In addition, the procedure must not be dictatorial. In other words, no single person can always determine the outcome no matter what others think. This is a very weak condition since it does not rule out situations in which a small group dominates the rest. (3) The process must satisfy a unanimity rule so that an option unanimously preferred to another is selected by society. (4) Finally, the procedure would rank any two alternatives solely on the basis of preferences for those alternatives. The presence or absence of other alternatives should not be relevant to the social choice over any pair of alternatives. Given these seemingly quite weak conditions, Arrow proved that no such process exists.

23. The seminal work is Black, 1963. For accessible treatments, see Feldman, 1980, pp. 164–70; Krehbiel, 1988, pp. 260–69; Mueller, 1989, pp. 63–66.

24. See Levine and Plott, 1977; Shepsle and Weingast, 1984.

25. Let S, B, and A stand for the status quo, the original bill, and the amended bill respectively. Suppose the three voters X, Y, and Z have the following preferences: X prefers A to B to S; Y prefers B to S to A; and Z prefers S to A to B. Then the bill is preferred to the status quo. However, if Z introduces an amendment, the amended bill will beat the original bill if everyone votes honestly. Once A has passed, however, the status quo will beat the amended bill.

26. Michael Ross, "Senate Kills Obstacle to Clean Air Bill Passage," *Los Angeles Times*, March 30, 1990. The bill did eventually pass as the Clean Air Act Amendments of 1990, Pub. Law 101–549, Nov. 15, 1990; 104 Stat. 2399, 101st Cong. S.1630.

27. For general proofs on the impossibility of strategy-proofness, see Gibbard, 1973; Satterthwaite, 1975. For a nontechnical overview, see Feldman, 1980, pp. 196–215.

28. See the discussion of minimum winning coalitions in Riker, 1962, pp. 32–76; and Riker and Ordeshook, 1973, pp. 176–201.

29. See, for example, Stigler, 1971; Rose-Ackerman, 1980a.

30. Bennett, 1979, pp. 1061–64, writing on statutory classification schemes, recommends the use of a cost-benefit test to judge a law's rationality. He recognizes the basic inconsistency between majority rule and wealth maximization (p. 1067), pointing out that politically weak groups such as children and prisoners are especially unlikely to have their interests considered in a majoritarian legislature.

31. Meade, 1965; Wicksell, 1883. Wicksell writes that "no one, however learned or sagacious he may be, can claim for the majority of the present possessors of capital and rent a right higher than that which lies in the instinct of self-preservation." (id. p. 43)

32. Buchanan, 1975; Buchanan and Tullock, 1962; Brennan and Buchanan, 1980.

33. See, for example, Krehbiel, 1987, 1988; Shepsle, 1987a, 1987b; Levine and Plott, 1977.

    The United States Congress first votes on amendments to a proposed bill and then pairs the bill as amended with the status quo. This procedure obviously constrains the set of laws that can be adopted. (Shepsle and Weingast, 1984) The selection of open or closed rules for amending bills on the floor affects the power of committees. (Gilligan and Krehbiel, 1987; Krehbiel, 1987) If the committee is more favorably disposed to the agency than the Congress (Niskanen, 1971), the agency can select a policy that keeps the committee from introducing legislation. This view of committees has been challenged by Krehbiel, 1989, who finds that committees are not generally differently constituted from the body as a whole. But see Hall and Grofman, 1990, who provide an intermediate view in which the committee's position relative to the chamber depends on the subject matter of the committee and the nature of the issues before it.

34. Some social choice scholars justify only a limited role for the courts on the ground that judges also operate in a self-interested manner and cannot be expected to seek to further general democratic values. Gely and Spiller, 1990, develop such a model to explain Supreme Court behavior. However, the conditions of employment for federal judges do, at least, make choices based on general principles possible. Under the Constitution, Article III, Sec. 1, judges have life tenure, and their salaries cannot be reduced by the legislature.

35. Mayhew, 1974. See also Arnold, 1990. According to Anton, 1989, p. 188: "In many regulatory programs . . . ambiguities of purpose are accompanied by exaggerated rhetoric and explicit rejection of cost or feasibility considerations, all of which suggests a politics of symbols rather than purpose."

36. The presidential veto and the two-thirds override rule constrain the options that can be enacted into law. (Ferejohn and Shipan, 1991) The veto, along with the need for both the House and the Senate to support a law, gives executive agencies freedom to act within limits. (McCubbins, Noll, and Weingast, 1987, 1989)

37. Douglas Arnold's (1990) analysis of the legislative process in the United States Congress suggests that courts should be cautious in interfering with legislative procedures in the name of democracy. Holding, as I do, that the extent of citizen control of government should be a central question of political science (p. 265), Arnold raises questions about some familiar reform proposals. Reforms designed to increase the openness of Congressional processes and restrict the bundling together of issues into omnibus bills may increase rather than decrease the impact of special interests. Lobbyists from organized interests are the most likely attendees at open meetings. (p. 274–75) Furthermore, when "many narrow issues are combined into an omnibus bill that helps to camouflage the group effects and accentuate the general effects, legislators pay greater attention to the general effects." (p. 272) For examples of both sorts, see id., pp. 131–32, 178, 220, 256–57.

38. The Federal Water Pollution Control Act of 1972, 33 U.S.C.A. §1251 et seq. states that "it is the national goal that the discharge of pollutants into the navigable waters be eliminated by 1985." (id. §1251 [9][1]) "A thorough reading of the Act, however, makes it apparent that the legislators were unwilling to accept the enormous social costs which this position, if taken seriously, would entail. As a result, the stated goal is merely a politically attractive mask. . . ." (Ackerman, Rose-Ackerman, Sawyer, and Henderson, 1974, p. 319)

    The Occupational Safety and Health Act of 1970, 84 Stat. 1590, 29 U.S.C.A. §651 et seq. (1975), states that its purpose is ensuring safe and healthful working conditions for every working man and woman in the nation.

    The 1970 Clean Air Act Amendments ruled out economic and technological factors as criteria for evaluating new air quality standards. The deadlines set for

automobile industry compliance were seen by many as unrealistic and have generated subsequent postponements and controversy. Anton, 1989, pp. 188–89.

39. See *Block v. Community Nutrition Inst.*, 467 U.S. 340 (1984). The case involved
the claim by a consumer group that it had standing to challenge certain milk market
orders issued by the Department of Agriculture under the Agricultural Marketing
Agreement Act of 1937. (7 U.S.C. §601 et seq.) Although the general purpose
section of the Act stated that it is the policy of Congress" (2) To protect the interest
of the consumer" and "(4) . . . To establish and maintain such orderly marketing
conditions . . . as will provide, in the interests of producers and consumers an orderly
flow of the supply thereof to market" (7 U.S.C. Section 602 [2] [4]), the Act makes
no "express provision for participation by consumers in any proceeding." (*Block*, p.
347) The Senate report quoted by the Court states that the milk market order scheme
was designed "to raise producers' prices." (S. Rep. 1011, 74th Cong., 1st Sess. 3
[1935]) Therefore, the Court concludes that not only do consumers have no right to
participate in the process of generating marketing orders within the agency, but they
also have no right to sue the Secretary. Handlers can represent their interests. (*Block*,
p. 352) Even if any savings the handlers obtain from a successful lawsuit are not
passed on, this is irrelevant, because the Court claims that the Act's intended benefits
to consumers are only indirect. (id., n. 3)

40. Cf. Judge Scalia's concurrence in *Hirschey v. FERC*, 777 F. 2d 1, 7–8 (D.C. Cir.
1985).

41. McCloskey, 1962, p. 39.

42. 348 U.S. 483 (1955). *Lee Optical* involves an Oklahoma law patently designed to
benefit optometrists and ophthalmologists at the expense of opticians. The act itself
stated: "It is the public policy of the State of Oklahoma that the citizens of Oklahoma
shall receive the best possible visual care through the efforts of well trained and
qualified [licensed] physicians . . . and optometrists . . . and that no unqualified
person shall be permitted to visually correct for compensation the eyes of another."
(59 Okla. Stat §941, chap. 24, pp. 521–22) The act, however, included provisions—
prohibiting opticians from fitting old lenses into new frames without a prescription
(§942), prohibiting advertising (§943), and preventing any provider of visual care
from renting space in retail establishments (§944)—that seem unrelated to this purpose. In finding the act constitutional, however, Justice Douglas, writing for the
Court, located public interest rationales that the legislature *might* have had for those
provisions. Thus the Court felt called upon to articulate a rationale but did not
believe it was required to determine that this actually was the rationale accepted by
a majority of the legislature. (pp. 487, 490, 491) The opinion did not claim that an
act whose only purpose was to benefit one group of sellers at the expense of another
would be constitutional. Instead, it articulated consumer protection rationales that it
found acceptable and consistent with the statute. At one point Douglas states that
"the law need not be in every respect logically consistent with its aims to be constitutional. It is enough that there is *an* evil at hand for correction, and that it *might be
thought* [by whom?] that the particular legislative measure was a *rational* way to
correct it." (id., pp. 487–88, emphasis added) The opinion quotes with approval
Chief Justice Waite in *Munn v. Illinois*, 94 U.S. 113, 134 (1877): "For protection
against abuses by legislatures the people must resort to the polls, not to the courts."

43. 336 U.S. 106 (1949). In *Railway Express* the Court upheld a New York regulation
banning advertising from the sides of vehicles except those which advertised the
business of the vehicle's owner. The regulation was promulgated by the Police
Commissioner under §435 of the New York City Charter, which provides that he can
issue traffic regulations "for the facilitation of traffic and the convenience of the
public as well as the proper protection of human life and health." (cited at 107–8, n.
1) The court looked to the "public safety" goal in the City Charter (id. at 109) and

found that local authorities "may well have concluded" that one type of sign was less of a threat to public safety than another. (id. at 110)

44. 437 U.S. 117, 124–25 (1978).

45. 439 U.S. 96 (1978)

46. Id. at 105, n. 12.

47. See e.g. *Reed v. Reed*, 404 U.S. 71, 75–76 (1971) striking down a difference based on gender as unrelated to statutory purpose; and *Weber v. Aetna Casualty and Surety Co.*, 406 U.S. 164, 172 (1972)—finding that exclusion of illegitimate children from a workmen's compensation award was against Equal Protection.

48. McCloskey, 1962, pp. 54–59.

49. Ely, 1970, p. 1207.

50. 363 U.S. 603, 612 (1960). See also *McDonald v. Boards of Election Commissions*, 394 U.S. 802, 809 (1969).

51. 413 U.S. 528, 533–38 (1973).

52. Id., pp. 535–37.

53. My discussion in this section was aided by Dolgenos, n.d.

54. However, early English cases did view the preamble as a means of discovering legislative intent. See especially *Brett v. Brett*, 3 Add 210, 216, (1826): "The key to the opening of every law, is the reason and spirit of the law . . . it is to the preamble more especially that we look for the reason, or spirit, of every statute; rehearsing . . . as it ordinarily does . . . in the best and most satisfactory manner, the object or intentions of the legislature." (Quoted in Singer, 1985, §47.04)

55. Singer, 1985, §§20.02, 47.04.

56. Dolgenos, n.d., pp. 35–36. On p. 25, he likens preambles to "press releases approved by the full Congress."

57. Singer, 1985, §20.03.

58. Id., §§20.03, 47.04. It is even subject to dispute whether the courts can refer to the preamble for the purpose of construing statutory language. The purposes stated in a preamble are entitled to weight but are not conclusive.

59. One especially mechanical doctrine is the finding that the preamble is not properly part of the statute and has no legal force because the enacting clause, which states the legal authority for the statute, generally follows the preamble. Policy statements fare a bit better here since they generally follow the enacting clause. This rule has been criticized even by the most conventional of commentators. (Singer, 1985, §§20.3, 20.5)

60. Ely, 1980, p. 129: Singer, 1985, §20.05.

61. Ruud, 1958, pp. 453–55, provides a list of state constitutional provisions as of 1958. See also Williams, 1987.

62. Williams, 1987, supports increased enforcement of these provisions after an analysis of the passage of the Pennsylvania Abortion Control Act. He also cites the critical literature. (pp. 92–93)

63. Minnesota Constitution, Article 4, Sec. 17.

64. *Wass v. Anderson*, 252 N.W. 2d 131, 135 (1977). See also *Bernstein v. Commissioner of Public Safety*, 351 N.W. 2d 24, 25 (Minn. App. 1984): "[W]e are reminded that the purpose of the restriction is to prevent deception as to the nature and subject of legislative enactments." In a case decided on other grounds a separate concurrence endorsed by two Justices argued that the Court should actively discourage "garbage or Christmas tree bills" which "appear to be a direct, cynical violation of our constitution." They believed that the court "should publicly warn the legislature that if it does hereafter enact legislation . . . which clearly violated Minn. Const. art IV, sec.

17, we will not hesitate to strike it down regardless of the consequences to the legislature, the public, or the courts generally." (*State ex. rel. Mattson v. Kiedrowski*, 391 N.W. 2d 777, 785, [Minn. 1986])

The South Dakota Supreme Court stated in *Independent Community Bankers Association v. State*, 346 N.W. 2d 737 (S.D. 1984), that two of the purposes of their single-subject provisions are to "prevent the unintentional and unknowing passage of provisions inserted in a bill of which the title gives no intimation," and to "fairly apprise the public of matters which are contained in the various bills and to prevent fraud or deception of the public as to matters being considered by the legislature." (quoted in *Simpson v. Tobin*, 367 N.W. 2d 757, 767 [S.D. 1985])

65. ". . . The well-known object of this section of the constitution was to secure to every distinct measure of legislation a separate consideration and decision, dependent solely upon its individual merits, . . . by preventing the combination of different measures, dissimilar in character, purposes and objects, but united together with the sole view, by this means, of compelling the requisite support to secure their passage." (*Wass v. Anderson*, 252 N.W. 2d 131, quoting *State v. Cassidy*, 22 Minn. 312, 322 [1875]) The South Dakota Supreme Court in *Simpson v. Tobin*, 367 N.W. 2d 757, 767 (S.D. 1985), interpreted their similar clause to mean that "there is no restriction on the scope of a single subject provided it is encompassed in the title." (id. at 767)

66. Lowenstein, 1983, pp. 957–63, makes this argument.

67. For a more general defense of logrolling, see Arnold, 1990, pp. 131–32, 256, 272.

68. Lowenstein, 1983, pp. 957–58. Compare Ruud, 1958, Rudd argues that the single-subject rule is helpful in reducing logrolling, because three bills will be harder to pass than one (id. at 449), and those who are part of the deal must openly acknowledge their participation.

69. Easterbrook, 1983b, 1984; Posner, 1974a, 1982b.

70. Posner, 1982b, p. 269.

71. Id. at 273.

72. Id. at 274.

73. Easterbrook, 1983b, p. 547.

74. *Securities Ind. Assn. v. Bd. of Gov. (Bankers Trust)*, 468 U.S. 137, 160 (1984) (dissent by O'Connor), cited in Easterbrook, 1984, p. 58, n. 149.

75. Easterbrook, 1984, p. 15.

76. In *Block v. Community Nutrition Inst.*, 467 U.S. 340, consumers failed to convince the Court that they should be given access to Department of Agriculture proceedings which regulated milk prices.

77. Macey, 1986.

78. Linde, 1976.

79. Id. at 223.

80. Id. at 227.

81. Referenda, of course, have their own problems related to the ways issues are framed and the rational ignorance of voters.

82. Linde, 1976, p. 253.

83. Id., pp. 231–33.

84. Bennett, 1979; Mashaw, 1980; Strnad, 1979; Sunstein, 1990a.

85. Bennett, 1979, p. 1071.

86. Id. at 1082.

87. Id. at 1083.

88. Jeff Strnad, 1979, in a student note written about the same time as Bennett's article, concentrates on state economic substantive due process. He argues that courts should

hold that the ends of allocation, stabilization, and certain kinds of redistribution are legitimate goals for laws with economic content. For laws that lack purposes falling into these categories the burden of proof would be on defenders of the law to convince the courts of the legitimacy of the law's purpose. In a lawsuit, the state would have the responsibility of articulating the ends. (p. 1505) These ends, however, would not have to be stated explicitly in the statutory language. Furthermore, given a legitimate goal, a statute may be struck down if less costly means of accomplishing the goal can be found. (p. 1506) Thus statutes that benefit narrow private interests under the guise of furthering public health could be struck down. (p. 1506) The state bears the burden of showing that the means relate to the ends.

89. Mashaw, 1980, p. 867.
90. Id. at 851.
91. Id. at 867.
92. Id. at 869.
93. Sunstein, 1990a, p. 139.
94. Id. at 139.
95. Id. at 140.
96. Id., pp. 139–40.

CHAPTER 5

The Power of the Purse

1. The legislature's own inability to control this problem is illustrated in "Pyrrhic Victory in the War on Pork," *Congressional Quarterly*, March 9, 1991, p. 590. Two representatives, saying that they were "serving notice on their colleagues that special interest provisions could no longer be sneaked into appropriations bills without due process," succeeded in striking a special purpose appropriation for North Dakota. The funds had been included by the Senate in the final fiscal 1991 agricultural appropriations act without being separately voted on by the House. They were earmarked for a German-Russian interpretive center at the birthplace of Lawrence Welk. The representatives' action angered the chairman of the Appropriations Committee and led to attempts by a North Dakota representative to strike special projects for the crusading representatives' home states.

    Tiefer, 1989, p. 1004, reports that when appropriations are passed through huge continuing resolutions, only the Appropriations Committee members are likely to know much about the bills' contents. In commenting on the 1986 continuing resolution, David Obey (D–Wis.), an appropriations subcommittee chair, said that "[t]here may be 10 people in this place who know what's in it." (Tiefer, 1989, p. 1004, quoting Gettinger, "Congress Returns to Tackle Biggest-Ever 'CR,' " *Cong. Q.* 44:2059 [1986]) According to Tiefer, Gettinger found that one member, Representative John Porter (R–Ill.), polled his house colleagues. Of the 124 responses, two-thirds said such bills were irresponsible, and 92 percent said they concentrated too much power in the hands of a few members.

    My proposals resemble provisions in some state constitutions that forbid substantive legislation in spending bills. For example, Article III, section 12, of the Florida constitution states: "Laws making appropriations for salaries of public officers and other current expenses of the state shall contain provisions on no other subject." (Quoted in *Department of Educ. v. Lewis*, [Sup. Ct. Fl., 1982]) 416 So. 2d 455,459 The Florida Supreme Court has stated that the purpose of this provision is to ensure "that every proposed enactment is considered with deliberation and on its own merits." (id. at 459) In contrast, some state constitutions explicitly exempt appropriations bills from their "single-subject" clauses. See Ruud, 1958, pp. 453–55.

2. Thus I accept the validity of Arnold's, 1990, p. 131–32, observation that omnibus bills may be necessary for the passage of certain kinds of broad-based compromises in the public interest.

3. "[I]n our constitutional system the commitment to the separation of powers is too fundamental for us to pre-empt congressional action by judicially decreeing what accords with 'common sense and public weal.' Our constitution vests such responsibilities in the political branches." (*TVA v. Hill*, 437 U.S. 153, 195 [1978]) See also Powell's dissent (p. 196): "It is not our province to rectify policy or political judgments by the Legislative Branch, however egregiously they may disserve the public interest."

4. House Rule XXI (2) provides:

> No appropriations shall be reported in any general appropriation bill . . . for any expenditure not previously authorized by law . . . Nor shall any provision in any such bill or amendment thereto changing existing law be in order.

See also Senate Standing Rule 16.4. (Tiefer, 1989, pp. 928–31, 978–94) According to Tiefer (p. 929), "Congress began observing the policies against legislation on appropriations in the 1810s."

5. *TVA v. Hill*, 437 U.S. 153, 190–91; *Andrus v. Sierra Club*, 442 U.S. 347, 359–61 (1979).

6. Tiefer, 1989, p. 981, notes that "[d]espite the rule, the Appropriations Committee reports large numbers of legislative provisions." He reports (p. 982, n. 165) that in 1978 the Democratic Study Group estimated that "[l]ast year the FY 1978 general and supplemental appropriations bill[s] carried nearly 200 new limitations and legislative provisions reported by the Appropriations Committee. These were in addition to previously enacted general provisions which are carried in appropriation bills year after year." He also reports that the Fiscal Year 1986 defense appropriations contained seventeen pages of provisions appropriating funds and twenty-two pages of "general provisions" consisting of "policy-directing language." (p. 982)

One major loophole is the Congressional understanding that "limitation riders" are not legislation and so do not run afoul of House Rule XXI or Senate Rule 16.4. As a consequence, limitations such as "none of the funds appropriated shall be used for abortions" were used increasingly in the Seventies as an important policymaking vehicle. The practice continued in the Eighties but was restricted by new House rules designed to restrict riders. (Tiefer, 1989, pp. 933, 977–78, 984–89)

Recent examples include the Omnibus Budget Reconciliation Acts and the 1990 supplementary appropriations for aid to Panama and Nicaragua. The Omnibus Budget Reconciliation Act of 1989 (P.L. 101–239, 103 Stat. 2106–2491) fills 386 pages of the U.S. Code. (*Congressional and Administrative News* for February 1990) Only a part of this space is taken up with the assignment of dollar amounts to particular programs or agencies. The rest includes substantive amendments to a wide range of underlying statutes. Some are written to apply only to the fiscal year in question, but others apply more broadly. In general, supplemental appropriations and continuing resolutions are frequent targets of special interest amendments. (Tiefer, 1989, pp. 1007–10)

The bill to appropriate funds for aid to Panama and Nicaragua was held up for weeks in the spring of 1990 as members added special interest appropriations. See "Add-Ons Hold Up Conferees on Supplemental Spending." *Congressional Quarterly*, May 12, 1990, pp. 1466–67; "Deal Near on Supplemental as House Lards the Bill," *Congressional Quarterly*, May 19, 1990, pp. 1532–34; and "A Pork-Heavy Supplemental Is Belatedly Sent to Bush," *Congressional Quarterly*, May 26, 1990, pp. 1630–33. The Act is Public Law 101-302 (H.R. 4404), 101st Congress, May 25, 1990. A summary is available in *Congressional Quarterly*, June 9, 1990, pp. 1818–22.

7. The budget process was established under the Congressional Budget and Impound-

ment Control Act of 1974, Pub. L. 93-344, 88 Stat 297, 2 U.S.C. §§681–88 (1982 and Supp.) See Stith, 1988b, pp. 615–25; Tiefer, 1989, pp. 849–920; and Schick, 1990, for descriptions of the budget process as it was before the amendments passed in the fall of 1990. The Budget Committees created by the 1974 act do not report either spending or revenue bills, but they do propose dollar limits by appropriations area which are then voted on by Congress in the form of budget resolutions. Until 1991 these resolutions were meant to bind the appropriations subcommittees.

8. Tiefer, 1989, p. 925.

9. The number of regular appropriations acts funded for the entire fiscal year in a continuing resolution grew over the Eighties. (There are meant to be thirteen regular appropriations acts.) The numbers by fiscal year were 1980, 3; 1981, 5; 1982, 4; 1983, 7; 1984, 3; 1985, 8; 1986, 7; 1987, 13; 1988, 13; 1989, 0. In 1989 a budget summit between the president and Congress speeded up the process (Schick, 1990, p. 181). See also Tiefer, 1989, pp. 861–63, 994–1006.

10. Tiefer, 1989, pp. 967, 1000.

11. Schick, 1990, p. 183, claims that the continuing budget resolutions are commonly loaded with legislative provisions, "including whole authorization bills, some of which may have had little chance of being enacted on their own." He points to the severe time pressures under which such resolutions are considered as one reason why such provisions can survive (id. p. 196, n. 30). See also Conlan, 1988, p. 119, who argues that the fiscal 1982 budget was "pasted together in a frenzied scramble of last-minute negotiations." The result, a complex document, poorly understood by most members, was voted on by the House under a closed rule.

12. Omnibus Budget Reconciliation Act of 1990, P.L. 101-508, 104 Stat. 1388, Title 13, Nov. 5, 1990. In fiscal 1991, 1992, and 1993 three separate limits have been set for domestic, defense, and international aid spending. In fiscal 1994 and 1995 overall spending limits have been imposed. If appropriations exceed the targets in fiscal 1991–1995, automatic spending cutbacks will go into effect, but only within the category of spending where the overshot occurred. The target spending limits exclude Operation Desert Storm and Social Security. Lawrence Haas, "New Rules of the Game," *National Journal*, November 17, 1990, pp. 2793–97.

13. Many programs are not permanently authorized but must be authorized at intervals by the relevant oversight committees which specify maximum spending levels. See Tiefer, 1989, pp. 961–66. On the relationship between enabling statutes, authorization laws, appropriations and budget resolutions, see id. at 849–1010.

14. Id. at 983. On the waiving of rules in general, see Bach and Smith, 1988.

15. Tiefer, 1989, gives examples at pp. 992–94.

16. Congressional Budget and Impoundment Control Act of 1974, P.L. 93-344, 88 Stat. 297 (1974), Sec. 2. Congress itself has, however, taken a step back from the 1974 process in reasserting the power of the appropriations committees under the 1990 budget law. Lawrence Haas, "New Rules of the Game," *National Journal*, November 17, 1990, pp. 2793–97.

17. The Antideficiency Act, 31 U.S.C. §1341 (Pub. L. 97-258, Sept. 13, 1982, 96 Stat 923), provides that no government employee may spend funds that have not been appropriated unless a contract or obligation has been "authorized by law." This act, first passed in 1870 and amended several times, complements the statement in Art. I §9 of the United States Constitution that "[n]o money shall be drawn from the Treasury but in Consequence of Appropriations made by Law."

18. For a description of what happened in those years, see Tiefer, 1989, pp. 859–63.

19. This leverage has become more powerful in the light of Attorney General Civiletti's opinions on April 25, 1980, and January 16, 1981, which according to Tiefer suggested "that most government departments would have to shut down at the outset of

the funding gap without awaiting the next payday." (Tiefer, 1989, p. 996) Arnold provides an example outside of the appropriations area. He describes how a program benefiting sugar producers was passed by being included by conferees in an omnibus farm bill that was reported to the floor for an up or down vote only two hours before the Congress was to adjourn for the year. (Arnold, 1990, p. 125)

20. The Gramm–Rudman process added an additional measure of brinkmanship. See Stith, 1988b. The act is the Balanced Budget and Emergency Deficit Control Act of 1985, Public Law No. 99-177, 99 Stat. 1037, and the Balanced Budget and Emergency Deficit Control Act of 1987, P.L. 100-119, 1987 U.S. Code, *Cong. & Admin. News* (101 Stat.) 754 (the act as amended is codified in scattered sections of 2, 31, and 42 (U.S.C.). Some of the brinkmanship has been removed by the 1990 changes in the budget process. See "Adding New Layers of Complexity to Budget," *National Journal*, November 17, 1990, p. 2796.

21. Tullock, 1959.

22. Arnold, 1990, pp. 177–92, describes the politics of tax and budget policy in the Reagan years and points out how consolidation can produce reasonable economic policies. According to him, "enacting particularistic policies is relatively easy, . . . enacting sound economics policies, and especially those that restrict group or geographic benefits, is considerably more difficult." He shows, however, that such general policies are regularly enacted by leaders who "invoke legislators' calculations about general benefits, and then develop and enforce procedures that ward off particularistic amendments." (id. at 192)

23. Conlan, 1988, pp. 1305–11, notes that budget-related measures now take up an increased proportion of Congressional activity. In 1975, 38 percent of roll calls in the House related to the budget. In 1981 and 1984, the shares were 60 percent and 61 percent respectively. By 1986 the share had fallen to 46 percent. According to Conlan, budget-related vehicles have become targets for extraneous legislation. Furthermore, since budgetary pressures have also increased, Conlan claims that Congress often seeks legislative provisions with little budgetary impact.

    Most legislative provisions in appropriations bills pass without challenge "either as old and settled or because the provisions represent favors that Senators do not quarrel over." (Tiefer, 1989, p. 992) For an example of a provision with no direct budgetary impact, Tiefer mentions a 1983 provision to give a federal island to the State of Washington. (id. at 992, n. 198)

    This problem also arose in the budget reconciliation process. See Tiefer, 1989, p. 891, who notes that a major issue in the current process is "the inclusion of 'extraneous' nonbudgetary provisions" in budget reconciliation bills reported out by committee. As Senator Byrd, then Minority Leader, observed in 1981, "such provisions can bypass the normal legislative process. . . . [They are] insulated from troublesome amendments, from the possibility of lengthy debate or a filibuster. . . ." (127 *Cong. Rec.* S6665 [daily ed. June 22, 1981], quoted by Tiefer, 1989, p. 891) Byrd supplied several examples:

    > The Senate Commerce Committee loaded seven extraneous provisions, from radio deregulation to establishment of an international telecommunications and information task force, onto their recommendations. The Senate Banking, Housing, and Urban Affairs Committee loaded on everything from a cutoff of new construction funds for cities that use rent control to an exemption from reserve requirements on checking accounts for Hawaiian savings and loans. [127 *Cong. Rec.* S6887-88 (daily ed. June 24, 1981), cited by Tiefer, 1989, pp. 891–92, n. 117]

    The difficulties noted by Byrd were controlled by the adoption in 1985 of the "Byrd Amendment" requiring a three-fifths vote to overturn a ruling that an amendment to a reconciliation bill was extraneous or not germane. (Tiefer, 1989, p. 893)

24. For example, in 1982 "the special rule for the key continuing resolution made only eight amendments in order. . . . However, the rule did not make in order a requested amendment to cut funding for the Tennessee–Tombigbee waterway, a project with strong backing among southern Democrats. The rule thus provided enough choice to be passed, but not enough to alienate project defenders who might well otherwise have killed the special rule." (Tiefer, 1989, p. 1001)

    In 1984, "[b]y a rare revolt," the House defeated the proposed special rule that would have allowed no amendments. As a result the continuing resolution became the vehicle for all sorts of stalled legislative initiatives. (id. at 1002)

    When budget resolutions are considered in the House, special restrictive rules are usually used. According to Tiefer (id. at 870), such rules do not usually arouse partisan controversy. In the Senate, budget resolutions are considered under provisions that severely limit debate time.

25. Tiefer, 1989, p. 868, describes the floor action in the House on the 1979 budget resolution, which was considered under an open rule. The resolution was on the floor for nine days in May 1979. About forty amendments were considered, and there were twenty-eight recorded votes. After that experience, special restrictive rules were used for subsequent resolutions.

    In 1955 the House Rules Committee refused to grant a rule for a supplemental appropriations bill waiving points of order. Chairman Cannon of the Appropriations Committee demonstrated the value to the membership of a restrictive rule by raising points of order as often as he could on his own bill whenever a provision contained legislation. The dollar value of the bill fell from $1.2 billion to $224 million when it finally passed. (id., pp. 971–72)

26. Stith, 1988b. Furthermore, the law was simply amended whenever the targets were not met. "Provisions Designed to Tighten Clasp on the Federal Spending Purse," *Congressional Quarterly*, October 6, 1990, pp. 3196–97. Under current law the deficit targets have been made advisory only, at least through fiscal 1993. "Adding New Layers of Complexity to Budget," *National Journal*, November 17, 1990, p. 2796.

27. *Andrus v. Sierra Club*, 442 U.S. 347, and *TVA v. Hill*, 437 U.S. 153, support the view that the appropriations process should focus on allocating funds, not on changing policy. See also *Environmental Defense Fund v. Froehlke*, 473 F. 2d 346, 353–54 (8th Cir. 1972): "NEPA [the National Environmental Protection Act] requires that construction projects be completed in accordance with its substantive provisions. An appropriations act cannot serve as a vehicle to change that requirement" (footnote omitted). The opinion supports this position by quoting House Rule XXI. The House and Senate rules are also quoted with approval in *Associated Electric Cooperative, Inc. v. Morton*, 507 F. 2d 1167, 1174 (D.C. Cir. 1974).

28. 442 U.S. 347, 359.

29. Id. at 362.

30. Id., pp. 360–61, quoting *TVA v. Hill*, 437 U.S. 153, 190. See also *Local 2677, American Fedn. of Govt. Emp. v. Phillips*, 358 F. Supp. 60, 74, n. 15 (D.C. Dist. Col. 1973): "[U]nder established Congressional procedures, substantive law provisions must be placed in authorization bills; they would be ruled out of order in an appropriations bill."

31. See *New York Airways, Inc. v. United States*, 369 F. 2d 743, 749 (Ct. Claims 1966): "As a general proposition Congress has the power to amend substantive legislation for a particular year by an appropriation act, although such procedure is considered undesirable legislative form and subject to a point of order." *City of Los Angeles v. Adams*, 556 F. 2d 40, 49 (D.C. Cir. 1977), states that "'we are bound to follow Congress's last word on the matter even in an appropriations law.'" See also *National Labor Relations Board v. Thompson Product*, 141 F. 2d 794, 797–99 (9th Cir. 1944),

arguing that while amendments via appropriations are permitted, an appropriations proviso did not the amend the statute but only limited appropriations for the fiscal year; *Skoko v. Andrus*, 638 F. 2d 1154, 1158 (9th Cir. 1979); *Republic Airlines, Inc. v. U.S. Dept. of Transp.*, 849 F. 2d 1315, 1320 (10th Cir. 1988); *Friends of the Earth v. Armstrong*, 485 F. 2d 1, 9 (10th Cir. 1973), *cert. denied*, 94 S. Ct. 933 (1974); *American Fedn. of Govt. Employees, AFL-CIO v. Campbell*, 659 F. 2d 157 (D.C. Cir. 1980), *cert. denied*, 454 U.S. 820 (1981); and *Director, Office of Workmen's Compensation Program v. Alabama By-Products Corp.*, 560 F. 2d 710, 719 (5th Cir. 1977).

　　Repetition from year to year in appropriations acts in one way to convince the courts that the substantive statute has been overridden. *U.S. v. Dickerson*, 310 U.S. 554 [1940]; *Skoko v. Andrus*, 638 F. 2d 1154, 1157

32. In *U.S. v. Dickerson*, 310 U.S. 554, 555, a case involving reenlistment bonuses, the Court states: "There can be no doubt that Congress could suspend or repeal the authorization contained in [the relevant statute]; and it could accomplish its purpose by an amendment to an appropriation bill, or otherwise." The most recent case is *U.S. v. Will*, 449 U.S. 200, 222 (1980), dealing with cost of living increases for judges, where an appropriations act is read as repealing a provision in an earlier statute.

33. The 1980 version in an amendment to the Labor–HHS appropriation stated that "none of the funds provided by this act shall be used to perform abortions" (with various exceptions, such as rape or incest). (Pub. L. 96-123, §109, 93 Stat. 926)

34. *Harris v. McRae*, 448 U.S. 297, 306–11 (1980). The opinion argues that Medicaid (Title XIX of the Social Security Act, 79 Stat. 343, as amended, 42 U.S.C. §1396 et seq. [1976 ed.] and Supp. II) should be viewed as a matching grant program that imposes no obligations on the states in the absence of federal matching funds. The original Act was viewed as establishing only a basic structure, with the details of funding priorities left to the appropriations process. In id. at 310, n. 14, the Court states:

> Since Title XIX itself provides for variations in the required coverage of state Medicaid plans depending on changes in the availability of federal reimbursement, we need not inquire, as the District Court did, whether the Hyde Amendment is a substantive amendment to Title XIX. The present case is thus different from *TVA v. Hill*, 437 U.S. 153, 189–193, where the issue was whether continued appropriations for the Tellico Dam impliedly repealed the substantive requirements of the Endangered Species Act prohibiting the continued construction of the Dam because it threatened the natural habitat of an endangered species.

The District Court, which found the Hyde Amendment unconstitutional, argued that the Hyde Amendment did substantively amend the Medicaid Act. (*McRae v. Califano*, 491 F. Supp. 630, 732 [E.D.N.Y. 1980]) The District Court opinion (id., pp. 742–844) includes a lengthy annex which summarizes the Congressional debate on the various versions of the Hyde Amendment between 1976 and 1980. The impropriety of including the amendment in an appropriations measure was raised by several speakers (id., pp. 745, 755, 757, 781), and points of order were raised. (id. at 772) Even Representative Hyde agreed that it was unfortunate to introduce the abortion issue into an appropriations bill. He justified his effort on the grounds that "there is no other vehicle that reaches the floor in which these complex issues can be involved." (id. at 773) Senator Magnuson made the following statement in 1979:

> It all comes back to appropriations. On every piece of legislation if it is a hot potato the legislative committees do not want to tackle, or someone gets frustrated because the legislative committee will not pass a piece of legislation that

they are for, they come down to the Appropriations Committee and try to attach it there. Frankly I am getting a little bit fed up. The abortion issues has been holding up the whole Government. It does not belong on the appropriations bill and particularly a continuing resolution bill. [id. at 839]

35. My proposal is essentially the reverse of Martin Shapiro's. Both of us focus on the same issue of the inconsistency between absolute statements of the program's value and subsequent finite appropriations. He would have courts accept appropriations decisions as valid priority setting exercises. Shapiro, 1988, p. 186, n. 20. I would have the courts highlight cases of grossly inadequate funding with the goal of toning down grandiose claims in the first place.

36. The judiciary cannot appropriate funds. It can determine if a legal obligation exists or if a constitutional requirement has not been fulfilled, but the courts have not actually ordered the spending of money by the federal government. The federal courts have, however, required spending by state and local governments that are in violation of the Constitution. See Frug, 1978, critically reviewing judicial opinions that use constitutional arguments to require spending by state and local governments.

37. P.L. 83-560, 42 U.S.C. §1441. This goal was criticized as impossible or overly expensive. See statement of Senator James P. Kern (R–Mo.) in *Congressional Record*, April 21, 1948, p. 4679 (Senate), cited by Weicher, 1980, p. 16.

38. Housing and Urban Development Act of 1968, Pub. L. 90-448, §2, Aug. 1, 1968, 82 Stat. 476, 12 U.S.C. §1701. After repeating the 1949 language, the Act goes on to state: "The Congress finds . . . that there exist in the public and private sectors of the economy the resources and capabilities necessary to the full realization of this goal."

39. Plotnick and Skidmore, 1975, p. 15. "Housing assistance, unlike, for example, public assistance in nutrition or health care, is a lottery. Any eligible family has only a small chance of winning at all, and like all lotteries, the prizes vary enormously." (Salins, 1987, p. 6)

The 1949 Act authorized 810,000 units to be built over the next six years. By 1960, five years after the target date, less than one-quarter of the authorized units had been produced. (Hayes, 1985, p. 93) The 1968 Act set a target of 26 million units, with one-fifth for low- and moderate-income households, and was followed by several high-production years, which were brought to a halt by the Nixon Administration. (id., pp. 105–6, 110–11; Sternlieb and Listokin, 1987, p. 29) Only 2.7 million low- and moderate-income units were produced. (Weicher, 1980, p. 16) In 1987 only 2.1 million (28%) of the poverty-level renter households lived in subsidized housing. (Apgar and Brown, 1989, p. 18)

40. The peak was 1.2 percent in 1968. (Hayes, 1985, p. 168) Spending is poorly correlated with units produced, because many subsidy payments are spread over the life of the housing unit. Subsidized housing production peaked in 1971, fell off dramatically in the early Seventies, and rose again in the later Seventies, only to fall in an uneven pattern in the Eighties. (id. at 150)

41. Id., pp. 93–96; Meehan, 1977, 1979. However, the absolute size of the federal commitment was not trivial. Between 1950 and 1986, 5 million units were built or rehabilitated, and federal outlays were $110 billion in 1986 dollars. (Salins, 1987, p. 1)

Housing quality has increased markedly since 1949, but most of this can be attributed to rising incomes, not federal policies. (Hayes, 1985, p. 73; Weicher, 1980, pp. 24–27) Between 1950 and 1980 the percentage of units lacking some or all plumbing fell from 34 to 2.2 percent; the percentage in poor physical condition fell from 9 to 3 percent (1977 data); the percentage overcrowded (more than 1.0 persons per room) fell from 15.8 to 4.2 percent; and the percentage of married couples without their own household went from 2.4 to 1.1 percent (1977 data). (U.S. Census figures cited in Weicher, 1980, p. 14; and 1987, p. 46) Since 1974, however, improvements in housing quality have slowed. (Apgar and Brown, 1988) Apgar and Brown (p. 16) report that 8.2 percent of owners and 18.7 percent of renter households (a total of 9.5 million households) lived in inadequate housing in 1983, down from 11.3 and 22.0 percent in 1974.

42. Hayes, 1985, p. 204, citing summary of the Housing Act of 1974, P.L. 93-383, Title I, in U.S. Department of Housing and Urban Development, *Block Grants for Community Development*, First Report on the Brookings Institution Monitoring Study of the CDBG Program, Washington, D.C., 1977.

43. Hayes, 1985, pp. 210–11.

44. Id. at 236.

45. Environmental and Energy Study Institute and Environmental Law Institute, 1985, p. ii. The number of deadlines totaled three hundred. In addition to the 14 percent that were met on time, 41 percent were completed after passage of the deadline; 27 percent had not been completed; no information was available on 15 percent; and 2 percent were deleted or extended but not yet satisfied by 1985. While some deadlines may deal with relatively trivial matters, others do not. For example, the preparation of State Implementation Plans is a key part of the Clean Air Act. None of them had been completed by the initial deadline of December 31, 1972. (Henderson and Peterson, 1978, p. 1463)

46. The courts' approach in such cases has been essentially to rewrite the statute to extend deadlines that have already passed. See, for example, *Environmental Defense Fund v. Thomas*, 627 F. Supp. 566 (D.C. Dist. Col. 1986), and *Delaney v. E.P.A.*, 898 F 2d 687 (9th Cir. 1990). In *Delaney*, however, the appeals court refused to accept the EPA's plan to give delinquent counties three years to carry out implementation plans under the Clean Air Act of 1977. The EPA argued that in spite of the clearly stated deadline in the 1977 Act, "Congress knew some states would not attain by the 1982 deadline and did not intend that states implement draconian measures." (id. at 690) The court did not accept this argument; however, since the case was brought after the deadline had passed, the most the court could do was require compliance as soon as possible using every available control measure.

47. Weingast and Marshall, 1988; Shepsle, 1987b.

48. Krehbiel, 1989. But see Hall and Grofman, 1990, who claim that representativeness varies across committees and across issues.

49. The revenue-sharing act was Title I of the State and Local Fiscal Assistance Act of 1972, P.L. 92-512. The Act simply mentioned payments of money to state and local government (I.A. 102) and required that they be used for "priority expenditures," which included a list of basic services and capital expenditures. (I.A. 103 [a]) The Act was repealed in 1986.

50. Such joint resolutions are extremely common. For example, the United States Code Service for December 1990 includes seventeen such resolutions for such causes as Visiting Nurse Associations, Geography, Rice, Philanthropy, and Women Veterans.

51. Outside of my concern are entitlement statutes that include formulas to determine benefit levels. In principle, Congress simply makes available sufficient funds to pay for the law as written. Spending levels can be reduced by amending the payment formula in the basic statute. (Tiefer, 1989, pp. 850–51)

52. See Henderson and Peterson, 1978, on the weakness of aspirational commands as a way of inducing compliance with environmental statutes. They do not deal with public perceptions of inflated programmatic rhetoric, but they do suggest that appeals to public welfare are inadequate even when backed by legal sanctions. They conclude that

　　the heavy reliance by Congress upon aspirational commands in recent years may reflect what some environmentalist writers have long and openly suspected—that in the final analysis, federal lawmakers lack the resolve to commit the resources necessary to implement their environmental policies effectively. . . . [T]hey have taken a relatively high sounding, seemingly low cost road, and have hoped for the best. [id. at 1470]

53. The Constitutional Court of the Federal Republic of Germany has adopted this practice in several recent opinions. (Kommers, 1989) The court can declare an act either null and void or incompatible with the Basic Law. In the latter case the unconstitutional practice remains in force during a transitional period when parliament is expected to rectify the situation." (id. at 61) Between 1951 and 1987, of the 391 legal provisions invalidated by the court, 144 fell into this category. (id. at 60) Kommers, p. 100, presents one example in which the court held a revenue-sharing formula invalid in 1986 but gave the parliament until fiscal 1988 to revise the law.

54. This practice is discussed in another context in Stith, 1988b, pp. 611–12. According to her, however, both the Congressional Budget and Impoundment Control Act and the Gramm–Rudman–Hollings process have given Congress a greater incentive to include more detailed line items in appropriations bills. (id., pp. 643–52)

55. If the legislature has not included a line item in an appropriations act, then the executive branch may refuse to fund a program. See *Intern. Union, United Auto., Aerospace v. Donovan*, 746 F. 2d 855, 861 (D.C. Cir. 1984). The opinion by then Judge Scalia argues that the executive's failure to fund a program is consistent with the underlying statute, which is read as giving discretion to the Secretary. It is not, however, so obvious as Scalia makes it seem that Congress intended to permit the Secretary to have discretion to repeal the law de facto in the absence of an explicit line item appropriation. Scalia, however, suggests that whatever the Congressional intent, the courts should avoid such issues:

To infer a "reasonable distribution" requirement, as appellees would have us do, is to assume that Congress has conferred upon us a task for which we are eminently unsuited and, in all likelihood, constitutionally incompetent. The distribution of public funds among competing social programs is an archetypically political task, involving the application of value judgments and predictions to innumerable alternatives, as opposed to the application of accepted principles to a binary determination. . . . If Congress ever clearly places it in our responsibility to decree what "reasonable" amounts should be expended on various programs, there will be time enough to consider how, and indeed whether, such a task can be performed; but we will assuredly not run out to interpret lump-sum appropriations as constituting such a mandate. [id., pp. 862–63]

Direct challenges to Scalia's position are difficult to find, but one Ninth Circuit opinion comes close. This case, *Rincon Band of Mission Indians v. Harris*, 618 F. 2d 569 (9th Cir. 1980), found that the Department of Health, Education, and Welfare and the Indian Health Service had violated California Indians' right of equal protection by allocating them too small a share of the funds for Indian health services. The low overall level of appropriations by Congress was not accepted as a justification for the allocation scheme or as an implicit ratification of the agencies' actions. The court did not require additional appropriations from Congress but did require that the agencies rework their allocation formula to give a share to California closer to its share of the nation's American Indian population. The executive was seen to have an obligation under the relevant substantive statute "to distribute rationally and equitably all of the available program funds." (id. at 937)

56. One example may be the consumers mentioned in the preamble to the statute at issue in *Block v. Community Nutrition Inst.*, 467 U.S. 340 (1984).

57. 501 F. 2d 848 (D.C. Cir. 1974).

58. *Pennsylvania v. Lynn* has not been adopted as a precedent outside of a few narrowly focused HUD cases. When a direct conflict with Congress exists over the propriety of an appropriation, courts have required the executive to spend the funds. See *Community Action Prog. Exec. Dir. Assn. of N.J., Inc. v. Ash*, 365 F. Sup. 1355 (D.C.N.J. 1973), and the impoundment cases. The courts have determined that if Congress appropriates money, it cannot be impounded by the president to fulfill macroeconomic goals. The President is not free to refuse to spend money appropriated for one purpose because of extraneous policy concerns. (See, e.g., *Train v. City of New York*, 420 U.S. 35 (1975); *Sioux Valley Empire Electric Association, Inc. v. Butz*, 504 F. 2d 168 (8th Cir. 1974); *National Coun. of Com. Mental H. Ctrs., Inc. v. Weinberger*, 361 F. Supp. 897 (D.C. Dist. Col. 1973); *State Highway Commission of Missouri v. Volpe*, 479 F. 2d 1099 (8th Cir. 1973); *State of Louisiana ex rel. Guste v. Brinegar*, 388 F. Supp. 1319 (D.C. Dist. Col. 1975).

59. *U.S. v. Louisiana*, 265 F. Supp. 703, 708 (E.D. La. 1966 (three judge court), *aff'd*, 386 U.S. 270 (1967).

60. The case has been taken to apply to federal administration of federal laws. It was cited in an Attorney General's opinion, January 16, 1981, justifying emergency spending by the executive branch at the beginning of the fiscal year in cases where Congress has failed to pass appropriations acts by the deadline. A narrow reading of the case, however, would see it only as saying that *under this particular statute* Congress meant to imply that the means would be available to carry it out.

61. *Puerto Rican Organization for Political Act. v. Kusper*, 490 F. 2d 575 (7th Cir. 1973); *Torres v. Sachs*, 381 F. Supp. 309 (S.D.N.Y. 1974); *Arroyo v. Tucker*, 372 F. Supp. 764 (E.D.Pa. 1974).

62. Much of the debate here concerns the status of government contracts. Does the existence of a contract signed by an executive branch official obligate the legislature to appropriate funds? The courts' answers have turned on the language of the contracts, the expectations of the parties, and the actions of the legislature. See *Fowler v. United Stats*, 3 Ct. Cl. 43, 1867 (damages awarded to contractor whose contract was canceled even through contract was for a larger sum than had been appropriated); *The Floyd Acceptances*, 74 U.S. 666 (1868) (government failure to honor acceptances for Army supplies upheld); *U.S. v. Corliss Steam-Eng. Co.*, 10 Ct. Cl. 494 (1874), *aff'd* 91 U.S. 321 (1875) (settlement arising from cancellation of valid contract is binding in spite of Congressional attempt to void settlement); *Louisiana ex rel. Hubert v. Mayor and Council of New Orleans*, 215 U.S. 170 (1909), upholding writ of mandamus to compel local government to levy taxes to satisfy debt obligations; *Seatrain Lines v. U.S.*, 99 Ct. Cl. 272 (1943) (proviso in appropriations bill forbidding payments under a valid contract entitles contractor to damages equal to its net losses); and *Blackhawk Heating & Plumbing Co. v. United States*, 622 F. 2d 539 (Ct. Claims 1980) (portion of contract overrun settlement agreement voided because of contract language making payment conditional on appropriated funds and because of subsequent legislation forbidding payment). See, especially, *New York Airways, Inc. v. United States*, 369 F. 2d 743, where the Court of Claims insisted that a subsidy be paid to airlines providing airmail services even though appropriations were insufficient. The same court argued, however, that the executive agency had no legal authority to make the payment. The plaintiff could obtain relief only from the Court of Claims. A subsequent case has read this opinion narrowly. (*Republic Airlines, Inc. v. U.S. Dept. of Transp.*, 849 F. 2d 1315, 1316, 1319]

63. According to the Attorney General (January 16, 1981), the Congress cannot deny the President obligational authority to carry out his constitutionally enumerated powers such as the "Power to grant Reprieves and Pardons for Offenses against the United States." (Art. II, §2, cl. 1) More generally, he concludes that the Antideficiency Act

exempts "obligations necessarily incident to presidential initiatives undertaken within his constitutional powers." Compare Stith, 1988a, pp. 1350–52, with Sidak, 1989.

While this claim has not been tested in court, a similar issue arose involving the federal judiciary. In 1986 the Justice Department concluded that "civil jury trials will have to be suspended on June 16 [1986] through the end of the fiscal year (September 30)," because Congress had failed to appropriate sufficient funds for juror payment. The Ninth Circuit held that "nationwide suspension of the civil jury trial system is unconstitutional." (*Armster v. United States District Court*, 792 F. 2d 1423, 1425 [9th Cir. 1986]) The court held that, while budget constraints provided a legal justification to limit the number of jury trials scheduled in any period (id. at 1428), "the availability of constitutional rights does not vary with the rise and fall of account balances in the Treasury. . . . [C]onstitutional rights do not turn on the political mood of the moment, the outcome of cost/benefit analysis or the results of economic or fiscal calculations." (id. at 1429) Even here, however, the court did not issue a writ ordering an appropriation but left it to the legislature to act in the light of the decision.

See also *Missouri v. Jenkins*, 110 S. Ct. 1651 (1990), which refused to impose a tax increase to fund a court-ordered school desegregation plan but upheld a Court of Appeals order authorizing local government institutions to raise funds in spite of state-imposed spending limitations. Compare *Griffin v. Prince Edward County School Bd.*, 377 U.S. 218, 233 (1964), permitting a District Court to order a county Board of Supervisors to levy taxes to finance school desegregation.

At the state and local level §1983 suits have been brought which claim that an individual's constitutional rights have been violated by the failure of a government to appropriate funds. In *Minton v. St. Bernard Parish School Bd.*, 803 F. 2d 129 (5th Cir. 1986), a case against a school board that refused to pay a damage judgment to an out-of-state plaintiff was permitted to proceed. A Louisiana statute forbade payment of a judgment without an appropriation. For a general discussion of federal court decisions that mandate state and local spending under the Constitution, see Frug, 1978.

64. Stith, 1988a, pp. 1392–93; *Reeside v. Walker*, 52 U.S. 272, 290–91 (1851) (state court judgment against the United States not binding in absence of appropriations); and *National Assn. of Regional Councils v. Costle*, 564 F. 2d 583, 589–90 (D.C. Cir. 1977) (federal courts have no power to revive spending authority that lapsed before commencement of suit). Even in contract cases judges claim that they are only determining legal liability, not ordering appropriations. *NARC v. Costle* at 590, n. 16, states that "the courts do not deal with questions of appropriations at all." All they do is determine legal liability. "If there is no . . . appropriation out of which a judgment can be paid, the courts still cannot order that it be satisfied, since 'the matter of whether or not an appropriation will be made rests solely upon the determination of Congress, and with that determination this court has nothing to do.' *Hetfield v. U.S.*, 78 Ct. Cl. 419, 422 (1933)." See also *Collins v. U.S.*, 15 Ct. Cl. 22, 35–36 (1879); *Geddes v. U.S.*, 38 Ct. Cl. 428, 444 (1903) ("The judgment of a court has nothing to do with the means—with the remedy for satisfying a judgment. It is the business of courts to render judgments, leaving to Congress and the executive officers the duty of satisfying them."); and *Glidden Company v. Zdanok*, 370 U.S. 530, 568–71 (1962) (inability of Court of Claims to enforce its judgments not inconsistent with Article III status). These opinions are an attempt to comply with Art. I, §9, cl. 7 of the Constitution, which states that "no money shall be drawn from the Treasury but in consequence of appropriations made by law."

65. "An authorization does not necessarily mean that a program will continue. Congress may decide to terminate a program before its authorization has expired, either indirectly by failing to supply funds through a continuing resolution or appropriation, or by explicitly forbidding the further use of funds for the programs as it did in the case

of the supersonic transport." (*Local 2677, American Fedn. of Govt. Emp. v. Phillips*, 358 F. Supp. 60, 75) See also *Guadamuz v. Ash*, 368 F. Supp. 1233, 1239, n. 26 (D.C. Dist. Col. 1973): "Legislation creating a new program is a two-stage process. Authorization bills merely provide the authority for programs. The Congress must still appropriate funds in an appropriations bill before the program can be operated." And *Local 2816, Office of Economic Op. Emp. U., AFGE v. Phillips*, 360 F. Supp. 1092, 1099 (N.D. Ill. 1973): ". . . until Congress actually appropriates funds for the fiscal year 1974 there is no obligation on the part of the defendants to carry out programs with regard to it."

66. 451 U.S. 1 (1981).

67. The "overall purpose" of the Act, as amended in 1978, is

> to assist [the] states to assure that persons with developmental disabilities receive the care, treatment, and other services necessary to enable them to achieve their maximum potential through a system which coordinates, monitors, plans, and evaluates those services and which ensures the protection of the legal and human rights of persons with developmental disabilities. [42 U.S.C.A. §6000(b)(1). The section was reworded in 1987, Pub.L. 100–146.]

68. Id. at §6010.

69. For example, the State of Pennsylvania, where Pennhurst is located, received only $1.6 million in annual appropriations. (*Pennhurst State School v. Halderman*, 451 U.S. 1, 24)

One aspect of the opinion that does not concern me here is the special problems raised when Congress creates a program to be administered by the states. The Court assumes "that Congress will not implicitly attempt to impose massive financial obligations on the States. . . . By insisting that Congress speak with a clear voice, we enable the State to exercise their choice [of whether to participate in the Federal program] knowingly, cognizant of the consequences of their participation." (id. at 17).

70. 397 U.S. 397, 413 (1970). Quoted in *Pennhurst*, 451 U.S. 1, 19.

71. The conversion of implicit repeals to de jure repeals would be consistent with cases finding that an explicit failure to fund a statutory provision amounts to repeal of that provision. The only troubling aspects of those cases is that they show that Congress is sometimes quite unconcerned with inconsistencies between promise and performance. Thus in *Friends of the Earth v. Armstrong*, 485 F. 2d 1, the Tenth Circuit upheld a congressional decision not to fund a project that would have prevented water from Lake Powell from entering the land area of the Rainbow Bridge National Monument. A proviso in the Public Works Appropriations Acts between 1962 and 1973 explicitly provided that no funds should be used "to prevent waters of Lake Powell from entering any National Monuments." Congress included this language in spite of statutory provisions which apparently required protection. The Appeals Court ruled that Congress had repealed these portions of the statute insofar as they applied to Rainbow Bridge. In dicta, however, the decision goes further to claim that appropriations acts are just as effective a way to legislate as ordinary bills. The discussion in the first part of this chapter has been an attempt to challenge that assertion. The court should have restricted itself to the facts of the case which concerned only the failure to fund a legislative provision, not the creation of a new program.

72. Jonathan Swift, "A Modest Proposal for Preventing the Children of poor People in Ireland from being a Burden to their Parents or Country; and for making them beneficial to the Publick. Written in the Year 1729," in Swift, 1958, pp. 488–96.

CHAPTER 6
Occupational Safety and Health

1. See Mendeloff, 1979, 1987; Viscusi, 1983.

2. Viscusi, 1983, pp. 1–5.

3. See, e.g., Fischoff, Slovic, Lichtenstein, Read, and Combs, 1978; Kahneman, Slovic, and Tversky, 1982.

4. Viscusi, 1983, pp. 37–58. The evidence for the theory is spotty. See Smith, 1979, who finds that only risk of death is incorporated into wage differentials, and Viscusi, 1978, who finds that workers do obtain wage premiums in risky jobs.

5. Lyndon, 1989; Mendeloff, 1979, pp. 13–15; Viscusi, 1983, pp. 59–87.

6. Mendeloff, 1979, pp. 12–13.

7. Compare the more general analysis of inalienability issues in Rose-Ackerman, 1985.

8. Frank, 1985, pp. 136–41. See p. 167 for the definition of a "prisoners' dilemma."

9. Viscusi, 1983, p. 83.

10. Mendeloff, 1979, pp. 32–33, 60.

11. Lyndon, 1989.

12. Viscusi, 1983, pp. 84–87, 157–59.

13. There is some evidence that the existing OSHAct, although it lacks the two-tier structure proposed here, operates de facto as a bargaining chip for unions. (Mendeloff, 1979, pp. 16–17, 91)

14. For a discussion of how the inconsistent treatment of new versus old technology biases investment decisions under other regulatory programs, see Huber, 1983.

15. For a fuller discussion of the reform of workers' compensation, see Viscusi, 1983, pp. 87–92, 159–60. This approach should be contrasted with the injury tax considered by the Council of Economic Advisers and other economists at the time of the debate on the OSHAct. See Mendeloff, 1979, pp. 25–31.

  The advantage of an injury tax is that, since workers are not compensated, they have an incentive to take care. However, it appears likely that employers are in the best position to evaluate risks and can influence the caretaking of workers through incentive payments and work rules. Thus, a reformed workers' compensation system which gave employers a greater safety incentive would not create insuperable moral hazard problems. Moore and Viscusi, 1989, show that even the current imperfect system gives employers an incentive to reduce fatality rates.

  My general perspective assumes that the Occupational Safety and Health Administration (OSHA) should concentrate on hazards that can be regulated generically by bringing to bear general knowledge about occupational hazards. Those health and safety problems that are, in fact, ideosyncratic to particular workplaces and particular employees should be handled by negotiations between workers and employers. These negotiations could be tilted in favor of workers by requiring employers to pay for harms through workers' compensation.

16. 29 U.S.C.A. §651 et seq. (1982).

17. Id. at §651(b) and (b)(7).

18. Id. at §652 (8).

19. Id. at §655(b)(5).

20. Id. at §655(a).

21. Id. at §655(b).

22. Id., §652 (8), states that an " 'occupational safety and health standard' means a standard which requires conditions, or the adoption or use of one or more practices, means, methods, operations, or processes, reasonably necessary or appropriate to provide safe or healthful employment and places of employment."

23. Id. at §655(b)(5).

24. Id., §657(c), requires employers to provide certain information to employees, but it stops short of requiring full disclosure, and §664 exempts trade secrets. Under §655(b)(7) regulations must include warning provisions. The Secretary of Health and Human Services must publish lists of hazards (§669[6]), and annual reports must be prepared by both the Secretary of Labor and the Secretary of Health and Human Services that provide extensive information (§675). The rule dealing with access to employee exposure and medical records is published at 29 CFR §1910.20 (1987). The hazard communication (labeling) rule is at 29 CFR §1910.1200 (1987). See Lyndon, 1989.

25. 29 U.S.C.A. §655.

26. Id. at §655(b)(7).

27. Id. at §§669, 671, 673.

28. While not coordinated with the OSHAct, the Toxic Substances Control Act, 15 U.S.C. §§2601, 2604 (1982), does contain prescreening requirements that apply to workplace hazards. However, reporting requirements are weak, and testing can be ordered by the Environmental Protection Agency only if an unreasonable risk exists. (Lyndon, 1989)

29. 29 U.S.C.A. §§669, 670, 671.

30. Id. at §656.

31. Id., §§659, 661.

32. See Mendeloff, 1979, 1987. Other analyses of OSHA's behavior are McCaffrey, 1982; Greenwood, 1984; Mintz, 1984; and Viscusi, 1983.

33. Mendeloff, 1979, pp. 94–120. This conclusion is controversial. See Robert Smith, 1976a, 1976b; and Viscusi, 1979. Studies finding that OSHA has had an impact on workplace safety are Cooke and Gautschi, 1981; and Smith, 1979.

34. Mendeloff, 1979, p. 91, makes this argument.

35. Mendeloff, 1987.

36. For example, the original benzene standard was issued on February 10, 1978, 29 CFR §1910.1028 (1979). The Supreme Court disallowed the rule on July 2, 1980. (*Industrial Union Dept., AFL-CIO v. American Petroleum Inst.* 448 U.S. 607 [1980])

37. In June 1988 OSHA began a rulemaking designed to provide a wholesale revision of the standards for hundreds of chemicals. The proposal has been criticized for relying too heavily on standards developed by the private American Conference of Governmental Industrial Hygienists and for lacking enforcement strength. Nevertheless, it appears to be a constructive step (53 FR 20,960 [June 7, 1988]; U.S. Office of Management and Budget, 1988b, pp. 297–98) The final rule was issued on January 19, 1989. (29 CFR 1910)

38. See E.O. 12291 (February 17, 1981). For an overview of pre-Reagan efforts to provide executive oversight, see Viscusi, 1983.

39. Viscusi, 1983. See, for example, OSHA Notice of Proposed Rulemaking to Revise Concrete and Masonry Construction Standards 50 FR 37,543 (1985); and OSHA Final Rule on Occupational Exposure to Formaldehyde 29 CFR §§1910.1926 (1987).

40. For example, cotton dust, 29 CFR §1910 (1987); grain elevators, 17 OSHR 1227 (January 6, 1988); asbestos, 15 OSHR 917 (January 30, 1986); ethylene oxide, 53 FR 11,414 (April 6, 1988). See also OSHA Proposal to Revise Air Contaminant Exposure Limits, 53 FR 20, 960 (1988).

In an interesting switch, firms in the smelting industry argued that OSHA's rule on airborne arsenic should be overturned because OSHA had not told them specifically what technology to employ. They argued that it was "unreasonable" for them to have to develop their own compliance plan. The Court of Appeals rejected this argument. (*ASARCO, Inc. v. OSHA*, 746 F. 2d 483, 498 [9th Cir., 1984])

41. *Industrial Union Dept., AFL-CIO v. American Petroleum Inst.*, 448 U.S. 607 (benzene); and *American Textile Mfrs. Inst. v. Donovan*, 452 U.S. 490 (1981) (cotton dust).

42. 452 U.S. 490, 508–9.

43. *American Petroleum Inst. v. OSHA*, 581 F. 2d 493 (5th Cir. 1978).

44. The process is described in *Industrial Union Dept.*, 448 U.S. 607, 639–46.

45. In U.S. Office of Management and Budget, 1987b, p. 650, only three substances— formaldehyde, benzene, and ethylene dibromide—are listed as reaching the final rule stage during that period. In U.S. Office of Management and Budget, 1986, p. 579, the same three substances plus asbestos are listed in the final rule category. Only the asbestos regulations were actually issued during that year (51 Fed. Reg. 22, 612 [1986], 29 C.F.R. 1910.1001, and they lacked controls on short-term exposures (53 Fed. Reg. 14,029 [1988], 29 C.F.R. 1926.58). In 1987 a benzene regulation was finally issued and accepted without court challenge. The benzene rule is a response to the 1980 Supreme Court case. (*Industrial Union Dept.*) 448 U.S. 607 (Final OSHA Rule on Occupational Exposure to Benzene, 52 Fed. Reg. 34460, Sept. 11, 1987, 29 C.F.R. 1910) A rule for formaldehyde was issued in February 1988, 29 CFR §§1910, 1926 (1987), but ethylene dibromide remained on OSHA's agenda.

46. Given the similarity of the underlying issues, the Fifth Circuit concluded:

> OSHA's failure to provide an estimate of expected benefits for reducing the permissible exposure limit, supported by substantial evidence, makes it impossible to assess the reasonableness of the relationship between expected costs and benefits. This failure means that the required support is lacking to show reasonable necessity for the standard promulgated. [*American Petroleum Inst. v. OSHA*, 581 F. 2d 493, 505]

However, the agency was not required to conduct "an elaborate cost-benefit analysis" so long as the benefits bear "a reasonable relationship" to the costs. (id. at 503) Thus the burden of proof was placed on the agency, but the standard imposed takes account of the imperfect information available.

In several cases decided before the benzene case, lower courts had found that the Consumer Product Safety Commission was required to balance benefits against costs in regulating hazardous products. The lower courts observed that the issue of workplace health and safety looked very similar to the issue of product safety. Part of the justification for this interpretation came from the common law of torts. See *Forester v. Consumer Product Safety Comm.*, 559 F. 2d 774 (D.C. Cir. 1977); and *Aqua Slide 'N' Dive Corp. v. Consumer Product Safety Comm.*, 569 F. 2d 831 (5th Cir. 1978).

47. 448 U.S. 607, 666.

48. Id., pp. 666–67.

49. Id., pp. 667, 670.

50. In *American Textile Mfrs. Inst. v. Donovan*, 452 U.S. 490, 514–22, Justice Brennan quotes extensively from the rhetoric in the *Congressional Record*. See also Justice Marshall's dissent in the benzene case, 448 F. 2d 607, 688 et. seq.

51. In areas other than toxic substances in the workplace, there is some evidence that this type of review may be possible under OSHA. Safety issues can still be decided on cost-benefit grounds. Courts have appeared more hospitable to policy analytic arguments when the method of compliance is at issue rather than the level of worker health and safety. See *Donovan v. Castle and Cooke Foods*, 692 F. 2d 641 (9th Cir.

1982) (hearing damage in cannery); and 18 OSHA 7 (June 1, 1988) (brief in lawsuit challenging grain elevator standards). For a summary of court cases using cost-benefit concepts see Heimann et al., 1990, pp. 608–18.

52. 29 U.S.C.A. 127 §651(b). The goal is "to assure so far as possible every working man and woman in the Nation safe and healthful working conditions and to preserve our human resources." In §651(b)(7) medical criteria are to be developed to "assure insofar as practicable that no employee will suffer diminished health, functional capacity, or life expectancy as a result of his work experience."

53. If we are ever to reshoulder the burden of ensuring that Congress itself make the critical policy decisions, these are surely the cases in which to do it. It is difficult to imagine a more obvious example of Congress simply avoiding a choice which was both fundamental for the purposes of the statute and yet politically so divisive that the necessary decision or compromise was difficult, if not impossible, to hammer out in the legislative forge. . . . It is the hard choices, and not the filling in of the blanks, which must be made by the elected representatives of the people. When fundamental policy decisions underlying important legislation about to be enacted are to be made, the buck stops with Congress and the President insofar as he exercises his constitutional role in the legislative process. [448 U.S. 607, 687]

See also his dissent in *American Textile Mfrs. Inst. V. Donovan*, 452 U.S. 490, 543 et seq. Compare Ely's similar position, 1980, pp. 131–34.

54. See, for example, Ackerman and Hassler, 1981, who argue for the adoption of this strategy in the environmental area.

CHAPTER 7
Proxy Shopping

1. National Academy of Public Administration, 1977; Aiken, Dewar, DiTomaso, Hage, and Zeitz, 1975; Weiss, 1981.

2. For example, monitoring of day care by public funding sources appears to be inadequate. See Jackson, 1973, pp. 35–40.

3. For example, one experiment with education vouchers placed parents on a school-districtwide advisory committee. Parents "tended to be absent, poorly informed, and deferential to the professionals" on the committee. (Cohen and Farrar, 1977, p. 88)

4. See, for example, Nelson and Krashinsky, 1973.

5. The term "proxy shopping" originated with Clark Havighurst, who sought to apply it to medical care. (Havighurst, 1970)

6. On housing allowances, see Friedman and Weinberg, 1982, pp. 66–95. For general reports on housing allowance experiments that included quality constraints, see Friedman and Weinberg, 1983; Lowry, 1983.

7. Food Stamp Act of 1977, 7 U.S.C. §§2011–29 (Supp. V 1981).

8. Since 1977 the food stamp program has given eligible households fixed-sum vouchers that must be spent on food. Certain kinds of food—e.g. liquor and most hot foods—cannot be purchased with food stamps (7 U.S.C. §2012 [g] [1982]), but otherwise beneficiaries can purchase anything they want, and neither stores nor the needy are required to report on the foods purchased with food stamps. For descriptions of the food stamp program, see Clarkson, 1975; MacDonald, 1977.

9. These tax-expenditure programs fall into two classes. First, some programs, such as tax credits for child care and energy conservation, directly lower individual tax bills. A second kind permits employees to exclude from their income the value of certain services, e.g. life insurance, medical care, legal services, and education.

10. Nevertheless, voucher plans have been proposed for programs that aid dependent people, although most retain considerable direct regulation of quality and price. See, e.g., Nelson and Krashinsky, 1973 (day care); Baker, Seltzer, and Seltzer, 1974 (mental retardation). See generally Pruger and Miller, 1973; Reid, 1972.

11. In a few situations mobility is restricted by law. Thus, some public subsidies for day care require recipients to send their children to specified centers. (Jackson, 1973, p. 21) For a critique of this practice, see Nelson and Krashinsky, 1973, pp. 63–64.

12. Moreover, I assume that representatives of the funding source cannot monitor service quality directly by becoming paying customers. Thus, this model is not applicable to most artistic and cultural activities, where donors are generally also paying customers. The funding source, however, has no problem determining who is eligible for subsidy. See Krashinsky, 1981, for discussion of the monitoring problems that arise when it is difficult to identify the needy.

13. This nonsatiation assumption should be contrasted with an alternative specification in which each person has a most preferred quality level. The suppliers' services would then be like the color spectrum. Each person has a most preferred "color" that he or she would choose if the price of colors were zero. The distinction between nonsatiation in quality and quality as "color" is equivalent to the distinction made in the industrial-organization literature between "quality dispersion" and "product variety" respectively. See Stiglitz, 1979. In the "product variety" case, the subsidized and unsubsidized would have to have similar "favorite colors" in order for a proxy shopping scheme to succeed.

14. See Pack and Pack, 1977, documenting both the coexistence of average income difference across communities and wide variation in incomes within communities.

15. Obviously, this payment scheme is feasible only if donated funds or tax revenues at least equal the required subsidy payment. Thus, a more complete model would analyze tax or donation decisions and consider their interaction with quality-control strategies.

16. A mathematical model in the Appendix to Rose-Ackerman, 1983b, develops these points more fully.

17. See, e.g., Fried, 1982; Michelman, 1969.

18. Hansen and Weisbrod, 1971, p. 117, propose a sliding-fee schedule in a study of higher education.

19. These firms could be either for-profits or "commercial" nonprofits as defined by Hansmann, 1980, pp. 840–41.

20. Studies indicate that a high proportion of food stamp recipients spend more than their food stamp allotment on food, so that the program essentially provides an income supplement. Except for very large households with six or more people, at least 65 percent of recipient families spend more than their food stamp allotment on food. See USDA, Science and Education Administration, 1981, p. 15. Clarkson, 1975, and MacDonald, 1977, however, conclude that food stamps lead to greater expenditures on food than an equivalent cash grant.

21. Feder, Holahan, Bovbjerg, and Hadley, 1982, pp. 273–76, report that "Federal spending on medical care rose twelvefold between 1965 and 1980 . . . [and] health's share of private incomes rose by 23 percent, from 6 to 7.4 percent. . . . Medical price increases . . . accounted for more than half the spending increases between 1965 and 1980 and three-quarters of the increase between 1975 and 1980." (id. p. 274) Of course, Medicaid and Medicare are not the only cause of price increases. Private insurance combined with the exclusion from federal income tax of employer payments to health insurance plans also played a role. (id. p. 276)

22. Anita Miller provided research assistance on this section. For a fuller analysis of policy problems in the field of mental retardation, see Rose-Ackerman, 1982b.

23. Scheerenberger, 1981, p. 5, reports that the average daily population of people in public residential facilities for the mentally retarded fell from 173,775 in 1967 to 139,410 in 1978. In 1967, 99 per 100,000 people in the total population were in such institutions. By 1978, the number was 65 per 100,000. (Lakin, 1979)

24. Nirje, 1976, p. 179; Wolfensberger, 1976. See generally, Balla, Butterfield, and Zigler, 1974; and Biklen, 1979, citing a number of studies published in the 1950s and 1960s that advocated deinstitutionalization.

25. Sigelman, Roeder, and Sigelman, 1981.

26. Biklen, 1979, pp. 49–50, reviews the history of public support for deinstitutionalization of the retarded in the United States.

27. See, for example, Etzioni, 1978, p. 14; and Throne, 1979.

28. Eliminating discrimination through training programs that emphasize equal treatment of clients could be a mixed blessing. A study of thirty institutions caring for the retarded classified certain practices as "institution-oriented" or "resident-oriented." (McCormick, Balla, and Zigler, 1975) Practices were labeled "institution-oriented" if they treated all children identically in the sense of creating rigid routines and regimented practices and providing little opportunity for self-expression and initiative. (id., pp. 4–5) Clearly, uniformity of treatment is not always the most effective or humane institutional objective. The difficulty, of course, is that if an institution becomes more "'resident-oriented" without a corresponding increase in personnel, the staff may concentrate on caring for the more "appealing" children and for those whose parents are most likely to complain about poor treatment. Therefore, the nondiscrimination condition may not be satisfied.

29. Of course, even the most well-informed parents will not be able to find out everything they would like to know about alternative methods of care. Professional opinion is divided, and much research needs to be done. There does not, for example, appear to be an adequate study of the impact of different kinds of community-based care. Cf. Wieck and Bruininks, 1980.

30. This may be true in spite of the lower hourly wage of poor people. The value of an hour spend monitoring may be low in dollar terms but high in utility terms since the hour must be subtracted from work or from time available to take care of home and family.

31. See U.S. Congress, 1972.

32. Havighurst, 1970, p. 730.

33. 42 U.S.C. §300e (1976). See Schneider and Stern, 1975.

34. 39 Fed. Reg. (1974), 37, 316; Schneider and Stern, 1975, p. 106.

35. According to Schneider and Stern, 1975, p. 110, "HMO's are under no obligation, and may well have no particular incentive, to seek to enroll" Medicaid and Medicare enrollees. Enrollees may have high expected health costs that are not reflected in government reimbursement formulas. The authors then go on to argue that the dual track system of health care will be unchanged by the act. (id., pp. 98–99)

36. Havighurst, 1970, p. 731 n. 48.

37. The main difficulty here is the possible violation of the mixing-and-sorting condition. Few HMO's may be established in low-income neighborhoods, and those in wealthier neighborhoods may be inconvenient for the poor to use.

38. Rose-Ackerman, 1978, pp. 85–108, 137–66.

39. Havighurst, 1970, p. 730.

40. Id., pp. 742–43.

41. Id. p. 730.

42. See, e.g., Bovbjerg, 1981; Marmor, Boyer and Greenberg, 1981.

43. See Andreano and Nyman, 1982; Nyman, 1987, p. 250.

44. Andreano and Nyman, 1982, pp. 18–19.
45. Chavkin and Treseder, 1977; Schneider and Stern, 1975, pp. 130–34. Mitchell and Cromwell, 1980, p. 2435, provide statistics on physicians who care for large numbers of Medicaid patients. They estimate that more than 30 percent of all Medicaid patients are cared for by physicians whose practice includes at least 50 percent Medicaid patients. These doctors provide only slightly shorter visits on average, but they do tend to be older, to be trained in foreign medical schools, and to have fewer credentials than other physicians.
46. Friedman, 1962. Some modest voucher-like experiments have begun, none of which bear much relationship to Friedman's original proposal. Given the political power of the existing public education system, most experiments are limited to public schools. (Chubb and Hanushek, 1990, pp. 222–24; Bowman and Pagano, 1990, pp. 18–19) Parents are still permitted to opt out of the system entirely by enrolling their children at parental expense in private schools.
47. Chubb and Hanushek, 1990, pp. 227–35; Chubb and Moe, 1990, pp. 206–29.
48. For a series of closely related models, see Schelling, 1978.
49. Chubb and Hanushek, 1990, pp. 227–35, 239–40. See also Chubb and Moe, 1990, chapter 6, pp. 206–29.
50. Starr, 1988, p. 14, n. 16.
51. Chubb and Moe, 1990, pp. 219–20.
52. Titmuss, 1971. He may, however, have overstated the quality-control benefits of gift giving. For example, Kessel, 1974, argues that a market system with liability imposed on blood banks would be most efficient.

CHAPTER 8

Tort Law in the Regulatory State

1. "[R]egulation can be as effectively exerted through an award of damages as through some form of preventive relief. The obligation to pay compensation can be, indeed is designed to be, a potent method of governing conduct and controlling policy." (*San Diego Building Trades Council v. Garmon*, 359 U.S. 236, 247 [1959])
2. One exception here is Calabresi, 1970, who stresses the interaction between tort law and statutory regulation.
3. *Larsen v. General Motors Corp.*, 391 F. 2d 495 (8th Cir. 1968). The statute is the National Traffic and Motor Vehicle Safety Act of 1966, Pub. L. 89-563, 80 Stat. 718 (1966), 15 U.S.C. 1381-1431 (1982), and Supp. III (1985)
4. Consumer Product Safety Act of 1972, Pub. L. 92-573 (1972), 86 Stat. 1207, 15 U.S.C.A. §§2051-83 (1982). The number of federal products liability cases filed rose 83 percent between 1974 and 1975. Priest, 1988b, p. 187.
5. The Occupational Safety and Health Act of 1970, 84 Stat. 1590, 29 U.S.C.A. §651 et. seq.
6. For evidence of this trend in the National Traffic and Motor Vehicle Safety Administration and the Consumer Product Safety Commission, see Mashaw and Harfst, 1990; Scanlon and Rogowsky, 1984.
7. Shavell, 1982; Shavell, 1987, pp. 277–90.
8. DES was a drug given to women to prevent miscarriage. Some of the daughters born to mothers who took DES developed cancers, which were attributed to the drug. Since an identical drug was produced by several manufacturers and since most plaintiffs could not identify the manufacturers of the drug taken in their individual cases, liability has been apportioned on the basis of firms' market shares. The

original articulation of this position is *Sindell v. Abbott Labs*, 26 Cal. 3d 588 (1980). For a recent variant, see *Hymowitz v. Eli Lilly*, 73 N.Y. 2d 487 (1989). See also Rose-Ackerman, 1990.

9. See, for example, *Mauro v. Raymark Industries, Inc.*, 561 A. 2d 257 (N.J. 1989); *Sterling v. Velsicol Chemical Co.*, 855 F. 2d 1188 (6th Cir., 1988).

10. Huber, 1988. See also O'Brien, 1987, pp. 62–68; Viscusi, 1984.

11. *Silkwood v. Kerr–McGee*, 464 U.S. 238, 283 (1984).

12. See Henderson and Eisenberg, 1990; Havenner, 1990; Litan and Winston, 1988.

13. On the history of Workers Compensation in the United States and the extent to which it replaced common law doctrines favorable to employers, see Weiss, 1934.

14. *Larsen v. General Motors Corp.*, 391 F. 2d 495, 506: "[T]he common law standard of [reasonableness] . . . can at least serve the needs of our society until the legislature imposes higher standards."

15. "Allowing a common law action holding manufacturers liable for failing to install air bags in motor vehicles would be tantamount to establishing a conflicting safety standard that necessarily encroaches upon the goal of uniformity specifically set forth by Congress in this area." (*Wood v. General Motors Corp.*, 865 F. 2d 395, 402 [1st Cir. 1988]) See also *Pokorny v. Ford Motor Co.*, 902 F. 2d 1116 (3d Cir. 1990). For a contrary state court finding, see *Gingold v. Audi-NSU Auto Union*, 389 Pa. Super. 328, 567 A. 2d 312 (1989).

16. *Wood v. General Motors Corp.*, 865 F. 2d 395, 404–6.

17. They have ruled, for example, that the Food, Drug, and Cosmetic Act does not preempt tort suits for damages. In *Abbot v. American Cyanamid Co.*, 844 F. 2d 1108 (4th Cir. 1988), the Court concluded that state tort suits were permitted because the FDCA regulations set only minimum standards for vaccines. In *Callan v. G. D. Searle & Co.*, 709 F. Supp. 662 (D.C. Md. 1989), and *Kociemba v. G.D. Searle & Co.*, 680 F. Supp. 1293 (D.C. Minn. 1988), federal district courts reached similar conclusions regarding claims involving intrauterine devices. Suits for both failure to warn and design defects were permitted. Similarly, another district court found that a tort claim by a woman injured by a ruptured silicone breast implant was not preempted. (*Desmarais v. Dow Corning Corp.*, 712 F. Supp. 13 (D.C. Conn. 1989])

   Several cases have considered whether the warnings required since 1965 by the Federal Cigarette Labeling and Advertising Act preempt state products liability suits against cigarette manufacturers. Five circuits have held that the act preempted some tort suits, with two circuits explicitly ruling out those based on the adequacy of warnings or the advertising and promotion of cigarettes. (*Cipollone v. Liggett Group, Inc.*, 789 F. 2d 181 [3d Cir. 1986], *cert. denied*, 479 U.S. 1043, [1987]; *Roysdon v. R. J. Reynolds Tobacco Co.*, 849 F. 2d 230 [6th Cir. 1988]; *Palmer v. Liggett Group, Inc.*, 825 F. 2d. 620 [1st Cir. 1987]; and *Stephen v. American Brands*, 825 F. 2d, 312 [11th Cir. 1987]) In *Pennington v. Vistron Corporation*, 876 F. 2d 414, 417 (5th Cir. 1989), the Fifth Circuit judged that while claims involving failure to warn were preempted, claims that the product was unreasonably dangerous were not. The New Jersey Supreme Court has permitted a case of inadequate warning, fraud in advertising, and design defect to go forward. (*Dewey v. R. J. Reynolds Tobacco Co.*, 121 N.J. 69, 577 A. 2d 1239 [N.J. Sup. Ct. 1990])

18. Cases involving the design of automobiles have left to the jury the question of whether compliance with a federal standard implied that an automobile was not defectively designed under principles of strict liability. (*Sours v. General Motors Corp.*, 717 F. 2d 1511, 1516–17 [6th Cir. 1983]; *Dawson v. Chrysler Corp.*, 630 F. 2d 950, 958 [3rd Cir. 1980]; *Shipp v. General Motors Corp.*, 750 F. 2d 418, 421 [5th Cir. 1985]; and *Pokorny v. Ford Motor Co.*, 902 F. 2d 1116. The statute states explicitly: "Compliance with any Federal motor vehicle safety standard issued under this subchapter does not exempt any person from any liability under common law."

(15 U.S.C. §1397 [c]) Air bags are a special case, because the agency expressly permitted firms to select an alternative to air bags. See *Wood v. General Motors*, 865 F. 2d 395.

19. The New York State Supreme Court has ruled that the Occupational Safety and Health Act sets floors, not ceilings, and hence does not preempt state criminal prosecutions. (*People v. Pymm*, 546 N.Y.S. 2d 871 [A.D. 2d Dept. 1989]) The Michigan Supreme Court found that state manslaughter charges against a supervisor whose employee died of carbon monoxide poisoning were not preempted. The court concluded that the Act was not comprehensive because of the low penalties for violations of its standards (*People v. Hegedus*, 432 Mich. 598; 443 N.W. 2d 127 [Mich. Sup. Ct. 1989]) Similarly, the Illinois Supreme Court permitted criminal prosecutions to go forward against a corporation and its top officers for exposing employees to toxic chemicals. (*People v. Chicago Magnet Wire Corp.* 534 N.E. 2d 962 [Ill. Sup. Ct. 1989], *cert denied*, U.S. Sup. Ct. Oct. 2, 1989)

20. Kolstad, Ulen, and Johnson, 1990, develop a model in which such behavior can be optimal in an uncertain world.

21. The injurer's compliance with that standard, however, would not preclude liability if some other negligent action caused the injury. (*Bradley v. Boston & Maine Railroad*, 56 Mass. 539, 543 [1948]) If a manufacturer obtained government approval for a new vaccine, for example, the firm would not be absolved of liability for injuries due to lax quality control in production.

22. See Calfee and Craswell, 1984.

23. See *Sours v. General Motors Corp.*, 717 F. 2d 1511, 1515; *Dawson v. Chrysler Corp.*, 630 F. 2d 950, 957; and *Shipp v. General Motors Corp.*, 750 F. 2d 418, 421. *Sours* at 1515 argues that there is no conflict between a common law tort that looks to the expectations of ordinary consumers and the risk/utility test.

24. Even though administrative remedies were available under the Surface Mining and Control and Reclamation Act of 1977, an Illinois court ruled that a state common law suit for damages from blasting was not preempted. (*Ginn v. Consolidation Coal Co.*, 107 Ill. App. 3d 564 [1982]) The court points out: "Tort liability is traditionally a function of State common law" (at 566), and there is no conflict with the statute because the standard for blasting is strict liability (at 567).

25. For examples, see Rose-Ackerman, 1989.

26. *Silkwood v. Kerr–McGee*, 464 U.S. 238, 276, n. 3. See also *McDougald v. Garber*, 73 N.Y. 2d 246, 253–254 (1989):

> [A]n award of damages to a person injured by the negligence of another is to compensate the victim, not to punish the wrongdoer. . . . [T]he temptation to achieve a balance between injury and damages . . . is rooted in a desire to punish the defendant [and] has no place in the law of civil damages.

27. Of course, punitive damages may reflect not punishment of the tortfeasor but a correction for the fact that only a fraction of victims sue. If the courts set the damages multiplier to correct for this, the earlier analysis of compensatory damages applies. The remedy would then have the same incentive effects as compensatory damages when all the injured sue.

28. For an overview, see Dudek and Palmisano, 1988, pp. 223–44; Hahn and Hester, 1989.

29. Clean Air Act Amendments of 1990, 104 Stat. 2399, Pub. L. 101-549, November 15, 1990, 101st Congress, S. 1630, Title IV, §401.

30. *State of New York v. Shore Realty*, 759 F. 2d 1032, 1041 (2d Cir. 1985).

31. *Silkwood v. Kerr–McGee*, 464 U.S. 238, 276 n. 3.

32. One argument often used to justify preemption, however, has little bite from a policy

analytic perspective. Courts sometimes stress the need for uniformity as a reason to permit statutes to preempt tort law. Yet sophisticated proposals for incentive-based regulation do not aim at uniformity in the treatment of injurers. Instead, fee levels reflect the relative benefits of risk reduction in different areas. Effluent fees, for example, might be set at high levels in pristine areas where the cost of moving from no to some pollution could be very high, and at lower levels in other areas that are already industrialized. When health effects are the primary concern, fee levels should reflect differences in population density. (Harrison, 1977) Thus the lack of uniformity introduced by tort suits is not in itself a reason to preempt tort actions. Rather, the argument must be that the variability in tort law bears little relation to variability in costs and benefits.

33. Private rights of action to compel a regulated entity to comply with an agency order are available under several environmental acts (for example, the Federal Water Pollution Control Act, 33 U.S.C.A. §1365). No damages are available (*Middlesex Cty. Sewerage Auth. v. Nat'l Sea Clammers Asso.*, 453 U.S. 1 [1981]), but the statute includes a very broad conception of who may bring a suit. Under the FWPCA any citizen may bring a suit where "citizen" is defined as "a person or persons having an interest which is or may be adversely affected." (33 U.S.C.A. §1365 [g]) The Act permits citizen suits when the EPA has neglected a nondiscretionary duty. The courts have interpreted this provision generously. In a recent case, for example, the EPA's claim that budgetary considerations had prevented issuance of an offshore oil drilling permit did not insulate oil companies from citizen suits. (*Kitlutsisti v. Arco Alaska, Inc.*, 592 Fed. Supp. 832 [D. Alaska 1984])

34. The CPSA states (15 U.S.C.A. §2072[a]):

Any person who shall sustain injury by reason of any knowing (including willful) violation of a consumer product safety rule, or any other rule or order issued by the commission may sue any person who knowingly (including willfully) violated any such rule or order in [a federal district court]. . . , shall recover damages sustained, and may, if the court determines it to be in the interest of justice, recover the costs of suit, including reasonable attorneys' fees. . . .

The question of whether §2072(a) preempts common law products liability suits does not appear to have been settled, but it may be largely irrelevant, given the lack of CPSC rules.

The CPSA requires that manufacturers, distributors, and retailers of consumer products report to the agency "defects" that create a "substantial product hazard." (§2064[b]) A firm that fails to do so is subject to penalties. (§2069) Several lawsuits have been brought alleging that such a failure should leave a firm open to suits for damages under §2072(a). Given the paucity of CPSC rules, such a reading of the statute would considerably expand the scope of damage remedies under the statute. The federal courts have been unsympathetic to these suits, arguing that damages cannot be claimed for violations of the statute itself and that the rules issued by the Commission with respect to the reporting requirement are interpretive rather than substantive or legislative rules and hence are not independently enforceable. (*Drake v. Honeywell, Inc.* 797 F. 2d 603 [8th Cir. 1986]: *Benitez-Allende v. Alcan Aluminio Do Brasil, S.A.*, 857 F. 2d 26 [1st Cir. 1988]; *Kukulka v. Holiday Cycle Sales, Inc.*, 680 F. Supp. 266 [E.D. Mich. 1988]; and *O'Connor v. Kawasaki Motors Corp., U.S.A.*, 69 9 F. Supp. 1538 [S.D. Fla. 1988]) The dismissal of damage actions for failure to report was given a different basis in *Zepik v. Tidewater Midwest, Inc.*, 856 F. 2d 936 (7th Cir. 1988).

The Surface Mining Control and Reclamation Act also contains a provision for damage suits (30 U.S.C.A. §1270 [f]), but a computer search found that it had not been used. When private actions are permitted but damages are not mentioned, the

Supreme Court has refused to infer the existence of a damage remedy. (*Middlesex Cty. Sewerage Auth. v. Nat'l Sea Clammers Asso.*, 453, U.S. 1)

35. *Silkwood v. Kerr–McGee* 464 U.S. 238, 251.

36. *Ferebee v. Chevron Chemical Co.*, 736 F. 2d 1529, 1539–43 (D.C. Cir. 1984).

37. See Viscusi, 1983, pp. 87–92, 159–60, for a suggested reform of the workers' compensation system.

38. Such actions would be analogous to those permitted under the Consumer Product Safety Act and the Comprehensive Environmental Response, Compensation, and Liability Act (Superfund). The CERCLA or Superfund includes a provision that makes generators of the hazardous waste liable for the "response costs" of "any other persons." (42 U.S.C. §9607 [a]) The courts have defined this term to exclude the costs of property damage, personal injury, or death. (*Ambrogi v. Gould, Inc.*, 750 F. Supp. 1233, 1238, 1259 [M.D. Pa. 1990]) The provision has been read as giving these "other persons" a private right of action to sue generators or current owners of contaminated sites. As the judge wrote in *City of Philadelphia v. Stepan Chemical Co.*, 544 F. Supp. 1135, 1143 (E.D. Pa. 1982), the Act as a whole

> is designed to achieve one key objective—to facilitate the prompt clean up of hazardous dumpsites by providing a means of financing both governmental and private responses and by placing the ultimate financial burden upon those responsible for the danger. The liability provision is an integral part of the statute's method of achieving this goal for it gives a private party the right to recover its response costs from responsible third parties which it may choose to pursue rather than claiming against the fund.

See also *Walls v. Waste Resource Corp.*, 761 F. 2d 311, 317–18 (6th Cir. 1985), and *Tanglewood East Homeowners v. Charles-Thomas, Inc.*, 849 F. 2d 1568 (5th Cir. 1988). Federal appeals courts have found that suits may be brought even though there has been no prior government involvement in the site. (*Tanglewood* at 1575, which cites previous cases) Thus, unlike the CPSA, where suits are tied to prior agency action, CERCLA has been interpreted as permitting private suits for violations of the law.

CHAPTER 9

Regulatory Takings

1. U.S.Const., Amendment V.

2. Ackerman, 1977; Peterson, 1989.

3. See id.

4. For a fuller treatment of these cases see Michelman, 1988, and Peterson, 1989. Peterson, 1990, argues that "takings decisions can best be explained by saying that a compensible taking occurs whenever the government intentionally forces A to give up her property, unless the government is seeking to prevent or punish wrongdoing by A." (id. at 59) Peterson argues that the federal courts define wrongdoing by looking to "societal judgements." (id. at 86) The courts themselves have failed to supply a consistent rationale for their decisions, but she is able to infer one from an evaluation of the outcomes. Peterson's analysis is purely positive. Even if she is correct as a descriptive matter, however, I would still argue for the reformed approach outlined in this chapter.

5. *Keystone Bituminous Coal Assn. v. DeBenedictis*, 480 U.S. 470 (1987).

6. *Kaiser Aetna v. United States*, 444 U.S. 164, 175 (1979) (quoted at 480 U.S. 470, 495) (citations omitted). Actually, Stevens is quoting from *Hodel v. Virginia Surface*

Mining and Reclamation Assn., Inc., 452 U.S. 264, 294 (1981), which quotes *Kaiser*. The internal quotation in *Kaiser* is from *Penn Central Transp. Co. v. New York*, 438 U.S. 104, 124 (1978). The Court repeats this language in *Pennell v. City of San Jose*, 485 U.S. 1, 10 (1988).

7. 480 U.S. 470, 508. Similar language is found in Brennan's majority opinions in *Andrus v. Allard*, 444 U.S. 51, 65 (1979): "There is no abstract or fixed point at which judicial intervention under the Takings Clause becomes appropriate. Formulas and factors have been developed in a variety of settings. Resolution of each case, however, ultimately calls as much for the exercise of judgment as for the application of logic."

8. *Pennell v. City of San Jose*, 485 U.S. 1, 15.

9. Michelman, 1968. Michelman's position is echoed by the Supreme Court in *Kaiser Aetna v. United States*, 444 U.S. 164, 175; and *Keystone Bituminous Coal Assn. v. DeBendictis*, 480 U.S. 470, 493, 499.

10. Michelman, 1968, pp. 1235–45, recognizes this point.

11. Justice Holmes in *Pennsylvania Coal Co. v. Mahon*, 260 U.S. 393, 413 (1922).

12. See Epstein, 1987. Epstein's own proposed reformulation of takings doctrine is, I believe, unsatisfactory. He has begged many of the most important questions. He does this by taking as relatively unproblematic the issue of how private property should be defined and using a definition that does not permit concerns with distributive justice to help determine the outlines of property claims. See Epstein, 1985, especially chapter 19, pp. 306–29, and the conclusion, pp. 331–50; Epstein, 1987, pp. 40–41, 44–45.

13. *Keystone Bituminous Coal Assn. v. DeBenedictis*, 480 U.S. 470, 484 (citing *Pennsylvania Coal Co. v. Mahon*, 260 U.S. 393, 413–14).

14. Rehnquist in dissent would have been willing to do this. He argues that in *Pennsylvania Coal* the general validity of the act "was properly drawn into question." (480 U.S. 470, 507)

15. *Pennell v. City of San Jose*, 485 U.S. 1, 8–15. The partial dissent, in contrast, would have reached the merits of the takings claim. (id. pp. 15–19.)

16. *First English Evangelical Lutheran Church v. County of Los Angeles*, 482 U.S. 304, 340, n. 17 (1987) (citations omitted). The internal quotation is from *San Diego Gas & Electric Co. V. San Diego*, 450 U.S. 621, 661 (1981) (Brennan, J., dissenting).

17. Levmore, 1990, p. 308, puts the point well: "[P]olitics works least well when it affects citizens who have difficulty influencing political bargains and . . . it is just when politics is least perfect that our legal system insists upon the use of markets. . . . Thus, the requirement of explicit compensation (in imitation of market transactions) for some takings might be understood as protective of individuals who cannot easily make politics part of their business."

18. *Loretto v. Teleprompter Corp.*, 458 U.S. 419 (1982). This decision found that the use of a few square inches of property on the outside of a building for a television cable connection constituted a taking. For a discussion of the courts' emphasis on physical occupation, see Ackerman, 1977.

Since *Loretto* makes clear that even the slightest physical invasion must be compensated, lawyers have tried to extend the definition of physical invasion to include, for example, monetary exactions and a regulation that required landlords to keep single room occupancy (SRO) buildings fully rented or pay a penalty. The Supreme Court refused to accept the former claim. It pointed out that if the government's fee was viewed as a physical occupation, then "so would be any fee for services, including a filing fee that must be paid in advance." (*U.S. v. Sperry Corp.*, 493 U.S. 52, 110 S.Ct. 387, 395, n. 9 [1989]) To the Court the fungibility of money is central.

It makes the remarkable claim: "Unlike real or personal property, money if fungible." (id.) The court does not tell us why fungibility is the touchstone or how it should be defined in a market economy.

The claim concerning SROs was accepted by the highest court in New York State. The majority saw the New York City law as requiring forced occupancy of one's property by strangers and therefore as being so extreme a regulatory measure as to constitute a physical occupation. (*Seawall Associates v. City of New York*, 542 N.E. 2d 1059, 1062–65 [N.Y. 1989])

19. For a fuller discussion of the issue of overinvestment, see Blume and Rubinfeld, 1984, pp. 618–20; Blume, Rubinfeld, and Shapiro, 1984. As Blume and Rubinfeld, 1984, p. 618, n. 144, argue: "Whatever the exact determination of compensation, it is important that the measure be one that cannot be directly affected by the behavior of the individual investors, since any compensation measure which can be affected by private behavior will create the possibility of inefficiency due to moral hazard."

20. Cf. Fischel and Shapiro, 1988, who analyze situations in which government actions produce demoralization costs.

21. See the critical analysis of this doctrine in Ackerman, 1977, pp. 130–36.

22. See *Penn Central Transp. Co. v. New York*, 438 U.S. 104. But see the New York State Court of Appeals decision in *Seawall Associates v. City of New York*, 542 N.E. 2d 1059. The New York high court found that both a physical and a regulatory taking had occurred when New York City attempted to aid the homeless by requiring owners of SRO facilities to keep them fully rented. Exemptions and buyout provisions in the law did not overcome this finding. While the court did not use my reasoning, the result is consistent with my framework, because the city law was designed to make use of existing buildings to further a public purpose.

23. Cf. Fischel, 1985, who gives an example. Legal doctrine in this area illustrates clearly the conflict between "scientific policymaking" and "ordinary observing" isolated in Ackerman, 1977.

24. Of course, there are exceptions. In *Chang v. United States*, 13 Cl. Ct. 555 (1987), the Claims Court denied compensation to engineers whose employment contracts in Libya had been voided by an Executive Order issued by President Reagan. The court argued that "the risk that employment in Libya might be interrupted by tension in the relations between that government and the United States can hardly be said to have been outside the reasonable contemplation of plaintiffs at the time they entered into their employment contracts." Furthermore, the engineers should have reasonably supposed that economic sanctions against Libya were possible.

25. A risk-neutral person is concerned only with the expected value of an investment opportunity and is indifferent to the variance or other measures of the dispersion of returns. Thus a risk-neutral person would be indifferent between $100 for sure and a gamble that paid $200 with a 50 percent probability and nothing otherwise. A risk-averse person would select the sure prize of $100 over a gamble with the same expected value.

26. Blume and Rubinfeld, 1984, pp. 584–99; and Fischel, 1988, p. 50.

27. See *Keystone Bituminous Coal Assn. v. DeBenedictis*, 480 U.S. 470.

28. Blume and Rubinfeld, 1984, p. 624.

29. Levmore, 1990.

30. See, e.g., Stigler, 1971; Peltzman, 1976; and Scholzman and Tierney, 1986.

31. See *Merced Irrigation Dist. v. Woolstenhulme*, 4 Cal. 3d 478 (1971).

32. Sax, 1964, pp. 64–65, 75–76; Michelman, 1968; Ackerman, 1977, pp. 52–53, 68, 79–80; Ely 1980, pp. 97–98; and Tribe, 1988, pp. 605–7.

33. *Monongahela Navigation Co. v. United States*, 148 U.S. 312, 325 (1893) (quoted in *Keystone Bituminous Coal Assn. v. DeBenedictis*, 480 U.S. 470, 5121 [Rehnquist,

C.J., dissenting]). See also *Armstrong v. United States*, 364 U.S. 40, 49 (1960): "The Fifth Amendment's guarantee that private property shall not be taken for a public use without just compensation was designed to bar Government from forcing some people alone to bear public burdens which, in all fairness and justice, should be borne by the public as a whole."

34. *Nollan v. California Coastal Comm.*, 483 U.S. 825, 842 (1987).

35. *Rochester Gas & Elec. Corp. v. Public Serv. Commn.*, 71 N.Y. 2d 313, 321 (1988).

36. Richard Epstein takes a contrary position, reading the takings clause as imposing severe restrictions on the ability of the government to redistribute wealth. See Epstein, 1985. But see Gray, 1986 (criticizing Epstein's position).

37. Cf. Tribe, 1988, pp. 607–13 (discussing the problematic nature of property in Supreme Court jurisprudence).

38. An instructive recent example is the attempt by the Corps of Engineers to use the Clean Water Act of 1972 to limit farmers' use of land protected from flooding by levees. The Corps argues that such farmland falls within the 1989 definition of wetlands and hence is under the jurisdiction of the Corps. In one such case the Corps sought to require a farmer to cede 25 percent of his land as a permanent wildlife easement. The farmer, who sued the Corps in federal court, argues:

> If my country needs my land for a public purpose, let them have it, but if they are going to take it for a public purpose, let them do it in a legal way and let the public pay for it, not send individual farmers into bankruptcy by taking away what they have spent much of their lives working for. [Quoted in William Robbins, "For Farmers, Wetlands Mean a Legal Quagmire," *New York Times*, April 24, 1990]

The farmer's preenforcement complaint was dismissed for lack of subject matter jurisdiction in an opinion which did not rule on the takings issue since it was judged not ripe for decision. (*McGown v. U.S.*, 747 F. Supp. 539 [E.D. Mo. 1990])

39. In upholding a fee charged to Sperry Corporation for use of the Iran–United States Claims Tribunal, the Supreme Court found that "Sperry has not identified any of its property that was taken without just compensation." (*U.S. v. Sperry Corp.*, 493 U.S. 52, 110 S.Ct. 387, 393)

40. *Mugler v. Kansas*, 123 U.S. 623, 665 (1887), quoted by Justice Stevens in his opinion in *Keystone Bituminous Coal Assn. v. DeBenedictis*, 480 U.S. 470, 491–92 and in his dissent in *First English Evangelical Lutheran Church v. County of Los Angeles*, 482 U.S. 304, 322.

41. *Keystone Bituminous Coal Assn. v. DeBenedictis*, 480 U.S. 470, 491; see also id. at 492, n. 22, citing cases holding that compensation is not required when the public action abates a public nuisance or stops illegal activity.

42. Coase, 1960; see also Tribe, 1988, p. 594: "Increasingly, deciding who had harmed whom seemed to open a choice to provide any determinate solution to the question of compensation" (citation omitted).

43. *Mugler v. Kansas*, 123 U.S. 623, 668–69.

44. *Keystone Bituminous Coal Assn. v. DeBenedictis*, 480 U.S. 470, 489.

45. *First English Evangelical Lutheran Church v. County of Los Angeles*, 482 U.S. 304, 325.

46. *Penn Central Transp. Co. v. New York*, 438 U.S. 104, 145 (Rehnquist, J., dissenting).

47. 480 U.S. 470, 512 (Rehnquist, J., dissenting), quoting *Curtin v. Benson*, 222 U.S. 78, 86 (1911).

48. *Nollan v. California Coastal Comm.*, 483 U.S. 825, 831, 858.

49. At least three current Justices, Kennedy, O'Connor, and Scalia, want to duck this question by upholding whatever determinations have been made by the states. In articulating this position, however, they have accepted the basic proposition that property rights are determined by law, not given a priori. See *Preseault v. I.C.C.*, 494 U.S. 1, 9 (1990).

50. For another application of this principle, see Rose-Ackerman, 1982c, p. 1036.

51. "We do know, however, that petitioners have never claimed that their mining operations, or even any specific mines, have been unprofitable since the Subsidence Act was passed. Nor is there evidence that mining in any specific location . . . has been unprofitable." *Keystone Bituminous Coal Assn. v. DeBenedictis*, 480 U.S. 470, 496)

52. *Nollan v. California Coastal Comm.*, 483 U.S. 825, 855.

53. *Pennell v. City of San Jose*, 485 U.S. 1, 11–12. The partial dissent is even clearer on this point. Scalia argues that "when excessive rents are forbidden . . . landlords as a class become poorer and tenants as a class (or at least incumbent tenants as a class) become richer. Singling out landlords to be the transferors may be within our traditional constitutional notions of fairness, because they can plausibly be regarded as the source or the beneficiary of the high-rent problem." (id. at 22) See also Levmore, 1990, p. 313, and the cases cited at n. 61 therein.

CHAPTER 10

Deregulation

1. Ronald Reagan in his first inaugural address stated: "Government is not the solution to our problems, government is the problem." Quoted in Harris and Milkis, 1989, p. 5. In his first Economic Report of the President, President Reagan wrote:

   Economic policy must seek to create a climate that encourages the development of private institutions conducive to individual responsibility and initiative. People should be encouraged to go about their daily lives with the right and the responsibility for determining their own activities, status, and achievements. [U.S. President's Council of Economic Advisers, 1982, p. 3]

   Reagan claimed that over the past decade "the government has spun a vast web of regulations" that has reduced productivity and raised prices. (id. at 3–4) The solution proposed was "a substantial reform of Federal regulation, eliminating it where possible and simplifying it where appropriate." (id. at 4–5)

   Immediately after taking office, Reagan established the President's Task Force on Regulatory Relief, which was to review major regulatory proposals, assess regulations currently on the books (especially those that were burdensome to the national economy or to key industrial sectors), and oversee the development of legislative proposals. (Eads and Fix, 1984, pp. 108–9)

2. U.S. President's Council of Economic Advisers, 1989, p. 196. See also Eads and Fix, 1984, pp. 69–80.

3. Eads and Fix, 1984, p. 1.

4. Id. The term "social regulation" is often applied to "the set of federal programs that use regulatory techniques to achieve broad social goals—a cleaner environment, safer and more healthful workplaces, safer and more effective consumer products, and the assurance of equal employment opportunities." (id. at 12) Economic regulation "refers to the programs that attempt to control prices, conditions of market entry and exit, and conditions of service, usually in specific industries considered to be 'affected with the public interest.'" Examples of the latter include regulation of airlines, telecommunications, and securities transactions. (id.)

5. *America's New Beginning: A Program for Economic Recovery*, U.S. Executive Office of the President, February 18, 1981. See also Harris and Milkis, 1989, pp. 3–16. For a more balanced argument in an official publication, see U.S. President's Council of Economic Advisers, 1982, pp. 29–46, 134–46. Murrey Weidenbaum, the Chairman of Reagan's first Council of Economic Advisers, is one of the moderates. In an assessment of the regulatory reform effort he is careful to state that he does "not equate regulatory reform with minimizing the costs of complying with regulation. . . . [Rather, he thinks] in terms of optimization, of moving toward more efficient regulatory activity (an approach that is guaranteed to upset our libertarian friends)." (Weidenbaum, 1984, p. 15)

6. One of the strongest statements of this position, under the heading "Ticking Regulatory Time Bomb," is in David Stockman and Jack Kemp, "Avoiding a GOP Economic Dunkirk," a memo prepared for the incoming president in December 1980. In that memo they write:

   McGovernite no-growth activists assumed control of most of the relevant sub-Cabinet policy posts during the Carter Administration. They have spent the past four years "tooling up" for implementation through a mind-boggling outpouring of rule-makings, interpretative guidelines, and major litigation—all heavily biased toward maximization of regulatory scope and burden. Thus, this decade-long process of regulatory evolution is just now reaching the stage at which it will sweep through the industrial economy with near gale force, preempting multi-billions in investment capital, driving up operating costs, and siphoning off management and technical personnel in an incredible morass of new controls and compliance procedures. ["Avoiding a GOP Economic Dunkirk," Memo to President Reagan, December 1980 reprinted in Greider, 1982, p. 146]

7. Statutes deregulating intercity buses and further deregulating financial institutions passed in 1982. The administration's role, while supportive, was not central. See U.S. President's Council of Economic Advisers, 1989, p. 196; Weidenbaum, 1984, pp. 15, 20–21.

8. The statute is the Hazardous and Solid Waste Amendments of 1984, Pub. L. No. 98-616 (amends the Solid Waste Disposal Act, as amended by the Resource Conservation and Recovery Act of 1976). In 1986 the Superfund and the Safe Drinking Water Act were reauthorized. Superfund Amendments and Reauthorization Act of 1986, Pub. L. No. 99-499; Safe Drinking Water Act Amendments of 1986, Pub. L. 99-339; Vogel, 1989, pp. 267, 276–77. These three environmental statutes, which impose regulations on the business community, were not mentioned in a list of Reagan's deregulation accomplishments. U.S. President's Council of Economic Advisers, 1989, p. 196.

9. Eads and Fix, 1984, p. 254; Vogel, 1989, p. 269. A canvass of the Reports of the Council of Economic Advisers during the Reagan years reveals the shifting interests of the administration. The first report in 1982 includes a chapter entitled "Reforming Government Regulation of Economic Activity," which takes a broad view of the needed reforms, ranging from the regulation of air pollution through agricultural marketing orders to health care and banking. (U.S. President's Council of Economic Advisers, 1982, pp. 134–66) In 1983 the Report contains a general chapter, entitled "The Burden of Economic Regulation," whose focus is more narrowly on price and entry regulation in specific industries. (U.S. President's Council of Economic Advisers, 1983, pp. 96–124) By 1984 the focus has further narrowed to financial market deregulation. (U.S. President's Council of Economic Advisers, 1984, pp. 145–74) Finally, in 1985, at the beginning of Reagan's second term, the report contains no chapter explicitly concerned with regulation. (U.S. President's Council of Economic Advisers, 1985) By 1986, however, regulation is back on the Council's agenda, and

the report contains a chapter entitled "Reforming Regulation: Strengthening Market Incentives." (U.S. President's Council of Economic Advisers, 1986, pp. 159–88) That chapter details the successes in the deregulation of the transportation sector and goes on to suggest both the deregulation of other sectors and the use of market incentives in social regulation. In 1987 a chapter entitled "Risk and Responsibility" argues for less government regulation of risk. (U.S. President's Council of Economic Advisers, 1987, pp. 179–207) By 1988 criticisms of airline deregulation were beginning to be heard. The Council's response was a chapter, entitled "Airline Deregulation: Maintaining the Momentum," that detailed the benefits of deregulation, acknowledged unforeseen problems, and proposed market-based solutions. (U.S. President's Council of Economic Advisers, 1988, pp. 199–231.) President Reagan's final economic report is a restrained assessment of past efforts which continues to call for increased deregulatory efforts. (U.S. President's Council of Economic Advisers, 1989, pp. 187–221)

10. Eads and Fix, 1984, p. 259. One exception is the mixed case of telecommunications. The Federal Communications Commission, an independent agency, took a deregulatory position. See Horwitz, 1989; Krogh, 1989; Tunstall, 1986.

11. Eads and Fix, 1984, pp. 140–48; Harris and Milkis, 1989, pp. 6, 113–24; Kraft and Vig, 1984, pp. 426–28; Lynn, 1985; Nathan, 1986, pp. 129–31; Crandall and Portney, 1984, p. 62; Goldenberg, 1985. Goldenberg points out that political appointees extended much farther down the ladder of the bureaucratic hierarchy than in previous administrations. Crandall and Portney (p. 62) claim that at the Environmental Protection Agency "[g]roups outside the agency prepared 'hit lists' of supposedly pro-environmental EPA employees and the new leadership appeared to respond to them by, for example, replacing several members of the EPA Science Advisory Board. Many senior employees left, while others became resentful and distrustful of the new team." Along with providing examples of unqualified appointees, Eads and Fix, 1984, p. 145, also provide counter-examples of some highly qualified and effective appointments.

12. Crandall and Portney, 1984, p. 62, state that at the EPA the positions of administrator and deputy administrator were not filled in the first six months of Reagan's term, "forcing the EPA to operate without clear, decisive policy guidance. This made it difficult to design new policies or solve old problems. It was also impossible to construct a legislative agenda without someone firmly in charge." The National Labor Relations Board had fewer than its complement of five members for much of the Eighties. (Kirk Victor, "Challenging Old Images," National Journal, October 27, 1990, p. 2605) The Consumer Product Safety Commission was without a full complement of commissioners for much of Reagan's presidency. (Federal Yellow Book, various years) See also McLaughlin v. Union Oil of California, 869 F. 2d 1039 (7th Cir. 1989) (Occupational Safety and Health Review Commission had lacked a quorum for seventeen months), and National Treasury Employees Union v. Bush, 715 F. Supp. 405 (D.C. Dist. Col. 1989) (Federal Labor Relations Authority had only one member since November 1988). In the latter case the District Court found that the federal courts could not legally direct the President to make an appointment.

13. On OSHA, see Chapter 6, n. 45. Crandall and Portney, 1984, p. 72, note that the EPA did successfully issue final rules in the water pollution area. However, by 1984 it had made less progress in the air quality program. While State Implementation Plans have been quickly approved, only one revision to the National Ambient Air Quality Standards had been proposed or made final by 1984. The administration was also slow in issuing New Source Performance Standards, and little progress was made under the Resource Conservation and Recovery Act.

14. Both at the Interior Department and at the EPA the first agency heads reorganized and downgraded enforcement activities. (Kraft and Vig, 1984, pp. 428–29; Crandall and Portney, 1984, p. 69) A General Accounting Office study found widespread

violation of water pollution permits over an eighteen-month period beginning in October 1980. Over the same period formal EPA enforcement actions declined by 41 percent. (Crandall and Portney, 1984, p. 69)

15. Weidenbaum argues that as "long as regulatory changes are seen as primarily a problem for business, there will be limited public support for reform." (Weidenbaum, 1984, p. 40) Vogel notes that the "relative strength of proregulation forces in Congress throughout the 1980s reflected in part a continued backlash against the administration's earlier deregulatory initiatives." (Vogel, 1989, p. 278)

16. See Ackerman and Hassler, 1981.

17. The economics and policy analysis literature is full of such proposals. For accessible discussions, see Ackerman, Rose-Ackerman, Sawyer, and Henderson, 1974; Ackerman and Stewart, 1988; Mendeloff, 1987.

18. See Weidenbaum, 1984, pp. 36–37, quoting Pertschuk, "The Case for Consumerism," *The New York Times Magazine*, May 29, 1983, p. 26. See also Tolchin and Tolchin, 1988.

19. Weidenbaum speculates that the Reagan administration may have reduced the chances for genuine reform:

> [T]he public and, especially, the organized environmental groups, were aroused by the strong language and public stands of Secretary of Interior James Watt. EPA Administrator Ann Gorsuch evoked a similar public response. . . . As a result, the entire spectrum of environmental organizations . . . became a solid phalanx of opposition to virtually every regulatory change proposed by the Reagan administration. [Weidenbaum, 1984, pp. 18–19]

This had, by the middle of Reagan's term in office, created a climate in which Congress did not trust agencies to carry out their statutory mandates. (id. at 38) Weidenbaum worried in 1983 that the administration's actions would "be leading inadvertently to a round of expanding governmental intervention." (id. at 39)

20. Exec. Order No. 12,291, 3 CFR 127 (1981), 5 U.S.C. §601 app. at 473–76 (1988); see Eads and Fix, 1984, pp. 108–12.

21. Exec. Order No. 12,498, 3 CFR 323 (1985), 5 U.S.C. §601 app. at 476–77 (1988).

22. Eads and Fix, 1984, pp. 45–68; Viscusi, 1983, pp. 150–55. For examples of presidential actions during the Ford and Carter administrations, see Exec. Order No. 11,821, 3 CFR 926 (1974), 12 U.S.C. §1904 at 592 (1976) (Ford order designed to force agencies to consider the inflationary impact of their regulations); Exec. Order No. 12,044, 3 CFR 152 (1978), 5 U.S.C. §553 at 70 (1976 and Supp. II 1978) (Carter order requiring regulatory analysis of every "major" rule proposed); see also Morrison, 1986, pp. 1067–68 nn. 7–8.

23. Harris and Milkis, 1989, pp. 104–5.

24. As Eads and Fix note, "OMB's actions were . . . vulnerable to being perceived as politicizing the technocratic process of translating legislative intent into implementing regulations." (Eads and Fix, 1984, p. 110)

25. See the contrasting views expressed in Morrison, 1986, and DeMuth and Ginsburg, 1986. A good summary of arguments on both sides is found in Verkuil, 1982. For White House attempts to respond to the critics, see Additional Procedures Concerning OIRA Review Under Executive Orders Nos. 12,291 and 12,498 (Revised), reprinted in U.S. Office of Management and Budget, 1988, App. III, pp. 529–43.

26. In cases where the Office of Information and Regulatory Affairs clashed publicly with agencies, the agencies emerged as winners. (Eads and Fix, 1984, pp. 135–38)

27. Harris and Milkis conclude that "the short-term impact of the OMB oversight may have jeopardized the prospects for long-term change in the substance of regulatory policy." (Harris and Milkis, 1989, p. 113)

28. See, for example, DeMuth and Ginsberg, 1986, pp. 1084–85.
29. Regulatory Impact Analysis Guidance, U.S. Office of Management and Budget, 1988, App. V, pp. 561–74.
30. See, for example, DeMuth and Ginsberg, 1986, pp. 1080–82; Sunstein, 1981.
31. See Chapter 3. Cf. Strauss and Sunstein, 1986.
32. See Eads and Fix, pp. 135–38, for evidence supporting the perception that cost-benefit analysis is but a technique to achieve the pro-business political objectives of the president. OMB sought revisions of 32 percent of the regulations submitted to it in 1986. While one-third of the requested changes were small, the rest were more substantial. (Conlan, 1988, pp. 208–9) No reliable study exists of the merits of OMB objections. Nevertheless, the existence of delays, at least, left the way open for critics to charge that the OMB actions and inactions were politically motivated.
33. See, e.g., Environmental and Energy Study Institute and the Environmental Law Institute, September 1985, finding that by mid-1985 only 14 percent of EPA's deadlines had been met, and Note, 1986, p. 1474, stating that EPA has frequently violated statutory deadlines for the implementation of federal hazardous waste litigation.
34. See, e.g., *Environmental Defense Fund v. Thomas*, 627 F. Supp. 566, 569 (D.C. Dist. Col. 1986) (court finds a sixteen-month delay "highly irresponsible" but accepts a proposed schedule for promulgation of the regulation in question); see also *Sierra Club v. California*, 658 F. Supp. 165, 171 n. 5 (N.D. Cal. 1987) (agency must show "utmost diligence" in efforts to meet statutory deadline for regulation promulgation).
35. *Environmental Defense Fund v. Thomas*, 627 F. Supp. at 571; Cf. *Public Citizen Health Research Group v. Tyson*, 796 F. 2d 1479, 1507 (D.C. Cir. 1986) (court notes that OMB involvement in agency rulemaking "presents difficult constitutional questions concerning the executive's proper rule [sic] in administrative proceedings," but finds "no occasion to reach the difficult constitutional questions presented by OMB's participation").
36. *Environmental Defense Fund*, 627 F. Supp. at 571.
37. See Administrative Procedures Act, 5 U.S.C. §706(2)(A) (1977); see also, for example, *Motor Vehicle Mfrs. Assoc. v. State Farm Mutual Ins. Co.*, 463 U.S. 29, 43 (1983) (agency cannot revoke a regulation without a "rational relationship between the facts found and the choice made").
38. Kahn, 1988, pp. xviii–xxiii, Tunstall, 1986.
39. U.S. President's Council of Economic Advisers, 1989, pp. 198–214.
40. Kahn, 1988, p. xviii.
41. Kahn writes that deregulation led to entry that

> produced marked declines in market concentration; it also set off price wars, business failures and consolidations, and labor unrest, along with other rapid changes in accustomed ways of doing business. . . .
> . . . [T]he fact that competitive markets—and especially markets suddenly opened to competition after decades of close regulation—tend to be more turbulent than regulated ones is in itself neither surprising nor dispositive of the comparative merits of the two institutions. [Id. at xviii]

See also Breyer, 1984, p. 15, disputing that "the fault lies primarily in deregulation" for the bankruptcy of Braniff Airlines and the financial troubles at Continental and Eastern airlines; and Rehn, "Charter Curbs Seen Hurting Competition," *Am. Banker*, April 11, 1989, at 2, discussing the views of the Comptroller of the Currency, Robert Clarke, that new banks must be permitted to enter the market for the sake of efficiency.
42. See Breyer, 1984, p. 15 ("The simple fact is that a competitive world leaves firms to sink or swim on the basis of their service, prices, and efficiency"); see also Cutler,

1982, p. 549 (reviewing Breyer, 1982), agreeing with Breyer's view that isolated failures should not defeat deregulation.

43. Thayer, 1987, p. 445, argues that deregulation "led to the scheduling of even more trips, thereby increasing service competition—more waste—at the same time that price-cutting wars began"; see also Breyer, 1987, pp. 1015–16, asserting that business travelers must realize that airports are more crowded because prices are lower and airlines are more efficient.

44. See Steiner, 1983, p. 1304: "The successful deregulation of airline rates does not lead to a sense that we should leave to the free market the question of whether DC-10 engines are attached in a proper way"; and Thayer, 1987, p. 151, arguing that "fixed routes and fixed terminals, with no duplication, would improve safety enforcement at a much lower cost. When facilities are not consolidated, the effectiveness of safety enforcement activity is inversely proportional to the number of operators."

45. As Kahn notes:

> [T]he upsurge of traffic need not have entailed the great increase in congestion that we have actually experienced. Responsibility properly rests, instead, with major failures of government policy—inadequate staffing of the Federal Aviation Administration with safety inspectors and flight controllers; failure to expand airport and air corridor capacity sufficiently; inefficient pricing of airport takeoff and landing "slots" at congested airports. [Kahn, 1988, p. xxii]

46. Id., p. xxii, n. 14.

47. Id.

48. See U.S. President's Council of Economic Advisers, 1988, Chapter 6, "Airline Deregulation: Maintaining the Momentum," pp. 199–229. This chapter does, however, discuss ways to relieve congestion through pricing landing slots.

49. See, e.g., Depository Institutions Deregulation and Monetary Control Act, 12 U.S.C. §3501 et. seq. (1980); Garn–St. Germain Depository Institutions Act, Pub. L. No. 96-221, 94 Stat. 132 (codified in scattered sections of 12 U.S.C.). See generally Note, 1988; Note, 1984.

50. See, e.g., "A Banking Puzzle: Mixing Freedom and Protection," N.Y. Times, Feb. 19, 1989 S3. "[W]ith the deregulation craze in full swing," "banks are going ahead willy-nilly . . . to enter new, and sometimes riskier, activities." See Litan, 1987, pp. 109–11; Lovett, 1989; Macey, 1989.

51. Barth and Bradley, 1988, pp. 46,47. See also Romer and Weingast, 1991, who argue that Congress should bear the blame for this state of affairs along with the president.

52. Barth and Bradley, 1988, p. 45.

53. U.S. President's Council of Economic Advisers, 1989, p. 204.

54. See, e.g., Kelman, 1981.

55. Eads and Fix note that "economists hoped that Reagan would embrace the concept as the principal vehicle for the regulatory relief he was pledging." (Eads and Fix, 1984, p. 104)

56. Hahn and Hester, 1989.

57. Eads and Fix, 1984, pp. 171–72; Tunstall, 1986.

58. An early statement of this view found in Schultze, 1977. See also Lave, 1981. Ackerman and Stewart, 1988, pp. 175–76, nn. 10, 11, summarize the studies of the saving that would be generated by the introduction of incentives schemes to control air pollution.

59. Clean Air Act Amendments of 1990, 104 Stat. 2399, Pub. L. 101-549, November 15, 1990, 101st Cong. S.1630, Title IV, §401.

60. See, for example, Mendeloff, 1979, pp. 25–31; Macaulay, 1989; Macaulay and Portney, 1984; Posner, 1972.

61. Tideman and Tullock, 1976. Ferejohn, Forsythe, and Noll, 1979.

62. Kneese and Schultze, 1974; Ackerman, Rose-Ackerman, Sawyer, and Henderson, 1974.

63. The Supreme Court has opened the way for the introduction of incentive-based plans by upholding the constitutionality of user fees promulgated by the Department of Transportation to cover the costs of administering federal pipeline safety standards. The Department was directed to set these fees by the Consolidated Omnibus Budget Reconciliation Act of 1985, Pub. L. No. 99-272, 100 Stat. 82 (codified at 49 U.S.C. App. §1682a [1982, Supp.V]). See *Skinner v. Mid-America Pipeline Co.*, 490 U.S. 212 (1989).

64. Harris and Milkis, 1989, pp. 124–25, report that from FY 1981 to FY 1985 the Federal Trade Commission lost 11 percent of its funding and over one-third of its permanent staff positions. The Consumer Product Safety Commission lost 16 percent of its funding and over 40 percent of its positions. The budget of the Environmental Protection Agency fell from $1,347 million to $1039 million between 1981 and 1983, and full-time employees fell by 1,500. By 1984 the EPA budget was no greater in real terms than it was in 1972 in spite of its increased responsibilities. (id., pp. 255–56) EPA's research and development fell by more than one-half in real terms between 1981 and 1984. (Kraft and Vig, 1984, pp. 430, 431) The overall budget of the federal regulatory agencies, after falling in real terms in the early years of the Reagan administration, rose slowly in real dollars after 1983. (U.S. President's Council of Economic Advisers, 1989, pp. 194–95) The Bush administration has supported increases in regulatory agency budgets especially for the EPA. Warren and Chilton, 1990.

65. See Harris and Milkis, 1984; Vogel, 1989. Vogel quotes a Washington attorney for the Chemical Manufacturers Association as stating, "The chemical industry certainly doesn't want to see EPA dismembered," and quotes a business lobbyist as saying, "We're in favor of intelligent implementation of the laws, but an agency in disarray can't do that." (Vogel 1989, pp. 266–67) Harris and Milkis, 1989, pp. 260–62, document business criticisms of the EPA under Anne Burford: "As far as the NAM [National Association of Manufacturers] was concerned, the lack of any clear intellectual framework for deregulation or sense of mission at the EPA cast Reagan, Watt, and Burford as despoilers of the environment catering to the whims of businesses at the expense of public health and environmental quality. This displeased business interests as much if not more than it displeased the Sierra Club." (id. at 262)

66. *Motor Vehicle Mfrs. Assn. v. State Farm Mutual Automobile Ins. Co.*, 463 U.S. 29 (1983). For other examples involving the EPA, see Harris and Milkis, 1989, pp. 263–64.

67. *Chevron, U.S.A., Inc. v. Natural Resources Defense Council, Inc.*, 467 U.S. 837 (1984); *Heckler v. Chaney*, 470 U.S. 821 (1985).

68. "An agency changing its course by rescinding a rule is obligated to supply a reasoned analysis for the change beyond that which may be required when an agency does not act in the first instance." (*Motor Vehicles Mfrs. Assn.*, 463 U.S. at 42) In a recent article Judge Wald argues that judicial review can

> dull somewhat the meat axe, 'damn the torpedoes, full speed ahead,' attitude that sometimes overtakes zealous political appointees advancing a political or ideological agenda. . . . [I]ts value may be greater . . . in times when the Executive is embarked on radical change. It is in such times that the temptation to cut corners, to mow down the intransigent opposition is greatest. [Wald, 1986, p. 543]

69. The Reagan administration made much of the reduction in *Federal Register* pages during its tenure. Total pages peaked at 87,012 in 1980 and reached a low of 47,418 in 1986. The total rose to 49,654 in 1987. Final rule documents fell from 7,745 in 1980 and 4,581 in 1987. (U.S. Office of Management and Budget, 1988, p. 558)

70. *McLaughlin v. Union Oil of California*, 869 F. 2d 1039.

CHAPTER 11
Decentralization

1. Quoted in Beam, 1985, pp. 418–19.

2. Exec. Order No. 12,612, 52 Fed. Reg. 41,685 (1987).

3. Beam, 1985, p. 415; Champion, 1985, pp. 444, 447. As Champion writes: "The president's initiative was not stillborn, but it never left the incubator." (id. at 444)

4. The Reagan administration proposed consolidating thirty-four programs into four block grants with FY 1984 funding of approximately $21 billion (a funding cut of 14 percent, according to the National Governors Association). The proposed legislation would hold funding levels constant until FY 1988. See Rochelle Stanfield, "Revised New Federalism Plan Would Do Little to Change Power, Authority," *National Journal*, March 5, 1983, p. 487; and U.S. Executive Office of the President, "President's Federalism Initiative Legislation Fact Sheet" (mimeographed), February 24, 1983.

5. For example, the Environmental Protection Agency asked the Justice Department to drop forty-nine pending enforcement actions, arguing (among other things) that enforcement should be left to the states. Under Medicare and Medicaid, the federal government sharply cut funds for nursing home inspections. Both examples are cited in Eads and Fix, 1984, pp. 128–53, 504–5. For more information on EPA activities, see Curtis and Creedon, 1982.

6. According to one article written in 1984: "Between 1983 and 1984 federal assistance to the states for air and water quality programs and hazardous waste control efforts would fall 28 percent in real terms under the administration budget, from $321 million to $230 million. Federal aid to states for environmental purposes would decline by 44 percent from 1981 levels under the proposed budget. . . . There is some evidence that the reduction in funds to the states may already be affecting compliance and enforcement." (Crandall and Portney, 1984, pp. 68–69)

7. For a persuasive presentation of this argument, see Conlan, 1988. See also Peterson, Rabe, and Wong, 1986, p. 219.

8. The growth had been vigorous since the end of the Korean War but was already beginning to abate at the end of Carter's presidency. In 1955 grants totaled $3.2 billion for 4.7 percent of federal outlays and 10.2 percent of state and local expenditures. See U.S. ACIR, *Significant Features of Fiscal Federalism*, 1988, vol. 2, p. 15, reproduced in Conlan, 1988, p. 156.

   The growth was fueled by the increased funding of social services and training programs and of health care for the poor under Medicaid. (Break, 1980, Table 4–3, p. 126, from Special Analyses of the Budget, Fiscal Year 1979, p. 182, and Fiscal Year 1980, p. 223)

9. U.S. Office of Management and Budget, 1990, Special Analysis H, p. H-22.

10. While total aid declined 8 percent and all aid to governments fell 24 percent between 1980 and 1985, real outlays for community and regional development were reduced by nearly 40 percent; real outlays for education, employment and training, and social services were cut by one-third. Particularly hard hit were many of the hallmark programs of the Great Society: community services, the descendant of the community action program, was cut nearly in half; local public works and regional development grants were practically eliminated; urban renewal and training and

employment services were cut by two-thirds. Within education, the largest cuts occurred in the 1960s programs of bilingual education, compensatory education, and the small stimulative grants consolidated into the Chapter Two education block grant. [Conlan, 1988, p. 157, and Table 8-3, p. 155]

11. Nathan, 1986, pp. 137–38.

12. Conlan, 1988, pp. 166–74.

13. The plan and negotiations over its design are described in Conlan, 1988, pp. 179–97.

14. U.S. Domestic Policy Council, 1986, p. 71.

15. Executive Order No. 12,612, 52 Fed. Reg. 41,685 (1987). The Executive Order was reaffirmed by the Bush administration on February 16, 1990. (Bowman and Pagano, 1990, p. 1)

16. Anton, 1989, pp. 228–29. In contrast, a bipartisan group under the auspices of the National Conference on Social Welfare issued a report in 1985 that called for virtual federal assumption of the costs of the major welfare programs with state administration. The group also supported grants to reduce fiscal disparities among states and localities. Both such policies have considerable support in the social science literature. (Anton, 1989, pp. 225–27)

17. Conlan, 1988, p. 207.

18. Id. at 207.

19. Id., pp. 161–62. The 1986 Tax Reform Act imposed limits on the tax exemption for municipal bond interest and eliminated the deductibility of state and local sales and personal property taxes. (id., I pp. 133, 145–47) Also costly to state and local governments were the cuts in federal income tax rates in 1981 and 1986. Cuts in marginal tax rates limit the degree to which the federal government shares tax burdens with the states. If state income taxes are deductible from federal taxable income, then a fall in marginal tax rates from, say, 50 percent to, say, 25 percent means that taxpayers pay 75 cents of every dollar of their state tax bill instead of 50 cents.

20. U.S. General Accounting Office, *Federal–State Relations: Trends of the Past Decade and Emerging Issues* (Washington, D.C.: GAO, March 1990), p. 28, quoted in Bowman and Pagano, 1990, p. 11.

    To take just one example, the Safe Drinking Water Act of 1985 (P.L. 99-339, S. 124; June 1986, 100 Stat. 642–67) strengthened the regulatory force of an earlier act enacted in 1974 (P.L. 93-523, 42 U.S.C. 300f. and following). Although under the jurisdiction of the Environmental Protection Agency, which is required to set limits for contaminants, the program is administered by the states with no direct federal financial help except for partial assistance with administrative and enforcement costs. The EPA estimates that the capital costs of the program to states and water companies will be $6 to $7 billion and the operating costs will be $2 to $3 billion per year. Kuzmack, 1990, pp. 69–76.

21. Conlan, 1988, p. 206. Crandall and Portney, 1984, p. 69, report on the decline in EPA enforcement activity in the water pollution area.

22. Eads and Fix, 1984, pp. 226–28.

23. Conlan, 1988, p. 206, argues that this happened in the regulation of surface mining and occupational health and safety.

24. Wolman and Teitelbaum, 1984, pp. 313–15, have documented the efforts by many groups to build up their state-level lobbying efforts.

25. Mitchell, 1990. State activism was, however, eventually restricted under the Nutrition Labeling and Education Act of 1990, 101 P.L. 535, H.R. 3562, which preempts state laws dealing with nutritional content while permitting states and localities to require health warnings.

26. See Litan and Winston, 1988.

27. The 1982 Federal Surface Transportation Assistance Act requires states to accept double-trailer trucks on interstate highways and on roads that provide access to them. In the field of nuclear power, the administration attempted to prevent states from implementing laws restricting the development of nuclear power and the disposal of radioactive wastes. See Smith, 1982. But the federal position has not always triumphed. See, for example, *Pacific Gas and Elec. Co. v. State Energy Resources Conservation and Development Comm.*, 461 U.S. 190 (1983), where California's position on regulating nuclear power was upheld. Preemptive drug labeling rules covered Reyes Syndrome for aspirin, warning labels on over-the-counter drugs, and tamper-resistant packaging. (Mitchell, 1990, p. 133, n. 65,) See also Anton, 1989, p. 211; and Conlan, 1988, pp. 201, 212–17.

28. U.S. ACIR, *Federal Preemption of State and Local Authority* (Washington, D.C.: ACIR Draft Report, 1989), cited in Bowman and Pagano, 1990, p. 11.

    The trend toward decentralized, nonstatutory lawmaking in the courts pushed the Reagan administration into proposing legislation that would preempt these judicial initiatives. As early as 1982 Reagan supported a bill proposed by Senator Kasten to supersede state product liability laws. (Conlan, 1988, pp. 213–14) The Kasten bill is summarized in Lipsen, 1991. In April 1986 the Reagan administration sent proposed legislation to the Senate setting a $100,000 cap on punitive damages and pain and suffering awards, limiting contingency fees, and restricting manufacturer liability. None of the bills was voted on by the full Senate. ("Administration Proposes Changes in Liability Law," *Cong. Q. Weekly Rep.*, May 3, 1986, p. 1002; Kincaid, 1987, pp. 10–11)

29. Some of the material in this section is derived from Mashaw and Rose-Ackerman, 1984. For a complementary typology that distinguishes between developmental and redistributive policies, see Peterson, Rabe, and Wong, 1986, pp. 11–20.

30. See, for example, Oates, 1972; Olson, 1979; Rothenberg, 1970; Tullock, 1969.

31. See, for example, Breton, 1965; Musgrave and Musgrave, 1973, pp. 614–20; Oates, 1972.

32. Outside the regulatory area, this issue has arisen most clearly in the severance taxes levied by coal-producing states on minerals produced within their borders. In *Commonwealth Edison Co. v. Montana*, 453 U.S. 609 (1981), these taxes were held to be constitutional. See McGrath and Hellerstein, 1982; Voegelin, 1982.

33. See Harrison, 1977, 1983.

34. See U.S. Advisory Commission on Intergovernmental Relations, 1982.

35. Peterson, Rabe, and Wong, 1986, pp. 103–5, distinguish between federal programs designed to foster economic development, where federal regulations requiring citizen participation met little resistance, and the more difficult task of fostering effective citizen and consumer participation in redistributive programs. (id. pp. 126–27, 178–84) Increased citizen participation has been one of the concerns of the EPA in judging state plans. (U.S. Environmental Protection Agency, 1982) When the Revenue Sharing law was reauthorized in 1976, one of the few changes was an attempt to tighten the citizen participation provisions. Some studies have shown that Revenue Sharing led to some increase in citizen participation, especially in large cities. (Break, 1980, p. 163)

36. The market, however, will not necessarily produce the optimal numbers of types of products. (Lancaster, 1979)

37. See Rose-Ackerman, 1980b, for an argument that state politicians have little incentive to support risky, scientifically valid experiments.

38. Tiebout, 1956.

39. Rose-Ackerman, 1983a, reviews research on multiple governments and cites the relevant sources.

40. See id. for a more detailed critique.

41. Even with a substantial federal role in welfare and health, there are wide variations in interstate spending. In education, where the federal role is modest, per capita (not per student) spending ranged from $1,526 to $540 in 1986 (excluding Alaska, with $2,309). (Anton, 1989, pp. 58–59) The data are from the *State Policy Data Book*, 1986.

42. Wolman and Teitelbaum, 1984, pp. 325–28.

43. See, for example, Musgrave and Musgrave, 1973, pp. 606–7; Olson, 1979; and Polinsky, 1972.

44. Winter, 1977. Easterbrook, 1983a, recognizes the limitations of interjurisdictional competition in the regulatory area but is relatively sanguine about the results.

45. The case of Mississippi is discussed in Lieber, 1975, pp. 138–47.

46. Schellhardt T. Jacobs, "War Among the States for Jobs and Business Becomes Even Fiercer," *Wall Street Journal*, July 18, 1983. See Mashaw and Rose-Ackerman, 1984, and Rose-Ackerman, 1981a, for an analysis of the implications of this competition for support for federal laws.

47. Consider, for example, the federal law that requires states either to form regional interstate compacts to handle the disposal of low-level nuclear waste or to dispose of it within their own states. (Low Level Radioactive Wastes Policy Act of 1980, 42 U.S.C. Section 2021 d[a] [Supp IV 1980])

48. National Governors' Association, Environment Subcommittee, "Report of Work Group on Delegation and Oversight," mimeographed, December 1982. In the environmental area federal support for research did indeed decline substantially, especially for long-term research, the type for which federal support is most justified. According to Crandall and Portney, 1984, p. 69,

> one must conclude that the scientific basis for environmental quality standards will deteriorate sharply; and understanding of possible new environmental problems, as well as knowledge about how current programs address existing problems, can be expected to diminish under the administration's [1984] budget.

49. There are, of course, constitutional limits to state action in this area. Although a law forbidding nonresidents from selling insurance was upheld more than seventy years ago (*La Tourette v. McMaster*, 248 U.S. 465 [1919]), changes in the interpretation of the Commerce Clause have made some of the more extreme forms of state protection illegal. (Monaghan, 1975, pp. 12–19) Nevertheless, the possibilities for developing state regulatory impediments to out-of-state competition remain substantial. See *Pacific States Box Corp. v. White*, 296 U.S. 176 (1935), and *Florida Avocado Growers v. Paul*, 373 U.S. 132 (1963). See generally Tribe, 1988, Chapter 6, pp. 218–412.

50. For example, funeral home owners lobbied against Federal Trade Commission regulations. The regulations finally promulgated by the FTC were upheld by Congress, but they were considerably less stringent than the original FTC proposals. See Funeral Practice Rule, vol. 40, *Federal Register* 39901, August 25, 1975; Pertschuk, 1982.

51. Eads and Fix, 1985, p. 152.

52. From Comments of the Chemical Manufacturers Association on EPA's proposed Consolidated Permit Regulations #189, September 12, 1979, p. 181, cited in Schnapf, 1982, p. 712, n. 136.

53. Vogel, 1989, p. 266; Fix, 1984.

54. *Business Week*, September 19, 1983, p. 124, quoted by Beam, 1985, p. 429. Beam illustrates this point with an example from the Occupational Health and Safety

Administration (OSHA). In November 1983 OSHA issued rules requiring firms to inform their employees of workplace hazards. The rules were supported by industry but opposed by labor because they would preempt state laws, some of which were tougher than the OSHA standards. (id., p. 439)

55. Quoted in W. John Moore, "Stopping the States," *National Journal*, July 21, 1990, pp. 1758–62.

56. Id. and W. John Moore, "Mineral Water Could Drown in Regulation," *Business Week*, June 1979, p. 11.

57. See Rose-Ackerman, 1981a, p. 161, n. 16.

58. See, for example, U.S. Domestic Policy Council, 1986.

59. The incentive to search for new ideas comes from the pressures of interstate competition, and there is no suggestion here that the states are "laboratories" carrying out scientifically valid experiments. See Rose-Ackerman, 1980b, for an argument that state politicians have little incentive to support risky experiments.

CHAPTER 12
Privatization

1. According to one observer, the adminstration's record on privatization resembles "selective hypocrisy." (Fitzgerald, 1988, p. 219)

2. See, in particular, the President's budget messages for the fiscal years 1987 and 1988. (U.S. Office of Management and Budget, 1987a, pp. M-6–9; and 1988a, Supp. pp. 2-38–51) "Privatization is a natural counterpart to other administration initiatives—such as federalism, deregulation, and an improved tax system—that seek to return the Federal Government to its proper role." (U.S. Office of Management and Budget, 1988a, pp. 2–44) In 1987, Executive Order 12607, September 2, 1987, created a Commission on Privatization, which reported in March 1988. (U.S. President's Commission on Privatization, 1988). For a general discussion and critique, see Tingle, 1988.

3. For example, an ambitious plan to sell federal land was drastically scaled back when it became clear that Western Republicans wanted to transfer title to the states for free and did not support sales to private interests. Ranchers who were using federal land for grazing recognized that they could well be outbid by recreational and energy businesses. (Nelson, 1989, pp. 143–61; Leshy, 1984, pp. 36–39)

4. Savas calls this "load shedding." (Savas, 1982) See also Savas, 1987, pp. 234–47.

5. Even the Reagan administration was not brave enough to propose selling the TVA, but in its budget for fiscal year 1987 it did propose the sale of five regional power administrations. (Kent, 1987, p. 6)

6. The U.S. President's Commission on Privatization, 1988, recommended that private ownership of the USPS be considered, with priority being given to employee ownership. The administration's proposed budget for fiscal year 1987 suggested the sale of government assets worth $8.5 billion, or 1 percent of the government's anticipated revenues for that year. The list included the sale of power administrations, airports, public housing, loans, petroleum reserves and railroads. (Kent, 1987, pp. 6–8)

7. U.S. President's Council of Economic Advisers, 1989, p. 212. Conrail was privatized in 1987. (Fitzgerald, 1988, p. 239) The Reagan administration made no major effort to sell off existing assets. Reagan did propose the sale of government loan assets to the private sector, but this proposal seems to have been viewed as a stopgap way of reducing the deficit. According to one observer, the program "appears to sacrifice good sense to the deficit god." (Tingle, 1988, p. 252) The assets would be sold for less than half their long-term face value, and the short-term gains of the sale would have

been canceled by the lost returns on the loans in the future. It was like "selling one's house to meet the fire insurance premium." (Priest, 1988a, p. 3)

8. On the sale of British state-owned enterprises, see Swann, 1988, pp. 189–292. A key tradeoff when a government firm is sold is the competitive structure of the market. The government can itself encourage competition by selling the public entity as several separate corporations or repealing regulations that give it a monopoly position. The temptation to retain the firm's monopoly position is high, however, since such actions will maximize the revenue to the government. See Vickers and Yarrow, 1989.

9. For a more general attempt to characterize the privatization issue, see Starr, 1988.

10. City and county governments have taken the lead in using outside contractors to provide services, and their use of contractors appears to be growing. The use of private firms is high in areas, such as vehicle towing and legal services, where a vigorous private market exists so that the government is not a monopsony buyer. It is also substantial in more specialized areas, such as trash collection, where the tasks to be performed can be specified with reasonable precision. Colman, 1989, pp. 396–397, reproduces a table based on a survey by the International City Management Association. For towing services, 80 percent (87% with franchising) were contracted out, compared with 51 percent for legal services, 44 percent (63% with franchising) for commercial solid waste collection, and 41 percent (55% with franchising) for street-light operation. At the low end, under 10 percent, were such services as police and fire, inspection, public relations, and secretarial services. For a general discussion see Colman, 1989, pp. 152–68. Allen et al., 1989, provide state case studies on correction services, state parks, human services, employment and training, vehicle maintenance, and transportation. The growth in contracting-out was found in a study by the National Center for Policy Analysis, discussed by Poole and Fixer, 1987, pp. 612–13. In the social welfare area, purchase-of-service contracts with nonprofit and for-profit providers are pervasive at the state and local level and have been encouraged by federal subsidy statutes. For a historical overview see Gibelman and Demone, 1989.

11. U.S. Office of Management and Budget, Office of Federal Procurement Policy, "Invitation for Public Comment, Proposed Revision to OMB Circular No. A-76 'Performance of Commercial Activities,' " 48 *Federal Register* 1376–79 (January 12, 1983); and U.S. Office of Management and Budget, "Issuance of OMB Circular No. A-76 (Revised) 'Performance of Commercial Activities,' " 48 *Federal Register* 37110–16, (August 16, 1983). The policy is thirty years old, but was not vigorously implemented by previous administrations. (Tingle, 1988, p. 233) Later the administration identified eleven thousand activities it wanted private contractors to perform, from moviemaking and geological surveys, to health services and air traffic control. (*New York Times*, March 11, 1985, cited in Gibelman and Demone, 1989, p. 46) In addition, several bills, H.R. 3357 (1986); H.R. 1606, 100th Cong. 1st Sess., 133 *Cong. Rec.* H1290 (1987); and S. 265, 100th Cong., 1st Sess., 133 *Cong. Rec.* S525 (1987), were introduced in Congress to codify this directive. On H.R. 3357, see U.S. General Accounting Office, 1986.

12. Tingle, 1988, pp. 234–46. The administration predicted that it would save $1 billion from A-76 review in 1988. This estimate includes savings from the review process itself even if activities continue to be performed by government. Tingle argues that these estimates are inflated because the data are flawed or have simply not been gathered. For example, in a General Accounting Office (GAO) study of twenty functions contracted out by the Department of Defense, GAO reported savings on seventeen even though all but one experienced cost increases. "GAO attributed cost increases in 12 of the 20 functions to ambiguities or actual errors in describing the scope of work already being performed by government employees, which formed the basis of the contractor's bid." (Tingle, 1988, p. 239, n. 34) Of particular importance

is the incentive that contractors have to underbid if they expect to be able to rene-gotiate the contract or obtain judicial relief. In general, government bears the risk of error. (id., pp. 239–40) See also Poole and Fixer, 1987, p. 622; U.S. President's Commission on Privatization, 1988, p. 134.

13. See U.S. Office of Management and Budget, "Commercial Activities Inven-tories," 53 *Federal Register* 46004 (November 15, 1988), which is a response to Executive Order 12615, "Performance of Commercial Activities," November 19, 1987.

14. "Regulators Say 80's Budget Cuts May Cost U.S. Billions in 1990's," *New York Times*, December 19, 1989.

15. "NASA's Reliance on Contractors Is Seen as Eroding Its Capabilities," *New York Times*, September 28, 1989, p. A1.

16. "Loss of $4 Billion Is Found in Audit of Mortgage Fund," *New York Times*, Sep-tember 28, 1989, p. A1. The Bush administration has proposed shifting the admin-istration of the Guaranteed Student Loan Program entirely to colleges and universities, eliminating banks and the costly subsidies they require to participate in the program. (*New York Times*, January 7, 1991)

17. An International City Management Association survey in 1982–84 found vouchers were used in elderly programs and paratransit operation/maintenance (3% each); day care, cultural/arts, and public health (2% each); and hospital operation, recreation, drug/alcohol, mental health/retardation, and child welfare (1%). The ICMA sur-veyed three thousand city and county governments and received replies from just under 50 percent. (cited in Colman, 1989, pp. 154, 166, 396–97)

18. One of the strongest advocates of privatization, E. S. Savas, served as Assistant Secretary of Housing and Urban Development in the early years of the administra-tion and actively promoted privatization goals, including vouchers. (Savas, 1987, pp. 122, 199–200) Savas's own experience in government illustrates the fine line between propriety and impropriety when the public and private sectors become intertwined. He left office after being criticized for allegedly using his staff to type and proofread his book and for appointing a panel that awarded a contract to a firm that had paid him consulting fees (Becker, 1988, p. 94, n. 35)

19. Struyk, Mayer, and Tuccillo, 1983, pp. 71–74; Rochelle Stanfield, "If Vouchers Work for Food, Why Not for Housing, Schools, Health and Jobs?" *National Jour-nal*, April 23, 1983, pp. 840–44. According to housing advocate Cushing Dolbeare, "Reagan has given vouchers a bad name" by associating them with budget cuts. (id. at 840)

20. Congress in 1983 approved an experiment covering 100,000 households. The Hous-ing and Community Development Act of 1987 (S.825) permanently authorized vouchers. (Ronald Elving, "Major Provisions of Housing Authorization Bill," *Con-gressional Quarterly*, January 2, 1988, p. 19) However, the number of new vouchers has not kept up with the reductions in new units subsidized. (Phil Kuntz, "Plan to Revamp Housing Policy Faces Same Old Problem: Funds," *Congressional Quarterly* April 2, 1988, pp. 892–94)

21. A Reagan-appointed panel on school financing endorsed vouchers in principle and recommended that federal aid to disadvantaged school children be given, not to school districts, but to the children themselves as vouchers or tuition credits. These credits could be used in either public or private schools. (U.S. Advisory Panel on Financing Elementary and Secondary Education, 1982, pp. 5–6) A minority of the panel objected to the voucher proposal because they suspected that the parents of the intended beneficiaries would not make the best educational choices for their children and because the plan undermined public schools. (id., pp. 13–15) See also the support for vouchers voiced in the report of the U.S. President's Commission on Privatization, 1988, pp. 85–99. While supporting the inclusion of private schools in

voucher plans, the Commission did articulate the need to ensure that civil rights be guaranteed. (id., p. 95)

22. Thayer, 1987.

23. For some examples see Rose-Ackerman, 1978, p. 111, n. 2, and pp. 118–19; and Thayer, 1987. Thayer's own rhetoric provides a counterweight to that of the determined privatizers. He calls privatization plans "conspiracies to loot the public treasury." (p. 147)

24. Savas, 1987, pp. 255–72. "Privatization may . . . increase supervisory costs even if it decreases service delivery costs." (Anton, 1989, p. 161)

25. Rose-Ackerman, 1987a.

26. "Because private contractors are usually less encumbered by union contracts and civil service regulations than local governments, officials have found that these services often cost less than they would if government employees performed them." (Anton, 1989, p. 159) For a discussion sympathetic to civil servant employees that also provides some examples, see Becker, 1988.

27. Sometimes private firms, in order to overcome opposition to privatization, simply rehire former civil servants to do their old jobs. See Kent, 1987, p. 18; Ring, 1987, p. 43; and Geis, 1987, p. 88. Even the OMB Circular includes a "right of first refusal," which "requires contractors to give qualified displaced Federal employees the right of first refusal for job openings on the contract." (*Fed. Register*, August 16, 1983, p. 37112)

28. Zeckhauser and Horn, 1989, pp. 17–19.

29. Geis, 1987, p. 78, argues that privatization of prisons might have the advantage of increasing the political clout of corrections.

30. Adams, 1982.

31. Zeckhauser and Horn, 1989, pp. 25–30.

32. "Absent competition, contracting-out simply replaces one bureaucracy with another." (Tingle, 1988, p. 241)

33. Ross, 1988, pp. 24–36. Zeckhauser and Horn, 1989, pp. 44–54, report a range of comparative results for several types of services, which point to the inefficiency of state-owned enterprises but also show that there are only small differences when the private firm is regulated.

34. Posner, 1972.

35. Ira Robbins, " 'Dungeons for Dollars': Private Enterprise Sees Money in Jails," *Legal Times*, November 27, 1989, pp. 28–29; and Ring, 1987. Geis, 1987, p. 89, provides a list of privately contracted penal facilities as of 1985.

36. One commentator recommends such conditions to limit opposition from public employees. "Quite often it is both necessary and desirable to include in contracts or franchises a provision for employee transfers to the new employer with employment guaranteed for a specified period." (Colman, 1989, p. 170) If such constraints are, in fact, political preconditions for contracting-out to occur, their costs should be included in any comparison of contracting versus in-house provision. (Hatry, 1989, p. 167) Even the U.S. President's Commission on Privatization, 1988, p. 139, recommends that when contracting-out is contemplated, the "federal work force should be assured that normally any staff reduction should be achieved through attrition." (Recommendation [6])

37. In Tennessee in 1982 only two firms responded to a request-for-proposal to manage a mental health institute. Officials believed that one reason for the low response was a condition that required all state employees to be retained at present pay levels for nine months and limited the contract to one year. Similarly, New Hampshire was unable to contract for the building and operating of a mental health complex because

the state insisted that the director be a state employee to whom all contractor personnel would report. (Chi, Devlin, and Masterman, 1989, p. 93)

38. Kent, 1987, p. 19; Ring, 1987, pp. 15–21.

39. These problems are outlined in Williamson, 1976. Zupan, 1989, shows empirically that monopoly pricing and operator opportunism are not serious problems in CATV contracts. However, efficiency problems remain. Operator profits are not eliminated, and nonprice concessions to local governments are costly.

40. See, for example, Klitgaard, 1988, pp. 134–5, who criticizes the U.S. Army's procurement procedures for their role in facilitating collusion by contractors.

41. Some of the studies are summarized in Savas, 1987, 121–62, and in Borcherding, Pommerehne, and Schneider, 1982, pp. 130–33.

42. "NASA's Reliance on Contractors Is Seen as Eroding Its Capabilities," *New York Times*, September 28, 1989, p. A1.

43. "Loss of $4 Billion Is Found in Audit of Mortgage Fund," *New York Times*, September 28, 1989, p. A1.

44. "Regulators Say 80's Budget Cuts May Cost U.S. Billions in 1990's," *New York Times*, December 19, 1989, p. A1.

45. The Ninth and Tenth Circuits have split on this issue. The firms sued, not only to delay enforcement, but also because they feared disclosure of trade secrets if employees of private contractors could observe production processes. The EPA has been using contractors to conduct inspections since 1973, so the issue is not a new one. (*U.S. v. Stauffer Chemical Co.*, 511 F. Supp. 744, 749 [M.D. Tenn. 1981]) However, the fact that lawsuits arose only in the Eighties suggests an increase in the importance of contractors. The suits were brought under Section 114(a)(2) of the Clean Air Act, 42 U.S.C. §7414(a)(2). Although the district court found for the EPA in one case, *U.S. v. Stauffer Chemical*, 511 F. Supp 744, the Courts of Appeals held for the company. (*Stauffer Chemical Co. v. E.P.A.*, 647 F. 2d 1075 [10th Cir., 1981]; *U.S. v. Stauffer Chemical Co.*, 684 F. 2d 1174 [6th Cir., 1982]) The latter case was appealed to the Supreme Court, but only on the issue of collateral estoppel. (*U.S. v. Stauffer Chemical; Co.*, 464 U.S. 165 [1984]) The EPA prevailed in *Bunker Hill Co., etc. v. U.S.E.P.A.*, 658 F. 2d 1280 (9th Cir., 1981). In only one case did the court, noting the inconsistency across statutes, raise the policy question of whether inspection tasks should properly be delegated to private firms. (*U.S. v. Stauffer*, 684 F. 2d 1174, 1189) At least one environmental act explicitly permits the use of outside contractors for inspections: Solid Waste Disposal Act Amendments of 1980, P.L. 96-482, discussed in *U.S. v. Stauffer*, 684 F. 2d 1174, 1188.

46. Leshy, 1984, p. 29.

47. Haspel, 1990.

48. Macauley and Portney, 1984.

49. Leshy, 1984, p. 32.

50. Id., p. 35. According to a Congressional Budget Office estimate, charging market rates for grazing and other commercial activity on federal lands would raise $65 million in 1991 and $160 million in 1995. Cited by Schultze, 1990, p. 55.

51. Macauley, 1989. See also Fitzgerald, 1988, pp. 251–54.

52. Chubb and Hanuchek, 1990, p. 229.

53. Gibelman and Demone, 1989, p. 32.

54. Rose-Ackerman, 1983c. See also James and Rose-Ackerman, 1986, pp. 50–62.

55. According to Lipsky and Smith, 1989–90, p. 627, "over 50 percent of federal social service expenditures is now devoted to nonprofit organizations; virtually none went to such sources in 1960." They concluded from a study of nonprofit agencies in Massachusetts that "the new public–private funding arrangement means increased gov-

ernment intrusion into the affairs of nonprofit agencies, thereby altering the character of social policy and the American welfare state." (id. p. 627)

56. Roberts, 1984.

57. Even lump-sum grants might, however, stimulate giving. See Rose-Ackerman, 1981b, reprinted in Rose-Ackerman, 1986, pp. 313–29.

58. Gibelman and Demone, 1989. Kramer, 1989, reports on a study which found that child welfare agencies in New York City "subsidized" government to the amount of $48 million or 16 percent of the agency's budget. We do not know, however, how much of this support would have been available in the absence of any public program. The notion that private agencies subsidize government presumes that government has a basic obligation to provide services at a particular level.

59. Rose-Ackerman, 1987b.

60. Gibelman and Demone, 1989, pp. 50–51.

61. Salamon, 1984.

62. Colman, 1989, pp. 148–60.

63. Id., pp. 145–48.

64. With its emphasis on shrinking government and using private firms to supply public services, the Reagan administration did not innovate in this area. (Musolf, 1989, p. 236)

65. Musolf, 1989.

66. The category identified by the National Academy of Public Administration as "private corporations" includes six nonprofit and six for-profit entities. The former are the Corporation for Public Broadcasting, Legal Services Corporation, National Park Foundation, National Home Ownership Foundation (never activated), Securities Investor Protection Corporation, and the United States Railway Association. The latter are the Communications Satellite Corporation, the Consolidated Rail Corporation (sold to private investors), the Federal National Mortgage Association, the National Corporation for Housing Partnerships, the National Railroad Passenger Corporation, and the Student Loan Marketing Association. Musolf would also add the United States Synthetic Fuels corporation to the list. (Id. at 250) In 1980 four of the nonprofits were wholly dependent on federal financing and gifts, and two of the for-profits depended heavily on government funding. (Id. at 233)

67. Colman, 1989, p. 150. A good example here is COMSAT, which is the United States signatory to INTELSAT, the international satellite consortium owned by 119 governments. COMSAT's major shareholder is A.T.&T. INTELSAT sells time on its own satellites, but it also plays a regulatory and information-gathering role. With the approval of the Federal Communications Commission, one private company, Pan American Satellite, launched its own satellite in 1988 and plans to launch more. Other companies are considering entering the business. Questions have been raised about whether COMSAT has an unfair competitive advantage because of its quasi-governmental stature. As a result of this concern, the FCC has required COMSAT to divide into two corporate entities, and mandated public disclosure of INTELSAT's statistical and technical information. Krogh, 1989; Edmund Andrews, "New Competition in the Sky, and Just in Time for the War," *New York Times*, February 10, 1991, Business Section, p. 12.2.

CHAPTER 13
Progressive Reform

1. Litan and Nordhaus, 1983, pp. 133–58, provide a cogent critique of regulatory budget proposals. They go on to propose a legislated regulatory calendar that would require executive submission and legislative assent for major regulatory proposals.

Even if their proposals could be designed to comply with the prohibition on legislative vetoes (*INS v. Chadha,* 462 U.S. 919 [1983]), it has some of the same failings as such vetoes. It does not give enough weight to the benefits of delegation to agencies in complicated regulatory areas, and it would exacerbate some of the currently perceived difficulties with rulemaking.

2. See, e.g., the Delaney Clause 21 U.S.C. §348 (c)(3)(A) (1982), requiring an absolute ban of any food additive found to induce cancer without regard to the costs of ban; *American Textile Mfrs. Inst. v. Donovan,* 452 U.S. 490 (1981), interpreting the OSHA as forbidding cost-benefit analysis in regulation of toxics; and *Union Electric v. EPA,* 427 U.S. 246 (1976), arguing that claims of infeasibility could not be used as reason for the EPA Administrator to reject a plan under the Clean Air Act.

Bibliography

AARON, HENRY. *Shelter and Subsidies.* Washington, D.C.: Brookings Institution, 1972.

ACKERMAN, BRUCE. *Private Property and the Constitution.* New Haven: Yale University Press, 1977.

———. *Social Justice in the Liberal State.* New Haven: Yale University Press, 1980.

———. "Beyond Carolene Products." *Harvard Law Review* 98:713–46 (1985).

ACKERMAN, BRUCE, and WILLIAM HASSLER. *Clean Coal/Dirty Air.* New Haven: Yale University Press, 1981.

ACKERMAN, BRUCE; SUSAN ROSE-ACKERMAN; JAMES SAWYER; and DALE HENDERSON. *The Uncertain Search for Environmental Quality.* New York: Free Press, 1974.

ACKERMAN, BRUCE, and RICHARD STEWART. "Reforming Environmental Law: The Democratic Case for Market Incentives." *Columbia Journal of Environmental Law* 13:171–99 (1988).

ADAMS, GORDON. *The Politics of Defense Contracting: The Iron Triangle.* New Brunswick, N.J.: TransAction Books, 1982.

AIKEN, M.; R. DEWAR; N. DiTOMASO; J. HAGE; and G. ZEITZ. *Coordinating Human Services.* San Francisco: Jossey-Bass, 1975.

ALLEN, J.; K. CHI; K. DEVLIN; M. FALL; H. HATRY; and W. MASTERMAN. *The Private Sector in State Service Delivery: Examples of Innovative Practices.* Washington D.C.: Council of State Governments and the Urban Institute, 1989.

ANDERSON, MARTIN. *The Federal Bulldozer.* Cambridge, Mass.: MIT Press, 1964.

ANDREANO, RALPH, and JOHN NYMAN. "A Modest Proposal for Paying Nursing Homes under the Medicaid Program." University of Wisconsin-Madison

Health Economics Research Center Research Reports Series. Madison, Wis., 1982.

ANTON, THOMAS. *American Federalism and Public Policy: How the System Works*. Philadelphia: Temple University Press, 1989.

APGAR, WILLIAM, JR., and H. JAMES BROWN. *The State of the Nation's Housing, 1988*. Cambridge, Mass.: Joint Center for Housing Studies, 1989.

ARNOLD, R. DOUGLAS. *Congress and the Bureaucracy*. New Haven: Yale University Press, 1979.

―――. *The Logic of Congressional Action*. New Haven: Yale University Press, 1990.

ARROW, KENNETH. *Social Choice and Individual Values*. New Haven: Yale University Press, 1951. Second edition, 1963.

AYRES, IAN. "Playing Games with the Law." *Stanford Law Review* 42:1291–1317 (1990).

AYRES, IAN, and ROBERT GERTNER. "Filling Gaps in Incomplete Contracts: An Economic Theory of Default Rules." *Yale Law Journal* 99:87–130 (1989).

BACH, STANLEY, and STEVEN SMITH. *Managing Uncertainty in the House of Representatives: Adaptation and Innovation in Special Rules*. Washington, D.C.: Brookings Institution, 1988.

BAKER, B.; G. SELTZER; and M. SELTZER. *As Close as Possible: Community Residences for Retarded Adults*. Boston: Little, Brown, 1974.

BALLA, DAVID; EARL BUTTERFIELD; and EDWARD ZIGLER. "Effects of Institutionalization on Retarded Children: A Longitudinal Cross-Institutional Investigation." *American Journal of Mental Deficiency* 78:530–49 (1974).

BARTH, JAMES, and MICHAEL BRADLEY. *Thrift Deregulation and Federal Deposit Insurance*. Research Paper 150. Washington, D.C.: Office of Policy and Economic Research, Federal Home Loan Bank Board, 1988.

BEAM, DAVID. "New Federalism, Old Realities: The Reagan Administration and Intergovernmental Reform." In Lester Salamon and Michael Lund, eds., *The Reagan Presidency and the Governing of America*. Washington, D.C.: Urban Institute Press, 1985, pp. 415–42.

BECKER, CRAIG. "With Whose Hands: Privatization, Public Employment, and Democracy." *Yale Law and Policy Review* 6:88–108 (1988).

BENNETT, ROBERT. " 'Mere' Rationality in Constitutional Law: Judicial Review and Democratic Theory." *California Law Review* 67:1049–1103 (1979).

BIKLEN, DOUGLAS. "The Case for Deinstitutionalization." *Social Policy* 10:48–54 (May–June 1979).

BLACK, DUNCAN. *A Theory of Committees and Elections*. London: Cambridge University Press, 1963.

BLAU, FRANCINE, and MARIANNE FERBER. *Career Plans and Expectations of Young Women and Men: The Earnings Gap and Labor Force Participation*. Working Paper No. 3445. Cambridge, Mass.: National Bureau of Economic Research, 1990.

BLUME, LAWRENCE, and DANIEL RUBINFELD. "Compensation for Takings: An Economic Analysis." *California Law Review* 72:569–628 (1984).

BLUME, LAWRENCE; DANIEL RUBINFELD; and PERRY SHAPIRO. "The Taking of Land: When Should Compensation Be Paid?" *Quarterly Journal of Economics* 77:71–92 (1984).

BORCHERDING, THOMAS; WERNER POMMEREHNE; and FRIEDRICH SCHNEIDER. "Comparing the Efficiency of Private and Public Production: The Evidence from Five Countries." *Zeitschrift für Nationalökonomie* 89:127–56 (1982).

BOVBJERG, RANDALL R. "Competition vs. Regulation in Medical Care: An Overdrawn Dichotomy." *Vanderbilt Law Review* 34:965–1002 (1981).

BOWMAN, ANN O'M., and MICHAEL PAGANO. "The State of American Federalism, 1989–1990." *Publius: The Journal of Federalism* 20:1–25 (1990).

BREAK, GEORGE. *Financing Government in a Federal System*. Washington, D.C.: Brookings Institution, 1980.

BRENNAN, GEOFFREY, and JAMES BUCHANAN. *The Power to Tax*. New York: Cambridge University Press, 1980.

BREST, PAUL. "Palmer v. Thompson: An Approach to the Problem of Unconstitutional Legislative Motive." *Supreme Court Review* 1971:95–133 (1971).

BRETON, ALBERT. "A Theory of Government Grants." *Canadian Journal of Economics and Political Science* 31:175–87 (1965).

BREYER, STEPHEN. *Regulation and Its Reform*. Cambridge, Mass.: Harvard University Press, 1982.

———. "Reforming Regulation." *Tulane Law Review* 59:4–23 (1984).

———. "Antitrust, Deregulation, and the Newly Liberated Marketplace." *California Law Review* 75:1005–47 (1987).

BROWN, JOHN PRATHER. "Toward an Economic Theory of Liability." *Journal of Legal Studies* 2:323–49 (1973).

BUCHANAN, JAMES. *The Limits of Liberty: Between Anarchy and Leviathan*. Chicago: University of Chicago Press, 1975.

BUCHANAN, JAMES, and GORDON TULLOCK. *The Calculus of Consent*. Ann Arbor: University of Michigan Press, 1962.

CALABRESI, GUIDO. "Some Thoughts on Risk Distribution and the Law of Torts." *Yale Law Journal* 70:499–553 (1961).

———. *The Costs of Accidents*. New Haven: Yale University Press, 1970.

CALABRESI, GUIDO, and JON HIRSCHOFF. "Toward a Test for Strict Liability in Tort." *Yale Law Journal* 81:1055–84 (1972).

CALABRESI, GUIDO, and A. DOUGLAS MELAMED. "Property Rules, Liability Rules and Inalienability: One View of the Cathedral." *Harvard Law Review* 85:1089–1128 (1972).

CALFEE, J., and R. CRASWELL. "Some Effects of Uncertainty on Compliance with Legal Standards." *Virginia Law Review* 70:965–1003 (1984).

CASS, RONALD. "Looking With One Eye Closed: The Twilight of Administrative Law." *Duke Law Journal* 1986:238–57 (1986).

CHAMPION, HALE. "Comments: The Big Impacts Were Indirect." In Lester Salamon and Michael Lund, eds., *The Reagan Presidency and the Governing of America.* Washington, D.C.: Urban Institute Press, 1985, pp. 443–47.

CHAVKIN, DAVID, and ANN TRESEDER. "California's Prepaid Health Plan Program: Can the Patient be Saved?" *Hastings Law Journal* 28:685–760 (1977).

CHI, KEON; KEVIN DEVLIN; and WAYNE MASTERMAN. "Use of the Private Sector in Delivery of Human Services." In John Allen, K. Chi, K. Devlin, M. Fall, H. Hatry, and W. Masterman, eds., *The Private Sector in State Service Delivery: Examples of Innovative Practices.* Washington, D.C.: Council of State Governments and the Urban Institute, 1989, pp. 75–102.

CHUBB, JOHN, and ERIC HANUSHEK. "Reforming Educational Reform." In H. Aaron, ed., *Setting National Priorities: Policy for the Eighties.* Washington, D.C.: Brookings Institution, 1990, pp. 213–47.

CHUBB, JOHN, and TERRY MOE. *Politics, Markets, and America's Schools.* Washington, D.C.: Brookings Institution, 1990.

CLARKSON, KENNETH. *Food Stamps and Nutrition.* Washington, D.C.: American Enterprise Institute for Public Policy Research, 1975.

COASE, RONALD. "The Problem of Social Cost." *Journal of Law and Economics* 3:1–44 (1960).

COHEN, DANIEL, and ELEANOR FARRAR. "Power to the Parents? The Story of Education Vouchers." *Public Interest* 48:72–97 (1977).

COLMAN, WILLIAM G. *State and Local Government and Public-Private Partnerships: A Policy Issues Handbook.* Westport, Conn.: Greenwood Press, 1989.

CONLAN, TIMOTHY. *New Federalism: Intergovernmental Reform from Nixon to Reagan.* Washington, D.C.: Brookings Institution, 1988.

COOKE, WILLIAM, and FREDERICK GAUTSCHI, III. "OSHA, Plant Safety Programs and Injury Reduction." *Industrial Relations* 20:245–57 (1981).

COOTER, ROBERT, and LEWIS KORNHAUSER. "Can Litigation Improve the Law Without the Help of Judges?" *Journal of Legal Studies* 9:139–63 (1982).

CRANDALL, ROBERT; HOWARD GRUENSPECHT; THEODORE KEELER; and LESTER LAVE. *Regulating the Automobile.* Washington, D.C.: Brookings Institution, 1986.

CRANDALL, ROBERT, and PAUL PORTNEY. "Environmental Policy." In P. Portney, ed., *Natural Resources and the Environment.* Washington, D.C.: Urban Institute, 1984, pp. 47–82.

CURTIS, THOMAS, and PETER CREEDON. *The State of the States: Management of Environmental Programs in the 1980s.* Washington, D.C.: National Governors Assn., Committee on Energy and Environment, 1982.

CUTLER, LLOYD. "Regulatory Mismatch and Its Cure." *Harvard Law Review* 96:545–54 (1982).

DEALESSI, LOUIS, and ROBERT STAAF. "Property Rights and Choice." In Nicholas Mercuro, ed., *Law and Economics.* Boston: Kluwer Nijhoff, 1988, pp. 175–200.

DEBOW, MICHAEL, and DWIGHT LEE. "Understanding (and Misunderstanding) Public Choice: A Response to Farber and Frickey." *Texas Law Review* 66:993–1012 (1988).

DEMSETZ, HAROLD. "The Exchange and Enforcement of Property Rights." *Journal of Law and Economics* 7:11–26, 1964.

———. "Toward a Theory of Property Rights." *American Economic Review, Papers and Proceedings* 57:347–59 (May 1967).

DEMUTH, CHRISTOPHER, and DOUGLAS GINSBURG. "White House Review of Agency Rulemaking." *Harvard Law Review* 99:1075–88 (1986).

DIVER, COLIN. "Policymaking Paradigms in Administrative Law." *Harvard Law Review* 95:393–434 (1981).

DOLGENOS, THOMAS. "Legislative Preambles." Draft student paper prepared for Professor Ruth Wedgewood, Yale Law School, New Haven, Ct., n.d.

DORFMAN, ROBERT, ed. *Measuring Benefits of Government Investments.* Washington, D.C.: Brookings Institution, 1965.

DOWNS, ANTHONY. *Residential Rent Controls: An Evaluation.* Washington, D.C.: Urban Land Institute, 1988.

DUDEK, DANIEL, and JOHN PALMISANO. "Emissions Trading: Why Is This Thoroughbred Hobbled?" *Columbia Journal of Environmental Law* 13:217–56 (1988).

EADS, GEORGE, and MICHAEL FIX. *Relief or Reform?: Reagan's Regulatory Dilemma.* Washington, D.C.: Urban Institute Press, 1984.

———. "Regulatory Policy." In J. Palmer and I. Sawhill, eds., *The Reagan Experiment.* Washington, D.C.: Urban Institute Press, 1985.

EASTERBROOK, FRANK. "Antitrust and the Economics of Federalism." *Journal of Law and Economics* 26:23–50 (1983a).

———. "Statutes' Domains." *University of Chicago Law Review* 50:533–52 (1983b).

———. "The Supreme Court 1983 Term: Foreword: The Court and the Economic System." *Harvard Law Review* 98:4–60 (1984).

EDLEY, CHRISTOPHER. *Administrative Law.* New Haven: Yale University Press, 1990.

ELY, J. H. "Legislative and Administrative Motivation in Constitutional Law." *Yale Law Journal* 79:1205–341 (1970).

———. *Democracy and Distrust.* Cambridge, Mass.: Harvard University Press, 1980.

ELY, RICHARD T. *Ground Under Our Feet: An Autobiography.* New York: Macmillan, 1938.

ENVIRONMENTAL AND ENERGY STUDY INSTITUTE AND ENVIRONMENTAL LAW INSTITUTE. *Statutory Deadlines in Environmental Legislation: Necessary But Need Improvement.* Washington, D.C., 1985.

EPSTEIN, RICHARD. *Takings: Private Property and the Power of Eminent Domain.* Cambridge, Mass.: Harvard University Press, 1985.

———. "Takings: Descent and Resurrection, 1988." *Supreme Court Review* 1:1–45 (1987).

ETZIONI, A. "Deinstitutionalization . . . A Vastly Oversold Good Idea. . . ." *Columbia*, Spring 1978, pp. 14ff.

FARBER, DANIEL, and PHILIP FRICKEY. "Integrating Public Choice and Public Law: A Reply to DeBow and Lee." *Texas Law Review* 66:1013–19 (1988).

———. *Law and Public Choice: A Critical Introduction*. Chicago: Chicago University Press, 1991.

FEDER, JUDITH; JOHN HOLAHAN; RANDALL BOVBJERG; and JACK HADLEY. "Health." In J. Palmer and I. Sawhill, eds., *The Reagan Experiment*. Washington, D.C.: Urban Institute, 1982, pp. 271–306.

FELDMAN, ALLAN. *Welfare Economics and Social Choice Theory*. Boston: Martinus Nijhoff, 1980.

FEREJOHN, JOHN. *Pork Barrel Politics*. Stanford, Calif.: Stanford University Press, 1974.

FEREJOHN, JOHN; R. FORSYTHE; and R. NOLL. "Practical Aspects of the Construction of Decentralized Decision-Making Systems for Public Goods." In Cliff Russell, ed., *Collective Decision Making*. Baltimore: Johns Hopkins University Press, 1979, pp. 173–88.

FEREJOHN, JOHN, and CHARLES SHIPAN. "Congressional Influence on Bureaucracy." *Journal of Law, Economics & Organization* 6:S1–S20 (1990).

FIORINA, MORRIS. *Congress: Keystone of the Washington Establishment*. New Haven: Yale University Press, 1977. (2d ed., 1989).

———. "Group Concentration and the Delegation of Legislative Authority." In Roger Noll, ed., *Regulatory Policy and the Social Sciences*. Berkeley: University of California Press, 1985, pp. 175–99.

FIORINA, MORRIS, and ROGER NOLL. "Voters, Legislators, and Bureaucracy: Institutional Design in the Public Sector." *American Economic Review— Papers and Proceedings* 68:256–66 (1978).

FISCHEL, WILLIAM. *The Economics of Zoning Laws: A Property Rights Approach to American Land Use Controls*. Baltimore: Johns Hopkins University Press, 1985.

———. "Property Rights and the Takings Clause." In H. Butler, W. Fischel, and W. Kovacic, eds., *Significant Business Decisions of the Supreme Court, 1986–1987 Term*. Washington, D.C.: Washington Legal Foundation, 1988, pp. 47–56.

FISCHEL, WILLIAM, and PERRY SHAPIRO. "Takings, Insurance, and Michelman: Comments on Economic Interpretations of 'Just Compensation' Law." *Journal of Legal Studies* 17:269–93 (1988).

FISCHOFF, BARUCH; PAUL SLOVIC; SARAH LICHTENSTEIN; STEPHEN READ; and BARBARA COMBS. "How Safe Is Safe Enough? A Psychometric Study of Attitudes Towards Technological Risks and Benefits." *Policy Sciences* 9:127–52 (1978).

FITZGERALD, RANDALL. *When Government Goes Private: Successful Alternatives to Public Services.* New York: Universe Books, 1988.

FIX, MICHAEL. "Transferring Regulatory Authority to the States." In G. Eads and M. Fix, eds., *The Reagan Regulatory Strategy: An Assessment.* Washington, D.C.: Urban Institute, 1984, pp. 153–79.

FRANK, ROBERT. *Choosing the Right Pond: Human Behavior and the Quest for Status.* New York: Oxford University Press, 1985.

FRIED, CHARLES. "Is Liberty Possible?" *Tanner Lectures on Human Values* 3:89–135 (1982).

FRIEDMAN, JOSEPH, and DANIEL WEINBERG. *The Economics of Housing Vouchers.* New York: Academic Press, 1982.

———, EDS. *The Great Housing Experiment.* Beverly Hills, Calif.: Sage, 1983.

FRIEDMAN, LEE. *Microeconomic Policy Analysis.* New York: McGraw-Hill, 1984.

FRIEDMAN, MILTON. *Capitalism and Freedom.* Chicago: University of Chicago Press, 1962.

FRUG, GERALD. "The Judicial Power of the Purse." *University of Pennsylvania Law Review* 126:715–94 (1978).

FURUBOTN, E., and S. PEJOVICH, EDS. *The Economics of Property Rights.* Cambridge, Mass.: Ballinger Publishers, 1974.

GEIS, G. "The Privatization of Prisons: Panacea or Placebo?" In B. Carroll, R. Conant, and T. Easton, eds., *Private Means and Public Ends: Private Business in Social Service Delivery.* New York: Praeger, 1987, pp. 76–97.

GELY, RAFAEL, and PABLO SPILLER. "A Rational Choice Theory of Supreme Court Statutory Decisions with Applications to the *State Farm* and *Grove City* Cases," *Journal of Law, Economics & Organization* 6:263–300 (1990).

GIBBARD, ALAN. "Manipulation of Voting Scheme: A General Result." *Econometrica* 41:587–601 (1973).

GIBELMAN, MARGARET, and HAROLD DEMONE, JR. "The Evolving Contract State." In H. Demone, Jr., and Margaret Gibelman, eds., *Services for Sales: Purchasing Health and Human Services.* New Brunswick, N.J.: Rutgers University Press, 1989, pp. 17–57.

GILLIGAN, THOMAS, and KEITH KREHBIEL. "Collective Decisionmaking and Standing Committees." *Journal of Law, Economics & Organization* 3:287–336 (1987).

GOETZ, C. J., and R. E. SCOTT. "Liquidated Damages, Penalties, and the Just Compensation Principle: Some Notes on an Enforcement Model of Efficient Breach." *Columbia Law Review* 77:554–94 (1977).

———. "The Mitigation Principle: Toward a General Theory of Contractual Obligation." *Virginia Law Review* 69:967–1024 (1983).

GOLDENBERG, EDIE. "The Permanent Government in an Era of Retrenchment and Redirection." In L. Salamon and M. Lund, eds., *The Reagan Presidency and the Governing of America*. Washington, D.C.: Urban Institute Press, 1985, pp. 381–404.

GOLDIN, CLAUDIA. *Understanding the Gender Gap*. New York: Oxford, 1990.

GRAY, THOMAS. "The Malthusian Constitution." *University of Miami Law Review* 41:21–48 (1986).

GREENWOOD, TED. *Knowledge and Discretion in Government Regulation*. New York: Praeger, 1984.

GREIDER, W. *The Education of David Stockman and Other Americans*. New York: Dutton, 1982.

GUNTHER, GERALD. "The Supreme Court—1971 Term." *Harvard Law Review* 86:1–48 (1972).

HADDOCK, D., and C. CURRAN. "An Economic Theory of Comparative Negligence." *Journal of Legal Studies* 14:49–72 (1985).

HAHN, ROBERT W., and GORDON L. HESTER. "Where Did All the Markets Go? An Analysis of EPA's Emissions Trading Program." *Yale Journal on Regulation* 6:109–53 (1989).

HALL, RICHARD, and BERNARD GROFMAN. "The Committee Assignment Process and the Conditional Nature of Committee Bias." *American Political Science Review* 84:1149–66 (1990).

HANSEN, W. LEE, and BURTON WEISBROD. "A New Approach to Higher Education Finance." In M. Orwig, ed., *Financing Higher Education: Alternatives for the Federal Government*. Iowa City, Iowa: American College Testing Program, 1971, pp. 117–42.

HANSMANN, HENRY. "The Role of Non-Profit Enterprise." *Yale Law Journal* 89:835–98 (1980).

HARRIS, RICHARD, and SIDNEY MILKIS. *The Politics of Regulatory Change: A Tale of Two Agencies*. New York: Oxford University Press, 1989.

HARRISON, DAVID, JR. "Controlling Automotive Emissions: How to Save More than $1 Billion Per Year and Help the Poor Too." *Public Policy* 25:527–53 (1977).

———. "The Regulation of Aircraft Noise." In Thomas Schelling, ed., *Incentives for Environmental Protection*. Cambridge, Mass.: MIT Press, 1983, pp. 41–143.

HASPEL, ABRAHAM E. "Drilling for Dollars: The New and Improved Federal Oil Lease Program." *Regulation* 13:62–68 (Fall 1990).

HATRY, HARRY. "Overall Findings and Recommendations." In John Allen, K. Chi, K. Devlin, M. Fall, H. Hatry, and W. Masterman, eds., *The Private Sector in State Service Delivery: Examples of Innovative Practices*. Washington, D.C.: Council of State Governments and the Urban Institute, 1989, pp. 163–68.

HAVEMAN, ROBERT, and JULIUS MARGOLIS. *Public Expenditures and Policy Analysis*. Chicago: Markham Publishing Co., 1970.

HAVENNER, ARTHUR. "Not Quite a Revolution in Products Liability." White Paper, Manhattan Institute. New York, 1990.

HAVIGHURST, CLARK. "Health Maintenance Organizations and the Market for Health Services." *Law and Contemporary Problems* 35:716–95 (1970).

HAYES, R. ALLEN. *The Federal Government and Urban Housing: Ideology and Change in Public Policy.* Albany: State University of New York Press, 1985.

HEIMANN, CHRISTOPHER, et al. "Project: The Impact of Cost-Benefit Analysis on Federal Administrative Law." *Administrative Law Review* 4:545–654 (1990).

HENDERSON, JAMES, and THEODORE EISENBERG. "The Quiet Revolution in Products Liability: An Empirical Study of Legal Change." *UCLA Law Review* 37:479–553 (1990).

HENDERSON, JAMES, and R. PETERSON. "Aspirational Commands." *Columbia Law Review* 78:1429–70 (1978).

HITCH, CHARLES J., and ROLAND N. McKEAN. *The Economics of Defense in the Nuclear Age.* Cambridge, Mass.: Harvard University Press, 1960.

HORWITZ, ROBERT G. *The Irony of Regulatory Reform: The Deregulation of American Tele-Communications.* New York: Oxford University Press, 1989.

HOVENKAMP, HERBERT. "The First Great Law and Economics Movement." *Stanford Law Review* 42:993–1058 (1990).

HUBER, PETER. "The New–Old Distinction in Risk Regulation." *Virginia Law Review* 69:1024–1107 (1983).

———. *Liability: The Legal Revolution and Its Consequences.* New York: Basic Books, 1988.

JACKSON, EMMA. "The Present System of Publicly Supported Daycare." In Dennis Young and Richard R. Nelson, eds., *Public Policy for Day Care of Young Children.* Lexington, Mass.: D. C. Health, 1973, pp. 21–46.

JAMES, ESTELLE, and SUSAN ROSE-ACKERMAN. *The Nonprofit Enterprise in Market Economies.* Chur, Switzerland: Harwood Academic Publishers, 1986.

JASKOW, PAUL, and ROGER NOLL. "Regulation in Theory and Practice: An Overview." In G. Fromm, ed., *Studies in Public Regulation.* Cambridge, Mass.: MIT Press, 1981, pp. 1–65.

JAYNES, GERALD, and ROBIN WILLIANS, JR., eds. *A Common Destiny: Blacks and American Society.* Washington, D.C.: National Academy Press, 1989.

KAHN, ALFRED. *The Economics of Regulation: Principles and Institutions.* Cambridge, Mass.: MIT Press, 1988.

KAHNEMAN, PAUL; PAUL SLOVIC; and AMOS TVERSKY, eds. *Judgment Under Uncertainty: Heuristics and Biases.* Cambridge, Eng.: Cambridge University Press, 1982.

KALMAN, LAURA. *Legal Realism at Yale, 1927–1960.* Chapel Hill: University of North Carolina Press, 1986.

KALT, JOSEPH and MARK ZUPAN. "Capture and Ideology in the Economic Theory of Politics." *American Economic Review* 74:301–22 (1984).

KATZ, AVERY. "The Strategic Structure of Offer and Acceptance: Game Theory and the Law of Contract Formation." Unpublished manuscript, October 1989.

KELMAN, STEVEN. *What Price Incentives?: Economists and the Environment.* Auburn, Mass.: Auburn House, 1981.

————. *Making Public Policy: A Hopeful View of American Government.* New York: Basic Books, 1987.

KENT, CALVIN. "Privatization of Public Functions: Promises and Problems." In Calvin Kent, ed., *Entrepreneurship and the Privatizing of Government.* New York: Quorum Books, 1987, pp. 3–22.

KESSEL, REUBEN. "Transfused Blood, Serum Hepatitis, and the Coase Theorem." *Journal of Law and Economics* 17:265–89 (1974).

KINCAID, JOHN. "The State of American Federalism—1986." *Publius* 17:1–33 (1987).

KLITGAARD, ROBERT. *Controlling Corruption.* Berkeley: University of California Press, 1988.

KNEESE, ALLEN, and CHARLES SCHULTZE. *Pollution, Prices, and Public Policy.* Washington, D.C.: Brookings Institution, 1974.

KOLSTAD, CHARLES; THOMAS ULEN; and GARY JOHNSON. "*Ex Post* Liability for Harm vs. *Ex Ante* Safety Regulation: Substitutes or Complements." *American Economic Review* 80:888–901 (1990).

KOMMERS, DONALD. *The Constitutional Jurisprudence of the Federal Republic of Germany.* Durham, N.C.: Duke University Press, 1989.

KORNHAUSER, LEWIS. "Unconscionability in Standard Forms." *California Law Review* 65:1151–83 (1976).

————. "Legal Rules as Incentives." In Nicholas Mercuro, ed., *Law and Economics.* Boston: Kluwer Nijhoff, 1988, pp. 27–56.

KRAFT, M., and NORMAN VIG. "Environmental Policy in the Reagan Presidency." *Political Science Quarterly* 99:415–39 (1984).

KRAMER, RALPH. "From Volunteerism to Vendorism." In H. Demone, Jr., and Margaret Gibelman, eds., *Services for Sale: Purchasing Health and Human Services.* New Brunswick, N.J.: Rutgers University Press, 1989, pp. 97–111.

KRASHINSKY, MICHAEL. *User Charges in the Social Services: An Economic Theory of Need and Ability.* Toronto: University of Toronto Press, 1981.

KREHBIEL, KEITH. "Sophisticated Committees and Structure-Induced Equilibria." In M. McCubbins and R. Sullivan, eds., *Congress: Structure and Policy.* New York: Cambridge University Press, 1987, pp. 376–402.

————. "Spatial Models of Legislative Choice." *Legislative Studies Quarterly* 13:259–319 (1988).

————. "Are Congressional Committees Composed of Preference Outliers?" *American Political Science Review* 84:149–63 (1989).

KROGH, GUY. "The Satellite Competition Debate: An Analysis of FCC Policy and an Argument in Support of Open Competition." *Syracuse Law Review* 40:867–92 (1989).

KRONMAN, ANTHONY. "Specific Performance." *University of Chicago Law Review* 45:351–82 (1978).

KUZMACK, ARNOLD. "The Safe Drinking Water Act: A Case Study." In Michael Fix and Daphne Kenyon, eds., *Coping with Mandates: What Are the Alternatives?* Washington, D.C.: Urban Institute Press, 1990.

LAKIN, CHARLES. *Demographic Studies of Residential Facilities for the Mentally Retarded: A Historical Review of Methodologies and Findings.* Project Report #3, Developmental Disabilities Project on Residential Services and Community Adjustment. Minneapolis: University of Minnesota, 1979.

LANCASTER, KELVIN. *Variety, Equity and Efficiency: Product Variety in an Industrial Society.* New York: Columbia University Press, 1979.

LANDA, JANET, and BERNARD GROFMAN. "Games of Breach and the Role of Contract Law in Protecting the Expectation Interest." *Research in Law and Economics* 3:67–90 (1981).

LANDES, WILLIAM, and RICHARD POSNER. *The Economic Structure of Tort Law.* Cambridge, Mass.: Harvard University Press, 1987.

LAVE, LESTER. *The Strategy of Social Regulation.* Washington, D.C.: Brookings Institution, 1981.

LEONE, ROBERT. "Regulatory Relief and the Automobile Industry." In G. Eads and M. Fix, eds., *The Reagan Regulatory Strategy: An Assessment.* Washington, D.C.: Urban Institute Press, 1984, pp. 87–105.

LESHY, JOHN D. "Natural Resource Policy." In Paul R. Portney, ed., *Natural Resources and the Environment: The Reagan Approach.* Washington, D.C.: The Urban Institute Press, 1984, pp. 13–46.

LEVINE, MICHAEL. "Revisionism Revised? Airline Deregulation and the Public Interest." *Law and Contemporary Problems* 44:179–95 (1981).

LEVINE, MICHAEL, and CHARLES PLOTT. "Agenda Influence and Its Implications." *Virginia Law Review* 63:560–604 (1977).

LEVMORE, SAUL. "Just Compensation and Just Politics." *Connecticut Law Review* 22:285–322 (1990).

LIEBER, HARRY. *Federalism and Clean Water.* Lexington, Mass.: D. C. Heath, 1975.

LINDE, HANS. "Due Process of Lawmaking." *Nebraska Law Review* 55:197–255 (1976).

LIPSEN, LINDA. "The Evolution of Products Liability as a Federal Public Policy Issue." In Peter Schuck, ed., *Tort Law and the Public Interest: Competition, Innovation and Consumer Welfare.* New York: Norton, 1991, pp. 247–71.

LIPSKY, MICHAEL, and STEVEN RATHGEB SMITH. "Nonprofit Organizations, Government, and the Welfare State." *Political Science Quarterly* 104:625–48 (1989–90).

LITAN, ROBERT. *What Should Banks Do?* Washington, D.C.: Brookings Institution, 1987.

LITAN, ROBERT, and WILLIAM NORDHAUS. *Reforming Federal Regulation.* New Haven: Yale University Press, 1983.

LITAN, ROBERT, and CLIFFORD WINSTON, EDS., *Liability: Perspectives and Policy.* Washington, D.C.: Brookings Institution, 1988.

LOVETT, WILLIAM. "Moral Hazard, Bank Supervision and Risk-Based Capital Requirements." *Ohio State Law Journal* 49:1365–95 (1989).

LOWENSTEIN, DANIEL. "California Initiatives and the Single-Subject Rule." *UCLA Law Review* 30:936–75 (1983).

LOWRY, IRA, ed. *Experimenting with Housing Allowances: The Final Report of the Housing Assistance Supply Experiment.* Cambridge, Mass.: Oelgeschlager, Gunn & Hain, 1983.

LYNDON, MARY. "Information Economics and Chemical Toxicity: Designing Law to Produce and Use Data." *Michigan Law Review* 87:1795–1861 (1989).

LYNN, LAWRENCE. "The Reagan Administration and the Penitent Bureaucracy." In L. Salamon and M. Lund, eds., *The Reagan Presidency and the Governing of America.* Washington, D.C.: Urban Institute Press, 1985, pp. 339–74.

MAAS, ARTHUR; MAYNARD HUFSCHMIDT; ROBERT DORFMAN; HAROLD THOMAS, JR.; STEPHEN MARGLIN; and GORDON FAIR. *Design of Water-Resources Systems.* Cambridge, Mass.: Harvard University Press, 1962.

MACAULEY, MOLLY. "Launch Vouchers for Space Science Research Opportunities." *Space Policy* 5:311–20 (1989).

MACAULEY, MOLLY, and PAUL PORTNEY. "Property Rights in Orbit." *Regulation* 8:14–18 (July–August 1984).

MACAVOY, PAUL. *The Crisis of the Regulatory Commissions.* New York: Norton, 1970.

MACDONALD, M. *Food Stamps and Income Maintenance.* New York: Academic Press, 1977.

MACEY, JONATHAN. "Promoting Public-regarding Legislation Through Statutory Interpretation: An Interest Group Model." *Columbia Law Review* 86:223–68 (1986).

———. "The Political Science of Regulating Bank Risk." *Ohio State Law Journal* 49:1277–98 (1989).

MARMOR, T. R.; RICHARD BOYER; and JULIE GREENBERG. "Medical Care and Procompetitive Reform." *Vanderbilt Law Review* 34:1003–28 (1981).

MARMOR, THEODORE, and JERRY MASHAW. *America's Misunderstood Welfare State: Persistent Myths, Enduring Realities.* New York: Basic Books, 1990.

MASHAW, JERRY. "Constitutional Deregulation: Notes Toward a Public, Public Law." *Tulane Law Review* 54:849–76 (1980).

———. "Administrative Due Process as Social Cost Accounting." *Hofstra Law Review* 9:1423–52 (1981).

MASHAW, JERRY, and D. HARFST. *The Struggle for Auto Safety.* Cambridge, Mass.: Harvard University Press, 1990.

MASHAW, JERRY, and SUSAN ROSE-ACKERMAN. "Federalism and Regulation." In G. Eads and M. Fix, eds., *The Reagan Regulatory Strategy: An Assessment.* Washington, D.C.: Urban Institute Press, 1984, pp. 111–52.

MAY, K. O. "A Set of Independent, Necessary and Sufficient Conditions for Simple Majority Rule." *Econometrica* 20:680–84 (1952).

MAYHEW, DAVID. *Congress: The Electoral Connection.* New Haven: Yale University Press, 1974.

MAYTON, WILLIAM. "The Possibilities of Collective Choice: Arrow's Theorem, Article I, and the Delegation of Legislative Power to Administrative Agencies." *Duke Law Journal* 1986:948–69 (1986).

McCAFFREY, D. *OSHA and the Politics of Health Regulation.* New York: Plenum Press, 1982.

McCLOSKEY, ROBERT. "Economic Due Process and the Supreme Court: An Exhumation and Rebuttal." *Supreme Court Review* 1962:34–62 (1962).

McCONNELL, MICHAEL. "The Counter-Revolution in Legal Thought." *Policy Review* 41:18–25 (Summer 1987).

McCORMICK, MARK; DAVID BALLA; and EDWARD ZIGLER. "Resident-Care Practices in Institutions for Retarded Persons: A Cross-Institutional, Cross-Cultural Study." *American Journal of Mental Deficiency* 80:1–17 (1975).

McCUBBINS, MATTHEW; ROGER NOLL; and BARRY WEINGAST. "Administrative Procedures as Instruments of Political Control." *Journal of Law, Economics & Organization* 3:243–77 (1987).

———. "Structure and Process, Politics and Policy." *Virginia Law Review* 75:431–508 (1989).

McGRATH, MIKE, and WALTER HELLERSTEIN. "Reflections on Commonwealth Edison Co. v. Montana." *Montana Law Review* 43:165–79 (Summer 1982).

McKEAN, ROLAND. *Efficiency in Government Through Systems Analysis.* New York: Wiley, 1958.

MEADE, JAMES EDWARD. *Efficiency, Equality and the Ownership of Property.* Cambridge, Mass.: Harvard University Press, 1965.

MEEHAN, EUGENE. "The Rise and Fall of Public Housing: Condemnation Without Trial." In Donald Phares, ed., *A Decent Home and Environment.* Cambridge, Mass.: Ballinger, 1977, pp. 5–42.

———. *The Quality of Federal Policymaking: Programmed Failure in Public Housing.* Columbia: University of Missouri Press, 1979.

MENDELOFF, JOHN. *Regulating Safety: An Economic and Political Analysis of Occupational Safety and Health Policy.* Cambridge, Mass.: MIT Press, 1979.

———. *The Dilemma of Toxic Substance Regulation: How Overregulation Causes Underregulation.* Cambridge, Mass.: MIT Press, 1987.

MICHELMAN, FRANK. "Property, Utility, and Fairness: Comments on the Ethical

Foundations of 'Just Compensation' Law." *Harvard Law Review* 80:1165–258 (1968).

———. "The Supreme Court, 1968 Term-Foreword: On Projecting the Poor Through the Fourteenth Amendment." *Harvard Law Review* 83:7–59 (1969).

———. "Takings, 1987." *Columbia Law Review* 88:1600–1629 (1988).

MINARIK, JOSEPH. "Family Incomes." In I. Sawhill, ed., *Challenge to Leadership*. Washington, D.C.: Urban Institute Press, 1988, pp. 33–66.

MINDA, GARY. "The Law and Economics and Critical Legal Studies Movements in American Law." In Nicholas Mercuro, ed., *Law and Economics*. Boston: Kluwer Nijhoff, 1988, pp. 87–122.

MINTZ, BENJAMIN W. *OSHA: History, Law and Policy*. Washington, D.C.: BNA Books, 1984.

MITCHELL, CHARLES P. "State Regulation and Federal Preemption of Food Labeling." *Food, Drug, and Cosmetic Law Journal* 45:123–41 (1990).

MITCHELL, JANET, and JERRY CROMWELL. "Large Medicaid Practices and Medicaid Mills." *Journal of the American Medical Association* 244:2433–37 (1980).

MONAGHAN, HENRY. "The Supreme Court 1974 Term. Forward: Constitutional Common Law." *Harvard Law Review* 89:1–45 (1975).

MOORE, M. J., and W. K. VISCUSI. "Promoting Safety Through Workers' Compensation: The Efficacy and Net Wage Costs of Injury Insurance." *Rand Journal of Economics* 20:499–515 (1989).

MOORE, THOMAS GALE. "The Beneficiaries of Trucking Regulation." *Journal of Law and Economics* 21:327–43 (1978).

MORRISON, ALAN. "OMB Interference with Agency Rulemaking." *Harvard Law Review* 99:1059–74 (1986).

MUELLER, DENNIS. *Public Choice-II*. Cambridge, Eng.: Cambridge University Press, 1989.

MUSOLF, LLOYD. "The Government-Corporation Tool: Permutations and Possibilities." In Lester Salamon, ed., *Beyond Privatization: The Tools of Government Action*. Washington, D.C.: Urban Institute Press, 1989, pp. 231–52.

MURRAY, CHARLES. *Losing Ground: American Social Policy, 1950–1980*. New York: Basic Books, 1984.

MUSGRAVE, RICHARD, and PEGGY MUSGRAVE. *Public Finance in Theory and Practice*. New York: McGraw-Hill, 1973.

NATHAN, RICHARD. "Institutional Change Under Reagan." In J. Palmer, ed., *Perspectives on the Reagan Years*. Washington, D.C.: Urban Institute, 1986, pp. 121–45.

NATIONAL ACADEMY OF PUBLIC ADMINISTRATION. *Reorganization in Florida: How is Service Integration Working?* Washington, D.C., 1977.

NELSON, RICHARD. *The Moon and the Ghetto*. New York: Norton, 1977.

NELSON, RICHARD, and MICHAEL KRASHINSKY. "Two Major Issues of Public Policy: Public Subsidy and Organization of Supply." In D. Young and R. Nelson, eds., *Public Policy for Day Care of Young Children.* Lexington, Mass.: D. C. Heath, 1973, pp. 47–70.

NELSON, ROBERT H. "Privatization of Federal Lands: What Did Not Happen." In Roger E. Meiners and Bruce Yandle, eds., *Regulation and the Reagan Era: Politics, Bureaucracy, and the Public Interest.* New York: Holmes & Meier, 1989, pp. 132–65.

NIRJE, BENGT. "The Normalization Principle and Its Human Management Implications. In R. Kugel and A. Shearer, eds., *Changing Patterns in Residential Services for the Mentally Retarded.* Washington, D.C.: President's Committee on Mental Retardation, 1976, pp. 231–40.

NISKANEN, WILLIAM. *Bureaucracy and Representative Government.* Chicago: Aldine, 1971.

NOTE. "Ownership of Member Banks by Mutual Fund Advisers Under the Glass–Steagall Act." *Fordham Law Review* 52:691–710 (1984).

NOTE. "Toxic Waste Litigation." *Harvard Law Review* 99:1458–1661 (1986).

NOTE. "Requiem on the Glass–Steagall Act: Tracing the Evolution and Current Status of Bank Involvement in Brokerage Activities." *Tulane Law Review* 63:157–91 (1988).

NYMAN, JOHN. "Improving the Quality of Nursing Homes: Regulation or Competition." *Journal of Policy Analysis and Management* 6:247–51 (1987).

OATES, WALLACE. *Fiscal Federalism.* New York: Harcourt Brace Jovanovich, 1972.

O'BRIEN, DAVID. *What Process Is Due? Courts and Science Disputes.* New York: Russell Sage, 1987.

OKUN, ARTHUR. *Equality and Efficiency: The Big Tradeoff.* Washington, D.C.: Brookings Institution, 1975.

OLSON, MANCUR, JR. *The Logic of Collective Action: Public Goods and the Theory of Groups.* 2d edition. Cambridge, Mass.: Harvard University Press, 1971. (First pub. 1965).

———. "The Principle of 'Fiscal Equivalence': The Division of Responsibilities Among Different Levels of Government." *American Economic Review—Papers and Proceedings* 69:479–87 (1979).

———. *The Rise and Decline of Nations.* New Haven: Yale University Press, 1982.

PACK, JANET, and HOWARD PACK. "Metropolitan Fragmentation and Suburban Homogeneity." *Urban Studies* 14:191–201 (1977).

PALMER, JOHN, and ISABEL SAWHILL, EDS. *The Reagan Record.* Cambridge, Mass.: Ballinger, 1984.

PELTZMAN, SAMUEL. "Toward a More General Theory of Regulation?" *Journal of Law and Economics* 19:211–40 (1976).

PERTSCHUK, MICHAEL. *Revolt Against Regulation: The Rise and Pause of the Consumer Movement*. Berkeley: University of California Press, 1982.

PETERSON, ANDREA. "The Takings Clause: In Search of Underlying Principles, Part I—A Critique of Current Takings Clause Doctrine." *California Law Review* 77:1299–1364 (1989).

———. "The Takings Clause: In Search of Underlying Principles, Part II—Takings as Intentional Deprivations of Property Without Moral Justification." *California Law Review* 78:53–162 (1990).

PETERSON, PAUL; BARRY RABE; and KENNETH WONG. *When Federalism Works*. Washington, D.C.: Brookings Institution, 1986.

PLOTNICK, ROBERT D., and FELICITY SKIDMORE. *Progress Against Poverty: A Review of the 1964–1974 Decade*. New York: Academic Press, 1975.

POLINSKY, A. MITCHELL. "Collective Consumption Goods and Local Public Finance Theory: A Suggested Analytic Framework." *Issues in Urban Public Finance*, Paper and Proceedings of the 28th Conference of the International Institute of Public Finance. New York, September 1972, pp. 166–81.

———. *An Introduction to Law and Economics*. 2d edition. Boston: Little, Brown & Company, 1989.

POOLE, ROBERT, JR., and PHILIP FIXER, JR. "Privatization of Public-Sector Services in Practice: Experience and Potential." *Journal of Policy Analysis and Management* 6:612–25 (1987).

POSNER, RICHARD. "The Appropriate Scope of Regulation in the Cable Television Industry." *Bell Journal of Economics* 3:98–129 (1972).

———. "Strict Liability: A Comment. *Journal of Legal Studies* 2:205–15 (1973).

———. "The DeFunis Case and the Constitutionality of Preferential Treatment of Racial Minorities." *Supreme Court Review* 1974:1–32 (1974a).

———. "Theories of Economic Regulation." *Bell Journal of Economics and Management Science* 5:335–58 (1974b).

———. *Tort Law: Cases and Economic Analysis*. Boston: Little, Brown & Company, 1982a.

———. "Economics, Politics, and the Reading of Statutes and the Constitution." *University of Chicago Law Review* 49:263–91 (1982b).

———. *Economic Analysis of Law*. Third edition. Boston: Little, Brown & Company, 1986.

———. *The Problems Jurisprudence*. Cambridge, Mass.: Harvard University Press, 1990.

PRIEST, GEORGE L. "Selective Characteristics of Litigation." *Journal of Legal Studies* 9:399–421 (1980).

———. "Introduction: The Aims of Privatization." *Yale Law and Policy Review* 6:1–5 (1988a).

———. "Products Liability Law and the Accident Rate." In R. Litan and C. Winston, eds., *Liability: Perspectives and Policy*. Washington, D.C.: Brookings Institution, 1988b, pp. 184–222.

PRIEST, GEORGE L., and B. KLEIN. "The Selection of Disputes for Litigation." *Journal of Legal Studies* 13:1–20 (1984).

PRUGER, ROBERT, and LEONARD MILLER. "Competition and the Public Social Services." *Public Welfare*, Fall 1973, pp. 16–25.

RABIN, ROBERT. "Administrative Law in Transition: A Discipline in Search of an Organizing Principle." *Northwestern University Law Review* 72:120–45 (1977).

REID, NELSON. "Reforming the Social Services Monopoly." *Social Work*, 17:44–54 (1972).

RIKER, WILLIAM. *The Theory of Political Coalitions*. New Haven: Yale University Press, 1962.

RIKER, WILLIAM, and PETER C. ORDESHOOK. *An Introduction to Positive Political Theory*. Englewood Cliffs, N.J.: Prentice-Hall, 1973.

RING, CHARLES. *Contracting for the Operation of Private Prisons*. College Park, Md.: American Correctional Association, 1987.

ROBERTS, RUSSELL. "A Positive Model of Private Charity and Public Transfers." *Journal of Political Economy* 92:136–48 (1984).

ROBYN, DOROTHY. *Braking the Special Interests*. Chicago: University of Chicago Press, 1987.

ROMER, THOMAS, and BARRY WEINGAST. "Political Foundations of the Thrift Debacle." In A. Alesina, ed., *Politics and Economics in the 1980's*. Chicago: University of Chicago Press, NBER Publications, 1991.

ROSE-ACKERMAN, SUSAN. *Corruption: A Study in Political Economy*. New York: Academic Press, 1978.

———. "Inefficiency and Reelection." *Kyklos* 33:287–306 (1980a).

———. "Risktaking and Reelection: Does Federalism Promote Innovation?" *Journal of Legal Studies* 9:593–616 (1980b).

———. "Does Federalism Matter? Political Choice in a Federal Republic." *Journal of Political Economy* 89:152–65 (1981a).

———. "Do Government Grants to Charity Reduce Private Donations?" In M. White, ed., *Nonprofit Firms in a Three Sector Economy*. Washington, D.C.: Urban Institute Press, 1981b, pp. 95–114.

———. "A New Political Economy?" *Michigan Law Review* 80:872–84 (1982a).

———. "Mental Retardation and Society: The Ethics and Politics of Normalization." *Ethics* 93:81–101 (1982b).

———. "Unfair Competition and Corporate Income Taxation." *Stanford Law Review* 34:1017–39 (1982c).

———. "Beyond Tiebout: Modeling the Political Economy of Local Government." In George Zodrow, ed., *Local Provision of Public Services After Twenty-five Years*. New York: Academic Press, 1983a, pp. 55–84.

———. "Social Services and the Market." *Columbia Law Review* 83:1405–38 (1983b).

————. "Unintended Consequences: Regulating the Quality of Subsidized Day Care." *Journal of Policy Analysis and Management* 3:14–30 (1983c).

————. "Inalienability and the Theory of Property Rights." *Columbia Law Review* 85:931–69 (1985).

————, ED. *The Economics of Nonprofit Institutions.* New York: Oxford University Press, 1986.

————. "Comment." *Journal of Policy Analysis and Management* 6:604–7 (1987a).

————. "Ideals Versus Dollars." *Journal of Political Economy.* 95:810–23 (1987b).

————. "Dikes, Dams and Vicious Hogs: Entitlement and Efficiency in Tort Law." *Journal of Legal Studies* 18:25–50 (1989).

————. "Market Share Allocation in Tort Law: Strengths and Weaknesses." *Journal of Legal Studies* 19:739–46 (1990).

ROSE-ACKERMAN, SUSAN, and MARK GEISTFELD. "The Divergence Between Social and Private Incentives to Sue." *Journal of Legal Studies* 16:483–91 (1987).

ROSS, DOROTHY. *Origins of American Social Science.* Cambridge, Eng.: Cambridge University Press, 1991.

ROSS, RANDY. *Government and the Private Sector: Who Should Do What?* New York: Crane, Russak & Co., 1988.

ROSSITER, CLINTON, ed. *The Federalist Papers.* New York: New American Library, 1961.

ROTHENBERG, JEROME. "Local Decentralization and the Theory of Optimal Government." In Julius Margolis, ed., *Analysis of Public Output.* New York: Columbia University Press, 1970, pp. 31–64.

ROWLEY, CHARLES. "Public Choice and the Economic Analysis of Law." In Nicholas Mercuro, ed., *Law and Economics.* Boston: Kluwer Nijhoff, 1988, pp. 123–74.

RUBIN, PAUL H. "Unenforceable Contracts: Penalty Clauses and Specific Performance." *Journal of Legal Studies* 10:237–47 (1981).

————. *Business Firms and the Common Law: The Evolution of Efficient Rules.* New York: Praeger, 1983.

RUUD, MILLARD H. " 'No Law Shall Embrace More than One Subject.' " *Minnesota Law Review* 42:389–455 (1958).

SALAMON, LESTER. "Nonprofit Organizations: The Lost Opportunity." In John Palmer and Isabel Sawhill, eds., *The Reagan Record: An Assessment of America's Changing Domestic Priorities.* Cambridge, Mass.: Ballinger, 1984, pp. 261–85.

SALINS, PETER. "America's Permanent Housing Problem." In Peter D. Salins, ed., *Housing America's Poor.* Chapel Hill: University of North Carolina Press, 1987, pp. 1–13.

SATTERTHWAITE, M. A. "Strategy-Proofness and Arrow's Conditions: Existence and Correspondence Theorems for Voting Procedures and Social Welfare Functions." *Journal of Economic Theory* 10:187–217 (1975).

SAVAS, E. S. *Privatizing the Public Sector: How to Shrink Government.* Chatham, N.J.: Chatham House Publishers, 1982.

———. *Privatization: The Key to Better Government.* Chatham, N.J.: Chatham House Publishers, 1987.

SAWHILL, ISABEL. "Poverty and the Underclass." In I. Sawhill, ed., *Challenge to Leadership: Economic and Social Issues for the Next Decade.* Washington, D.C.: Urban Institute Press, 1988, pp. 215–52.

SAX, JOSEPH. "Takings and the Police Power." *Yale Law Journal* 74:36–76 (1964).

SCANLON, TERRENCE, and ROBERT ROGOWSKY. "Back-Door Rulemaking: A View from the CPSC." *Regulation* 8:27–30 (July–August 1984).

SCHEERENBERGER, RICHARD. "Deinstitutionalization: Trends and Difficulties." In Robert Bruininks, C. Edward Meyers, Barbara Sigford, and K. Charlie Lakin, eds., *Deinstitutionalization and Community Adjustment of Mentally Retarded People.* Washington, D.C.: American Association of Mental Deficiency, 1981, pp. 3–13.

SCHELLING, THOMAS. *Micromotives and Macrobehavior.* New York: Norton, 1978.

SCHICK, ALLEN. *The Capacity to Budget.* Washington, D.C.: Urban Institute Press, 1990.

SCHMID, A. ALLEN. "Law and Economics: An Institutional Perspective." In Nicholas Mercuro, ed., *Law and Economics.* Boston: Kluwer Nijhoff, 1988, pp. 57–86.

SCHNAPF, DAVID. "State Hazardous Waste Programs Under the Federal Resource Conservation and Recovery Act." *Environmental Law* 12:678–743 (1982).

SCHNEIDER, ANDREAS, and JOANNE STERN. "Health Maintenance Organizations and the Poor: Problems and Prospects." *Northwestern University Law Review* 70:90–138 (1975).

SCHOLZMAN, KAY LEHMAN, and JOHN T. TIERNEY. *Organized Interests and American Democracy.* New York: Harper Row, 1986.

SCHULTZE, CHARLES. *The Public Use of the Private Interest.* Washington, D.C.: Brookings Institution, 1977.

———. "The Federal Budget and the Nation's Economic Health." In Henry Aaron, ed., *Setting National Priorities: Policy for the Nineties.* Washington, D.C.: Brookings Institution, 1990, pp. 19–64.

SCHWARTZ, ALAN. "A Reexamination of Nonsubstantive Unconscionability." *Virginia Law Review* 69:1053–83 (1977).

———. "Specific Performance." *Yale Law Journal* 89:271–306 (1979).

SCHWARTZ, ALAN, and LOUIS WILDE. "Intervening in Markets on the Basis of

Imperfect Information: A Legal and Economic Analysis." *University of Pennsylvania Law Review* 127:630–82 (1979).

———. "Imperfect Information in Markets for Contract Terms: The Examples of Warranties and Security Interests." *Virginia Law Review* 69:1387–1485 (1983).

SCHWARZ, JOHN E. *America's Hidden Success.* New York: Norton, 1988.

SEN, A. K. *Collective Choice and Social Welfare.* San Francisco: Holden-Day, 1970.

———. *On Economic Inequality.* Oxford: Clarendon Press, 1972.

SHAPIRO, MARTIN. *Who Guards the Guardians? Judicial Control of Administration.* Athens, Ga.: University of Georgia Press, 1988.

SHAVELL, STEVEN. "Damage Measures for Breach of Contract." *Bell Journal of Economics* 11:466–90 (1980a).

———. "Strict Liability Versus Negligence." *Journal of Legal Studies* 9:1–25 (1980b).

———. "The Social Versus the Private Incentive to Bring Suit in a Costly Legal System." *Journal of Legal Studies* 9:333–39 (1982).

———. "The Design of Contracts and Remedies for Breach." *Quarterly Journal of Economics* 98:121–48 (1984).

———. *Economic Analysis of Accident Law.* Cambridge, Mass.: Harvard University Press, 1987.

SHEPSLE, KENNETH. "The Positive Theory of Legislative Institutions: An Enrichment of Social Choice and Spatial Models." *Public Choice* 50:135–78 (1978).

———. "Institutional Arrangement and Equilibrium in Multidimensional Voting Models." In M. McCubbins, and T. Sullivan, eds., *Congress: Structure and Policy.* Cambridge, Eng.: Cambridge University Press, 1987a, pp. 346–75.

———. "The Institutional Foundations of Committee Power." *American Political Science Review* 81:85–104 (1987b).

SHEPSLE, KENNETH, and BARRY WEINGAST. "When Do Rules of Procedure Matter?" *Journal of Politics* 46:206–21 (1984).

SIDAK, J. GREGORY. "The President's Power of the Purse." *Duke Law Journal* 1989:1162–1253 (1989).

SIGELMAN, LEE; PHILLIP ROEDER; and CAROL SIGELMAN. "Social Service Innovation in the American States: Deinstitutionalization of the Mentally Retarded." *Social Science Quarterly* 62:503–15 (1981).

SINGER, NORMAN. *Sutherland Statutes and Statutory Construction.* Fourth edition, 1985 Revision. Volume 1A. Wilmette, Ill.: Callaghan, 1985.

SMITH, REBECCA. "Federal Limitations on State Power to Regulate Radioactive Waste." *Montana Law Review* 43:271–78 (1982).

SMITH, ROBERT S. *The Occupational Safety and Health Act: Its Goals and*

Achievements. Washington, D.C.: American Enterprise Institute for Public Policy Research, 1976a.

———. "The Impact of OSHA Inspections on Manufacturing Injury Rates." *Journal of Human Resources* 14:145–70 (1976b).

———. "Compensating Wage Differentials and Public Policy: A Review." *Industrial and Labor Relations Review* 32:339–52 (1979).

SPITZER, MATTHEW. "Radio Formats by Administrative Choice," *University of Chicago Law Review* 47:647–687 (1980).

STARR, PAUL. "The Meaning of Privatization." *Yale Law and Policy Review* 6:6–41 (1988).

STEINER, GEORGE. *The State of Welfare*. Washington, D.C.: Brookings Institution, 1971.

———. "The Legalization of American Society: Economic Regulation." *Michigan Law Review* 81:1285–1306 (1983).

STERNLIEB, GEORGE, and DAVID LISTOKIN. "A Review of National Housing Policy." In Peter D. Salins, ed., *Housing America's Poor*. Chapel Hill: University of North Carolina Press, 1987, pp. 14–44.

STEWART, RICHARD. "The Reformation of American Administrative Law." *Harvard Law Review* 88:1667–1813 (1975).

STIGLER, GEORGE. "The Theory of Economic Regulation." *Bell Journal of Economics and Management Science* 2:3–21 (1971).

———. "Free Riders and Collective Action." *Bell Journal of Economics and Management Science* 5:359–65 (1974).

STIGLITZ, JOSEPH. "Equilibrium in Product Markets with Imperfect Information." *American Economic Review* 69:339–45 (May 1979).

STITH, KATE. "Congress' Power of the Purse." *Yale Law Journal* 97:1343–96 (1988a).

———. "Rewriting the Fiscal Constitution: The Case of Gramm–Rudman–Hollings." *California Law Review* 76: 593–668 (1988b).

STOKEY, EDITH, and RICHARD ZECKHAUSER. *A Primer for Policy Analysis*. New York: Norton, 1978.

STRAUSS, PETER, and CASS SUNSTEIN. "The Role of the President and OMB in Informal Rulemaking." *Administrative Law Review* 38:181–207 (1986).

STRNAD, JAMES, III. "State Economic Due Process: A Proposed Approach." *Yale Law Journal* 88:1487–1510 (1979).

STRUYK, RAYMOND; NEIL MAYER; and JOHN TUCCILLO. *Federal Housing Policy at President Reagan's Midterm*. Washington, D.C.: Urban Institute, 1983.

SUNSTEIN, CASS. "Cost-Benefit Analysis and the Separation of Powers." *Arizona Law Review* 23:1267–82 (1981).

———. "Factions, Self-Interest, and APA: Four Lessons Since 1946." *Virginia Law Review* 72:271–96 (1986).

———. *After the Rights Revolution*. Cambridge, Mass.: Harvard University Press (1990a).

————. "Paradoxes of the Regulatory State." *University of Chicago Law Review* 57:407–41 (1990b).

SWANN, D. *The Retreat of the State: Deregulation and Privatization in the UK and US*. Ann Arbor: University of Michigan Press, 1988.

SWIFT, JONATHAN. *Gulliver's Travels and Other Writings*. New York: Random House, 1958.

THAYER, FREDERICK. "Privatization: Carnage, Chaos, and Corruption." In B. Carroll, R. Conant, and T. Easton, eds., *Private Means and Public Ends: Private Business in Social Service Delivery*. New York: Praeger, 1987, pp. 145–70.

THRONE, JOHN. "Deinstitutionalization: Too Wide a Swath." *Mental Retardation* 17:171–75 (1979).

TIDEMAN, NICHOLAS, and GORDON TULLOCK. "A New and Superior Process for Making Social Choices." *Journal of Political Economy* 84:1145–59 (1976).

TIEBOUT, CHARLES. "A Pure Theory of Local Expenditures." *Journal of Political Economy* 64:416–24 (1956).

TIEFER, CHARLES. *Congressional Practice and Procedure: A Reference, Research, and Legislative Guide*. Westport, Conn.: Greenwood, 1989.

TINGLE, MICHAL LAURIE. "Privatization and the Reagan Administration: Ideology and Application." *Yale Law and Policy Review* 6:229–57 (1988).

TITMUSS, RICHARD. *The Gift Relationship: From Human Blood to Social Policy*. London: George Allen & Unwin, 1971.

TOLCHIN, M., and S. TOLCHIN. *Buying into America*. New York: New York Times Books, 1988.

TRIBE, LAWRENCE H. *American Constitutional Law*. 2d ed. Mineola, N.Y.: Foundation Press, 1988. First pub. 1978.

TULLOCK, GORDON. "Problems of Majority Voting." *Journal of Political Economy* 67:571–79 (1959).

————. "Federalism: Problems of Scale." *Public Choice* 6:19–29 (1969).

TUNSTALL, JEREMY. *Communications Deregulation: The Unleashing of America's Communications Industry*. Oxford: Basil Blackwell, 1986.

U.S. ADVISORY COMMISSION ON INTERGOVERNMENTAL RELATIONS. *Regulatory Federalism: Process, Impact and Reform*. Washington, D.C., mimeographed, December 1982.

U.S. ADVISORY PANEL ON FINANCING ELEMENTARY AND SECONDARY EDUCATION. *Toward More Local Control: Financial Reform for Public Education*. Washington, D.C., 1982.

U.S. CONGRESS, HOUSE, SUBCOMMITTEE ON PUBLIC HEALTH AND ENVIRONMENT OF THE COMMITTEE ON INTERSTATE AND FOREIGN COMMERCE. *Health Maintenance Organizations*. Parts 1-4, Hearings on H.R. 5615 and H.R. 11728, 92d Cong., 2d Sess., 1972.

U.S. DEPARTMENT OF AGRICULTURE, SCIENCE AND EDUCATION ADMINISTRATION. *Food Consumption and Dietary Levels of Low-Income Households*, November 1977–March 1978. Washington, D.C.: GPO, 1981.

U.S. DOMESTIC POLICY COUNCIL. *The Status of Federalism in America: A Report of the Working Group on Federalism of the Domestic Policy Council.* Washington, D.C., November 1986.

U.S. ENVIRONMENTAL PROTECTION AGENCY, OFFICE OF POLICY AND RESEARCH MANAGEMENT. *Improving Delegation of EPA Programs to the States.* Washington, D.C., mimeographed, December 1982.

U.S. GENERAL ACCOUNTING OFFICE. *Federal Productivity: Potential Savings from Private Sector Cost Comparisons.* Report to Congress. Washington, D.C.: GPO, December 1986.

U.S. OFFICE OF MANAGEMENT AND BUDGET. *Regulatory Program of the United States Government: April 1, 1986–March 31, 1987.* Washington, D.C.: GPO, 1986.

———. *Budget of the United States Government, Fiscal Year 1987.* Washington, D.C.: GPO, 1987a.

———. *Regulatory Program of the United States Government: April 1, 1987–March 31, 1988.* Washington, D.C.: GPO, 1987b.

———. *Budget of the United States Government, Fiscal Year 1988.* Washington, D.C.: GPO, 1988a.

———. *Regulatory Program of the United States Government: April 1, 1988–March 31, 1989.* Washington, D.C.: GPO, 1988b.

———. *Budget of the United States Government, Fiscal Year 1990.* Washington, D.C.: GPO, 1990.

U.S. PRESIDENT'S COMMISSION ON PRIVATIZATION. *Privatization: Toward a More Effective Government.* Washington, D.C.: GPO, 1988.

U.S. PRESIDENT'S COUNCIL OF ECONOMIC ADVISERS. *Economic Report of the President Together with the Annual Report of the Council of Economic Advisers.* Washington, D.C.: GPO, 1982, 1983, 1984, 1985, 1986, 1987, 1988, 1989.

VELJANOVSKI, CENTRO. "The Role of Economics in the Common Law." *Research in Law and Economics* 7:41–64 (1985).

VERKUIL, PAUL. "Symposium on Presidential Intervention in Administrative Rulemaking." *Tulane Law Review* 56:811–17 (1982).

VICKERS, JOHN, and GEORGE YARROW. "Privatization in Britain." In P. MacAvoy, W. T. Stanbury, George Yarrow, and R. Zeckhauser, eds., *Privatization and State-owned Enterprises: Lessons from the United States, Great Britain and Canada.* Boston: Kluwer Academic Publishers, 1989, pp. 209–45; comments, pp. 246–72.

VISCUSI, W. K. "Labor Market Valuations of Life and Limb: Empirical Evidence and Policy Implications." *Public Policy* 26:359–86 (1978).

———. "The Impact of Occupational Safety and Health Regulations." *Bell Journal of Economics* 10:117–40 (1979).

——— *Risk by Choice.* Cambridge, Mass.: Harvard University Press, 1983.

―――. "Structuring an Effective Occupational Disease Policy: Victim Compensation and Risk Regulation." *Yale Journal on Regulation* 2:53–81 (1984).

VOEGELIN, WARY VICTOR. "Commerce Clause v. Coal Severance Taxation." *West Virginia Law Review* 84:1123–34 (1982).

VOGEL, DAVID. *Fluctuating Fortunes: The Political Power of Business.* New York: Basic Books, 1989.

WALD, PATRICIA. "The Realpolitik of Judicial Review in a Deregulation Era." *Journal of Policy Analysis and Management* 5:535–46 (1986).

WARREN, MELINDA, and KENNETH CHILTON. "Higher Budgets for Federal Regulators." *Regulation*, 13:21–25 (Fall 1990).

WEICHER, JOHN C. *Housing: Federal Policies and Programs.* Washington, D.C.: American Enterprise Institute, 1980.

―――. "Private Production: Has the Rising Tide Lifted All Boats?" In Peter D. Salins, ed., *Housing America's Poor.* Chapel Hill: University of North Carolina Press, 1987, pp. 45–66.

WEIDENBAUM, MURREY. "Regulatory Reform Under the Reagan Administration." In G. Eads and M. Fix, eds., *The Reagan Regulatory Strategy.* Washington, D.C.: Urban Institute Press, 1984, pp. 15–41.

WEIMER, DAVID, and AIDAN VINING. *Policy Analysis: Concepts and Practice.* Englewood Cliffs, N.J.: Prentice Hall, 1989.

WEINGAST, BARRY, and WILLIAM MARSHALL. "The Industrial Organization of Congress; or Why Legislatures, Like Firms, Are Not Organized as Markets." *Journal of Political Economy* 96: 132–63 (1988).

WEISS, HARRY. "Employers' Liability and Workmen's Compensation." In Elizabeth Brandeis, ed., *Labor Legislation:* Vol. 3, *History of Labor in the United States, 1896–1932.* New York: Macmillan, 1934, pp. 564–610.

WEISS, JANET. "Substance vs. Symbol in Administrative Reform: The Case of Human Services Coordination." *Policy Analysis* 7:21–45 (1981).

WICKSELL, KNUT. *Value, Capital and Rent.* New York: A. M. Kelley, 1883. English edition, 1954, reprinted 1970.

WIECK, C., and R. BRUININKS. *The Cost of Public and Community Residential Care for Mentally Retarded People in the United States.* Minneapolis: University of Minnesota, manuscript, 1980.

WILEY, JOHN. "Antitrust and Core Theory." *University of Chicago Law Review* 54:556–89 (1987).

WILLIAMS, ROBERT. "State Constitutional Limits on Legislative Procedure: Legislative Compliance and Judicial Enforcement." *Publius: The Journal of Federalism* 17:90–114 (Winter 1987).

WILLIAMSON, OLIVER. "Franchise Bidding for Natural Monopolies—In General and With Respect to CATV." *Bell Journal of Economics* 7:73–104 (1976).

―――. *The Economic Institutions of Capitalism.* New York: Free Press, 1985.

WILSON, JAMES Q. "The Dead Hand of Regulation." *The Public Interest* 25:39–58 (1971).

———. *The Politics of Regulation*. New York: Basic Books, 1980.

WINTER, RALPH K., JR. "State Law, Shareholder Protection, and the Theory of the Corporation." *Journal of Legal Studies* 6:251–92 (1977).

WOLFENSBERGER, WOLF. "The Origin and Nature of Our Institutional Models. In R. Kugel and A. Shearer, eds., *Changing Patterns in Residential Services for the Mentally Retarded*. Washington, D.C.: President's Commission on Mental Retardation, 1976, pp. 35–82.

WOLMAN, HAROLD, and FRED TEITELBAUM. "Interest Groups and the Reagan Presidency." In Lester Salamon and Michael Lund, eds., *The Reagan Presidency and the Governing of America*. Washington, D.C.: Urban Institute Press, 1984, pp. 297–329.

ZECKHAUSER, RICHARD, and MURRAY HORN. "The Control and Performance of State-owned Enterprises." In P. MacAvoy, W. T. Stanbury, George Yarrow, and R. Zeckhauser, eds., *Privatization and State-owned Enterprises: Lessons from the United States, Great Britain and Canada*. Boston: Kluwer Academic Publishers, 1989, pp. 7–58.

ZUPAN, MARK. "The Efficiency of Franchise Bidding Schemes in the Case of Cable Television: Some Systematic Evidence." *Journal of Law and Economics* 32:401–56 (1989).

Cases Cited

Abbot v. American Cyanamid Co., 844 F. 2d 1108 (4th Cir. 1988), 225

A.F. of L. v. American Sash Co., 335 U.S. 538, 69 S. Ct. 258 (1948), 199

Ambrogi v. Gould, Inc., 750 F. Supp. 1233 (M.D. Pa. 1990), 228

American Fedn. of Govt. Employees, AFL-CIO v. Campbell, 659 F. 2d 157 (D.C. Cir. 1980, cert. denied, 454 U.S. 820 (1981), 211

American Petroleum Inst. v. OSHA, 581 F. 2d 493 (5th Cir.. 1978), 220

American Textile Mfrs. Inst. v. Donovan, 452 U.S. 490, 101 S. Ct. 2478 (1981), 220, 249

Andrus v. Allard, 444 U.S. 51, 100 S. Ct. 318 (1979), 229

Andrus v. Sierra Club, 442 U.S. 347, 99 S. Ct. 2335 (1979), 69, 70, 207, 210

Aqua Slide 'N' Dive Corp. v. Consumer Product Safety Comm., 569 F. 2d 831 (5th Cir. 1978), 220

Armster v. United States District Court, 792 F. 2d 1423 (9th Cir. 1986), 216

Armstrong v. United States, 364 U.S. 40, 80 S. Ct. 1563 (1960), 231

Arroyo v. Tucker, 372 F. Supp. 764 (E.D. Pa. 1974), 215

ASARCO, Inc. v. OSHA, 746 F. 2d 483 (9th Cir., 1984), 220

Associated Electric Cooperative, Inc. v. Morton, 507 F. 2d 1167 (D.C. Cir. 1974); cert. denied, 423 U.S. 830 (1975), 210

Benitez-Allende v. Alcan Aluminio Do Brasil, S.A., 857 F. 2d 26 (1st Cir. 1988), cert. denied, 489 U.S. 1018 (1989), 227

Bernstein v. Commissioner of Public Safety, 351 N.W. 2d 24 (Minn. App. 1984), 204

Bi-Metallic Inv. Co. v. State Bd. of Equalization, 239 U.S. 441, 36 S. Ct. 141 (1915), 199

Blackhawk Heating & Plumbing Co. v. United States, 622 F. 2d 539 (Ct. Claims 1980), 215

Name Index

Subject Index

Abortion, Hyde Amendment, 69, 211n

Administrative law, 190–192. *See also* Judicial review; entries for specific subjects of regulation

adjudication, 40–42

Administrative Procedures Act, 13, 40, 41

deregulation in the eighties, 149–158

judicial review of agency actions, 38–42, 93–96

non-delegation doctrine, 95–96

rulemaking, 39–42, 119

Airlines, deregulation of, 11, 15, 153–154

Air pollution. *See also* Environmental protection

Clean Air Act Amendments of 1970, 202n, 249n

Clean Air Act Amendments of 1990, 226n; defeat of Byrd Amendment, 49; tradeable pollution rights in, 128, 155, 191

Appropriations. *See* Congress, U.S.

Automobiles

regulation of exhaust gases, 202–203n

safety: airbags, 10, 123, 225n, 226n; automobile design, 225n; National Transportation Safety Administration, 224n; torts versus regulation, 119, 123, 124

Blood, sales or gifts of, 116, 224n

Budget process. *See* Congress, U.S.

Bush, George, administration of, 155, 238n, 245n

Cigarettes, federal labeling law and tort suits concerning, 225n

Common law, economic analysis of, 19–27. *See also* Contract law; Property rights; Torts

Community Development Block Grant program, 71

Congress, United States, 43–79. *See also* Statutes

judicial prohibition of in toxic
substances regulation under
OSHA, 93–95
in occupational safety and
method of compliance, 220n
Council of Economic Advisers,
U.S. President's. *See* President, U.S.
Courts. *See* Administrative law;
Judicial review; Supreme
Court, U.S.

Democracy, 33–38, 43–79, 95–
96, 115–116, 137–142, 189–
190. *See also* Congress,
U.S.; Majority rule; President, U.S.
Distributive justice
and compensation of tort victims, 129–130
and cost-benefit analysis, 18
and educational vouchers,
114–116
and federalism, 169
and progressivism, 6, 18, 39,
192
and property rights, 201n
and social service provision,
104, 105–106
and takings clause, 140–143
wealth, distribution of, 12, 21,
23, 36, 50, 192
and workplace health and
safety, 88–89

Economics. *See* Cost-benefit
analysis; Efficiency; Law and
economics; Market failure
Education, elementary and secondary
desegregation of, 115–116,
216n

interstate variations in spending
on, 242n
proxy shopping, unworkable in,
114–116
voucher plans in, 114–116,
224n, 245n
Efficiency, 7, 15, 16, 18, 33, 36,
49, 187, 190–192. *See also*
Law and economics; Market
failure; Regulation
of the common law, 20–27
and decentralization, 163–173
and deregulation, 151–158
in health and safety regulation,
85–88
and privatization, 175–182
in product regulation, 118–
131
in social service delivery, 97–
117
in takings law, 135–140
Environmental protection, regulation of. *See also* Air pollution; Hazardous waste; Water
pollution
citizen participation, 241n
deadlines, failure to meet, 71,
152
enforcement efforts: contracting
out inspections, 178, 247n;
downgrading of, under Reagan, 234n
federal grants to states, fall in,
239n
federal spending on, 238n
personnel policy in Reagan administration, 234n
research and development
spending, fall in federal
spending on, 242n
state and federal, 162, 242n
statutory deadlines, 213n

Printed in the United States
By Bookmasters